La Ciudad de Los Terrenitos
of the Little Landers
Monte Vista, Los Angeles County, California

Notes:

Water piped in street in front of each lot.
Lot measurements shown are NET and do NOT run to center of street.
The construction of Club House is already under way.
Construction of $5,000 School House has already been authorized at a recent election.
Lots 186 and 187 are reserved for Colony Store now in process of organizing. Lot 255 is reserved for Hotel Site.
For prices and terms address:

HOUSE OF THE LITTLE LANDERS
929 South Figueroa Street, Los Angeles, Cal.

Phones:
Home 55299
Main 2192

The Little Landers of Los Angeles cheering Old Glory and their own flag at the celebration of the corner stone laying of the Club House at Los Terrenitos, April 12, 1913, with 208 already on the ground.

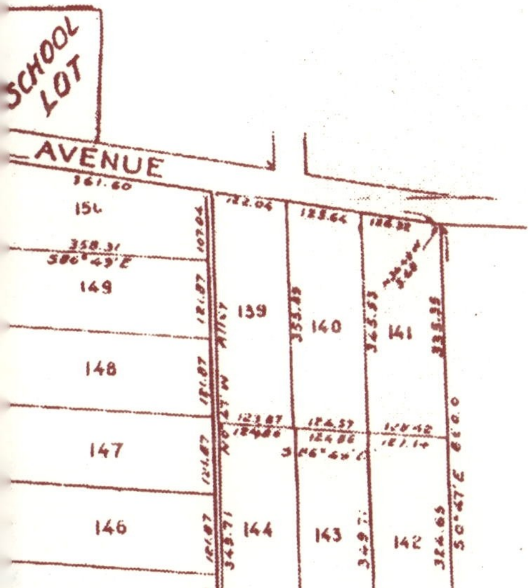

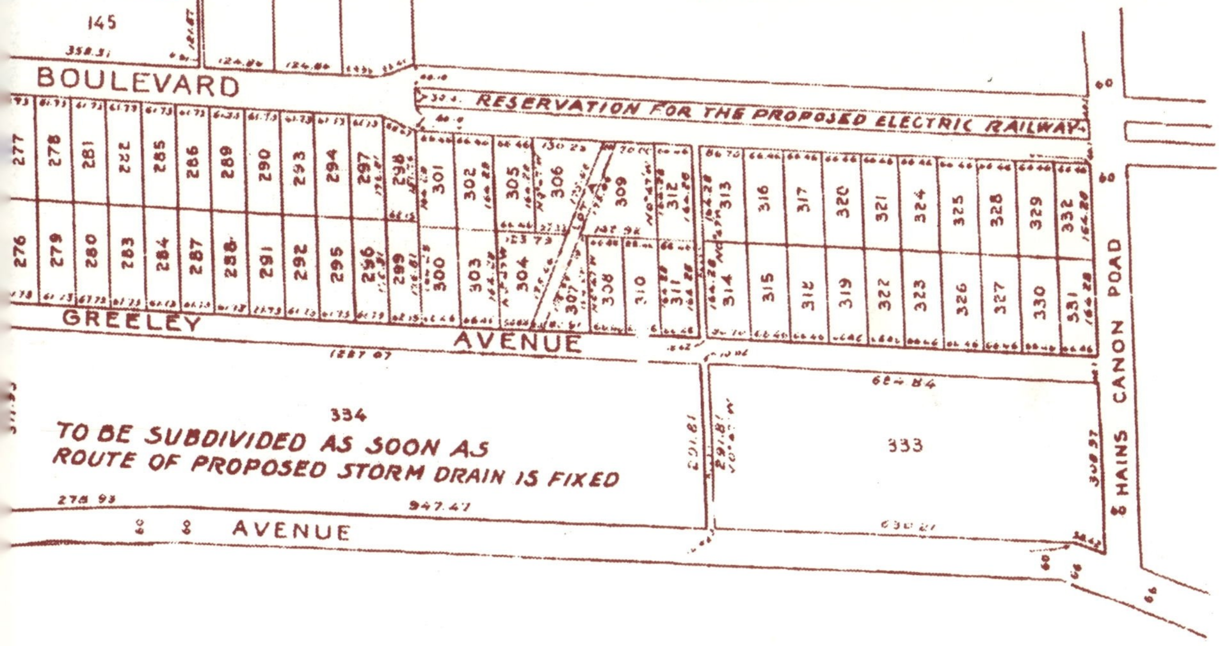

Founding Sisters

Unidentified group leaving Bolton Hall.
Note "Tin Lizzies" parked along Sunset Boulevard, c. 1915.

(*opposite*) Elsie Ellenberg, with gun, and sister Frances, with rabbit, on Mt. Gleason Avenue, looking east, c. 1914.

Founding Sisters

Life Stories of Tujunga's Early Women Pioneers

1886–1926

by
Mary Lou Pozzo

ZINNIA PRESS
Tujunga, California
2005

Founding Sisters
Life Stories of Tujunga's Early Women Pioneers
1886–1926

Published by
ZINNIA PRESS
P.O. Box 226
Tujunga, California 91043

Text copyright © 2005 by Mary Lou Pozzo.
All rights reserved.
No part of this book, including interior design, cover design and icons,
may be reproduced or transmitted in any form, by any means
(electronic, mechanical, photocopying, recording or otherwise)
without the prior written permission of the publisher.

The photographs reproduced in this book
are under copyright to the photographers and institutions
named herein and may not be reproduced in any form without
obtaining permission from the photographers and institutions.

Library of Congress Control Number: 2004102649
ISBN 0-9717922-0-8

Library of Congress Cataloging-in-Publication Data
Pozzo, Mary Lou, 1945–
    Founding sisters : life stories of Tujunga's early women pioneers, 1886–1926 / Mary Lou Pozzo.—1st ed.

    p.cm.
Includes selected bibliographical references and Index.
ISBN: 0-9717922-0-8
1. Women pioneers—California—Los Angeles—
Biography. 2. Frontier and pioneer life—California—
Los Angeles. 3. Tujunga (Los Angeles, Calif.)—
Biography. I. Title.

F868.L8P69 2002   979.4'9304'092'2
                            QBI33-209

Text face is Centaur, 1,500 copies printed on acid-free, 60-lb. natural paper.

Design and production
The Arthur H. Clark Company
Spokane, Washington

Printed in the United States of America
10 9 8 7 6 5 4 3 2 1

Table of Contents

Foreword	9
Early Photographs Gallery	11
From Rancho to Colony	31
The Hope of the Little Lands	59
Tujunga—What's in a Name	93
Oh! To Be a Happy Little Lander	105
The Edenization of Tujunga	111
Earth, Wind, and Fire: Facing the Elements	123
Silenced Voices	127
Women Pioneers A through Z	143
Appendixes	423
Names at Laying of Cornerstone	425
Population	427
Sunland Rural Telephone Company	429
Street Names	431
Name Changes for the Sunland-Tujunga Area	433
Origins of Little Landers	434
And the Name Lives On	435
Where They Lived (map)	436
The Tujunga Women's Heritage Trail	437
Final Residence	439
Photo Gallery	441
Where They Worked	441
Amusements	446
Health Care	470
Tujunga Timeline	477
In Gratitude	481
Selected Bibliography	483
Index	487

Dedicated to the Women in My Life

My Grandmothers	MINNIE KOSMELLA
	JENNIE SORENSEN
My Mother	VIOLET STRAUB
My Mentor	VIOLA CARLSON
My Best Friend	DUKIE MARIE

The Women Pioneers of Tujunga
1886–1926

Adam, Anna	1873–1955	The Walker
Begue, Franciscoa	1867–1940	Mother Tujunga
Blake, Catherine	1888–1981	First Catholic Church
Bolton, Alice Carr	1881–1968	Postmaster's daughter
Bryson, Laura	1878–1960	Community activist
Buck, Edna	1854–1916	Early pioneer
Chapman, Nana	1892–1983	Postmaster of Tujunga
Colby, Lillian	1854–1927	Ladies of the Canyon
Colby, Nellie	1872–1914	
Dean, Lydia May	1850–1938	Dry goods store owner
Fehlhaber, Helena	1866–1938	Oak Grove proprietress/ Early recycler
Frish, Marie	1881–1969	} The
Souto, Anna	1883–1969	} Girls
Gilbert, Zoe	1895–1995	Pioneer with a pen
Hansen, Marie Huber	1891–1993	Hansen's Lodge
Hatch, Mabel	1880–1957	Insurance agency owner/ Verdugo Hills Cemetery
Lamson, Alice	1877–1964	Photo colorist
Lichtenthaler, Jennie	1862–1927	Business woman
Linaberry, Cora Belle	1859–1945	Bird's Acre owner
Livingston, Hilda	1863–1958	Early pioneer
Maygrove, Gladys	1903–1985	Musician

FOUNDING SISTERS

McGroarty, Ida	1866–1940	Civic leader/ Philanthropist/ Costume designer
Millspaugh, Nora	1857–1950	Original "Little Lander"/ Kindergarten teacher
Mingay, Emma	1846–1924	Civil War captain's wife
Morgan, Bertha	1882–1959	Tujunga City Clerk
Morgan, Flora	1865–1931	Friend to the Aged
Morgan, Frances R.	1867–1959	Newspaper publisher
Parcher, Frances M.	1903–1970	Dance Studio owner/ Philanthropist
Osgood, Myra	1864–1941	Haines Canyon Water Company
Parcher, Nannie	1859–1941	Publisher's mother
Pasko, Beth	1894–1947	Poet/Librarian
Phillips, Mary	1895–1981	The Turtle Lady
Rutherford, Helen	1865–1940	Early conservationist
Smith, Virginia T.	1880–1963	Dr. Smith, Medicine Woman
White, Flora P.	1879–1960	Mortuary owner
Wieman, Alma	1854–1939	First Methodist Church
Wornum, Jenny	1851–1923	Evangelist
Zachau, Jean	1885–1961	Tujunga homesteader

> The soul selects her own society.
> —*Emily Dickinson, 1886*

Foreword

It all started innocently enough, with a question to the late Tujungan historian, Sarah Lombard, while we were walking our dogs in the Big Tujunga Canyon. Her book, *Rancho Tujunga*, had left me wanting to know more about the early women pioneers in our area. I was curious about the woman walker who celebrated her good health each birthday with a 42-mile round-trip walk to Exposition Park. Who, for example, was Flora Morgan and why was a trail in our Verdugo Mountains named for her? Sarah's wonderful book didn't specify many names nor elaborate on the details of their lives. I wondered what struggles these women had to meet head-on. My curiosities led me away from the archives of Bolton Hall Museum to Bades Mortuary in Tujunga, and I became a frequent visitor to their basement archives. Had it not been for their meticulously preserved records, our local pioneer voices would have remained silent.

Soon, my little research project took on the look of a lifetime's work and a "real" book. From the very start, it has been exciting. After locating Flora Morgan's granddaughter in Ashland, Oregon, I knew that the voices of our early pioneer women must be heard, and there were many oral histories to be gathered.

Each moment of researching and writing this book has been a stimulating adventure. Traveling to Alaska to obtain information on Ida Blake was an added bonus. For the past decade, I have been immersed in the life stories of these women. It has been my joy to know some of these remarkable women and their families personally. They asked me into their homes and took me into their lives. This book of memories is a celebration of their unique and colorful lives and their courage as they lived and worked in a man's world.

Some of the pioneer women are well known, while others are all but forgotten. They all were part of the rich tapestry that is Tujunga's history. Yes, the pioneer women of Tujunga were the quintessential American heroines: strong, self-reliant, ingenious, and sometimes a little eccentric. Although some of their homes and workplaces have disappeared from view, their footprints remain upon the land.

I hope this is the first of many biographies of women pioneers who showed no small amount of courage in journeying to Tujunga and civilizing a barren and rocky land. Every attempt has been made to let the women tell their own stories through their own words: in letters, diaries, journals and short stories. The photographs of the women and the images of their daily lives show us a portrait of all the joys and all the struggles of life at the turn of the twentieth century. I have tried to recreate their stories, alternately compelling and sometimes mundane, often humorous but always authentic, stories mostly through unpublished photographs, oral histories and their own written words.

My apologies for any women not included in this initial account. My sincerest hope is that many more people will now step forward and share their families' genealogies and remembrances.

> The farther backward you can look,
> the farther forward you are likely to see.
> —*Winston Churchill*

Early Photographs Gallery

EARLY PHOTOGRAPHS GALLERY

The arrival of the first Southern Pacific train, c. 1876.
Courtesy of the Los Angeles Public Library.

(*above*) The Railroad Rate War of 1886 and 1887 began a national rush to southern California. In one year the Southern Pacific Railroad deposited 120,000 passengers in Los Angeles. *Courtesy of Title Insurance & Trust.*

(*left*) The western entrance to Tujunga was through Sunland. Train passengers disembarked at the rustic Roscoe "flag stop" and journeyed by foot, horse or buggy for four and one-half dusty miles to Sunland, c. 1918. The town of Roscoe became Sun Valley in 1949. *Courtesy of the Southern Pacific Railroad.*

(*opposite*) In 1911, you could take the Glendale Suburban Electric System car to Verdugo Park in Glendale. Then, after arriving in Montrose, you took an auto stage to Tujunga over a bumpy dirt road. "The Western Empire Land Banking and Home Securing Plan—So True—So Plain That a Child Can Understand" brochure. *Unless otherwise noted, all photos courtesy of Bolton Hall Museum Archives.*

EARLY PHOTOGRAPHS GALLERY

The Glendale Suburban Electric System to Verdugo Park

FOUNDING SISTERS

EARLY PHOTOGRAPHS GALLERY

(*opposite, top*) 1913 was a year during which a few unconnected but transformative events occurred. November 5, 1913, 40,000 people gathered to greet the first water arrival over the Los Angeles Aqueduct. This picture was taken just as the water arrived after a 250-mile journey in the northwest section of the San Fernando Valley.

(*opposite, bottom*) On April 12, 1913, the cornerstone of Bolton Hall was placed. M. V. Hartranft, in dark suit (*far right*), addresses the Little Landers while William E. Smythe sits to Hartranft's left with hands folded on his lap. White tent in distance stood on the site of Camp Creemore, founded in 1910 for convalescents.

(*right*) The raising of the Little Landers flag on April 12, 1913. The cornflower blue and white flag flew proudly in front of the "Clubhouse." *The Record-Ledger.*

With high hopes and flags flying, Little Landers cross the dry Big Tujunga River, c. 1914.

17

FOUNDING SISTERS

ROCKY BEGINNINGS
Pay $3 and Start In.
Get a bag of cement, a trowel and—
Come build a home of your own.
—*Marshall V. Hartranft, c. 1914*

EARLY PHOTOGRAPHS GALLERY

Looking west from Valmont Street. The post office of Little Lands, left of Bolton Hall, c. 1914.

The "Clubhouse" in 1915. Note the outdoor plumbing (right of the flagpole).

EARLY PHOTOGRAPHS GALLERY

In this 1918 photograph, Tujunga is waiting for the population to arrive.

(*opposite, top*) This photograph was taken March 12, 1915, during a day devoted to the "spring cleaning" of Bolton Hall.

(*opposite, bottom*) This 1914 photograph shows: Foothill Boulevard (1), corner of Commerce and Greeley (2), Commerce Avenue (Sunset) (3), Tujunga Canyon Boulevard (4) and Birds Acre (just above 5). *The Record-Ledger.*

FOUNDING SISTERS

(*above*) "FOR MAN AND BEAST" was the name given to the water fountain and horse trough, which used to stand at the corner of Valmont and Commerce Avenue. The original Bolton Hall Women's Club conceived the idea of the trough, c. 1916.

(*left*) In 1921, American Legion Post 250 bought Bolton Hall for $5,500.00 from the Commonwealth Homebuilders Association. After moving into the building in August, the First Moon Festival took place in September to raise funds for the purchase of the building. By 1926, the building became City Hall. Moon Festival Brochure, 1922.

(*left*) The belfry at Bolton Hall that once housed the famous bell, so dearly loved by early residents, c. 1918.

EARLY PHOTOGRAPHS GALLERY

(*above*) Last known photograph of the Bolton Hall Bell. The Bell was stolen during a daring mid-day robbery at Travel Town in Griffith Park, Los Angeles. It was one month after the Little Landers Historical Society requested its return to Tujunga. *The Record-Ledger.* (February 27, 1964).

(*right*) Cy Mays examines the Bolton Hall Bell after an exhaustive climb to remove it from the bell tower. *The Record-Ledger* (September 1957).

23

FOUNDING SISTERS

(*left*) M. V. Hartranft ran this advertisement in the *Record-Ledger Newspaper* in 1922.

(*below*) George Harris sitting beside the hand-carved, eucalyptus wood mantel at Bolton Hall, bearing the inscription "To the Spiritual Life of the Soul." c. 1914.

(*opposite, top*) May Noonan and Marie La Bow stand beside their tent, where they lived while building their home, c. 1922.

(*opposite, bottom*) While permanent homes were being built, tent living was popular and economical. Looking north on Mt. Gleason Avenue (Walnut). Al Reed's sandwich shop (right) at corner of Mt. Gleason and Summitrose (Summit Avenue), c. 1920.

EARLY PHOTOGRAPHS GALLERY

Looking north on Sunset (Commerce Avenue) from Verdugo Hills, south of Michigan Boulevard.
Note Lamson Studio on Greeley Street, c. 1916.

EARLY PHOTOGRAPHS GALLERY

Looking east into Tujunga. Note oak tree in the middle of Michigan Avenue (Foothill Boulevard), c. 1925.

Looking south at the corner of Commerce and Valmont, c. 1925.

Looking south on Commerce Avenue (Sunset Boulevard), Tujunga's "Main Street." c. 1926.

EARLY PHOTOGRAPHS GALLERY

With streets paved and lights installed, business was booming
on Commerce Avenue, c. 1926. *The Record-Ledger.*

> If you want to get the feel of working class Southern California
> in the 1920s and 1930s, you cannot get it anymore in Hollywood.
> The epicenter of "Old Wide-open Southern California" is in
> the Sunland-Tujunga area.
> —*David Gebhardt and Robert Winter,* Architecture in Los Angeles

Don Francisco López, first owner of Rancho Tujunga and the man who discovered gold in Placerita Canyon.
The Viola Carlson Collection.

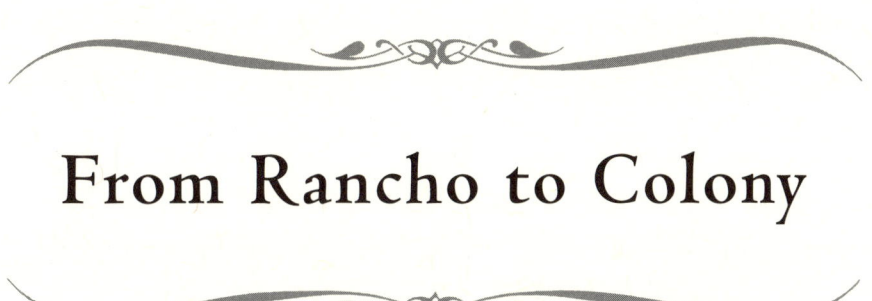

From Rancho to Colony

*I*n just seventy-three years, the eastern portion of Rancho Tujunga, now known as the City of Tujunga, emerged from the rancho era and became the Little Lands Utopian Colony.

The rise from rancho to utopian colony is a story that is colorful and dramatic, involving dreams, discoveries, heartache, the decline of the Californios, gold and lost riches, speculation, lawsuits, water rights, subdivision, and growth. Such a story mirrors the history of southern California and the entire state.

The story of the West and the land has generally been written by men about men: explorers, trappers, miners, soldiers, bandits, journalists, ranch owners, and homesteaders. It would take the combined efforts of four remarkable women—Anna Barclay Kirby, Elizabeth MacVine, Viola Carlson, and Ethel Duquette Watt—to tell the true story of Rancho Tujunga. Of record, Rancho Tujunga and portions of it were owned by twenty-six men and five women. It is interesting to note that of the five women owners, three were Hispanic and two were of European/American ancestry.[1] Of the eight hundred Mexican land grants in California, sixty-six were granted to women. The names of the female owners of Rancho Tujunga have long been forgotten but the names of their male counterparts are remembered in street names and city sections, such as Olvera, Hoover, Chapman, Wicks, Trifuño, Sherman, López, and Glassell. As a partial owner of the rancho, Elizabeth B. MacVine did have a street in neighboring Sunland named for her. Unfortunately, the sign maker converted her name to "McVine."

As we look back on the years of Spanish occupation (1784–1822), life in pastoral California can best be described as simple and feudal. During the entire Spanish period, only thirty ranchos were granted to citizens. In actuality, the land grants were little more than grazing rights. Governor Pedro Fages approved the first major land grants in 1784 to three retiring San Diego soldiers, Jose Maria Verdugo (Rancho San Rafael, 36,403 acres), Juan Jose Dominguez (Rancho San Pedro, 75,000 acres) and Manuel Nieto (Rancho Los Nietos, 158,000 acres). The ranchos, which were also called *haciendas* or *estanceas*, were primarily granted as rewards for military service and to increase the livestock and agricultural resources for the *pueblos*.[2] The Spanish period ended in 1822 when California was notified of Mexico's victory over Spain in the Mexican war for independence. The rancho era did not begin until the secularization of the missions was completed in 1836. The primary land use, during both the Spanish and Mexican eras, was cattle grazing. Cattle were the chief source of wealth, trade, and food. Sun-dried strips of beef became *carne seca*, a mainstay of the ranchers' diet.[3] Horses and sheep were also grazed on rancho acreage. The *Dons* and their wives lived in relative opulence; the *gente de razon* were rich in land and cattle but did very little purchasing with cash.[4] Producing few manufactured products, i.e., wine, cloth, and soap, forced the Californios to be dependent on foreign trade.

31

The "Yankee" traders often sold their goods to the Californios at triple the true value. The traders tempted the Californios with furniture, jewelry, salt, fireworks and timber, all of which helped the families enjoy their wealth and status. As the hide and tallow trade began to decrease in the late 1850s, the elite Californios found themselves in serious debt. The declining prices of cattle and exorbitant customs charges greatly increased the price of consumer goods. More and more cattle had to be slaughtered for "California bank notes" or "leather dollars."[5]

Life on the ranchos was enlivened by rodeos, bullfights, rooster pulls, bull and bear fights, horse races, and gambling. Few days would pass without the celebration of a particular Saint's Day or other religious holiday, a *baile* (dance), a *fandango* (an evening of singing and guitar playing) or a wedding, which could be a week-long celebration. Food and drink were consumed to excess with little thought to the future, and life was lived for the moment. The Californios exemplified the tendency of Latin Americans to make pleasure the chief end of work.[6]

The one institution that the *rancheros* took pride in, above all else, was their large families. As Margaret Mead asserted, "To be Spanish American is to belong to familia."[7] Historian Robert Cleland stated, "The rancho provided a home for a host of poor relations, entertained strangers as well as friends . . . and begat as many sons and daughters as the Hebrew patriarchs of old."[8] Of the thirty or so land grants during the Spanish era, most consisted of ex-mission land comprising some 8 million prime acres. By the time the 1848 Treaty of Guadalupe Hidalgo was signed, ending the Mexican era, some eight hundred Mexican land grants had been awarded, amounting to almost 14 million acres of land. In the last year of the Mexican era, 1846, Governor Pío Pico made eighty-seven grants, mostly to personal friends.

In March 1851, the Spanish and American legal systems collided. The United States Land Commission was created to rule on the validity of Californios' Mexican land titles. If a claimant failed to appear before the commission in San Francisco, he could forfeit his claim. Not one of the land commissioners spoke or wrote Spanish, so the burden of proof was on the rancho owner. Since most of the original boundary markers had disappeared over the years, there was great confusion. Accurate land surveying was not yet put into practice. The process of proving title to land grants was costly and time consuming. Most rancho owners had to mortgage their property and borrow money at high interest rates in order to defend their title. They were inundated with proposals from land-hungry Americans. Squatters on the Californios' disputed land were prevalent, and confrontations leading to violence and death were common.[9] Although the Treaty of Guadalupe Hidalgo guaranteed the Mexican residents of California United States citizenship and title to their land, most of them would not survive the Americanization process economically.[10] An invasion of grasshoppers, a major flood and drought from 1862 through 1864, and a smallpox epidemic brought the rancho era to an end as the land was traded for every necessity and commodity. "Ranchos like Malibu and Centinella exchanged for wines and groceries, the Los Alamitos Rancho bought with hides and tallow, the La Cañada Rancho deeded for attorney's fee. Ranchos were exchanged for horses, wines, surveyor's fees and many ranchos for mortgages."[11]

By the 1880s, most of the Mexican land grants had been traded, divided, and sold. With the advent of the transcontinental railroad, trains delivered home seekers and health seekers at an astonishing rate, replacing the sheep and cattle. The colorful rancho period sank into the history books. It would not surface again until the 1920s when Charles Lummis, John Steven McGroarty, *The Mission Play*, the Ramona pageant, and the California Auto Club would popularize once more the romance of the ranchos.

In 1886, Frank H. Barclay built the 45-room Monte Vista Hotel in the Monte Vista Colony (present-day Sunland). His hotel boasted a fireplace in every room and a two-story privy. Like most promoters of his time, he sponsored excursions from the city of Los Angeles and would then give the pitch to prospective land buyers from the cupola at the top of the hotel. He wooed the buyers with barbeques and piano recitals, but few bought land. When all was said and done, he went bankrupt in the great land boom and bust of the late 1880s.

The real story of Rancho Tujunga would not be known until 1959. In 1956, Anna Barclay Kirby, the daughter of developer Frank H. Barclay, gave her friend and neighbor, Viola Carlson, some papers and maps that would ultimately rewrite the history of the rancho. The papers given to Viola, a registered nurse, mother of five children, and a tireless student of California history, included an abstract of the 6,660.71-acre Mexican land grant encompassing present-day Lake View Terrace, Shadow Hills, Sunland, and Tujunga. Also included was a copy of the original *diseño* (map) from which Viola was able to locate the López Adobe in Little Tujunga Canyon. The next few years passed quickly as Viola verified the documents, had them translated from Spanish to English, and located the petition for Rancho Tujunga in San Francisco and Washington, D.C., as well as the complete Expediate of Rancho Tujunga from the United States District Court, Northern District of California in San Francisco.[12] Viola deposited her Rancho Tujunga papers, made in the mid-nineteenth century, at the San Fernando Mission Archives and the Huntington Library.

Three years after the gift of history from Anna Kirby, Viola and her husband Mel would make a miraculous discovery. Using the old López *diseño* (map), they began searching in the Little Tujunga Canyon for the 118 year old López Adobe. As she and Mel peered through the trees on Colonel Harper's Middle Ranch, they saw the adobe. "It was sitting just left of the caretaker's cottage, at the base of a hill."[13] They entered the adobe and spotted a readable copy of the *Los Angeles Times* dated March 8, 1899. It was glued to the cupboard, placed there so many years before by the Duquette family.[14] When the Duquettes moved from the adobe, the Vioro family came to live there until 1924. Later, the property was purchased by film director Cecil B. DeMille and renamed the Paradise Ranch. Mr. DeMille used the López Adobe as a storage facility, unaware of the building's historical significance.

In 1960, Viola interviewed Ethel Duquette Watt of Pasadena, the last known López Adobe resident, and recorded her story. The 76-year-old Ethel recalled vividly that day, March 4, 1899, when at the age of fifteen years she moved with her family into the "old López Adobe." The spunky retired nurse remembered what life was like in an old adobe at the turn of the century:

> The Adobe had three rooms, a four foot wide porch and large flat stones at the kitchen door. About fifteen feet from the porch was a trellis of grapes. Every adobe had its olive, fig and pomegranite [*sic*] trees, the large leaf prickly pear cactus, and oleander bush, rosemary, lemon verbena plants and a lemon tree. Gold of atter [*sic*] rose, plus geraniums of all kinds if the yard was large enough. The "must" was first and last the tomatoes and chilies plus corn, pole beans, which were often planted after the corn came through the ground, the corn acting as a pole for the beans. These were followed by onions, garlic, cucumbers, water and musk melons. We used to gather the wild green mustard and mushrooms following the sheep camps. I have gathered gallons of them and water cress in the streams, and the dried corn stocks in the fields for winter kindling—a scarce commodity.
>
> The early Californians used to make the most delicious tea from the very small leaves on the tips of the branches of both the orange and lemon trees. They used both but preferred the orange. In the fall of the year, as the chilies just showed the first bit of red, they were picked, strung on stout string and hung from the adobe roof. They were a beautiful red and shown like they had been polished. When the wind blew they looked like red pygmies dancing in the breeze. At the end of the adobe was an old, purple lilac bush.
>
> Every adobe, every sheep camp had its outdoor eating place; four or more poles latched together with brush over them for shade, and the oil cloth covering the table—always a garish hue—very colorful. At the sheep camps the tables were void of cover on the tables. I can still taste the cold mutton, sour dough bread plus the glass of claret which for me was always weakened with water, at which I always rebelled.
>
> The backyards of these old adobes would be tamped down so hard; they were sprinkled daily and swept with a broom and we danced on them.[15]

Prior to the rediscovery of the adobe in 1959, noted anthropologist Dr. Mark Harrington, with the help of Martin Feliz and Roger Little, had found the López Adobe in 1933 and made a quick sketch of the three rooms and the large eucalyptus trees surrounding them. At that time, history books, newspapers, and

Early photograph of the López Station situated among the fields of wild mustard and roaming cattle in San Fernando. By 1912, it would be under the Sepulveda Dam, c. 1870s. *The Viola Carlson Collection.*

local residents had always believed that the hills and valleys of Sunland and Tujunga were a part of the San Rafael Spanish land grant, owned by the Verdugo family and consisting of the modern cities of Glendale, Eagle Rock, and La Cañada-Flintridge. Dr. Harrington's papers were filed at the Southwest Museum. After years of research, Viola confidently declared that Rancho Tujunga was a Mexican land grant to Pedro and Francisco López in 1840. The brothers had petitioned the Honorable Assembly of the Department of the Californios for a land grant "known by the name of *Arroyo de Tejunga*, bounded at the South by the *Sierra Madre* and the *Sierra Burdugos* [*sic*], at the East by oak woodland and at the West by the *Partequelo.*"

Who were the López family, whose names can still be found on streets and canyons of the San Fernando Valley? The brothers were Pedro and Josef Francisco de Garcia López, both born at the Mission San Gabriel to Maria Dolores Salgado López and Juan Bautista López.[16] Francisco was born on March 9, 1802, the eighth of ten children. Pedro was born in 1805. The boys were the grandsons of Claudio and Maria Louisa Cota López. Claudio was the *majordomo* (manager) of the San Gabriel Mission from 1821 through 1830 and moved to the Pueblo of Los Angeles in 1826 to become *alcalde* (mayor). Ancestors of the López family were of Spanish heritage and had arrived in Mexico City from Spain. They moved to Baja California before coming north to the San Gabriel Mission.

Pedro and Francisco had the dress and manners of fine gentlemen. Although Francisco would take a more prominent place in the history of the San Fernando

(*above*) The cattle brand of Francisco López (upper left corner).

(*right*) The cattle brand of Pedro López.

Valley and the state of California, Pedro was appointed the *majordomo* of the San Fernando Mission when the Mexican government took possession in 1834. The López family acquired several ranchos and adobes in the area and the brothers were often in need of additional grazing land for their cattle, horses and sheep.

Francisco studied at the university in Mexico City. He took courses in history, literature, languages, and mining. He then moved to Santa Barbara on September 10, 1822, and married Maria Antonita Feliz. In 1823, their daughter was born at the Santa Barbara Mission. Sadly, just prior to her second birthday, she passed away in San Fernando.

Nicknames had to be given to the various Francisco Lópezes in order to keep their identities separate. Francisco "Chico" had a ranch in Antelope Valley, while the first co-owner of Rancho Tujunga was called Francisco "Cuso." Cuso spent much of his time hunting and prospecting for silver, gold, and other metals. As he was considered an experienced miner, he was chosen to guide the eminent mineralogist Andres Catillero on his visit to the province in 1840. Francisco "Cuso" was convinced that gold-bearing stratum started in Mexico and extended north up the California coast.

Francisco's niece, Jacopa, and her husband, Antonio del Valle, settled in the upper Santa Clarita Valley. Rancho San Francisco Xavier was granted to the del Valles in 1839. Uncle Francisco leased a portion of their 49,000 acres to graze his cattle. After just two years of marriage, Jacopa's husband died and Francisco was appointed *majordomo* of the rancho and executor of the estate. Antonio's 33-year-old son Ignacio, from a previous marriage, was awarded the Camulos section of the rancho (13,000 acres in present-day Ventura County), while Francisco's relatives gained the remainder of the rancho. Although the López family acreage increased, Francisco "Cuso" would be remembered in history not for being the first co-owner of Rancho Tujunga, but for an event that occurred on his fortieth birthday. A full six years before James Marshall discovered gold at Sutter's sawmill on the American River in January 1848, Cuso made the first documented discovery of gold in California, March 9, 1842, in Placerita Canyon on the backside of the San Gabriel Mountains, thirty-five miles northwest of Los Angeles. His discovery became a legend in the history of early Spanish California.

Perhaps the finest account of this magnificent discovery was written by the late historian Jerry Reynolds. He sets the stage for this golden moment thus:

The long rainy winter was coming to an end on March 9, 1842, as a brilliant sun rose from behind jagged deep blue mountains far to the east where the Rio Santa Clara was

FOUNDING SISTERS

The proud López family and early notables pose for a fiftieth wedding anniversary photograph for Doña Catalina (2) and Don Geronimo López (3), c. 1890.

After inspecting the stock, and taking a hard stroll up and down the mountains, he [López] felt rather fatigued, and, as the hour of noon had arrived, he selected a shady tree under which to rest and have lunch. Recently the tree has been acclaimed the oldest in Southern California. It is an oak, said to be 500 years old. He alighted from his horse, and his servant spread a *sarape* [sic], or Mexican blanket, on the ground, unsaddled his master's horse and placed the saddle on one end of the sarape [sic], that it might serve as a head rest [sic]. The boy then made the coffee and served the lunch. After a lengthy *siesta*, *Don* Francisco awoke and suddenly remembered his wife's request. Taking a knife from his belt, he went to the slope nearby and began to dig up some of the wild onions. Noticing some yellow particles clinging to the roots, he examined them wonderingly. He shook the earth from the roots, set them down and started to dig again with vigor. Upon examining the earth closely, he suddenly started to his feet and shouted, "Gold! I have found it at last! Gold! Gold!"[18]

born. A long, narrow valley came to life, dotted by wide branching oak trees sprouting their first leaves over a carpet of lush emerald green grass. Early wildflowers were beginning to blossom—the snowy white Castilian rose, yellow Spanish broom and golden poppy splashed the landscape with color. Francisco López strode out of the red-roofed Casa de Rancho, which perched on a bluff overlooking the confluence of the St. Clair and Castaic creeks. He sampled the brisk, invigorating air. It was his 40th birthday, and he planned to inspect the herds of cattle and do a little hunting, then return to his ranch house for some festivities his wife had planned that evening. *Dona* Maria Antonia asked him to gather some herbs and spices growing in the canyons as she handed a picnic lunch, tied in a neat bundle, to his Indian *mozo*, Juan.[17]

Mr. Reynolds continues by quoting Francisco's grand-niece, Francisca López Belderrain:

After a night of celebrating Cuso's birthday and his discovery of gold, he and other family members traveled to the Pueblo of Los Angeles to put the gold in the safe at Abel Stearns's general store. Stearns, a wealthy businessman, then sent a sample and a mining claim to Governor Alvarado. The governor had jewelry for his family made from part of the sample and sent the remainder to Mexico City. Francisco's claim was denied, since it was on private property. Stearns then sent Alfred Robinson to Washington, D.C., to get an assay report. The mint at Philadelphia found the 18.34 ounces of gold to be of high quality and then used it to produce gold coins.

Just how much gold was removed from this area during the boom years of 1842–47 is not known. According to Abel Stearns, production varied but averaged between $6,000 and $8,000 per year. After the American victory in the Mexican-American War of 1847, the majority of miners returned to Mexico. By today's exchange rate the total production of the mine would be approximately $7,280,000. The following year, Francisco discovered gold in Santa Feliciana Canyon (now covered by Lake Piru). Remembering his past mistakes, he filed for a land grant in the traditional manner. He was awarded Rancho Temescal, consisting of 3,560 acres.

What was the fate of the centuries-old "Oak of the Golden Dream"? In the late 1930s, the plaque showing the tree's designation as California Registered Landmark No. 168 was stolen. This famous tree was rededicated in 1946 and again on November 15, 1992. On that occasion, two hundred members of Los Pobladores, descendents of the founding families of Los Angeles, the Ancient Order of E Campus Vitus, and the Santa Clarita Valley Historical Society placed a final monument to the tree in a colorful ceremony.

Francisco's son, Francisco Ramon, married Eduarda Villa but the couple remained childless, with only nieces and nephews to carry on the López traditions. Pedro López's daughter, Catalina, and her husband, Geronimo López, built a large home on their forty acres near the San Fernando Mission. Known as López Station, where the Butterfield Overland Mail stage stopped twice a week until 1874, it also housed a general store and the valley's first post office and was home to the valley's first English-teaching school. The station was always lively with the López's thirteen children, but the tireless Catalina proved to be a gracious hostess. Catalina's brother, Valentin, built his sister and brother-in-law a two-story adobe in 1883 at the northwest corner

The famous oak of the Golden Dream in Placerita Canyon, north of Mission San Fernando where Francisco López discovered gold on March 9, 1842. A small gold rush followed as evidenced by the mining operation tailings surrounding the tree, c. 1876. *The Viola Carlson Collection.*

of Maclay and Pico streets. Catalina died at the age of 86 years in 1918, and her husband died in 1921. In 1975, the adobe was opened to the public and now houses the San Fernando Valley Historical Society.[19] Pedro López served for many years not only as the *majordomo* of the San Fernando Mission but also as a Judge of the Plains, the equivalent of today's sheriff.

On December 5, 1840, Governor Juan B. Alvarado granted the brothers, Pedro and Francisco, Rancho Tejunga. Sunland-Tujunga is now situated on all of the rancho, lots 45 and 46 of the Rancho La Cañada and public lands in Township 2, North Ranges 13 and 14 west of the San Bernardino meridian. The land grant consisted of 1½ square Mexican leagues or 6,660.71 acres. The minute neighbors Jose Maria Villa and Julio Verdugo heard of the new grant, they insisted it was on their land. After an inspection, the López claim was upheld and Verdugo and Villa withdrew their protests. As a condition of the new grant, the brothers had to build and occupy an adobe on their property. They chose to have their ranch manager live in the small home. Now the López cattle could roam freely. The ancient Indian village of Tuhunga, vacated since 1800, was on the northeast portion of Rancho Tejunga. The name Tejunga had been accepted by the Spanish and Mexican governments, and Rancho Tejunga was acknowledged by the Mexican government as the official name of the land surrounding the Indian village.

On May 13, 1845, Rancho Tejunga was traded to a Fernandiño, Jose Miguel Trifuño, for Rancho de Cahuenga. The Cahuenga rancho consisted of only 388 acres but was situated in the heart of Rancho Providencia, much closer to the routes leading to the Pueblo of Los Angeles. Trifuño had been a captain of the guard at Mission San Fernando and was married to a Californio, Rafaela Cañedo. Their marriage produced five children.[20] On May 17, 1850, Jose Miguel and his wife sold one-half of Rancho Tujunga back to Francisco López for $200. Three months later, the Trifuños sold the other half of the rancho to well-known Los Angeles merchant David W. Alexander for $200. On September 27, 1851, Francisco "Cuso" sold his one-half to Augustin Olvera for $400. When Francisco died the following year, a claim was filed at the General Land Office of the United States by David Alexander, Augustin Olvera, and the heirs of Francisco López, for title of Rancho Tujunga. In October 1853, David Alexander sold his share of the rancho for $120.

In September 1855, Francis Mellus sold to Augustin Olvera his one-half of Rancho Tujunga for $1 plus Olvera's interest and right in Rancho de Cahuenga. The investments made by Alexander and Mellus marked the beginning of the American period of ownership. Olvera then mortgaged Rancho Tujunga to Leon Hoover for $1,000. On April 15, 1859, Vincent Hoover bought Rancho Tujunga at a sheriff's auction to redeem the mortgage on which Olvera defaulted. The property sold for $1,600. The following year, on August 16, 1860, Francisco's wife, Maria, sold all her rights in Rancho Tujunga to Augustin Olvera for $500.

On March 14, 1868, Rita G. de la Ossa received a possessory claim for 160 acres of Rancho Tujunga. Two months later, Vincent Hoover sold his acreage to Wake Bryarly and William F. O'Neal for $2,000. Bryarly and O'Neal, from Virginia City, Nevada, then sold the property (February 6, 1869) to William M. Fileston for $6,666 in gold coin, with payments due in gold coin for the next year. Just one month after the big sale, Wake Bryarly died suddenly in San Francisco, intestate (the court awarded his wife Mary his estate the following year). Five months later, William F. O'Neal sold to Mary his one-quarter share of the rancho for $2,200 in gold coin. Mary became sole owner of one-half of Rancho Tujunga.

Six months later, Augustin Olvera quit claimed his rights to Augusto Martiñon for $1. Seven days later,

In 1823, you would have spent 21 days walking from the San Diego Mission to the San Francisco Mission. Each Mission and bell were spaced one day apart along the route of "El Camino Real." *Golden California— Official State Travel Magazine* (Autumn 1993).

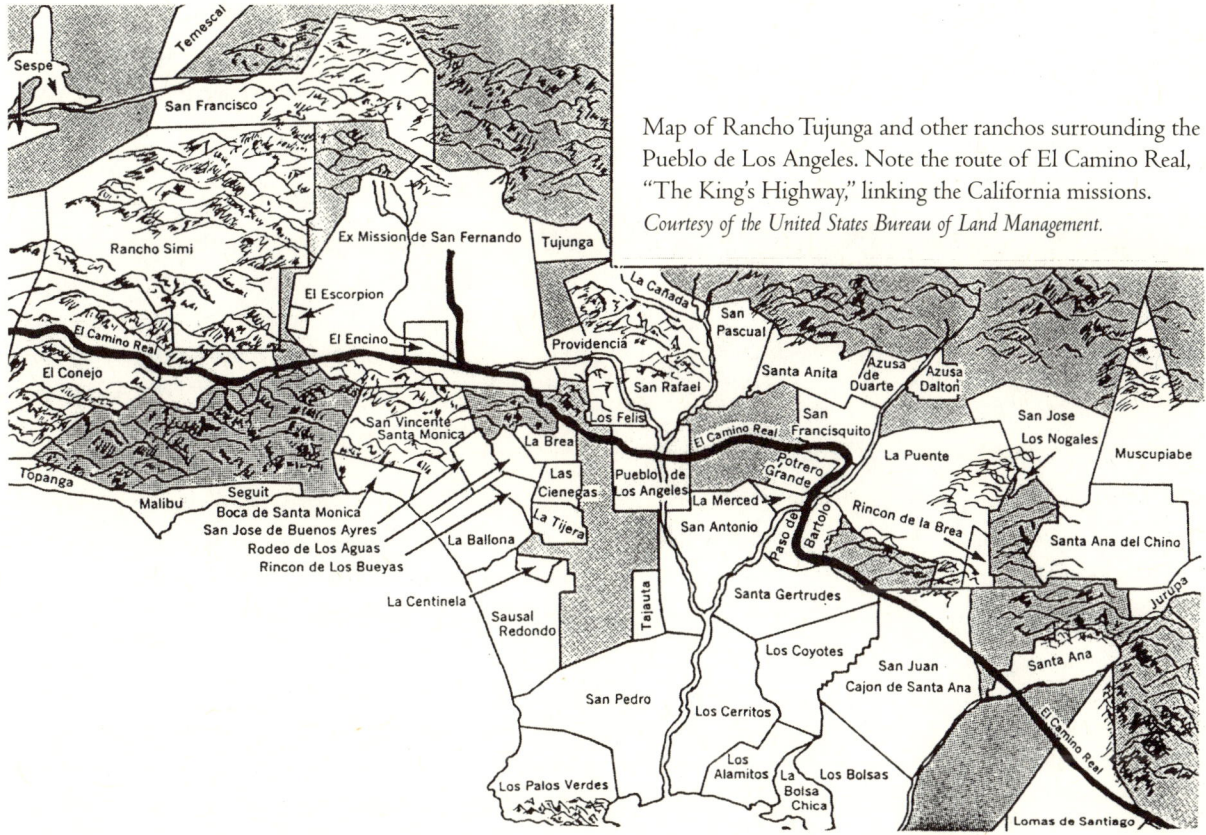

Map of Rancho Tujunga and other ranchos surrounding the Pueblo de Los Angeles. Note the route of El Camino Real, "The King's Highway," linking the California missions. *Courtesy of the United States Bureau of Land Management.*

William M. Fileston sold to George F. Emery, J. W. Hobson, and Vernon Seaman three-quarters of the rancho for $1 and a promise to complete the payments to Mary Bryarly. On September 13, 1871, Mary Bryarly filed suit against William M. Fileston, George Emery, and J. W. Hobson for lack of payment. Fourteen days later the court ordered that the property must be sold. An attorney, George Smith, from the law firm of Glassell, Chapman and Smith, conducted the sale. The description of Rancho Tujunga was posted on the front door of the Bella Union Hotel in downtown Los Angeles and on the door of the downtown courthouse. Mary won her lawsuit against Fileston and also her court fees. Three years later on May 22, 1875, Mary, an astute businesswoman, sold her one-half of the rancho to Andrew Glassell for $5,250.[21] He advertised "Rancho Tejunga" throughout American and European cities.

Settler John Cox was the first Tujunga resident of record in 1883. His home was located at the corner of Haines Canyon and Tujunga Canyon Boulevard. On June 22, 1883, Andrew Glassell sold his 2,300 acres (three-eighths of the rancho), the Monte Vista Tract, to General Sherman Page (founder of Pacific Electric Interurban Railway) and F. C. Howes for $40,000. Just three years later, General Page and Mr. Howes sold their acreage to Frank H. Barclay, Charles McCreary, B. F. George and W. Kierulff for $66,500.

From the time Frank Barclay and his partners bought the Monte Vista Tract in the summer of 1886, the buying and selling of the old Rancho Tujunga land was extensive. In one day, December 17, 1886, the following transactions occurred: William Lacy sold to Ferdinand F. Frazier (20 acres for $2,500); Ferdinand F. Frazier sold to F. H. Barclay for $3,000; and by the end of the day, John MacVine and his wife, Elizabeth (Bury) MacVine, bought 40 acres for $8,000.

Page and Howes filed a claim for water on the Big Tujunga Creek on June 27, 1888. Their water line start-

39

FOUNDING SISTERS

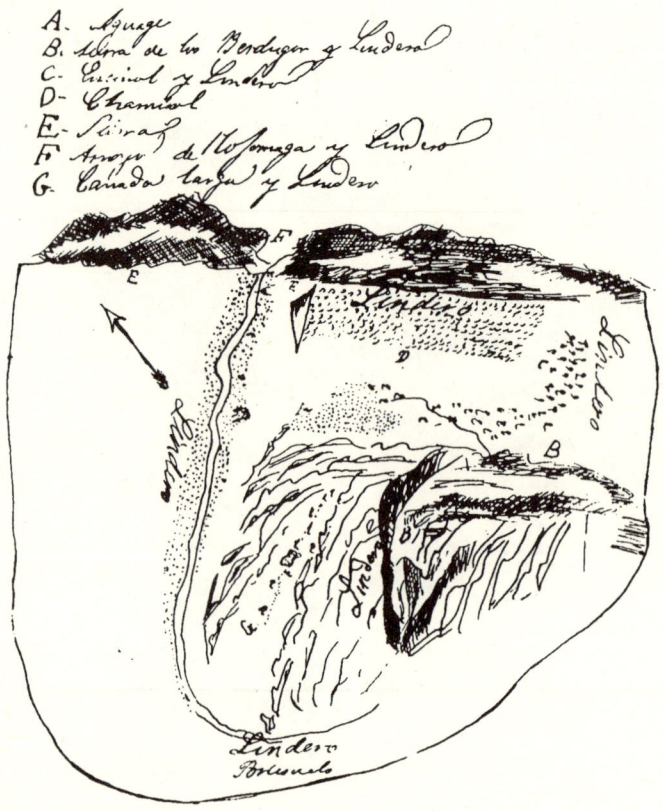

A - Aguage - *Spring*
B - Sierra de los Berdugos y Lindero - *Verdugo mountains and Boundary*
C - Encinal y Lindero - *Oak grove and Boundary*
D - Chamisal - *Chaparral*
E - Sierra - *Mountain range*
F - Arroyo de Tujunga - *Tujunga Canyon*
G - Canada larga y Lindero - *Wide canyon and Boundary*
Lindero Portesuelo - *Gateway Boundary*

Copy of the original *diseño* (map) that accompanied the petition for Rancho Tujunga, prepared by Francisco López. *The Viola Carlson Collection.*

(*opposite*) Early map indicating the location of the López Adobe in Rancho Tujunga, c. 1850.

ed in Pipe Canyon, went across the Johnson Ranch, and ended at a water main in Lot 12 of the village of Monte Vista. The village was platted in 1888.

The other five-eighths of Rancho Tujunga was sold to banker and developer Moses L. Wicks, who was involved in several boomtowns in 1885. Before Wicks filed his subdivision plan, portions of the rancho were sold to Jacob Shelly, John M. Warner, and the Reverend J. S. Flory in 1884 and early 1885. The eastern portion of Rancho Tujunga was platted by King, Dexter and Gilbert in 1888.

The Civil War had set into motion two events that would change the history of the West Coast. The economic decline brought about by the war forced a large-scale emigration from the South and Midwest. By the end of the war, the California towns of San Diego, Los Angeles, and Santa Barbara were also on the wane. Congressional passage of the Pacific Railroad Act in 1862 started the westward expansion of the railways. The completion of the transcontinental rail line to San Francisco in 1869 began to change the California economic outlook. Within a short time, some seventy thousand passengers arrived on the West Coast. As they traveled south by steamer and stagecoach, they were impressed by the beauty of the land. Letters sent back home often were printed in newspapers and spoke of the land south of the Tehachapi Mountains as "a sun kissed agrarian paradise." The national panic of 1873 left behind a trail of lost fortunes and financial ruin, and the collapse of the Temple Workman Bank in Los Angeles left the economy of the city destroyed. In 1876, the population of Los Angeles was 16,000 people. Just four years later, the total had dropped to 11,183 people.

The selling of California would be accomplished by the emerging railroads, and the *New York Herald* and *Harper's Magazine* travel writer, Charles Nordhoff. His 1872 guide, *California: for Health, Pleasure, and Residence: A Book for Travellers and Settlers*, would sell three million copies, including translations into many foreign languages. His book also provided hope to the weary farmer and listed land prices and information on housing, transportation and schools. A special chapter was written for invalids and would later be responsible for filling the trains with "coughing pilgrims."[22]

The rate wars between the Santa Fe Railroad and the Southern Pacific Railroad made national and international news. By March 6, 1887, the rate from Missouri to California had been bargained down to $1. Tales of drought and smallpox epidemics were soon forgotten. The railroads were now surprised to find out they did not have enough cars to transport the people. They soon put into service "immigrant trains," which consisted of sixteen cars pulled by two engines. Each car featured folding chairs that flattened to beds. Stoves were provided so that coffee and food could be cooked. Most families carried their food in big wicker hampers. The bonding between families was much as it had been during the period of prairie schooners and wagon trains. Large groups going to a specific colony would take an excursion train.

Both the Santa Fe and Southern Pacific Railroads had hundreds of "Zulu" cars. These cars operated on freight trains. Usually one member of a family would ride the "Zulu" car along with the family's household belongings, while the remainder of the family rode the immigrant train. In the case of the Wiemans, the entire family and their possessions arrived in one boxcar.

The Santa Fe Railroad arrived in Los Angeles via Colton and Pasadena on May 31, 1887. Brass bands, speeches, and beer greeted the new arrivals. Soon flag-draped trains, exuberant auction sales accompanied by brass bands, and free lunches became the norm. Tourists, home seekers, and "coughing pilgrims" overwhelmed the citizens of Los Angeles. Once home to cattle rustlers and proclaimed the "queen of the cow towns," Los Angeles now became a cosmopolitan city. Between 1880 and 1890, the population of California rose from 517,000 to 1,200,000 people.

Those seeking the American dream were Anglo-Saxon and primarily from the Midwest. The culture of the Californios and Indians was superceded by the new arrivals—baseball replaced bailes and band concerts in the park replaced *fandangos*. A schoolteacher, Patric Tonner, wrote:

> The Indian for a thousand years
> These lovely ales possessed.
> The Spaniard for a century
> The native race oppressed.
> And now, the blue-eyed savior
> From o'er the distant main,
> With steady step is driving back
> The dark-eyed race of Spain.[23]

The once sleepy *pueblo* of Los Angeles was now a town in a hurry to grow up. Two thousand real estate offices

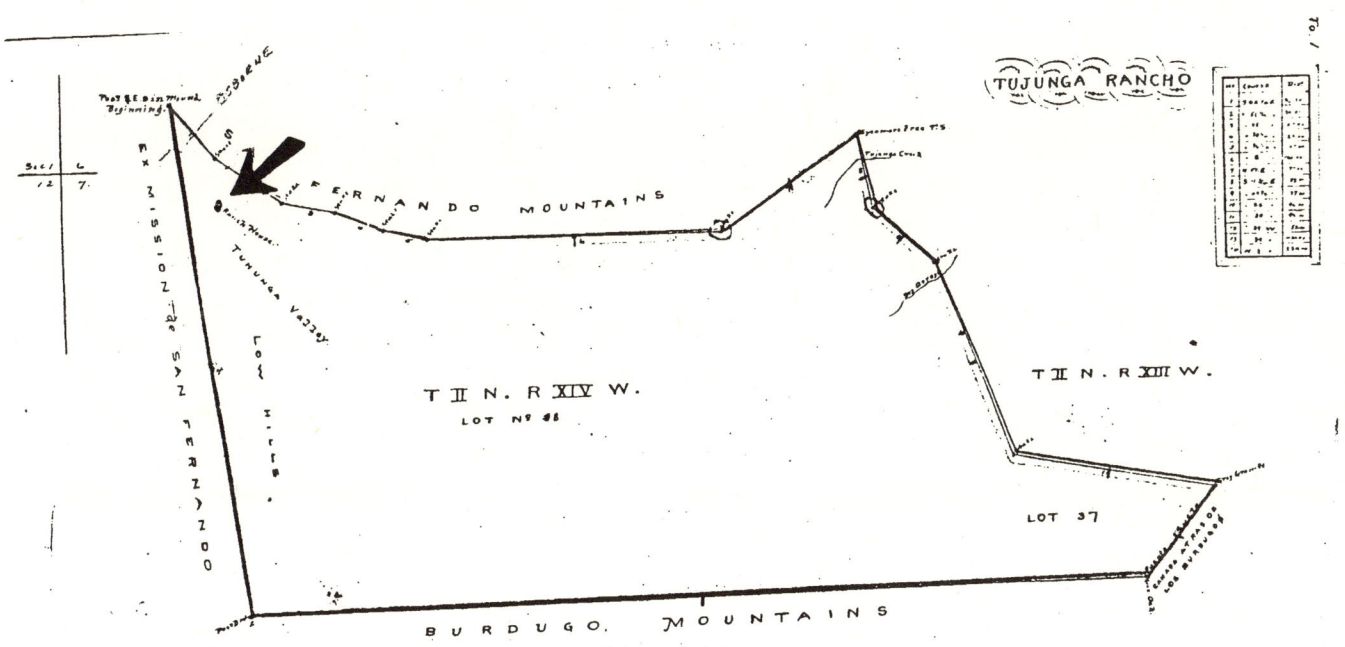

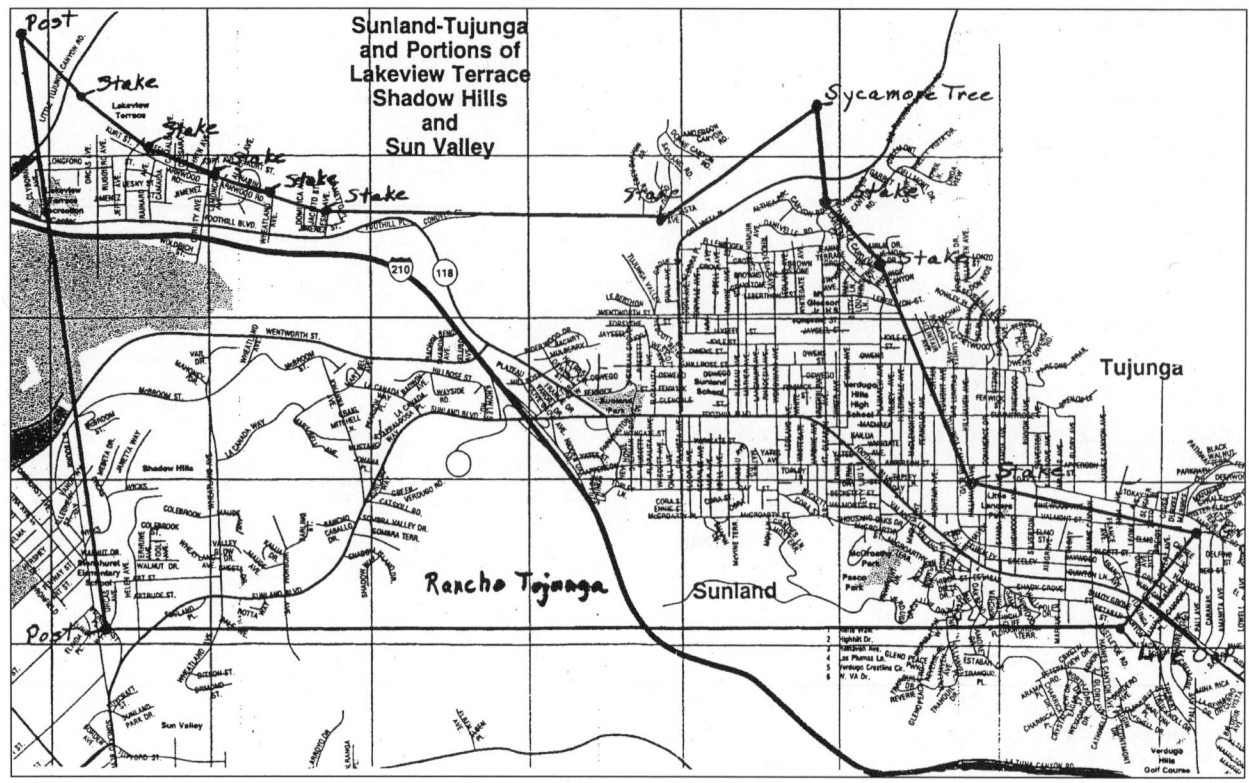

1858 map of Rancho Tujunga superimposed onto a 1989 map of the area. *Created by Jackie Karvis in 2002.*

sprang up almost overnight. The professional land promoters or "escrow Indians" roamed the streets of downtown Los Angeles ready to "scalp" the newly arrived innocents. Just as the forty-niners had salted their mines with fool's gold, these promoters were not above placing oranges on Joshua trees or other greenery near the rail routes.

Many of the real estate transactions were never recorded and the easy flow of money prompted fraud and corruption. Years later, most promoters were redeemed when property values greatly increased. One of the most prominent promoters of the day was Moses L. Weeks, who, at the age of thirty-five years, had land holdings that went from Balloña Creek (Playa del Rey) to the northern portion of the San Fernando Valley, including Rancho Tujunga. The boom brought greater amounts of people, and they were responsible for a richer economic structure. In Los Angeles folklore, the word "real" meant real estate.[24]

The new immigrants brought the morals and customs of America's heartland, large amounts of capital, and the ability to adjust to a new land. Sarah Comstock made a good analogy when she stated, "Los Angeles could never have accomplished the feat of getting that way by a slow and gradual growth. Rather, it is the result of several inundations which have stratified like lava."

The infrastructure of Los Angeles was so overburdened that four new schools of higher education had to be built. More homes, an upgraded water system, libraries, and new churches led to an intensification of civic pride. Los Angeles could boast of having a new urban profile. In 1885, at the start of the boom years, the streets of Los Angeles were illuminated by electric lights.

The brief glory of the real estate boom was due not so much to the competitive rate wars of the railroads

> IT IS OUR MANIFEST DESTINY to overspread
> the continent allotted by Providence
> for the free development of
> our yearly multiplying millions.
> —Jane Cazeau, reporter, 1845

but more to the railways history of land acquisition and sales. European investors joined midwestern farmers who had experienced six years of successful harvests. Railroad agents went far beyond America's eastern coast to spread the word of western land. All of Europe knew about California and every sea-going passenger was given "the pitch." Railroad pamphlets promoting California often showed the wide variety of foods grown in the regions, especially oranges. Speakers, pamphlets, books, and booklets describing California's wonderful climate would circulate throughout the United States, Canada, and Europe. Travelers and tourists returning to dingy cities and cold weather would remember the Sunshine State, where the scent of roses and orange blossoms permeated the air. Just as M. V. Hartranft would later teach the public to pronounce Tujunga as Tu-hoon-ga, so would Los Angeles teach the new arrivals the proper pronunciation of her name:

> The Lady would remind you, please,
> Her name is not Lost Angie Lees—
> Nor Angie anything whatever.
> She hopes her friends will be so clever
> To share her fit historic pride,
> The G shall not be jellified.
> O long, G hard, and rhyme with "yes"—
> And all about Loce Ang-el-ess.[25]

During June, July, and August 1887, over $38 million was exchanged in real estate transactions in Los Angeles County. Enthusiasm continued, but by the first few months of 1888, the boom collapsed, leaving in its wake ghost towns like Joyful, Dundee, Monte Vista, Ivanhoe, Lordsburg, Ramona, and Raymond.

From 1886 through 1888, Los Angeles County had 1,770 tract maps, subdivisions, and replats filed. Most of these were on the perimeter of Pasadena or Los Angeles. Of the one hundred towns that were plated, sixty-two faded from memory. Haste and speculation resulted in a plethora of lawsuits and bankruptcies, keeping the attorneys of Los Angeles busy. Once the railroad promoters stepped aside, the Boards of Trade and the Los Angeles Chamber of Commerce took over the promotion of the Southland. The Chamber of Commerce organized costly exhibits at the Chicago Fair, the Atlantic Exposition, and the Omaha and St. Louis fairs. For two years the chamber sponsored a "California on Wheels" train that visited every major city in the South and Midwest. By 1900, Los Angeles was the best-advertised city in the nation, and visiting

Interior of Pullman sleeping car on Pacific Railroad, c. 1887.
From an early California travel guide.

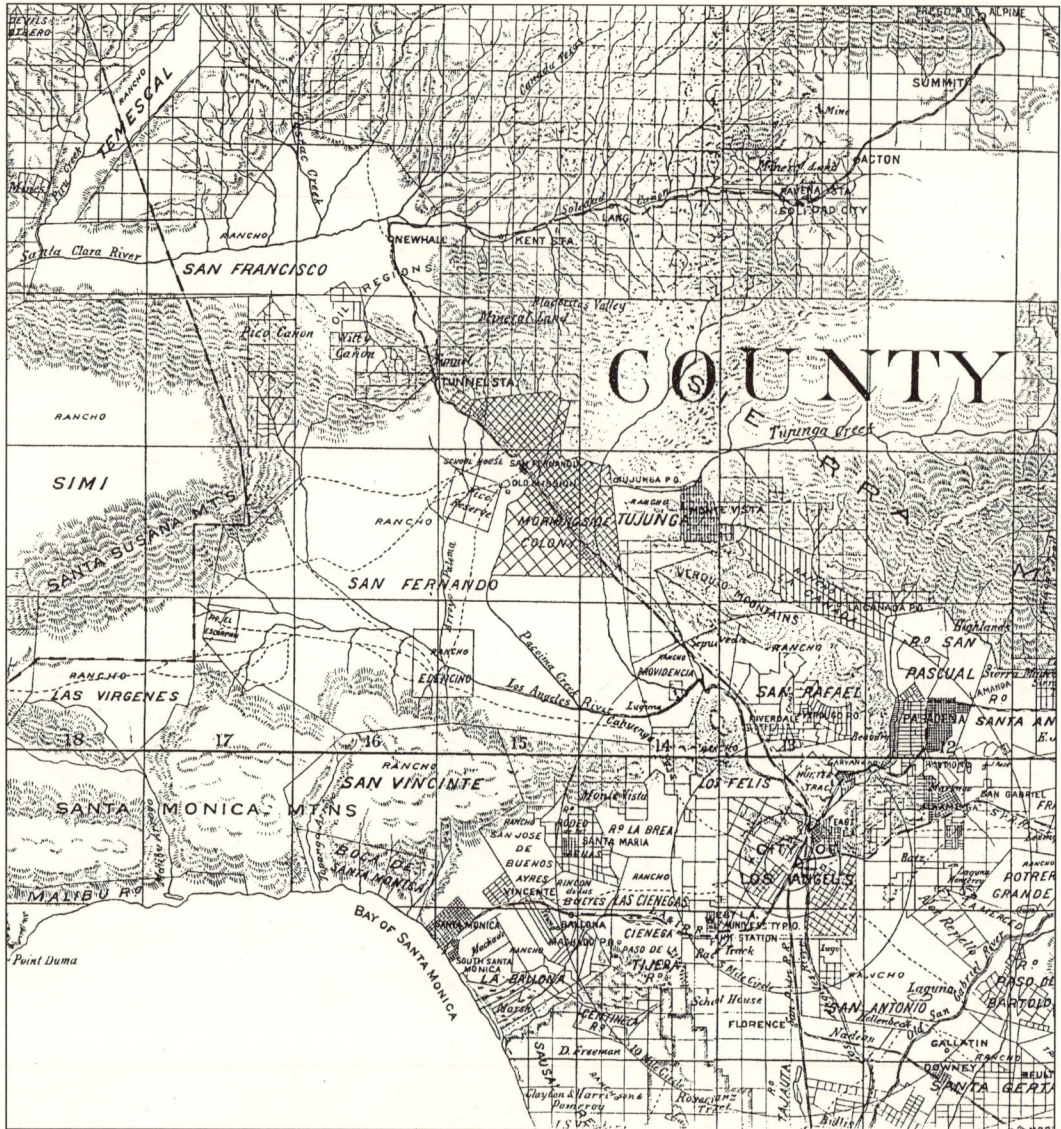

California became the rage. The new interurban Pacific Electric Cars took tourists to the beach, the mountains, *The Mission Play* in San Gabriel and the ostrich and alligator farms. The third wave of immigrants made Los Angeles a tourist town. Curio stores, freak exhibits, special excursion buses, and a schedule of "must-sees" were now available to visitors.

Though the climate of southern California has been blamed for the eccentric social behavior of its citizens, sociologist Franz Boas said, "The study of the cultural history of any particular region shows clearly that geographical conditions by themselves have no creative force and are certainly no absolute determination of culture. It would be the volume and velocity of the migration to Los Angeles that would create the region's cultural landscape."[26]

Each wave of migration brought new modes of living that would be superimposed or placed side by side with the old. *Los Angeles Times* columnist and Tujunga resident Harry Carr wrote, "In cities like New York, where the area is restricted and there can be no spread, old buildings are torn down to make way for new. But

FROM RANCHO TO COLONY

(*right*) Frank and Mary Barclay's home in Los Angeles. (top to bottom) Edith, Anna and the ill-fated Mary Lenore, c. 1883.

(*opposite*) In this 1886 map, compiled by Howland and Koeberle, Tujunga Creek and Rancho Tujunga appear with the final and official spelling. *Map courtesy of the Huntington Library.*

Southern California has rarely bothered to remove the old."[27]

Southern California's large population of cults and cultists has always been fodder for the press and the nation. In 1895, Mrs. Charles Steward Daggett wrote, "The millennium has already begun in Pasadena and that even now, there are more sanctified cranks to the acre than any other town in America."[28] Julia M. Sloane wrote in 1925, "Los Angeles is full of people with queer quirks and they aren't confined to gardeners."

The Monte Vista subdivision was unique in that its water supply was assured. Page and Howes advertised,

> Monte Vista. The most beautiful tract in Southern California. Magnificent Scenery. Healthful Clime. Bountiful soil. Pure Mountain Water. Home of the Fig, the Olive, the Orange, Lemon, Prune and Vine. *No Fogs! No Frosts! No Insect Pests!*

Another of their ads ran, "Tejunga Park! This desirable tract . . . for sale. $35 to $100 per acre." And still another read,

> Monte Vista—New Colony and Health Resort. Nature's Sanitarium. Dry, invigorating air, pure mountain water—abundant and never failing. Elevation 1,500 feet above sea level. Consumption and all kindred diseases cured without medicine.

In 1884, Frank Barclay built the two-story, five-bedroom Park Hotel at the corner of Sherman Avenue (Sherman Grove) and Central Avenue (Fenwick Street) in Monte Vista. The Barclays— Frank, Mary and daughters, Anna (Frankie), Edith (LuLu) and Mary Lenore—lived at the Park Hotel while the magnificent Monte Vista Hotel was being built. When the Barclays moved into the Monte Vista in 1887, Frank had his good friend Ben Willis and his wife, affectionately known as "Aunt Randy," run the Park Hotel.

In Barclay's advertisement in the *Los Angeles Times*, the charming Park Hotel and its salubrious climate were described as "small, but neat and clean, reasonable and facing a grand oak grove." The price for a night's lodging was $2.50.[29] Frank was an avid hunter and could often be seen hunting the many rabbits that resided in the grove of Monte Vista Park. Little is known of his wife, but Monte Vista Village was in love with his daughters. Anna (Frankie) was described as "energetic, madcap and ahead of her time." She was a legend in the village and its most famous "tom boy."[30] Daughter Mary Lenore, just twenty years old, met an early death. She went to a party in Burbank in the family's horse and carriage. After spending the night, she started home early the

45

(*top*) The earliest known photograph of the Monte Vista Hotel. Mary Barclay on porch, Anna, Dicky and cousin Ethel in small cart pulled by burro, Edith and Mary Lenore in the large horse drawn cart, c. 1886. *Courtesy of Author.*

(*above*) F. H. Barclay's highly publicized lithograph of Monte Vista, c. 1889.

(*left*) Early photograph of Monte Vista Park, c. 1888. *Courtesy of Author.*

next morning. Mary had epilepsy and, on the way back to Monte Vista, suffered a grand mal seizure and fell over the side of the carriage. Her head wedged between the wheel and the shaft of the carriage so that as her horse moved forward, her skull was crushed. Several hours later, Miss Phillips, a mail carrier for the village, came upon the gruesome scene. She removed Mary from the wheel, put her in the carriage and took her home to a grieving family and community.[31]

In 1890, the Monte Vista Hotel was sold to Quinton Rowley, brother of Sunland early pioneer Loren Rowley. While Loren and his wife Virginia built their home on Hillrose Avenue, they lived in Quinton's hotel. Although the hotel was bought as an investment, Quinton encouraged Loren and his family to live there. Two of Loren and Virginia's children were born at the hotel: Robert, their second child, in 1898 and Dorothy, their first daughter, in 1902.[32] Robert was

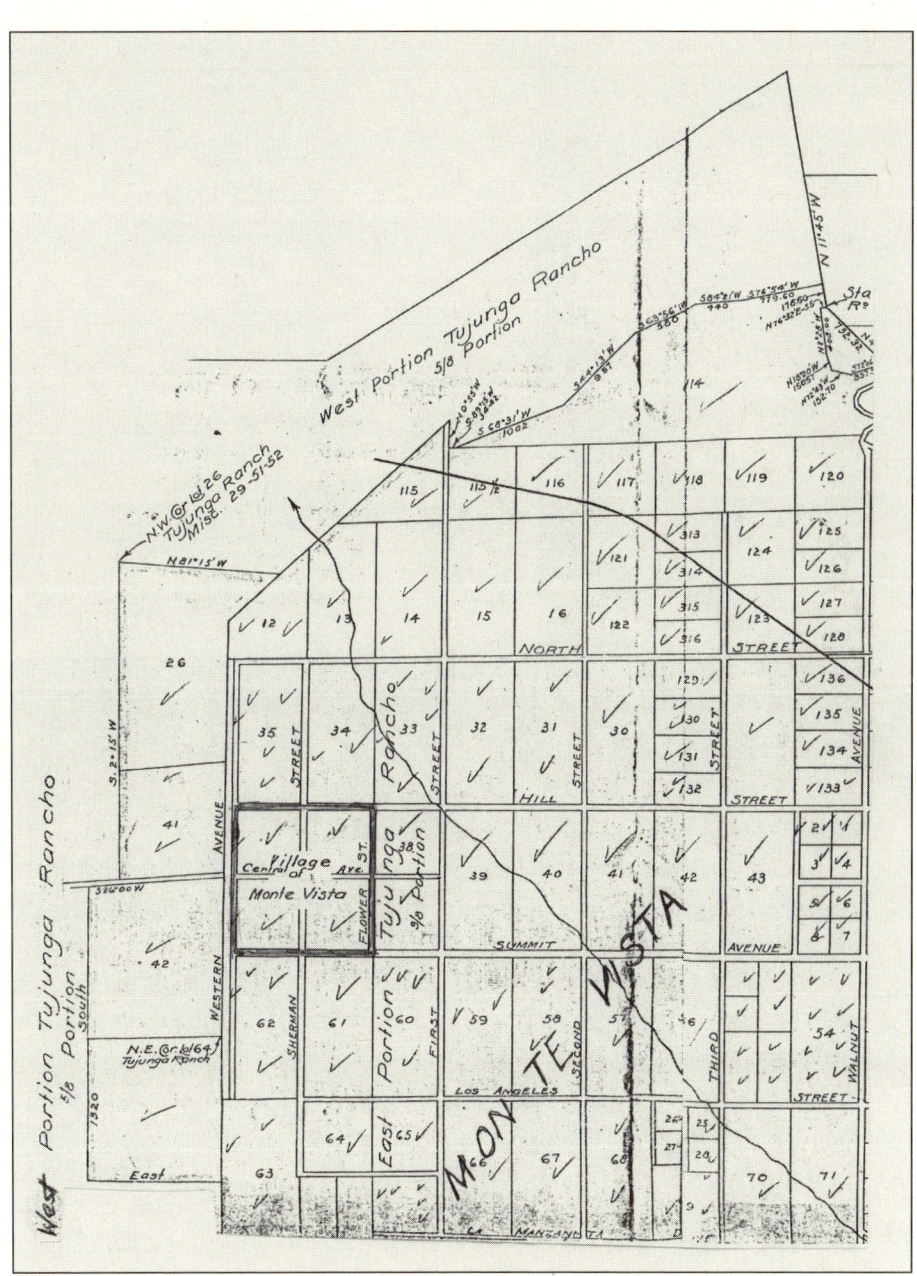

Early map of F. H. Barclay's Monte Vista Village. Water from the Big Tujunga Canyon entered at lot number 13, c. 1890.

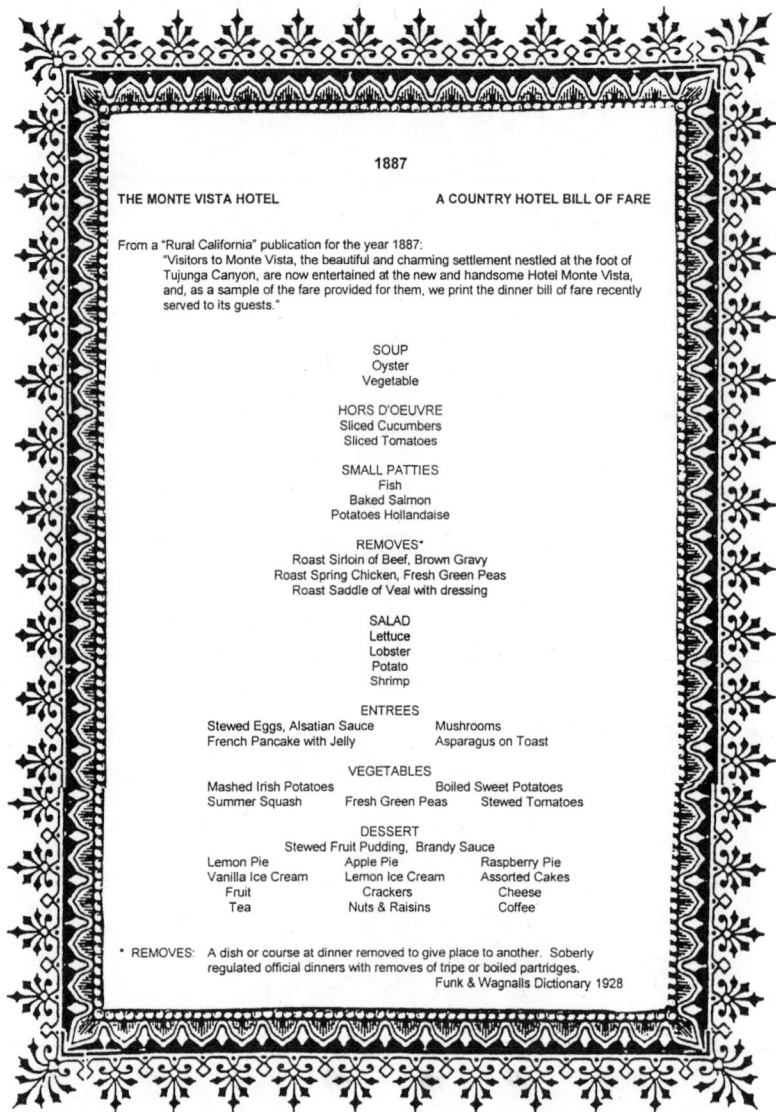

renowned for climbing on the roof of the old hotel and for sliding down the banister at breakneck speed.[33]

The Barclays experienced a serious reversal of fortune by 1899 and were forced to move back into the Park Hotel before eventually moving to Los Angeles. Anna Brandsetter and her husband bought the Park Hotel and moved in with their 3-year-old son, Herbert, in 1907. The 13 acres that surrounded the hotel were planted in "peach trees, lemon trees, grape vines and orange trees."[34] The Brandsetters renamed the hotel the Monte Vista Park Hotel. In 1924, Anna's husband died and she married Sid Jump. The Jumps' suburban hotel took in lodgers until the 1930s. Anna and her husband both passed away in 1965.[35] The home was rented to various families for years but suffered irreparable damage in the Sylmar earthquake of 1971. Eventually the hotel was demolished.

The Barclay family, although residing in Los Angeles, continued to be a presence in the Sunland-Tujunga area. When daughter LuLu married Earl Mauk at

The elegant Monte Vista Hotel in Sunland opened in 1887.
Guests enjoyed weekend stays, fine dining, dances and wedding receptions.
The hotel had thirty sunny rooms and well-tended tennis courts. By 1920, the hotel
closed and reopened as a home for undernourished children. The building was razed in 1964.

The magnificent Monte Vista Hotel, minus the cupola built by Frank Barclay, c. 1887.

With the cupola removed, the hotel became a Volunteers of America guest home for the elderly. This was followed by a home for undernourished children and then Cypress Manor Rest Home. It was demolished in 1964, c. 1920.

(*right*) Aunt Randy and Uncle Ben who lived in the Park Hotel. *Courtesy of Author.*

(*below*) The Park Hotel, where Frank and Mary Barclay and their daughters lived while the Monte Vista Hotel was being built and the land subdivided, c. 1920s.

Bolton Hall on June 15, 1915, it was the social event of the year. Gladys and Bing Maygrove served as flower girls and sister Anna (Frankie) as matron of honor. "It was a wedding as beautiful as any I have been to. Flowers, music and the lovely setting on the inside with only acres of sagebrush and rocks on the outside."[36] The Reverend W. H. Wieman, pastor of the Church Federation of the Little Landers, solemnized the wedding.

Bolton Hall which is the common meeting ground of the colony, is a large handsom [*sic*] building that serves as the center of church and social life for the dwellers in the community. It was beautifully decorated. Toward the eastern end of the building, where the dias [*sic*] stands, a large central arch had been constructed with evergreens and the tall striking blooms of the yucca palm, interwoven with a variety of flowers and ferns, and relieved here and there with white bells. A large white bell was suspended from the keystone of the

(*clockwise from above*) Early photograph of west entrance into Monte Vista Park.

Frank Barclay's original office in Monte Vista.

Anna Barclay's home in Sunland, c. 1919. *Photos courtesy of Author.*

arch. Two smaller arches supported the central one and converted the place of the ceremony into a miniature garden of Allah. Every window of the hall was a bower of floral beauty. The organ loft was decorated in similar style and the strains of sweet music breathed from a labyrinth of roses.[37]

Frank Barclay became superintendent of the Glendale Montrose Railroad and later superintendent of the Little Lands Colony in the Monte Vista Subdivision of the Western Empire. Anna would live in Tujunga until her death in 1956.

In late 1888, the railroads stepped aside with their large promotions and the Los Angeles Chamber of Commerce, started by General Harrison Grey Otis (*Los Angeles Times* publisher) along with other prominent businessmen, took over the primary job of promoting the area. Marshall V. Hartranft, a land broker, conveniently located his California Home Extension Association office in the downtown Los Angeles Chamber of Commerce building.[38] The Chamber's showroom held a giant elephant made of walnuts and magnificent displays of produce from the "agrarian paradise" known as southern California.

The discovery of oil and the growth of the movie industry lured more job seekers to this "promised land." Between 1920 and 1930, 2 million people moved to California, with 72 percent settling in southern California. Los Angeles recorded a 115 percent increase in its population. Eight new cities, including Tujunga, joined

(*clockwise from top, left*) Hulda, Anna Barclay and Ed Bloomfield in the Big Tujunga Canyon. *Courtesy of Author.*

Aunt Randy and a young Anna Barclay. *Courtesy of Author.*

Elizabeth MacVine's home and ranch located on the south side of Manzanita Drive.
Each week she opened her home for use as a library, c. 1918

Historian Viola Carlson stands in front of the newly discovered López Adobe in Little Tujunga Canyon, c. 1959.

FOUNDING SISTERS

Los Angeles County. Automobile travel and all-weather highways contributed to the boom of the 1920s, just as the Santa Fe Railroad had to the boom of the 1880s.

For one hundred years, southern California had been sold by the acre, the mile, the lot and, finally, by penny postcards. The 1920s saw the colorful postcards boasting of the beaches, mountains, orange groves, beautiful homes, and the bounty of the land. These "penny promoters" (postcards cost one cent to mail and were referred to as "penny postcards") lured tourists and those seeking new homes.

In 1907, the California Fruit Growers Exchange, with support from the railroad, started a major advertising campaign in Iowa. Their slogan was "Oranges for Health—California for Wealth." Sunkist Growers produced colorful fruit crate labels that would further draw people to California and facilitate an increase in the population. California now became synonymous with health. In the same year, Homer Hansen, who had recovered his health in the Big Tujunga Canyon, had the western portion of Rancho Tujunga surveyed and platted and began development of Hansen Heights and Tujunga Terrace (now known as Shadow Hills and Lake View Terrace).

By 1911, Marshall V. Hartranft had purchased 2,300 acres of the rancho and began selling lots in Glorietta Heights. He made his own home in Sunland in 1907 and would remain there until his death in 1945. By 1913, the remaining acreage of Rancho Tujunga was being marketed and sold as a utopian colony.

Tujunga would not be the quintessential California story. It would share that honor by joining the ranks of other fleeting secular utopian colonies, such as Kaweah in eastern Tulare County and Llano del Rio in the Antelope Valley, and religious groups, including the Theosophists at Point Loma, the Harrisites at Fountain Grove, the Fellowship Farms Colony northeast of Puente, and the Mormon colony in San Bernardino. From 1850 to 1950, California would give birth to more utopian colonies than any other state.[39]

The story of Tujunga was revealed, in large part, by the gifts of two women. Anna Barclay Kirby's gift of papers to Viola Carlon in 1959 began a search for the

FROM RANCHO TO COLONY

OLD ADOBE FOUND

It was an exciting moment when historian Viola Carlson peered through the trees on Col. Harper's Middle Ranch in the Little Tujunga Canyon and discovered the crumbling remains of the López Adobe built in 1841. It originally consisted of three rooms and a long veranda, c. 1959.

beginnings of the land grant. Elizabeth Bury MacVine, one of the few women owners of Rancho Tujunga, left her papers on the rancho to her good friend Mrs. Aikens, who presented them to the Little Landers Historical Society in 1968. This gift helped rewrite much of Tujunga's history. Tujunga would hold a unique place in the history of California. While the San Fernando Valley would have a patron saint in Mother Cabrini, Tujunga—always distinctive, always colorful—would choose San Ysidro, a Spanish, Jewish farmer as their patron saint. San Ysidro had no specific religious order. He was a simple farmer, born in Madrid, who spent his life working beside his wife for one landowner. His kindness to animals and his intelligence was well known and, though not a monk, he passed his days in truthful work and prayer.[40]

By March 17, 1913, Tujunga was the only utopian city in Los Angeles County.

Notes

[1] Leonard Pitt and Dale Pitt, *Los Angeles A–Z, an Encyclopedia of the City and County* (Berkeley: University of California Press, 1997), 419–22.

[2] Iris W. Engstrand, *The Legal Heritage of Spanish California* (Santa Barbara Museum Archives Library, 1994), 227–31.

[3] Robert Glass Cleland, *From Wilderness to Empire—A History of California* (New York: Alfred A. Knopf, 1946), 134.

[4] "People of reason" referred to Spanish-speaking Christians.

[5] The value of "leather dollars" fluctuated from one dollar to three dollars.

[6] Pitt, loc. cit.

[7] Margaret Mead, *Cultural Patterns and Technical Change* (New York: New American Library, 1955), 153.

[8] Robert Glass Cleland, *Cattle on a Thousand Hills: Southern California 1850–1880* (San Marino: Huntington Library, California, 1951), 43.

[9] The Preemption Act of 1841 was, in essence, a guarantee of the option to buy land that a squatter had improved, should the court reject the original "rancho" claim, and to buy it at a minimum price prior to public auction.

[10] Paul W. Gates, "California's Embattled Settlers," *California Historical Quarterly* 41 (June 1962): 99–103.

[11] Palmer Conner, *The Romance of the Ranchos* (Los Angeles: Title Insurance and Trust, 1941), 2.

[12] Viola Carlson, "Rancho Tujunga, a Mexican Land Grant of 1840," *Brand Book Twenty—Rancho Days in Southern California*, Kenneth Pauley, ed. (The Westerners, Los Angeles Corral, 1977), 63–78.

[13] Dick Degnon, "State Reported Viewing Site for Monument," *The Record Ledger* (1959).

[14] Viola Carlson, "They Shall Build a House," six-page undated treatise, Bolton Hall Museum, Tujunga, Calif.

[15] In 1958, the property was donated to Hathaway Home for Children. The López Adobe eventually disintegrated from floods, earthquakes, and time.

[16] Marie E. Northrup, *Spanish-Mexican Families in Early California: 1769–1850* (New Orleans: Polyanthus, 1976), 181.

[17] Jerry Reynolds, "The Golden Dream of Francisco López," *The California Historian* 49 no. 2 (Winter 1944): 12–16.

[18] Francisca López Belderrain, "First Gold in California," *Touring Topics* (November 1930): 32–34.

[19] W. W. Robinson, "The Spanish and Mexican Ranchos of San Fernando Valley," *Southwest Museum Leaflet* no. 31 (1966): 8–9.

[20] José Miguel's story took on tragic overtones. One son died, while another went to prison. José went mad and his wife was forced to sell their rancho. After he died, Rafaela married an Apache Indian and bore him a son. Doyce B. Nunis, Jr., *Mission San Fernando, Rey de España, 1797–1997—A Bicentennial Tribute* (Historical Society of Southern California, 1997), 276.

[21] Viola Carlson, "Chain of Title of the Rancho Tujunga," six-page unpublished abstract.

[22] Eventually the author moved to California and the bucolic Ojai Valley. He founded the town of Nordhoff that in 1916 became Ojai. His grandson, Charles B. Nordhoff, wrote *Mutiny on the Bounty*, with partner James Norman Hall, in 1932.

[23] Gloria Ricci Lothrop, "The Boom of the '80s Revisited. Land Policy and Land Use in Southern California," *Southern California Quarterly* 80 nos. 3–4 (Fall–Winter 1993): 288.

[24] For an in-depth description of the speculative frenzy, see Theodore S. Van Dyke, *Millionaires of a Day: An Inside History of the Great Southern "Boom"* (New York: Howard and Hulbert, 1890).

[25] Carey McWilliams, *Southern California—An Island on the Land* (Salt Lake City: Peregrine Smith Books, 1946), 116.

[26] Ibid., 227.

[27] Ibid., 228.

[28] Ibid., 247.

[29] Monte Vista Hotel Advertisement, *Los Angeles Times* (July 1, 1887).

[30] Robert Rowley personal interview. Viola Carlson, Spring 1964.

[31] "Killed on the Road," *Los Angeles Times Newspaper* (undated), Bolton Hall Museum clippings file.

[32] On February 1, 2003, Dorothy Rowley McCollum celebrated her 101st birthday.

[33] Personal interview with Dorothy Rowley by Viola Carlson, Joan Conrad, and the Author, February 17, 1996.

[34] "Six Persons Owned Valley When Anna Jump Arrived," *The Record-Ledger* (September 30, 1954).

[35] During the "Old Timers' Week" festivities, the Jump home was opened to the public for tours. Herbert led the tours of the home, which retained most of its original furniture and charm. "Old Jump Home Open to Tours During S-T Old Timers Week," *The Record-Ledger* (August 8, 1968).

[36] Gladys Maygrove, "Maygrove Remembers" (unpublished memoirs), 3.

[37] *Glendale Evening Newspress* (June 25, 1915).

[38] For all intents and purposes, Hartranft's mother Hetty was the California Home Extension Company. She was the president and her son Marshall was the secretary. Sarah Lombard, "Friends of the Library," *The Record-Ledger* (1976).

[39] Robert V. Hine, *California's Utopian Colonies* (San Marino: The Huntington Library, 1953), 6.

[40] San Ysidro was named for St. Isadore—the farmer, patron saint of the plow or agriculture (1070–1130). Cannonized in 1622, he would later be called the Patron Saint of Little Homes. Robert Ellsworth, *All Saints—Daily Reflections on Saints, Prophets and Witnesses for Our Time* (New York: The Crossroad Publishing Company, 1997), 213.

(*opposite, top*) The only known photograph of the George and Emily Duquette Watt home. It once belonged to the López family, c. 1890. *Courtesy of Sarah Lombard.*

(*opposite, center*) The ruins of López Adobe, once located in Rancho Tujunga. Time and earthquakes have leveled the structure, c. 1959.

(*opposite, bottom*) Elizabeth and John MacVine gave good friend D. Aikens (*third from the left*) a copy of the Rancho Tujunga 1850 Purchase, copied from old land records. (*left to right*) Roberta M. Stewart, President of the Little Landers Historical Society, Irene Loudal (*seated*), Librarian of Tujunga Branch of Los Angeles County Library, and Cora Corrigan, President of the Public Relations Council, c. 1968. *The Record-Ledger.*

FROM RANCHO TO COLONY

> A little land and a living surely is
> better than desperate struggle
> and wealth possibly.
> —*Bolton Hall, 1908*

BOLTON HALL (1854–1938).
Bolton Hall, a New York attorney, was an author, reformer and idealist. He founded the Free Acres Colony in New Jersey in 1909. His book *A Little Land and a Living* (1908) was the inspiration for the Little Lands Colony.

The Hope of the Little Lands

*I*n 1889, France amazed the world with its elaborate World's Fair in Paris and the debut of the Eiffel Tower. Not to be outdone by the French, Americans celebrated the four hundredth anniversary of Christopher Columbus' voyage with a World's Fair of their own in Chicago in 1893. Americans were given the chance to show the world their cultural and technological advances. The Chicago fair, The Columbian Exposition, cemented Americans' love affair with technology, foretelling the fate of American cities at the dawn of a new century. From May through October 31, 1893, 27 million visitors marveled at Edison's electricity, engineer George Ferris' revolving wheel, architect Daniel Hudson Burnam's buildings, and the landscaped grounds designed by New York City Central Park's creator and urban planner Frederick Law Olmstead. In the gathering economic storm, the fair showed American cities all that they could become and was the largest attended event in the modern history of the world.

The World's Fair had an affect on how Americans perceived their municipalities. Citizens were no longer content to live in smoke-blackened, overcrowded cities. The magnificent "White City" on Lake Michigan would forever change architecture and, in truth, became the origin of urban planning. Even "Cracker Jack" and "shredded wheat" could trace their beginnings to the fair. Visitors included Frank Lloyd Wright, Helen Keller, Susan B. Anthony, Annie Oakley, Archduke Ferdinand of Austria (in disguise), Harry Houdini, Nicolai Tesla, Ignacy Jan Paderewski, Thomas Edison, Scott Joplin, Clarence Darrow, Teddy Roosevelt, Indians from Buffalo Bill's Wild West Show, and a professor from Princeton named Woodrow Wilson. From farms and cities throughout the nation, people flocked to America's Dream City. Lucille Rodney of Galveston, Texas, couldn't afford transportation so she walked the thirteen hundred miles to Chicago, following along railroad tracks.

This fair would come to symbolize America's rush toward the new century. Fredrick J. Turner declared "The American frontier" was now officially closed.[1] The modern era had begun, when cities would reflect great architecture and social inclusion. No record exists as to whether William E. Smythe, founder of the Little Landers movement, attended the fair, but we do know he was in Chicago at that time for an irrigation congress before he left for Los Angeles. The fair would give birth to many new inventions and a lifetime of memories along with being an inspiration to millions of visitors. Just as Daniel H. Burnham would invite George Washington Ferris to debut his carnival ride at the fair, William E. Smythe would later invite George Washington Harris to create magic in his utopian dream of the Little Lands Colony, Los Terrenitos, in 1913, where Harris built Bolton Hall. While visiting the fair, Elias Disney (Walt Disney's father) and Frank L. Baum (creator of *The Land of Oz*) were able to visually observe a clean and fanciful city that would be the inspiration for Fantasyland in Disney-

59

land Park. Disney was so caught up in the fever of the fair that he wanted to name his son Columbus. Fortunately Mrs. Disney prevailed and they named their baby Roy.

President Harrison declared October 12 a national holiday in honor of Columbus. Smythe's friend and inspiration, socialist minister Francis Bellamy wrote the "Pledge of Allegiance to the Flag" in honor of the 400th anniversary of Columbus' discovery of the New World. It was recited at the dedication of the land used for the fair on October 21, 1892. On June 22, 1942, the seventy-seventh Congress declared Bellamy's pledge the official "Pledge of Allegiance to the Flag."

The year the Chicago Fair closed was a pivotal year for American labor. Samuel Gompers and Eugene V. Debs inspired workers to unionize, rally, picket and strike.[2] For many Americans, the end of their dreams came the same year as the Chicago Fair, when from April to December the stock market crashed, banks failed and were seized, silver prices plummeted, and riots took place throughout the country. Despite the grand Chicago World's Fair, America experienced the greatest economic depression in its history.

By the time the nineteenth century drew to a close and the "Gilded Age" came to an end, industrialism and capitalism had alienated the majority of American citizens.[3] The period between 1880 and 1910 was dominated by "new" money and the conspicuous accumulation of possessions, with the new millionaires often losing sight of the common man. As the nation moved away from farms and villages, crowding into cities, the pace of American life gained momentum and became chaotic. This dramatic shift in lifestyle created a nostalgic yearning for the past and non-machine made wares. It was no coincidence that the new arts and crafts movement, with its simple lines and rustic materials, appealed to so many Americans. City dwellers longed for a simpler life and handmade products, such as fabrics, books, and furniture. The Industrial Revolution had created a decaying affect on their lives and the products in their homes. It was an age of tenements, sweatshops, and exploitive child labor. Social conditions in large cities would be comparable to urban life in today's third-world countries. The wealthy were able to turn a blind eye to the poverty and grim realities of city life and factory work. Interestingly, these same affluent people were fascinated with the poor and ethnic communities. In secret, the upper crust would take midnight "slumming tours." Malnourished beggars were called "cranks" and were often removed from the streets and sent to mental institutions. "Never have the lines between the two classes—those who have wealth and those who do not—been more distinctly drawn. Whether we like it or not, it is an incontrovertible fact that a large portion of our population is discontented and does not hesitate to express its feelings."[4]

The excesses (large ornate palaces, hotels and restaurants) of the "Gilded Age," so called by Mark Twain, and the adoration of machine-made gizmos allowed for the easy embrace of the arts and crafts movement as well as the "back to the soil" movements. All of the nation's land was owned by just 1 percent of the population. The majority of urban dwellers lived in grinding poverty. The climate was ripe for social experiments and utopianism—it was the time for a new social order. The years 1900 through 1926 would be known as the Progressive Era. During this period, muckrakers exposed corruption: Ida Tarbell reported on the monopoly in the oil business, Upton Sinclair (*The Jungle*, 1906) wrote of the shocking conditions of the meat industry, and Frank Norris (*The Octopus*, 1901) condemned the large railroads.

The spirit of Henry David Thoreau would reappear when New York socialist Bolton Hall advised in his *Three Acres and Liberty* that "Men forced to drop out of the city's ranks by the pressure of an over strenuous life, might consider the vast and unknown possibilities of the very small farm intensely cultivated."[5] It is said that every age has had its utopias, from Plato's time to the twenty-first century, but nineteenth-century America and twentieth-century California produced a plethora of secular and non-secular utopian experiments. Most utopias were aimed at building a new world or a new order, to exist solely as a social experiment. Utopian colonies were meant to reform the world but, more often than not, reformed the soul of those who participated in the grand experiments.[6]

Why did the period prior to World War I create a

climate where utopias and dreamers flourished? Economic turmoil, lack of foreign involvements, and hard times fueled the illusions and frustrations of middle-class America. Writers such as Edward Bellamy[7] and Bolton Hall[8] would greatly affect the philosophers, social reformers, and politicians of the age.

Bolton Hall's *A Little Land and a Living* (1908) and *Three Acres and Liberty* (1909) would become the blueprint for William E. Smythe's agricultural utopian communities. The books were widely read and shared among the Little Landers colonists. However, just one line in *Three Acres and Liberty* would seal the fate of all the colonies: "In a small plot, the character of the soil is of little importance." William Ellsworth Smythe, a leading advocate of irrigation and a gifted and prolific writer and orator, maintained that a man could support himself and a family of four on a single acre of irrigated land.[9]

Smythe's message encompassed a simple agrarian life enriched with cultural programs, which would provide the benefits of both rural and urban living. "Country life has failed on its spiritual side," he said. "What is wanted is a form of country life that shall bring the people reasonably close to the great towns, both for market and social advantages; that shall permit the numerous neighbors the organization of a rich up-to-date social and intellectual life—full, elevating and satisfying."[10]

To understand the Little Landers movement, one needs to look back on the forces that compelled Smythe to become the nation's leading advocate of irrigation and the founder of four "back to the soil" colonies in California. When 1891 dawned, leaving behind the "great die-up of 1887" and the "drought of 1890" that severely affected the Plains states, readers of the *Omaha Weekly Bee* newspaper were greeted with the front-page headline "Plans for Irrigation in Nebraska." It was written by a young transplanted New Englander, William E. Smythe. As a teenager, he was inspired by Parton's biography of Horace Greeley;[11] in 1888, Smythe took Greeley's advice and moved west.[12] He became editor and publisher of the *Kearney Expositor*. By 1891, he was an editorial writer for the *Omaha Bee*.[13] Shocked by the consequences of Nebraska's severe drought and the sight of farmers shooting their livestock in order to save them from starvation and abandoning their farms within view of streams, he "discovered irrigation" after a tour of the irrigated Greeley Temperance Colony in Colorado. He also toured the Maxwell Land Grant in New Mexico and set out with an aggressive campaign to let people know "they had to irrigate not to emigrate":[14] "I had taken the cross of a new crusade. To my mind, irrigation seemed the biggest thing in the world. It was not merely a matter of ditches and acres, but a philosophy, a religion and a program of practical statesmanship rolled into one."[15] Smythe's urgent message caught the ear of those Americans who yearned for the independence and personal fulfillment that they believed a small piece of agricultural land would provide. Their enthusiastic response to his urgent cry produced a California statewide social group that became known as the Little Landers movement. The movement was William E. Smythe's utopian dream: a combination of irrigation theory, populist ideals, and manifest destiny.

At Nebraska's State Irrigation Convention, Smythe proposed a National Irrigation Congress. He then resigned from the *Omaha Bee* and started *Irrigation Age*, a journal he put together after the first National Congress in Salt Lake City in 1891. It would be the October 1893 Congress held in Los Angeles that would give him a national pulpit for his views. The congress was an event that might have been staged by P. T. Barnum. The Los Angeles Chamber of Commerce rented the

> I remember our beautiful scheme of a noble and unselfish life, and how fair, in that first summer, appeared the prospect that it might endure for generations, and be perfected, as the ages rolled away, into the system of a people, and a world. More and more, I feel that we had struck upon what ought to be a truth. Posterity may dig it up, and profit by it.
>
> —*Nathaniel Hawthorne*, The Blithedale Romance, 1852

61

Aerial view shows the unique double horseshoe design of New Plymouth, Idaho. The colony started in 1896. Each colonist purchased twenty acres of land, c. 1978.

City's Grand Opera House. The entrance was flanked on either side by 16-foot-high cornstalks, proof of what irrigation could accomplish. At the conference, two men with divergent views about the future of the West would speak. William E. Smythe and John Wesley Powell would forever be linked to the issue of water and the arid west.[16] Powell saw California's reliance on imported water as a trigger for economic collapse. He was against the promise of creating an Eden in the desert. He saw a Federal Irrigation Program as the only salvation for the area, but his scientific reports were dismissed as too cautious and his warnings of economic collapse were ignored. As the crowd "booed" Powell, he prophetically pronounced, "There's not enough water, boys. There's just not enough."

As California struggled to transform itself from a semi-arid wilderness into the most populous state in the Union, Smythe saw irrigation as its only salvation. Investment capital had disappeared with the national panic of 1893. The following year, the United States Congress passed the Carey Act, which gave public lands to the individual states for irrigation. The more successful legislation would occur in 1902 when the Newlands Reclamation Act was passed. Now money derived from government land sales would be funneled into large-scale projects that consisted of dams and large areas of irrigated land in the West. The last irrigation congress that Smythe headed was in Albuquerque in 1895. He then turned his energy toward colonization as a better way to renew national interest in the irrigation movement. His philosophy for colonization was that only small land holdings, under a national policy of water reclamation, would assure an independent middle class.

At the National Irrigation Congress, held in Chicago in 1894, the New Plymouth Society of Chicago (under Smythe's direction) was formed. Smythe and William J. Shawhan joined forces to create the New

Plymouth Colony in 1896. Shawhan had been granted 325 acres of land in the Payette Valley of Idaho under the Desert Land Act of 1877. This became New Plymouth Farm Village. In 1908 the name was shortened to New Plymouth.[17] Smythe believed his colony, based on the European farming communities, would help overcome the isolation of life on the northwestern plains: a life that often led to insanity and "prairie sickness." Rather than 160-acre farms, the 40-acre sites were laid out in a horseshoe configuration to lend itself to a better social life for the colonists and the avoidance of "prairie fever."

The timing was right for Smythe's first colony, as the nation struggled through a rough economic period. The Payette Valley colony was located twelve miles from the town of Payette and the railroad. The semi-arid land was cleared, homes built, and crops and fruit trees planted. The colonists only had to wait for their envisioned "spiritual life of the soil."[18] The New Plymouth settlers enjoyed all the social aspects of the colony plan.[19]

State of California utopian colonies, 1850–1950.

At the age of 39, William E. Smythe came to northern California. The distinguished gentleman with the Van Dyke beard started two new colonies in northern California, one in Tehama County and one at Standish in Lassen County.[20] Unable to get clear water rights to the land, he was powerless to attract many settlers or capital. While struggling to establish the colony in Standish, he wrote *The Conquest of Arid America* (1899), destined to become a classic in Western literature.

Little Lands Colony—Standish

In the 1890s, Smythe was president of the Associated Colonies of New York, a group whose main goal was to colonize the arid lands of the West, with their first venture being New Plymouth. In 1897, the group incorporated the Honey Lake Valley Colonial Irrigation Company and the Susan River Irrigation System of Edward Purser; thus, the second planned utopian colony of Standish was formed in the highlands of California. The colony was based on a design of European communities, where everyone would reside inside the colony and leave during the day to work in the surrounding fields. There were new colonists every one hundred feet along the frontage of the boulevard. This helped avoid the dreaded isolation and inevitable hunger for social contact, which had in part driven folks from the farms to the cities.[21] Although the Standish Colony was started, it lasted just a few years. In February 1898, eager colonists had dedicated the 240-acre townsite. But by August 1901, the Bank of Lassen County had won a large judgment against the colonists.[22]

In 1901, a new phase of Smythe's career came about when Charles Lummis offered him the "Twentieth Century West" department of his magazine *Out West*. He also became vice president of the California Water and Forest Association. While touring the state on the association's behalf, he met Marshall Valentine Hartranft, a land developer from Sunland, with whom he would later join forces to develop the second Little Lands Colony in Tujunga. During this statewide speaking tour, Smythe came to San Diego to lecture. He fell in love with the beautiful "City of the Silver Gate" and moved

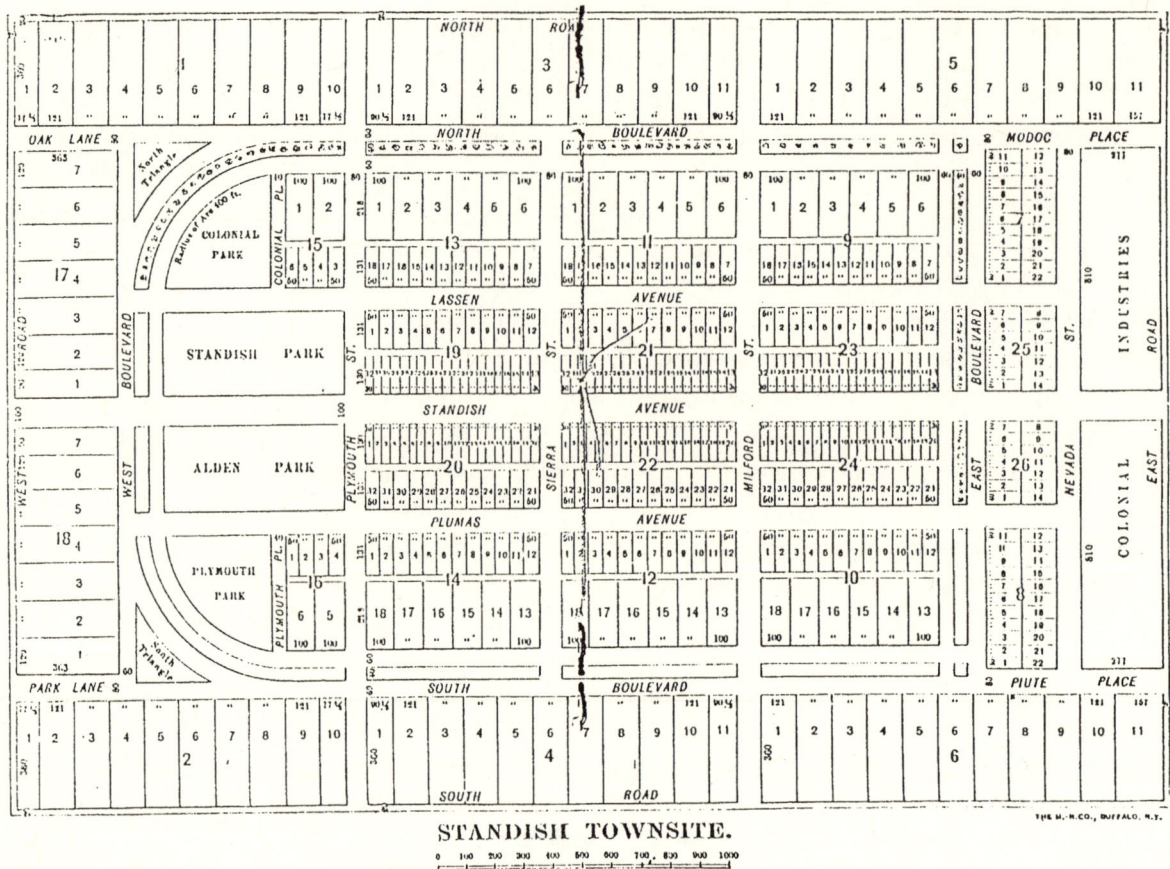

Standish Colony map. Note the names of the four parks. Unknown date.

Little Lands Colony—Standish

Photograph of Standish in the early 1900s, looking down Milford Street (now known as A3).
(*left to right*) Highway 395, boarding house, store (until 1995, now empty),
and the colony's hotel. *Map and photo courtesy of Edith Summers.*

wife Harriet, son Bensil, and daughter Margaret to their new home. The following year, another son, William Smythe Jr., was born. After securing a job with the *San Diego Union* newspaper, Smythe decided to run for Congress. It was 1902 and the eighth district, encompassing most of southern California, was newly created. He campaigned for this seat by supporting the placement of all water development under the control of the state and for public ownership of all water utilities. Nicknamed "Windy Willie," Smythe lost the election because of fears in the agricultural community that he was going to do away with their existing riparian water rights. He also worked tirelessly for the San Diego Chamber of Commerce, promoting the area and the Imperial Valley. In 1907, he authored *History of San Diego, 1542–1908*, a book that helped San Diegans realize the importance of preserving their past.[23]

San Ysidro

The year 1907 saw America in the grip of another national panic. Banks closed, farmers declared bankruptcy, and thousands of city dwellers were out of work. Smythe and a partner created the Consolidated Realty Company of San Diego that year. For the first of his Little Landers' lectures, on July 28, 1908, Smythe rented the Garrick Theater in downtown San Diego. Here he proposed a Little Landers colony to be built in San Ysidro. The timeliness of his speech proved to be a boon to the Little Landers movement. He felt this "back to the soil" movement would free people from the social bondage of the cities, or, as Jack London had called them, *The People of the Abyss* (1901). By 1907, because of reduced rail fares, thousand of tourists and home seekers were arriving in southern California. A third of the immigrants returned east, disappointed—yet in their disappointment Smythe saw a way for their financial wellbeing. His co-operative agricultural colony would provide for their security. The colony would also benefit the city of San Diego by bringing new residents to the area and agricultural prosperity to a barren land. A road would be built connecting San Ysidro to National City.

William E. Smythe and his partner, George P. Hall (the ex-horticultural commissioner of San Diego

Utopian Colonies

	Colony Name		Associated City
1	Icaria Speranza	1881–1886	Cloverdale
2	Altruria	1894–1895	Cloverdale
3	Fountain Grove	1875–1934	Cloverdale
4	Army of Industry	1915–1918	Sacramento
5	Winter's Island	1895–1898	San Francisco
6	Tuolumne Farms	1945–1950	Modesto
7	Holy City	1918–1952	Monterey
8	Kaweah	1884–1892	Visalia
9	Temple Home	1898–1922	San Luis Obispo
10	Joyful	1884–1885	Bakersfield
11	Pisgah Grande	1915–1920	Santa Barbara
12	Llano del Rio	1914–1918	Palmdale
13	San Bernardino	1851–1857	San Bernardino
14	Fellowship Farm	1912–1926	Puente
15	Modjeska's Colony	1876–1877	Anaheim
16	Point Loma	1897–1940	Oceanside
17	San Ysidro *	1909–1917	San Diego
18	Los Terrenitos *	1913–1918	Tujunga
19	Monte Vista Colony *	1916–1918	Cupertino
20	Hayward Heath *	1916–1918	Hayward
21	Standish	1898–1901	Standish

* Indicates a Little Landers Colony

County), purchased 550 acres in the Tia Juana Valley, fifteen miles south of San Diego and two miles north of the international border, for $15,000. At Hall's suggestion, the site of California's first Little Landers Colony was selected. One-fourth of the Colony's acreage was on a dry creek bed with alluvial soil. The rest of the acreage was on a mesa above the creek bed. Smythe urged the colonists to build their farms on the dry creek bed and their homes on the mesa above, but few heeded his suggestion. The original town of Tia Juana had been wiped out in a disastrous flood in 1891. After the flood, the Mexican population moved south, to higher ground, while the American settlement that remained was known as Tia Juana, California. Smythe was aware of the treacherous past of the dry riverbed.

The land for the new colony was surveyed and laid

FOUNDING SISTERS

out in a modest townsite with streets, a park, post office, clubhouse, and civic center; land was set aside for a school. Building lots were 25 feet by 140 feet and sold for $250. Full-acre lots cost between $350 and $550. Terms were for one-half the amount down and the balance to be paid in eight quarterly payments, 6 percent interest on the portion owing with 5 percent for all cash paid down.[24] Formal incorporation of the San Ysidro Colony occurred on August 1, 1908. The capital stock of the company was $100,000 and ten thousand shares of stock were authorized for distribution on January 11, 1909.

At the time of the land purchase, the old adobe of the Ybarra Ranch was still standing and would act as the clubhouse for the San Ysidro Colony until Redwood Hall was built on the mesa and dedicated in 1908. The new clubhouse was committed under the slogan "A Little Land and a Living." Prominently displayed on the wall was Smythe's "Hope of the Little Lands." San Ysidro's Clubhouse, with double fireplaces, was the community center for the colony and provided a library, church services, night school classes, musical and literary programs, dinners, and town hall meetings.[25]

The Smythe family moved from El Cajon into the colony and had a grand housewarming party on July 4, 1909. Their home was a single large room with adjacent tents serving as sleeping rooms and kitchen. There were covered passages connecting the tents to the main room. After the success of her housewarming, Harriet, first lady of the colony, decided to open her home to the wives and mothers of the colony each Thursday afternoon for social gatherings. It was her vision to level social barriers with good food, music, and conversation. She felt gracious living was possible in any location. Her keen interest in astronomy prompted her to urge the colony to build a planetarium.

In December 1910, the colony itself was incorporated, with 70-year-old George P. Hall as president and William E. Smythe as vice president. Hall had contributed the land within the colony for the Little Landers' Park and the larger-than-life statue of General Ulysses S. Grant.[26] On April 11, 1913, the San Ysidro Colony celebrated the eighty-ninth birthday of the late President Grant. The celebration included a large street parade with marching Civil War veterans, United States Army soldiers from nearby Fort Rosecrans, colonists, and many visiting dignitaries.

In 1911, a major problem became apparent when there was insufficient capital to provide a proper irrigation system. San Ysidro was one of the first colonies (cities) to apply for an irrigation district under the new law of 1911. Despite Smythe's friendship with and plea to Governor Hiram Johnson, the commissioner of Irrigation Districts moved so slowly that several planting seasons were missed before the district was approved. While awaiting the decision on the bond measure, Smythe traveled to Alaska with Interior Secretary Walter Fisher. The $25,000 irrigation bond was even-

Colonists sold their excess produce at the Little Landers Market at
6th Avenue and C Street, San Diego, from 1911 to 1915.

Little Landers from the Mother Colony at San Ysidro had a much bigger store for their produce.
Little Landers Market at 6th and C Street in San Diego.

WILLIAM ELLSWORTH SMYTHE, 1861–1922.
(*above, left*) A young William E. Smythe, c. 1890.

tually issued to pay for the new pumping system that would deliver water to each lot. A forty-horse-power engine and centrifuge pump were used to lift water to a reservoir and the colony's irrigation system. Visitors from around the world, including the progressive democrat from Wisconsin, Robert LaFollette, came to the colony to view what appeared to be a success. LaFollette expressed a desire to return to Wisconsin and start his own Little Lands Colony. Instead, LaFollette left with Smythe that year to campaign for the senator's presidential bid.

By the end of 1911, there were about sixty-nine families located in the Colony. The Smythe family would reside there from 1909 to 1911. The unrest of the Industrial Workers of the World (I.W.W.) insurrection and Pancho Villa's army in Mexico caused many families on the Mexican side of the border to move to the United States. The time period of 1907 through 1910 would be marked by industrial strife in San Diego and Los Angeles. There was seething unrest as the *Los Angeles Times* fought for an open shop and women battled in the suffrage movement. Dr. John R. Haynes, reformer in the Progressive movement, helped get the initiative, referendum, and recall as part of the Los Angeles charter.

After the *Los Angeles Times* bombing case, San Diego experienced its own liberal movement. When the city government copied Los Angeles with a restricted free-speech law in 1912, the I.W.W. and hundreds of "wobblies" descended on San Diego and mounted their soapboxes to deliver their message.[27] Jails quickly filled with "free speechers" and the city formed a vigilante committee to keep protesters at bay. "Red Emma" Goldman arrived in San Diego to deliver numerous speeches but was escorted out of town and placed on a train for Los Angeles. By 1915, the free speech fight was won and she was allowed to return to San Diego.[28]

By the end of 1910, the battle between labor and management had escalated to an all-out war in Los Angeles. The passing of the anti-picketing ordinance forced most of the trades to go on strike. The *Los Angeles Times* stepped up its campaign to keep Los Angeles an open shop city. The Socialist Party joined forces with the unionists and reported signing up one hundred members a day. The timing of the bombing of the *Los Angeles Times* building further agitated the already tense situation. The bombing would be called "the crime of the century." Open shop was critical in keeping a cheap labor pool in Los Angeles, where wages were 40 percent below those of San Francisco. It was a common sight to see workers marching in parades, chanting the slogans of the Socialist Movement.

Job Harriman, one of the key figures in the fight to unionize Los Angeles, launched his own "brave new world" in a utopian community in the Antelope Valley. The Llano del Rio Cooperative experiment lasted four short years. Harriman's colony was more of a

68

worker's sóviet, with workers being paid $4 per day out of the net earnings of the farms. His colony had May Day parades and was advertised in *The Western Comrade*. The colony's downfall was water. Where Smythe's colony had too much, Harriman's had not enough.

As author and lawyer Carey McWilliams would say,

> Throughout the period from 1890 to 1937, Los Angeles was the last citadel of the open shop, the white spot of the nation, the paradise of the professional patriot and the red baiter. The large masses not part of a strong trade union were given to invent new forms of social discontent. Frustrations often led to fantasy and Southern California was built by boosters and real estate hawkers as paradise.[29]

With the creation of the racetracks and the gambling at Tijuana and Agua Caliente, many employees chose to move north. As 1912 progressed, San Ysidro (two miles from the Mexican border) was evolving from a farming community into a town. That year brought the construction of forty-seven new houses, so that by 1913 there were 116 families and about 300 people living in the Colony.[30]

William Smythe was forced to travel and lecture extensively to offset the bad publicity his colony was subject to during the beginning of the Mexican Revolution and the arrival of the "wobblies." Worried that people would think of his colony as Marxist, new promotional literature mentioned that the colony did not endorse social fads and fancies, each purchaser held title to his own property, and the co-operative marketing agreement was voluntary. This was an agricultural colony, neither socialist nor communist. It also mentioned that this was the first colony in a planned nationwide string of Little Landers colonies.

In 1912, Smythe was back in the newspaper business, writing editorials for the Scripps newspapers from an office in San Diego. He traveled throughout the West speaking for irrigation, reclamation, big dams, and water for the West. His *Little Lands in America Magazine* was read throughout the United States. The Little Landers' story went along with Smythe to the 1911 National Irrigation Congress in Chicago and later to the 1915 Panama-California Exposition in San Diego, where three Little Landers' one-acre farms, with a typical

Just living is not enough, said the butterfly.
One must have sunshine, freedom and a little flower.
—Hans Christian Anderson

home and buildings for goats and chickens were displayed. Smythe was busy planning more colonies (in Tujunga and farther north) with new partner, Marshall Valentine Hartranft.

Smythe was initially hired by Hartranft early in 1912 to help promote the Western Empire Home Extension Plan in Tujunga. Hartranft considered himself a land broker, not a developer. In 1907, he purchased 1,728 acres of land in the Tujunga Valley that had formerly belonged to Vanderbilt University in Nashville, Tennessee. The university had planned to build a college on the acreage. Hartranft's theory was that "population creates land values." He was convinced the formula for wealth was the trio of population, residential land, and transportation. He also believed that every adult citizen was worth $1,500 to the community. Land for development was purchased through his Western Empire Suburban Farms Association that was established in 1910. Hartranft filed claim on the water rights of Haines Canyon and Blanchard and Blue Gum canyons in Tujunga and bought the water rights from Philip Begue in the Haines Canyon watershed. He also bought the water rights in the Big Tujunga Canyon from Mary Ann Johnson. After subscribers purchased their bonds, roads were constructed, sagebrush cleared, and irrigation and domestic water was provided. Bond holders had two choices; they could wait until the land was paid for and take a profit or they could exchange it for land at $300 per acre in bonds. With each bond, the owner had one share in the Western Empire Suburban Farms Association and one share in the water company.

This method of land distribution had been successful for Hartranft previously in Greenfield (Monterey County) in 1904, Clark Colony (Salinas Valley) in 1905, Alspaugh (Tulare County) in 1906, Wasco (Kern County) in 1907, Elysian Garden (Los Angeles) in 1908, Valley Oaks in 1910–11, and Mountain View in 1908. Hartranft's ninth project was Monte Vista, which in 1913 became Los Terrenitos Colony (Little Lands). Smythe and Hartranft joined forces to create the second Little Landers Colony on Hartranft's land. Hartranft resided in Sunland beginning in 1907, but Smythe never lived in Los Terrenitos, although he attended the laying of the cornerstone of Bolton Hall in 1913. Hartranft, like Smythe, was a prolific writer and also ran for several political offices. Both Hartranft's Home Extension Colonies and Smythe's Little Landers Colonies had great appeal to retirees and people with little savings. In 1916, a third Little Landers colony was formed. Some sixty families bought 500 acres near the San Francisco Bay town of Hayward in Alameda County. It was called Hayward Heath.[31] The acreage was selected from a tract of 2,300 acres in the Hayward Hills. Land sold for $325 to $1,200 per acre. In promotional literature, the condition of the soil was described as "no soil, in its natural state, is good enough for the Little Lander, and none is such that it cannot be made good enough by work and artificial environment, for the soil is like folks. It wants to be loved and the more you love it, the more it will love you."[32]

In 1914 a Little Lander of the San Ysidro Colony complained to a state engineer that the $25,000 irrigation bond provided a faulty irrigation system and asked for a state investigation. The colony then began to get

(*left*) Little Landers' farms in San Ysidro, c. 1911.

(*below*) Little Landers and their flag in the community park. George P. Hall bought the statue of President Grant and the large base, c. 1910.

unfavorable publicity from the *National Farm Journal* and *The Country Gentleman*, and Smythe had to make some changes. In February 1915, the co-operative store at San Ysidro ran into debt and was returned to private enterprise for management. The market corporation ceased to exist that year. In May 1915, President Hall succumbed to old age. The following year, a Little Lander accused Smythe of permitting "any dear, old lady with $500 or $600 to settle upon a stone pile . . . and try to make a living on it."[33]

Smythe stated he "never felt comfortable in the role of the real estate huckster" and he immediately divested himself from his realty company and the sale of land. For all his commitment and sacrifice, he received $47.50 in salary for five years' work at the San Ysidro Colony.

In San Ysidro, despite the many internal and external problems facing the colonists, they were finding some success growing many varieties of fruits and vegetables suited to the climate of the area. These included figs, oranges, lemons, guavas, apricots, peaches, and avocadoes. The most enterprising farmers were those who raised chickens, ducks, rabbits, and goats. San Ysidro colonist Philip Sanger and his partner grazed as many as two thousand goats on the upland pasture adjacent to his tract. He was the first to sell goat's milk in San Diego and marketed it through the colony's store. A short-term experiment with canning rabbit meat met with little success. It was estimated that 50 percent of the colonists had to supplement their incomes with outside employment. But it appeared they had survived their early pioneer trials and were headed to becoming a permanent colony in San Diego. Smythe's managerial skill was not the real disaster for the Colony. That came in the form of one Charles Mallory Hatfield, whose "moisture acceleration" experiment would bring the colony to a disastrous end.

In 1916, San Diego was in the grip of a severe drought. City officials promised Mr. Hatfield $10,000 if he could fill the Lake Moreno Reservoir by a specific date. Hatfield, the "rainmaker," "water magician," "cloud coaxer," "precipitator," would become one of California's first folk heroes. Born in Oceanside, California, he derived his ideas about the science of *pluviculture* (the craft of rainmaking) from an 1871 treatise written by Edward Powers. After some experiments, Hatfield was able to produce a quantity of moisture by placing a secret mix of chemicals in a large cauldron on top of a 24-foot tower.

The drama of Hatfield's experiment began on January 5, 1916, when a series of storms inundated the San Diego area and all of southern California. More than sixteen inches of rain fell in just two days. Not only did Hatfield fill the eighteen million-gallon Moreno reservoir, it then collapsed and killed some twenty people. Two San Ysidro colonists, Mrs. Max Kastner and her sister-in-law, Miss Anna Kastner, were drowned while being evacuated from their home by boat. At the San Ysidro Colony, twenty-five homes and the prized pumping plant were destroyed.[34] During a second storm, Hatfield then stated, "When we started, there were 112 bridges in San Diego and when we got through, there were only two left; imagine that!" There wasn't a train into San Diego from Los Angeles for thirty-two days.[35] His actions brought about $5 million in lawsuits against the City of San Diego. Naturally, the city refused to pay his fee for the moisture experiment. Hatfield sued the city for his $10,000 fee and his lawsuit dragged on in the courts for the next twenty-two years before it was finally dismissed.[36] He never received a single penny for his efforts. Hatfield and his brother Paul did lay claim to the fact that, as a result of the two storms, thirty-five inches of rain fell in the Lake Moreno Reservoir.

The second storm, with winds recorded at 55 to 62 miles per hour, lasted from January 25 through January 30. An additional six inches of rain fell in the lower areas. The level of the lower Otay Reservoir rose more than twenty-seven feet in just ten days. William Smythe did not abandon his colony in their time of need. He arrived during the storm and worked with his family in the large emergency tents, which were set up for the storm's refugees. Outside money, food, and clothing arrived from citizens of San Diego. Smythe's daughter Margaret became custodian of food and clothing contributions, and Isaac Irwin, from the Citizen's Savings Bank of San Diego, was in charge of the cash donations. At six o'clock in the evening on January 27, the lower Otay dam burst. It took two and one-half hours

FOUNDING SISTERS

The interior of the first Little Landers Clubhouse.
William Smythe (4th from left) and partner George P. Hall (5th from left), c. 1914.

Charles Hatfield and the platform that held his cauldron and the secret chemicals, c. 1916.

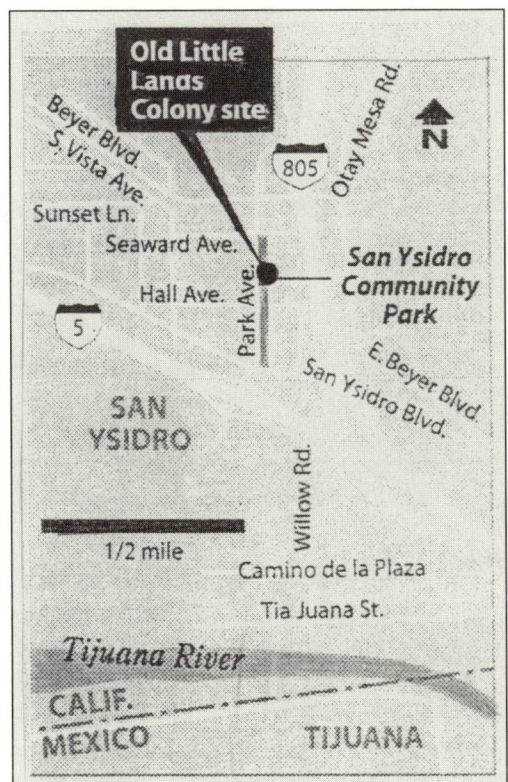

(*above*) The site of the first Little Landers Colony in San Ysidro. *Map courtesy of* San Diego Union-Tribune.

(*right*) Smythe's daughter, Margaret and her groom, fellow Little Lander Harold Champ, on their wedding day in San Ysidro (undated).

for the thirteen billion gallons of water to empty, flooding everything in its seven-mile path to the bay. One hundred Little Landers lost their homes. Once again the city of San Diego became isolated. All mail and supplies had to be delivered by ocean going vessels.[37] The San Ysidro refugee camp took care of 135 colonists and many outsiders who had lost everything in the flood. William Smythe was eventually ordered to leave the camp, suffering from exhaustion and pneumonia.[38]

The San Ysidro Colony never recovered from the disastrous flood. Although a new pumping plant was installed for domestic water and irrigation to the mesa lands, by 1918, a new economic disaster struck. The finances of the colony were depleted and the remaining colonists were asked for additional money to get clear title to their land. The Little Landers Incorporated became extinct in 1917 for failure to pay the state franchise tax. In less than a year after the statewide investigation of the agricultural colonies, Smythe was delivered a second blow. Just months shy of her fifty-seventh birthday, Harriet Bridge Smythe died at their home in San Francisco after a two-day struggle with peritonitis, brought on by appendicitis.[39] Her body was shipped from San Francisco to San Diego for burial. An exhausted and saddened William E. Smythe left California, never to return. He was called to Washington, D.C., to assist Interior Secretary Franklin Lane's abortive Soldier Homestead Colony program. He left the struggling colonies and colonists without a leader and their main inspiration.

Later, while residing in New York, Smythe wrote *City Homes and Country Lanes—Philosophy and Practice of the*

Smythe's son, William E. Smythe Jr. and son Bensil's daughter,
Julia Smythe Woods, in the San Ysidro Colony (undated).

William E. Smythe and W. E. Smythe Jr. in their lovely home in the San Ysidro Colony.
Note the beautiful hanging tapestries (undated).

THE HOPE OF THE LITTLE LANDS

George Washington Harris
1872–1945
The Builder

Marshall Valentine Hartranft
1872–1954
Land Developer

William Elsworth Smythe
1861–1922
Founder of the Little Lands Colonies

"The Trinity"
Pen and ink drawing by David E. Smith, c. 1983.
Illustration courtesy of Donna Larson.

Home-in-a-Garden in 1921 and dedicated the book to his late wife. His new quest was to help men secure suburban garden homes through his American Homesteaders Society. While working at his desk in his Fifth Avenue apartment, on October 6, 1922, he succumbed to a massive heart attack. Both Smythe and his business partner, Hartranft, would pass away while working at their desks.

With William Smythe's departure from the state of California, his four surviving Little Lands Colonies faded into the history books. By the mid 1920s, few Little Landers still resided in the Los Terrenitos Colony, and none were to be found in Hayward Heath or Cupertino.

Tujunga

The lessons of San Ysidro were not learned, and each Little Lands Colony was formed on progressively poorer soil. "Handkerchief farming" on a tiny plot of land was too labor intensive and most colonists were forced to rely on savings or outside employment. A few colonists remained bound and determined to make a go of their land. To be a Little Lander was to try to conquer the land and be strong of health. The Little Lands Colony in Tujunga would be considered the most successful of Smythe's colonies. By 1915, Tujunga had 500 settlers and 200 constructed homes. When it became apparent that they could not make a living on their one-acre plots, they were able *(continued on page 84)*

(*above*) April 12, 1913, would be the date the Little Landers used as the beginning of the colony. To the left of the cornerstone (*second row*) is George Harris (the builder) in a white shirt and to the right of the cornerstone (elevated area) is M. V. Hartranft in a black frock coat, looking pensive with his chin in his hand and William Smythe, left of Hartranft, with his hands outstretched.

(*left*) Land broker M. V. Hartranft on the patio of his Lazy Lonesome Ranch, c. 1934.

Land without population is a Wilderness;
But, population without Land, is a Mob.
—*Marshall V. Hartranft*

View looking northwest from M.V. Hartranft's "Lazy Lonesome Ranch," located at junction of McGroarty Drive and Day Street in Sunland. Structure on far right is Monte Vista Hotel and Park. Prospective landowners often stopped at the ranch for a barbecue lunch before looking at lots, c. 1907.

In this 1922 booklet, "My Hand-Made Home in the Hills," M. V. Hartranft used a photograph of his hillside home in Sunland for the cover.

GRAPES OF GLADNESS

By

M. V. Hartranft

YOU ARE NOT BROKE
Though you have no money.

You are worth $1,000 in California land values just because you sit in that auto. Los Angeles has many skyscrapers worth a million dollars each, only because a million law-abiding, refined people dwell there. California still has room for any who can feed themselves from our endless-chain gardens, instead of from the State Treasury.

California's refreshing and inspiring answer to John Steinbeck's "Grapes of Wrath".

"Two men looked out from
 their prison bars,
One saw the mud, the other
 the stars."

THE HOPE OF THE LITTLE LANDS

(*clockwise from top, this page*) Distribution Day at Home Extension Hall that occupied almost all of the ground floor of the Chamber of Commerce Building in Los Angeles, c. 1914.

A group of unidentified, potential buyers hearing the "pitch." c. 1913. The first lots went on sale March 17, 1913.

Smythe and Hartranft sold land/trust deed bonds at the Los Angeles Chamber of Commerce Building at 126 South Broadway in a block that now houses the *Los Angeles Times Newspaper*, c. 1910. *From Author's collection.*

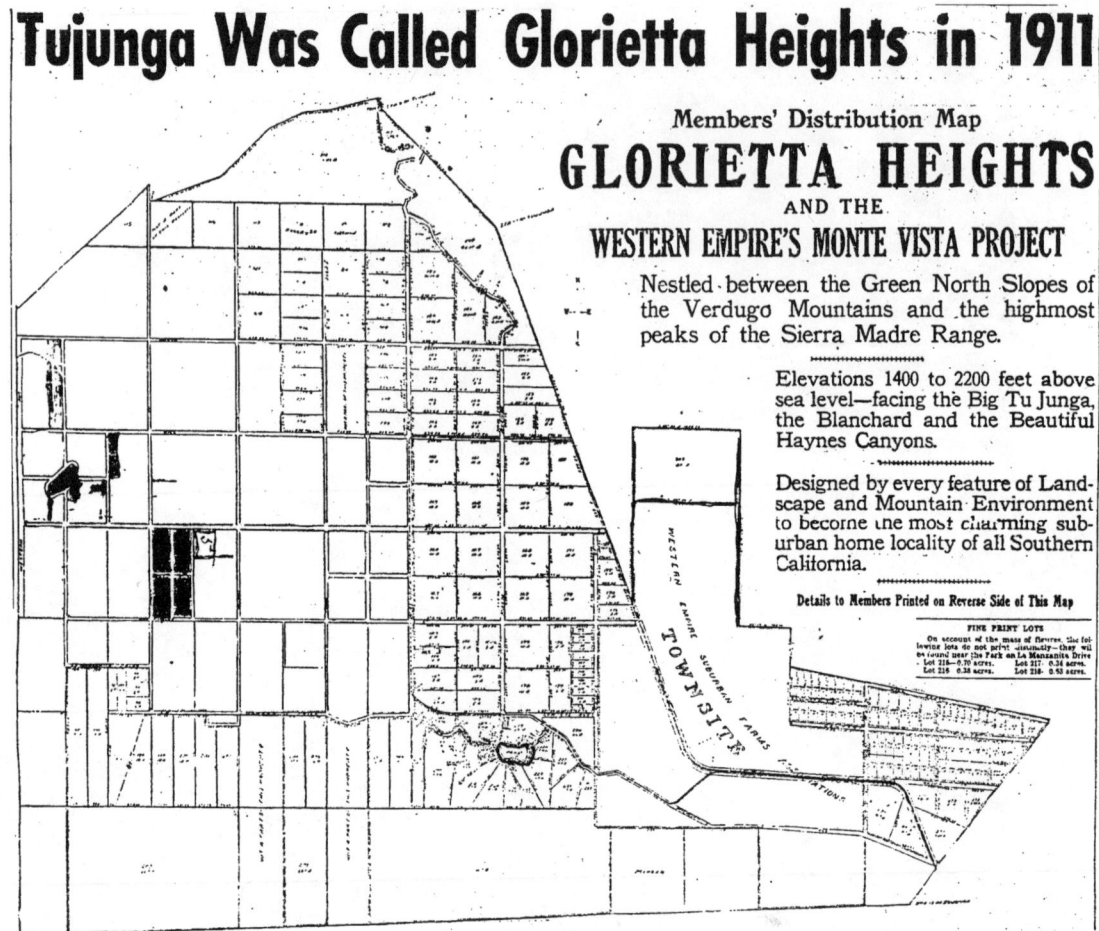

(*opposite, top*) Hartranft's advertisement for the new colony. *Los Angeles Evening Express* (May 3, 1913).

(*opposite, bottom*) Touring map to Tujunga, "The Little Yosemite." *The Record-Ledger* (1920s).

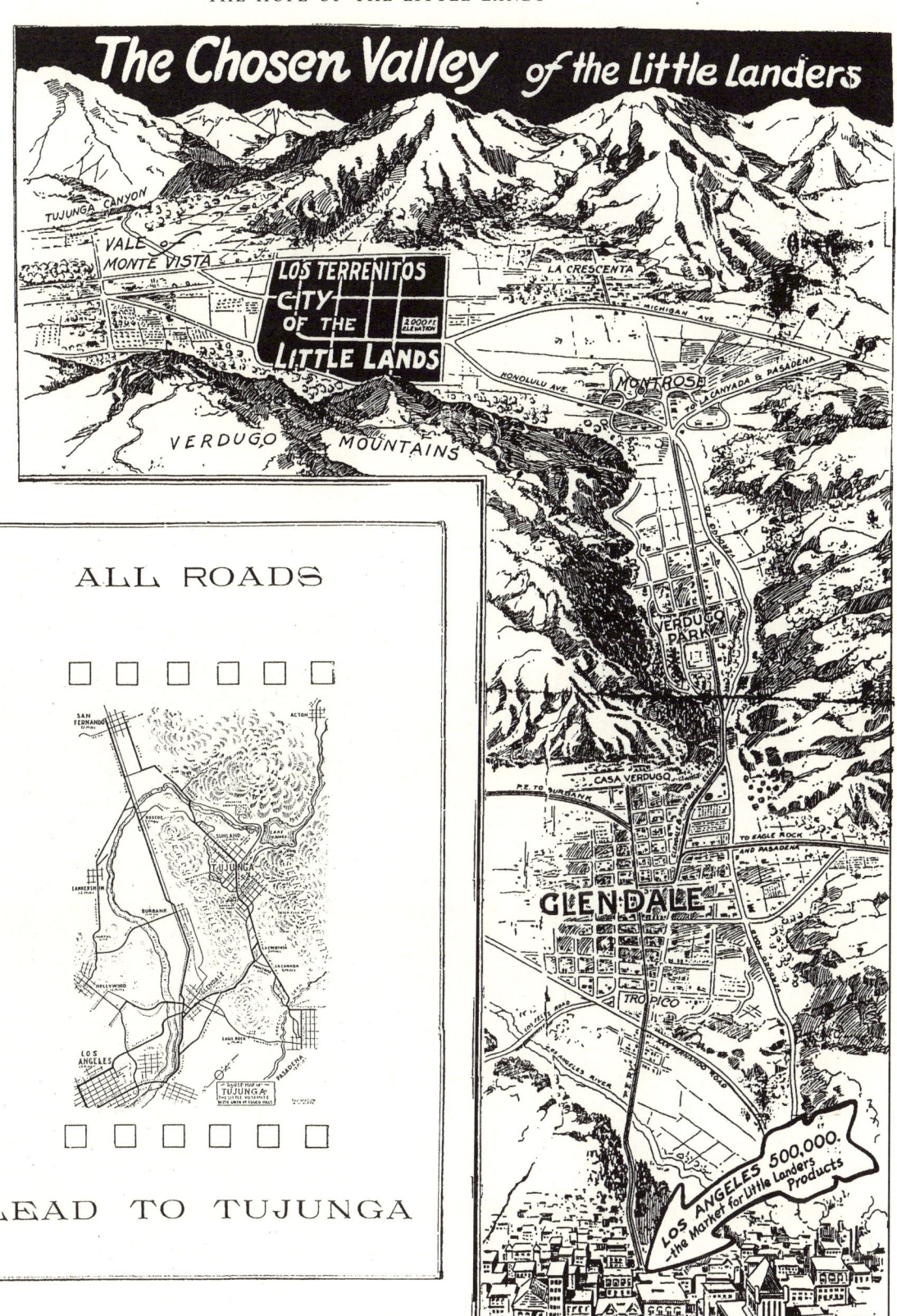

FOUNDING SISTERS

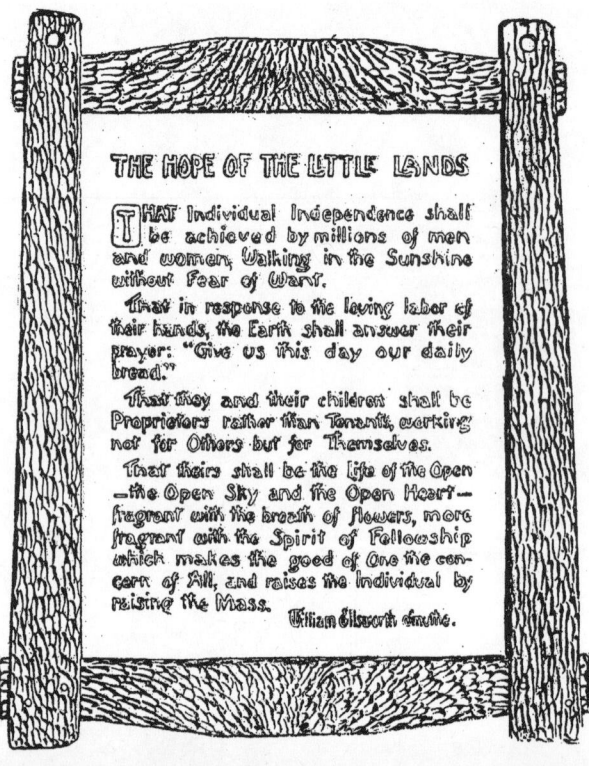

(*left*) This is the message on a hand-tooled, copper tablet, hanging in Bolton Hall since its dedication in August 1913. It was William Smythe's utopian dream for the Little Lands.

(*below*) The Hope of Little Lands copper tablet hanging to the right of the main entrance to Bolton Hall. Note the organ loft and the arts-and-crafts-style lanterns, c. 1916.

Beautiful Homes of Robert Oliver and Levert Goddard

(*above*) Some artistic examples of using the "free building materials" in the area. *The Record-Ledger* (February 1929).

(*left*) Early rustic house built on Marcus Avenue. The structure would later serve as a church and arts and crafts store. c. 1910.

Those who come out to Tujunga need never fear it will take on city ways and be spoiled. No paved walks, asphaltic avenues, or grotesque street electroliers will ever be found to offend the eye, or mar the virginal, rustic charm of the community.

"Homespun boulevards" and walks, their excellence unrivalled, made of honest, rugged, yellow gravel will guide our wandering footsteps and rubber-tired motors, as long as the majority of Tujunga folks can voice and opinion. And at night, here and there among the trees overhanging the footpaths, a cheery little light will speed you safely on your way; if it so happens that you are in haste.

To those innumerable others who, like Mr. Carr, have been "hoping for such a spot—but did not know it was so near," this folder is dedicated. Rainbow's End for the discerning may be found here at Tujunga. Its advantages are many—its deficiencies, if any, have not as yet been discovered.

—In M. V. Hartranft's 1922 brochure, "My Hand-Made Home in the Hills," Tujunga was described as having everything but a "yellow brick road."

to subdivide their acreage into urban lots. Each plot could be subdivided into eight lots that would bring from $400 to $800 each. This contributed to the creation of a suburb of Los Angeles and urban sprawl, which in turn contributed to the very loneliness and isolation the experiment had hoped to avoid. However, most colonists made a profit on their original investment and left contented with the Little Lands experiment.

Hayward Heath

Smythe's third colony, Hayward Heath, was built on a hillside of sandy soil over clay. The colony officially began in 1917 as subdivision number one, where 350 one-acre plots awaited those willing to follow Smythe's dream. With just one road into the hilly plots, a faulty water system, frequent high winds, and an abundance of mud, the fate of the colony was sealed.

Back in 1914, Smythe "had taken from a tract of 2,300 acres, about 500 acres for his utopian colony in the Hayward Hills. By 1915, he was advertising land at prices ranging from $325.00 to $1,200.00 per acre. By 1916, sixty families were living on the land. A demonstration garden was set aside under the direction of a Mr. Taylor and was established to provide proof of what a Little Lander could produce. Mr. Taylor educated the colonists on extensive farming methods."[40] Despite clever advertisements about living in Hayward Heath, most investors went bankrupt and eventually called the colony "Hungry Heath."[41]

> Take a trip to Hayward Heath Bunny Farm, it's a sight worth seeing.
> New Zealand, Flemish, Checkered Giants
> Get in the habit—eat rabbit.

Some one-acre plots produced berries, chickens, rabbits, pigeons, citrus and vegetables. Yet not all colonists were committed to the soil.

There was something magic about the hilly terrain. Of course, some people left for one reason or another, but others came. They were from all walks of life. For instance, at one time there was a thriving house of ill-fame at the intersection of Grandview and Dobble Avenues, right across the street from the home of the Baptist minister.

The Reverend Mr. Hill built his own house. It consisted of two rooms, one above the other with the stairs on the outside of the house. In passing the house I would speculate that the upper room was Mr. Hill's bedroom. It reminded me of a song my father sang to the accompaniment of his banjo:

Smythe's great-grandson, Bill, in front of portrait of William Ellsworth Smythe in Bolton Hall Museum, c. 1996. *Courtesy of Author.*

THE HOPE OF THE LITTLE LANDS

"Oh, I lived too high for comfort
in my bedroom near the sky;
They put me up there—I never knew
quite why.

There's an old square box for a table,
and a chair tied up with string,
And a terrible thing for a bed
upon an old wire spring.
They make Dutch cheese in the cellar
that sends up a tough perfume,
And the bedbugs bite one summer's night—
Upstairs in my bedroom!"

Well, the minister's house was too high for comfort and safety. One night, in a north wind, his house began to rock. One final big gust toppled it over. The Reverend Mr. Hill moved away, saying the Lord had plainly shown him this was the wrong location.

Probably there was no connection between the two events but shortly after Mr. Hill left, the District Attorney closed down the bawdy house.[42]

Hayward Heath, like all of Smythe's other colonies, had a clubhouse where town hall meetings were conducted, dances and other social events were held, and the bell rang out to bring children to school and alert residents of fire. During the prohibition years, Hayward Heath stayed wet and several stills were raided by the Federal Revenue agents. A few of the ladies living

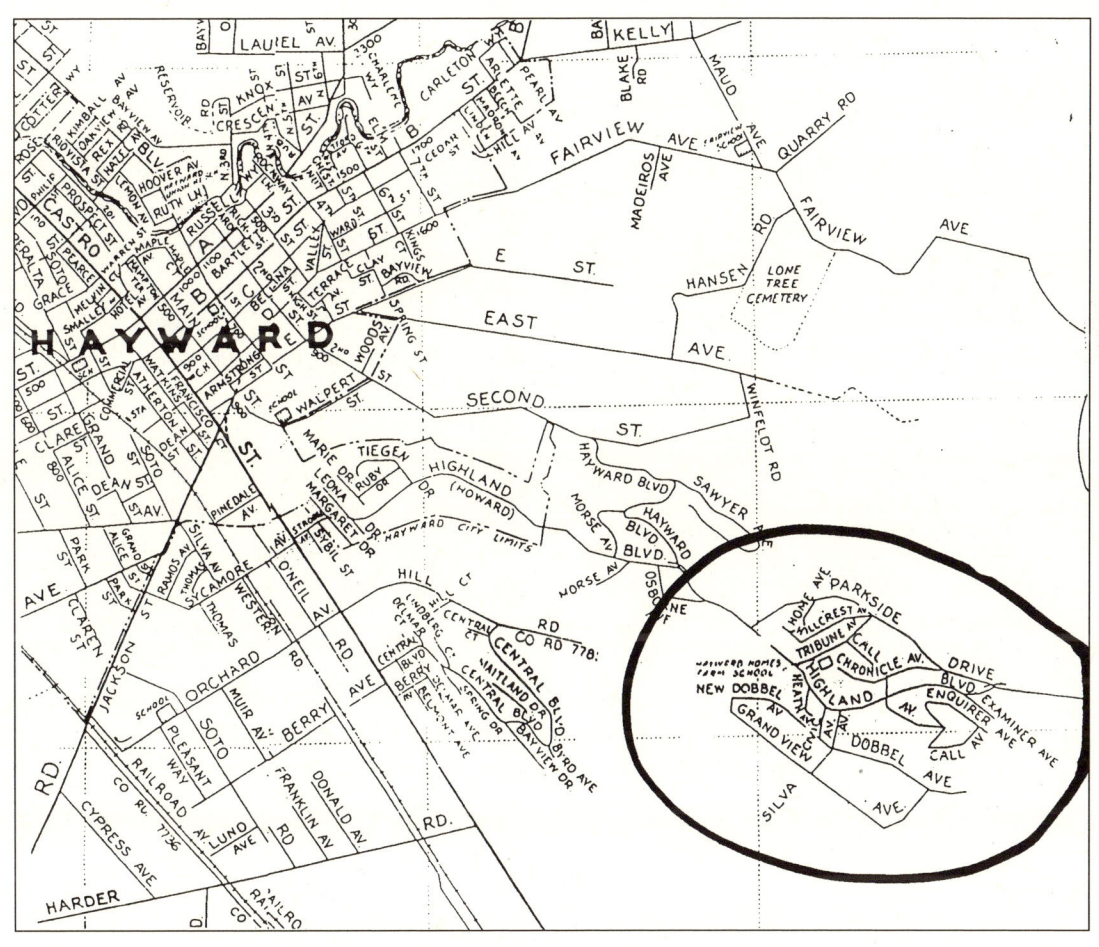

Current map of Hayward showing location of Hayward Heath Little Landers Colony.
Courtesy of Hayward Historical Society.

85

Hayward Heath colonists standing in front of a redesigned Little Landers flag. Undated photograph.
Courtesy of Hayward Historical Society.

in the colony were not interested in being farmers. Society had many names for them, such as "soiled doves," "sporting women," and "painted ladies." Little is known about the colony's bawdy house. Each woman had a name and a story, but their voices remain silent.

Men generally wore bib overalls, and one woman who worked out of doors was recorded as wearing a faded blue cotton dress and poke bonnet. Another woman, Mrs. Knox, who raised goats, wore a faded blue poke bonnet on her head, a feed sack over her shoulders and sacks tied around her legs. Very few cars existed in the colony, so bachelor Henry Merkel used his Model-T flat bed truck to haul produce, chickens, goats, and even colonists.[43]

September 1918 saw the young men going off to war and the arrival of the deadly flu of 1918. Although six miles from the city, several of the Little Landers of Hayward Heath succumbed to the flu. "Anyone leaving his house had to wear a white cotton mask. It was mandatory on the streets and in public buildings."[44]

"In 1925, historian Henry Anderson visited the Hayward site to find only five of the original settlers still upon their lands. A few abandoned cabins, a deserted school house, and what was left of the 'model acre farm' and the cottage used by Mr. Taylor."[45] Pearl Parker Hartley and her husband, Ted, moved to higher ground, about a quarter-mile from the state university, and lived in their cottage for sixty years.

The Little Landers disbanded and abandoned their houses. Their land proved to be unsaleable at any price. Despite their loses, few held William Smythe responsible or lacking in honesty and sincerity. "Mr. Smythe did not witness the final outcome of Hayward Heath. In February 1919, he became associated with the late Franklin K. Lane, then Secretary of the Interior, in connection with a plan to extend the reclamation movement to the entire United States, and thus passed from the picture of the Little Landers' colonies."[46]

Monte Vista (Cupertino)

The fourth colony, Monte Vista, near Cupertino in Santa Clara County and thirty-four miles south of San Francisco, was launched in 1916 and lasted a few years. The "Little Orchard Sections" were 200 feet in length

THE HOPE OF THE LITTLE LANDS

Bird's eye view of the Pan-Pacific International Exposition in San Francisco, c. 1915. *Courtesy of Richard Thomas.*

> The true basis for any serious study of the art of architecture is in those indigenous structures, the humble buildings everywhere, which are to architecture what folklore is to literature or folksongs are to music.... All are happily content with what ornament and color they carry, as naturally as the rocks and trees and garden slopes which are with them.
>
> —*Frank Lloyd Wright, 1910*

TIME TABLES

HOW TO REACH MONTE VISTA

The pleasantest way to make the trip down the peninsula from San Francisco is aboard a comfortable and speedy auto bus of the line maintained by the Peninsular Land and Investment Company. The line will be added to as travel increases, and a low commute rate is to be established for residents of Monte Vista whose employment requires daily trips to the city.

AUTO BUS LEAVES 57 POST STREET
DAILY
AT 10:00 A.M. ONLY

RAILWAY SERVICE

The Southern Pacific runs trains from 3rd and Townsend St. via the Mayfield Cut-off daily at 8:10 A.M. and 4:10 P.M.

Connecting at Palo Alto with the trains of the Peninsular Electric Railway for Monte Vista, the Southern Pacific runs trains from 3rd and Townsend St. at 6:30; 7:00; 9:00 and 10:40 A.M. and 1:20; 3:25; 5:20; 6:05; 8:10; 10:00 and 11:45 P.M.

and 100 feet in width. Of course, promotional literature listed the soil and weather as far and above average.[47]

The dream of the Little Landers' movement was finally terminated in 1917, when the California Commission on Land Colonization and Rural Credits, headed by Smythe's old friend, Elwood Mead, investigated the commercial exploitation of the poor and elderly who joined irrigation colonies throughout California. William E. Smythe was called upon to testify. The commission stated that his colonies were not fraudulent but unfavorable publicity soon followed. A new Little Lands Colony was being planned near Palo Alto, but the business partners pulled out after hearing the bad publicity. The Runnymede Colony, founded near Palo Alto in 1916 by Charles Weeks and Peter Faber, was not a Little Landers Colony. Smythe was hired to promote the Charles Weeks' Poultry Colony and that led to some confusion as to how many Little Lands Colonies there actually were.

Following World War I, and the demise of the Little Landers Colony, in Tujunga M.V. Hartranft created the California Home Extension Association. He re-

THE HOPE OF THE LITTLE LANDS

The Lumberman's Building and House of Hoo-Hoo, once located
in the Forestry Court of the Panama Pacific International Exposition, consisted of
the eight commercial woods of the Pacific coast. The building was resurrected in Cupertino
and became the clubhouse of the Little Landers, c. 1915. *Courtesy of Richard Thomas.*

The masthead of the Little Lands Colony newsletter in Cupertino,
featuring their clubhouse, The House of Hoo-Hoo. The House was erected by
the Artic Brotherhood, an organization of 999 lumber dealers. The large black cats, composed of
California minerals, had sparkling eyes and tails that moved mechanically, c. 1916. *Courtesy of Gail Hugger.*

89

subdivided his original 1911 tract, which hadn't sold its ten, five and two acre parcels, and created thirty, forty and fifty foot lots. These lots were in response to the post-war demand for cheap home sites with no building restrictions.

> With lots selling under $200 each on terms of $10 down and $4 per month with no building restrictions, mechanics, clerks, business and professional men speedily realized that the money they could save by escaping the mounting rents would buy homes at Tujunga and leave a good surplus toward living expenses.
>
> The slogan "bring a trowel and a bag of cement and build your own" was interpreted literally every holiday and weekend by the new "homesteaders," [sic] As soon as they could escape from their daily tasks in the city they steered for Tujunga and their "little farms in the foothills."
>
> Highways were lined with autos of all sizes and makes with lumber lashed to the fenders, bags of cement on the running boards and provisions and camp equipment piled high on the back seats. In numerous instances families gave up high-priced apartments and camped in tents for months while husbands and fathers gradually built more substantial dwellings during the hours they could spare from their employment in the city.[48]

The Little Landers arrived at their colonies with high hopes, even in their darkest hours. Hope was never in short supply. The colonies would share Smythe's dream of a little land and a living, his creed "The Hope of the Little Lands," the Little Landers cornflower blue flag with the white star of hope pointing to a refuge for the weary and a better living, a co-operative store and a clubhouse where town meetings, church services, dances, educational classes and evenings of entertainment could be held. Records indicate J.S. Lewis, the builder in San Ysidro, was sent to Tujunga where he built Zoe Gilbert's home. Mr. and Mrs. William Hevener were so successful with their ducks, poultry, and rabbits that they were sent from San Ysidro to Hayward Heath in 1915.[49] Tujunga resident George Harris was sent to the Monte Vista Colony in Cupertino. These transplanted Little Landers were to act as inspiration and teachers to the new colonists.

As Professor Hines[50] states, "You have to remember that success and failure are very tricky terms: these people always contended that these were the happiest times in their lives. The Little Landers experience paid off in dividends of improved health and joyous social interaction."[51] Tujunga resident Tom Theobold (1916–2003) recalled, "It was a grand dream that was never fulfilled." The Little Landers left the legacy of commitment to the land and their belief in William E. Smythe's "Hope of the Little Lands."

Notes

[1] Frederick Jackson Turner (1861–1932), a professor at Harvard University and the University of Wisconsin, was one of the first educators to teach a course of the American West. He theorized that the settling of the west played a large part in forming the American character. He won the Pulitzer Prize posthumously in 1933 for his work *The Significance of Sections in American History*.

[2] Eugene Victor Debs (1855–1926), Indiana born labor leader who founded the American Railway Union (1893), Socialist Democratic Party of America (1897) and the Industrial Workers of the World (1905). A gifted orator, he ran for president of the United States on the Socialist Party platform in the elections of 1900 through 1920. His anti-war sentiments led to a ten-year federal prison sentence and he became the only presidential candidate to run for office from prison.

[3] The "Gilded Age" (1878–1889) was a period after the Civil War when industrial giants in oil, steel, and electrical power emerged. The expansion of the railroads brought about a national market economy. A large blue-collar work force surfaced, fueled by foreign immigrants.

[4] William Stephens Rainsford, *New York Journal* (January 23, 1897).

[5] M. H. Dunlos, *Gilded City—Scandal and Sensation in Turn-of-the-Century New York* (New York: Harper Collins, 2000).

[6] In Faber's Book of Utopias, utopia was defined as "no where or no place." Usually it was interpreted to mean an ideal and good place. Distopia meant a bad place.

[7] Edward Bellamy's (1850–1898), *Looking Backwards, 2000–1887*, became the manifesto of the national movement and the emergence of the People's Party.

[8] Bolton Hall (1854–1938), Presbyterian minister, attorney, socialist and ardent single tax reformer. As a Christian Socialist and follower of Henry George, he started an agricultural utopian colony named Free Acres in New Jersey in 1909. He was the main inspiration to William E. Smythe.

[9] Although a master of public speaking, granddaughter Julia C. (Smythe) Woods remembers him at home pacing the floor and practicing his speeches out loud. Letter to author from Julia (Smythe) Woods dated April 2, 1992.

[10] William E. Smythe, *The Conquest of Arid America* (1899 and 1905), still remains in print with several revised editions.

[11] In 1913, Smythe named a street in Tujunga Greeley Street after his childhood hero. Horace Greeley (1811–1872) was founder of the *New York Tribune*.

[12] Greeley adopted the phrase, "Go west young man, go west," which originated with John Soule. John Babstone Lane Soule, a journalist from Indiana first coined the expression in an editorial in The Terre Haute Express (1851).

[13] For a comprehensive look at William E. Smythe's life see George Wharton James' book, *Heroes of California—The Story of the Founders of the Golden State as Narrated by Themselves of Gleaned from Other Sources* (1910).

[14] *Land Of Sunshine Magazine*, 13, December 1900.

[15] Smythe, op. cit.

[16] John Wesley Powell (1834–1902) was a one-armed Civil War veteran who explored the Grand Canyon and Colorado River in 1869 and 1871. He served as Director of the United States Geological Survey from 1881 to 1894 and the Bureau of Ethnology until 1902.

[17] It progressed to city status in 1948. New Plymouth is located fifty miles east of the state capital of Boise. As with the Little Lands Colony in Tujunga, the sale of alcohol was prohibited.

[18] For further information and photographs on New Plymouth, Idaho, visit their website at http://www.npidaho.com.

[19] Author's telephone conversation with Beth Earles, New Plymouth City Clerk, on March 14, 2003. The town's population has remained consistent for the last few decades. Current population is 1,900 people.

[20] The town of Standish was named after the pilgrim father, early American colonist Miles Standish. Refer to Henry Wadsworth Longfellow's poem "The Courtship of Miles Standish" (1858). Smythe would continue to use names such as Standish and New Plymouth to symbolize the new century's pilgrims and colonies. As of 2003, Standish's population is 70 residents. Tujunga is 40,000 residents and San Ysidro is 28,000 residents.

[21] Information courtesy of Edith Summers, Standish resident and member of the Lassen Historical Society in Susanville, California. July 15, 2003.

[22] Tim I. Purdy, "Utopian Town is Now Known As Standish," *Lassen Chronicles* (April 27, 1997).

[23] William E. Smythe, *History of San Diego, 1542–1908*. It is still regarded as an accurate and important record of San Diego's early history.

[24] Herbert Hensley, "The Little Landers of San Ysidro," *Chula Vista—The Early Years*, The Chula Vista Historical Society, IV (1994).

[25] Little Landers Park, the San Ysidro Women's Club, and San Ysidro Library still exist, although the original redwood Clubhouse is gone. Author's telephone interview with Joyce Kettrick (97 years young), San Ysidro historian, June 4, 2003. Smythe's home is still in existence at 216 East Park, next to the 805 freeway.

[26] The leaders of the San Ysidro Colony were eager to maintain cordial relations with the leaders of San Diego. President Grant's son was a prominent businessman in the area and builder of the deluxe Grant Hotel. In 1918, when the colony's finances were low, someone discovered that the statue was stamped out of sheet copper and therefore valuable. It was then sold as scrap metal.

[27] From 1908 to 1913, the Industrial Workers of the World recruited about one thousand migratory laborers as it urged a radical reform of the economy. Believing in the Marxist concept of class struggle, it threatened California and its municipalities. The term "wobblies" was a derisive term newspapers used to describe the radical members. Some said the I.W.W. stood for the "I Won't Work" movement.

[28] In 1919, anarchist Emma Goldman was deported and exiled to Russia.

[29] Carey McWilliams, "Southern California—an Island on the Land," *The Politics of Utopia*, 293. Travel folders luring tourists to the Golden State failed to mention California as a hotbed of social unrest.

[30] Lawrence B. Lee, "The Little Landers Colony of San Ysidro," *Journal of San Diego History* (1975): 26–51.

[31] The area was named for Hayward Heath in Sussex Downs, England, a region noted for its agriculture.

[32] Henry S. Anderson, "The Little Landers Colonies: A unique Agricultural Experiment in California," *Agricultural History* 5, no. 4 (October 1931): 148.

[33] Stories from disgruntled colonists began to circulate and were published nationally. The dream was beginning to vanish. *San Francisco Examiner* (July 23, 1916).

[34] The Redwood Clubhouse, built on the high mesa, did not wash away and was later used as a Women's Club and neighbor to the San Ysidro Library in Little Landers Park. Author's interview with Joyce Kettrick, June 5, 2003.

[35] Cecilia Rasmussen, "Cloud Coaxer had a Stormy Career in Parched Deserts," *Los Angeles Times* (May 6, 2001).

[36] Charles Hatfield went on to obtain contracts to produce rain from many cities throughout California. His rainmaking activities ended in 1928 when Los Angeles secured water from the Colorado River. Mr. Hatfield died during the rainy winter of 1958 in the desert town of Pearblossom. He was ridiculed, divorced by his wife, shunned by the public, and died in obscurity. His brother, Paul A. Hatfield, donated six volumes of his brother's writing (without the secret formula) to the San Diego Public Library, California Room.

[37] Richard F. Pourade, *The History of San Diego—Gold in the Sun*, 110–112, 208–217.

[38] Lee, op. cit.

[39] Death Certificate, State of California, June 3, 1918.

[40] Letter to Beulah Linnell (Hayward) from John Whelan, *Adobe Trails* (Fall 1980).

[41] "Agriculture dominated Hayward life in 1919," *The Daily Review* (January 29, 1984).

[42] Pearl Parker Hartley (Hayward Little Lander), *We Were This Way* (self-published, 1979), 14–15.

[43] Ibid., p. 46.

[44] Ibid.

[45] Whelan letter, op. cit.

[46] Anderson, op. cit., pp. 149–150.

[47] "The House of Hoo-Hoo," Volume I, August 1916. The Cupertino Colony Newsletter, 12 pp. The name Hoo-Hoo is derived from a building that was located in the center of the Forestry Court at the Panama Pacific International Exposition in San Francisco. The outside of the building was composed of eight log columns, 26 feet high and 42 inches in diameter. The unusual building housed the Monte Vista Board of Trade and large displays of the produce grown in the colony. Cupertino resident and librarian Gail Hugger reports the building burned to the ground in 1960. George Washington Harris, the builder of Bolton Hall, was listed as a resident of their colony.

[48] Helen Wilson, "1920 Started the Flapper Era," *The Record-Ledger Golden Anniversary Edition* (May 14, 1970). Bolton Hall Museum Library.

[49] *Journal of San Diego History* 21, no. 1 (Winter 1975): 44.

[50] Robert V. Hines' book, *California's Utopian Colonies* (1953), is considered the quintessential reference book on the state's utopian colonies.

[51] Henry Chiu, "Utopia: Little Lands Rocky Soil Provided Settlers Little Living," *The Los Angeles Times* (January 7, 1996).

TUJUNGA

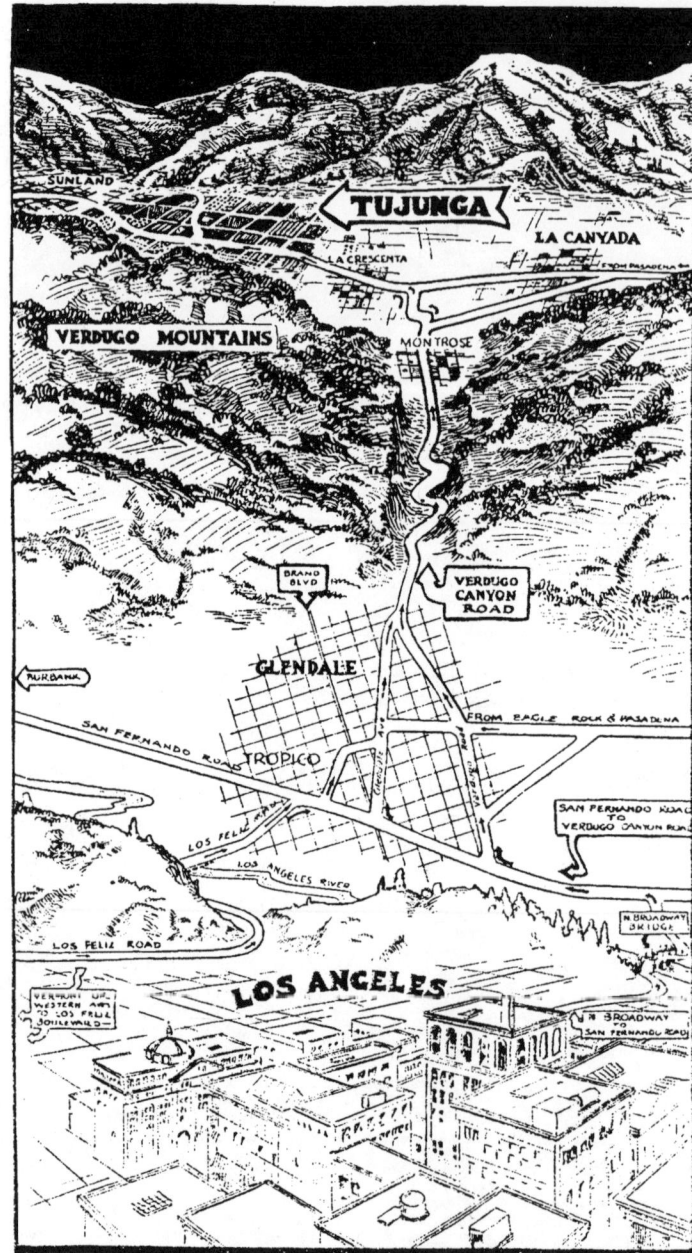

In this 1921 promotional brochure, M. V. Hartranft would teach the world to pronounce the name "Too-hoon-gah."

Tujunga—What's in a Name

The spelling, pronunciation and meaning of the word Tujunga has vexed travelers, mapmakers, real estate promoters, and residents since the word first came into print.

The many definitions of the word have included Big Thunder, an Indian Mother's Smile, Place of the Old Woman, and Mountain Range. The first record of the original Indian village in the area would appear in the journal of Padre Vicente De Santa María who, along with Gaspar de Portola and Father Juan Crespi, first crossed into the San Fernando Valley in the summer of 1769. He noted that there was an Indian village near the mouth of the Big Tujunga Canyon.

The earliest recorded contact of Tongva Indians and Europeans was in the mid-sixteenth century. From 1519 to 1521, Spain invaded and conquered Mexico with an army led by Hernando Córtez. After the conquest, Spain claimed all of Mexico and the unknown lands to the north. These lands included much of the southwest United States.

The viceroy of Mexico, Antonio de Mendoza, urged Juan Rodriguez Cabrillo to explore the entire Pacific coast north of Mexico. After Cabrillo's 1542 expedition, when he met the Tongva Indians on Catalina Island, Sebastian Viscaíno would again meet the Indians on Catalina Island in 1602.

For the next century and a half, California would remain virtually unexplored. When rumors began circulating about the Russians coming south from Alaska and the English, along with other nations, entering the Pacific region including California, Spain decided to occupy California. *Presidios* (forts) and missions were to be developed in rapid succession. The Jesuits, who established the missions in Baja California and explored portions of Arizona and Utah, were expelled from the New World. Spanish king Carlos III deemed them too powerful. The Jesuits were replaced by the Franciscan order. Franciscan missionary Junípero Serra founded the first mission in San Diego in 1769. The governor of Baja California, Gaspar de Portola, led an expedition to Monterey Bay that would be the first party of white men to cross into the San Fernando Valley. Portola entered the valley via the Cahuenga Pass and members of the expedition stopped near the populous Indian village of Siutcanga and greeted more than two hundred Indians, including women and children, near the large pool of water.[1] The group of fifty-seven men spent several peaceful nights in the Encino area and noted the friendly and cooperative Indians living there.[2] The Indians brought presents and nourishment to the weary travelers, who camped by the spring surrounded by a dense forest.[3]

Outside of the Indians in the Great Valley in Mexico, the concentration of Indians from San Diego to Santa Barbara was the largest in North America. The Tongvas numbered approximately 5,000. Noted authority A. L. Kroeber said, "They [Gabrielinos] seem to have been the most advanced group south of Tehachapi, except perhaps the Chumash." When the Spanish arrived in California, the entire native population of the

FOUNDING SISTERS

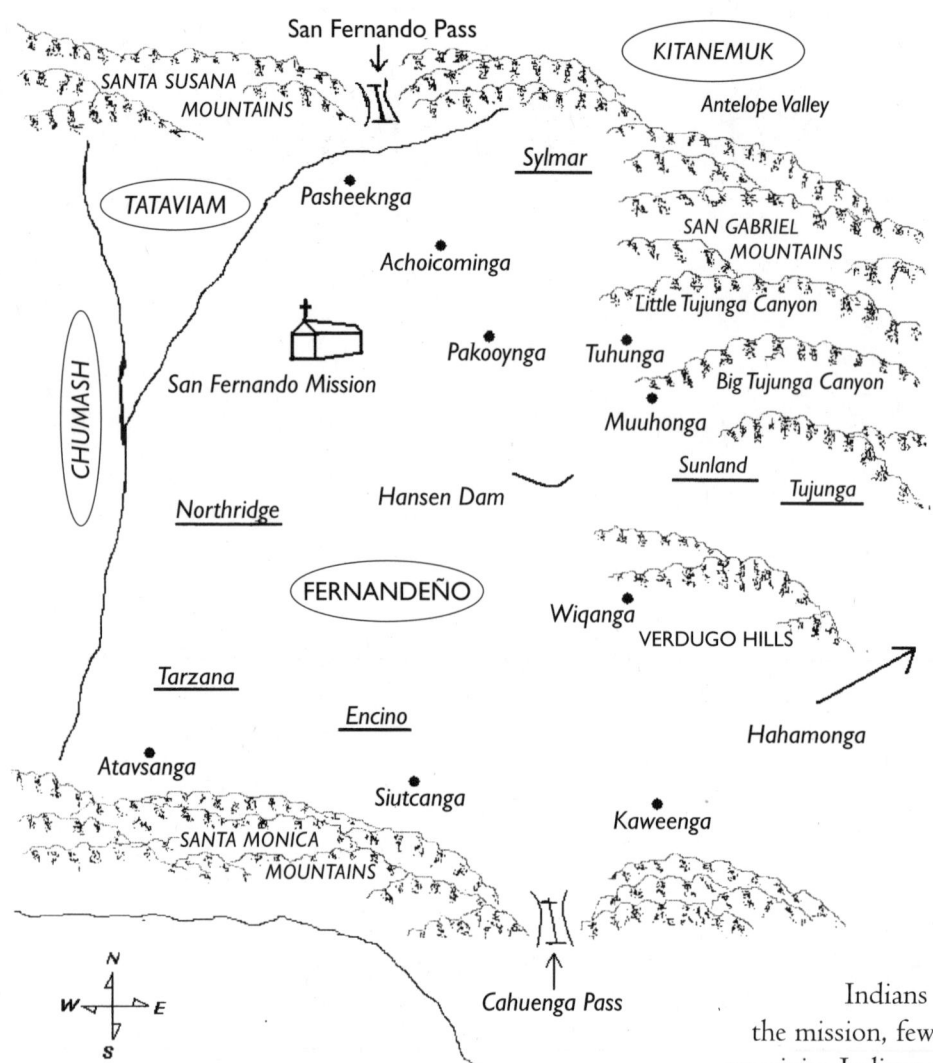

Indian villages in the San Fernando Valley prior to 1805. *Map by Martine Prado.*

Gabriel Mountains in the San Fernando Valley. Muuhonga was located at the mouth of Big Tujunga Canyon in Sunland and Tuhungna was located near the mouth of Little Tujunga Canyon in Lake View Terrace. Tuhungna would later appear in the marriage and baptismal records at the San Fernando Mission (Mission San Fernando Rey de España, 1797–1834, founded by Padre Fermin Lasuén) as Tejunga (the Spanish form of Tujunga) and Tujubit.[4] By 1801, the village of Tuhunga (435 A.D.–1801) had ceased to exist. One by one, as the missions were founded, large plots of land for livestock and crops were granted so that the missions would become self-sustaining. In 1822, there were over 1,000 Tongva/Gabrielinos and Tataviam and Fernandeño Indians living at the San Fernando Mission.

Ultimately the Church's plan for the Indians failed. After the secularization of the mission, few Indians received land grants. The remaining Indians drifted into the pueblo of Los Angeles or traveled to the surrounding mountains and the Mojave Desert. Horace Bell, in *Reminiscences of a Ranger— Early Times in Southern California (1851–1854)*, recounted how Indians in Los Angeles were paid for their ranch work with a liquor called *aguardiente*. Saturday and Sunday would be occupied with drunken fights and disruption. By Sunday evening, the sheriff, along with special Indian deputies, would herd the troublemakers into jail. On Monday mornings, a weekly slave auction was held. The slave mart in Los Angeles was much like those in New Orleans and Constantinople, except the slave in Los Angeles was sold fifty-two times a year for as long as he lived, generally not more than two or three years. The going price for each slave was one to three

state was estimated to be 300,000. By the early 1900s, that population was reduced to less than 30,000. In the Los Angeles County area, there were approximately eighty Indian villages or *rancherias* established near streams, rivers, and natural sheltered areas. Two important Tongva villages were located at the base of the San

"TUJUNGA"

Tujunga, an Indian mother's smile,
    The town is like the name—
You can travel many a weary mile
    And find nothing just the same.

The way Tujunga came about—
    Here's how 'twas told to me,
And there's not even a tiny doubt
    'Tis true as true can be.

One dark night some angels seven
    Were searching from on high
For a little piece of Heaven
    That had fallen from the sky.

When suddenly the leader pointed
    To a diadem in the air;
Not one of all the seven doubted
    The lost was found a-nestling there.

Next day 'twas proven by the band
    Like nothing ever seen before—
Mountain rear guard, right and left hand,
    A dream valley just at the front door.

Tujunga, a little piece of Heaven,
    Come to earth, an ever-changing toy,
And like the smile so seldom given,
    It fills each heart with Peace and Joy.

Mary E. Smith, The Record Ledger, *January 24, 1924*

---

dollars per week. "Those thousands of honest, useful people were absolutely destroyed in this way." In just over one hundred years, much of the native population and its culture had disappeared.[5]

In 1868, noted California historian Hubert Howe Bancroft said the earliest spelling of the Indian village's name was Tuyunga.[6] In the Uto-Aztec dialect, the ending "nga" means "the place of" and the word root "tux-u'u" means "old woman." John P. Harrington, noted ethnologist of the Smithsonian Institute and the Southwest Museum, said the meaning of Tujunga was "old woman, our mother, the earth."[7] In a legend retold by Juan Menendez's (one of the last remaining Fernandeño descendants) mother, "*Ra wiyawi* was the name of the *capitán* of Tuhunga, the *calandria* (meadowlark)." Harrington's wife, Corabeth Tucker Harrington, recorded the legend in a mixture of Spanish, English, and Fernandeño the evening of November 9, 1917, at the old Calabasas *adobe*. The legend describes how Tuhunga became named Tuxuunga, "old woman place," because the wife of *Ra wiyawi* turned herself into stone out of grief for her dead son and daughter. The areas covered by the legend include most of the San Fernando Mission land.[8] When the town of Tujunga was established in 1913, few residents could remember seeing a Native American in the area. Elsie Ellenberg, who lived on Mt. Gleason Avenue in the early 1900s, remembered seeing a few Indians living on the dirt road leading into the Big Tujunga Canyon. Tujunga would make famous its own Indian, an Osage named Big Chief White Horse Eagle (1826–1937). He lived in a tent with his wife, Queen WA-The-NA, and 100 cats at Marcus and Foothill Boulevard in the 1930s. He starred in the Western classic movies *The Covered Wagon* (1923) and *The Iron Horse* (1924).

Martin Feliz, a consultant of John P. Harrington,

learned from an old Fernandeño woman named Espír-tu (one of three grantees of the Mexican land Rancho El Escorpion)[9] that an early name for Little Tujunga Canyon was La Reiña or "The Queen." It was said that the queen came in the form of a whale and was petrified at the mouth of the Canyon. By going to Sunland, you can see the 25-feet-long red rock "petrified queen."

Historian José Zalvidea said that the Muuhonga was located "about two and a half miles from San Fernando." He related a story of Muuhonga in which "all the fish and animals of the sea" were invited to a large fiesta. Once there, they were murdered by their hosts, all shot with arrows. "There the rocks at Muuhonga resembled people with heads bent forward, as if shot. Only the turtledove escaped by making a tremendous leap, landing at Santa Catalina Island." José Zalvidea translated the name Muuhonga to be *tiraron jarazos* ('they shoot arrows'). In contrast, José de los Santos Juncos said the Tongva word *muhu* means 'owl.' Therefore, in fact, Muuhonga means 'Place of the Owl.' Logically, the 'Place of the Owl' (Sundland) was located near the 'Place of the Old Woman' (Lake View Terrace).

Los Angeles (La Reiña de los Angeles—Queen of the Angels) was founded on September 4, 1781, by the Spanish governor Felipe de Neve, along with a priest from the San Gabriel Mission (1776) and eleven families of settlers who had been recruited from the Sinaloa and Sonora areas of Mexico. Mission San Gabriel built a second church in the new Los Angeles pueblo that can still be seen today at the corner of North Main Street and Sunset Boulevard, facing the old Main Plaza. The Indian village near the Los Angeles River was named Yang-na. The Spanish period, which lasted from 1769 through 1822, created two-dozen ranchos, but by the close of the Mexican period (1822–1848) almost eight hundred ranchos had been granted. In many instances, the Mexican land grants were for land granted in the Spanish period, mainly grazing rights.

When Mexico won her independence from Spain in 1822, California became a province of the newly formed Republic of Mexico. Because the Indian village of Tuhunga was so close to the San Fernando Mission, they were converted rapidly. In 1798, large numbers of Tongva children were baptized and slowly their parents converted as well. The last year of the missions saw the conversion of twenty-four adults over the age of twenty-one years and only one child. A total of ninety Tuhuvitam were baptized. The last resident of the Tuhunga village, Julian (the 50-year-old leader or "Captain") was removed on February 1, 1801. The once vital village of Tuhunga became silent.[10]

By 1834, the secularization of the missions was complete. A civil administrator was assigned to the ex-mission land. "The secularization of the Franciscan missions, issued August 9, 1834, assigned one-half of the mission lands and property to the Indians (neophytes) in grants of 33 acres of arable land along with land 'in common' sufficient to 'pasture their stock'. In addition, one-half of the mission herds were divided proportionately among the neophyte families."[11] Many Mission Indians did not retain title to their land. By 1840, the City of Los Angeles had 1,610 Native Indians and the whole of California had 92,597 Indians. Their numbers were reduced by disease, changes in their diets and the obliteration of their culture and language. Several Indians remained in the area working on ranchos, while many more drifted into Los Angeles, the mountains surrounding the city or the desert of the Antelope Valley.

The ancient Fernandeño villages of Tuhunga and Muuhonga now had become part of the Mexican land grant of Rancho Tejunga. By 1848, the United States had finally won the war with Mexico. With the signing of the Treaty of Guadalupe Hidalgo in January 1848, Mexico ceded all of California, New Mexico, and Arizona to the United States. In 1850, California entered the Union as the thirty-first state. In 1875, the name of the old village and rancho was recorded as Teyunga. More confusion arose in 1886 when a new map by Howland and Koeberle referred to the new post office in Monte Vista (Sunland) as the Tujunga Post Office.

The Tuhunga Indian village was one of the oldest habitation of Indians known in southern California. Its history would remain a mystery until 1945, when the Loyd McFee family was attempting to enlarge their

Just a few of the artifacts uncovered in the McFee garden, c. 1945.

garden and their plow began to unearth the original Tuhunga village. So many bowls and artifacts emerged that they knew they had discovered a major archeological site. The Southwest Museum, which had housed and displayed Indian items since 1909, was summoned. The archeologists found fragments of stone bowls, mortars, pestles, and *maños* from six to thirty-six feet below the surface of the soil. Other discoveries included human, whale, and animal bones (rabbit was a favorite meal), stone pipes, awls, game pieces, fishing hooks, and arrowheads of obsidian, quartz and jasper, as well as hair ornaments made of abalone shell.[12] Small amounts of cremated remains were found in soapstone bowls. Later, it would be determined that the site had been used for the mourning ritual and was a reburial site. Ceremonies held an important place in Tongva life. Death received the greatest ritual attention with many significant ceremonies to help free the spirit of the deceased from this world and aid it on the journey to an after life. Every year in August, when the week of visiting, dancing, singing, and feasting was completed, the Tongvas would make life-size images of the dead and burn them.

In 1963 and 1964, and later in 1968, the anthropology department of the University of California at Los Angeles would excavate the ancient village of Tuhunga. In 1968, U.C.L.A. joined forces with the Department of Recreation and Parks of the State of California to remove and retrieve the majority of the artifacts before the concrete lanes of the 210 Freeway would permanently seal over the ancient village of Tuhunga.

The northeastern section of the site was determined to be the oldest. The forty shards of Arizona red-on-brown Hokam pottery jars, made in the seventh and eighth centuries, indicated the Tongva's extensive trade network with other native groups. Human bones were found in the oldest part of the site. It would be centuries later that cremation would be used by the village residents. The settlement apparently had been occupied for a long time, as debris of black ash, firestones, and miscellaneous refuse was almost three feet deep.[13]

Time and the freeway have erased much of the true evidence of this prehistoric site that existed from 435 A.D. to 1801 in the San Fernando Valley. The village of Tuhunga had perhaps as many as three hundred Indian residents. They lived in multi-family circular, dome-shaped dwellings that were covered with tulles or reeds from the river. The Fernandeño and Gabrielino/Tongva were culturally of the Shoshone and linguistically of the Uto-Aztec family, distantly related to the Utes, Paiutes, New Mexico Pueblos, Yaquies, and Aztec.[14]

It was estimated that 9,000 Tongva lived in the Los Angeles Basin. Remains of Tongva villages have been found in the watershed of the Pacoima, Los Angeles, Santa Anna, and Rio Hondo rivers, from Long Beach to Encino.[15]

"The town of Tujunga is the result of three distinct periods of evolution. The area was first plated in 1888 by King, Dexter Gilbert and King. In the early 1900s there were three known families living in the area, the Begues, John Cox, and the Fehlhaber family."[16] In 1915, when the Little Landers Colony applied for a new post office, a movement began to select a new name. Little Lander Mabel Hatch recalled,

Project director Nelson Leonard III (*center*) observes Chuck Irwin (U.C.L.A.) and Nancy Heller (U.C. Davis) uncovering a large pottery bowl that measured more than two feet in diameter. *The Record-Ledger* (August 29, 1968).

Nobody wanted to continue being called Little Landers. Whatever magic had been attached to the words in the beginning had long since fallen from them. We did a lot of talking and quarrelling about it and finally decided to call a mass meeting. That meeting was a good deal like a political convention. Everybody went with his mind made up and his lines of influence spread. There were all sorts of suggestions but I remember only one, "Fairy Dell." My aunt, fresh from wrestling with a rock as big as a house, snorted so loudly at this suggestion she could be heard all over the hall. There was a suppressed giggle of sympathy. I don't remember how we ever came to agree on Tujunga, there was bitter opposition to it because of its harsh sound and the booby trap in the pronunciation. But I think we were just worn down. However, years later we came to feel it probably was the right name after all because of its historic background.[17]

When the colonists first bought their acreage in "Los Terrenitos" or the "Little Lands Colony," they agreed on little, but all agreed the name had to go. In July 1916, the residents approved the name Tujunga and it became official on August 8 of that year. Very few had any idea what the word Tujunga meant or its origin. M. V. Hartranft, in his 1922 brochure, urged people to pronounce it Too-hoon-gna. John S. McGroarty and several prominent citizens would later claim they suggested the name Tujunga. As years passed, no one could remember who had actually suggested the name. In October 1923, John McGroarty wrote a letter to the postmaster of San Fernando asking for clarification of the correct spelling. By January 1924, he had an answer that clouded the issue further. C. Hart Merriam, chairman of the United States Geographic Board, wrote him that the Monte Vista Post Office was called Tuhunga in 1887. He said he preferred the Indian version, as opposed to the Spanish version, Tujunga. The board, at that time, would not be able to issue a final correct spelling. "It is quite in order, however, for the organizations to add the weight of their opinions in an effort to reach some final decision that everybody will accept for all the time."[18] To this day, people still struggle with the pronunciation of the town's name. Tujunga citizens have grown weary explaining to out-of-state residents that Tujunga is not located in Mexico.

"Boosting for Tujunga"
by Eliz. M. Shaner

Tujunga, we've discovered,
Has legends old and grand,
And her mountains and her valleys
Are the finest in the land.
So come out here and see us,
From city and from shore;
We'll tell you of her golden weather
And all her ancient lore.

Chorus:
We're boosting for Tujunga,
Yes, boosting right along;
We're boosting for Tujunga,
Boosting two thousand strong.
(Repeat Chorus)

If a ripe old age is wanted
With contentment and with peace,
At Tujunga buy a piece of land,
You do not want to lease.
She has water, soil and climate
Found in no other clime,
So come out here and live with us
And life will be sublime.

Chorus

FOUNDING SISTERS

The Meaning of Tujunga

T the TEMPLE where all may kneel,
U the UNITY all may feel,
J the JOY all may share,
U in UNITING in thankful prayer,
N for NATURE's blessings lent,
G to GREET those weary bent,
A to the ACME of Content.

—Lorraine Hunter, The Record Ledger, 1923.

(*above*) "Singing" Jimmy Smith, the man who put Tujunga on the map, c. 1930s.

(*below*) Tujunga's favorite troubadour, "Singing" Jimmie Smith, c. 1931.

100

In the halcyon days of the 1920s, when motorists were discovering the joy of Sunday drives, Tujunga began to be noticed. The fern caves and wonders of the Big Tujunga Canyon began to appear in the motoring magazine *Touring Topics* issued by the Automobile Club of Southern California. The fern caves were featured in the May issue of *National Geographic Magazine* in 1925. Soon articles appeared in *Journeys Beautiful*, published by the Motor Transit Company, and *Seeing California Magazine*.[19]

It would take a unique man to make the word Tujunga well known. In the late 1920s, local musician, troubadour, and Kiwanis member "Singing" Jimmie Smith put Tujunga on the minds and hearts of people throughout the United States. Jimmie and his portable traveling organ appeared at state Kiwanis conventions all over the United States. With his song "The Best Little Town in the U.S.A.," he taught folks how to pronounce Tujunga and spell it, too.[20]

In 1932, to add to the confusion over the name Tujunga, some street names were changed when Tujunga was annexed to the City of Los Angeles.[21] Those residents opposed to annexation had their names, applied to various streets, removed from the maps.

Sunland became connected to Tujunga with a hyphen. Today, we think of Sunland-Tujunga as sister cities. This was not always so. The Sunland folks wondered about these Tujunga people—moving up there amongst all those rocks and building a clubhouse with a library and having cultural events. Julia Granger Sharp, who was born in 1906 and grew up in Sunland, recited a jingle the Sunland children used to sing about the perils of venturing into Tujunga: "In Los Terrenitos I lost my goat, also my vest and hat and coat." Julia said, "We in Sunland always thought of the Los Terrenitos folks as more or less the elite."[22]

Hilda Livingston's son Chan said, "We were different from the people who came into Tujunga. Starting in 1909, Hartranft began a promotion called Little Landers in the dry-wash area that is now Tujunga. It was a colony for people who came up there for their health or to retire."[23] While the population of Tujunga grew rapidly, as the small lots were swept up by retirees and health seekers, the town of Monte Vista grew slowly. The large ranches of Sunland were owned and worked by a much younger population. The Sunland folks always looked at the Little Landers folks as rather odd and a little gullible because they purchased acreage that was more rocks than usable soil. "On occasion, I remember them being referred to as those Tujunga knotheads. Looking at the situation today, those Sunland families were not about to disrupt their peaceful way of life... they were not about to concern themselves with the complications, troubles and monetary problems of the growing pains of a new Tujunga."[24]

> Whether in song or verse, everyone had their own idea of the true meaning of the word "Tujunga."

Since Bolton Hall served as the clubhouse for all church services, concerts, meetings, and dances, the Little Landers' families were much closer to one another than the residents of Sunland, whose ranches were larger and whose only meeting place was under the oak trees of Monte Vista Park. Chan said those Little Landers were an entirely different type than the younger "dirt farmers" of Monte Vista (Sunland) who had to earn a living. Little Landers came with an inheritance or wealth acquired from their previous businesses.[25]

As the years passed, the Sunland and Tujunga residents attended church and social functions together, danced together at Bolton Hall, and their children were schooled together and married one another. The towns' names merged and they now shared more than the hyphen in their name. The sister cities, both located in the Vale of Monte Vista or Tujunga Valley, shared a rich history and geographic location.

Tu–jun–ga: A Legend

In the undiscovered archives
Of the green hills of Verdugo
Is this legend of the gone days
When the hills were not so old;
Once there was an Indian chieftain
"Who was sour and harsh and bitter,"
With long years of tribal problems
All his heart grown hard and cold.

"Never smiled he on his people,"
"Never spoke he without snarling,"
Till 'twas said he'd learned the language
Of some old wolf starved and lame.
Ruled he with a will of iron.
"Every squaw, papoose and warrior"
Did his wish with dread and fearing
Lest his wrath break forth like flame.

And the mother scared her papoose
"Into proper, right behavior"
"When she plainly, sharply threatened"
To involve the old chief's wrath.
Far to the northward and to eastward
"Lived the harsh chief and his people,"
Till at last the war dance sent forth
All the braves on the war path.

Joined the tall and fierce Tulares
"With the Piutes and the Monos,"
Gainst the sour chief and his people
"In a red determined strife,"
"Took the lands of his ancestors,"
"Slew and scattered all his people,"
Deemed they had forever blotted
All from off the book of life.

But the chieftain lived to wander
With a small and feeble remnant
And what hardship and starvation
None can tell how they passed through.
Grown more harsh and stern and bitter
The old leader led them onward
Till the Green Hills of Verdugo
In their beauty came in view.

Their tired way they wended westward
Twixt great mountains and green foothills
Up the strange and tilted valley
"All forlorn and without hope,"
Camped they on the sloping summit
East of the sparse live oak forest
Where the village of Tujunga
Clusters now upon the slope.

In the morning somewhat early
Rose the vanquished restless chieftain;
With great gloom upon his spirit
Strode he forth to muse alone;
Then he saw the mighty mountains
And the green foothills below them;
Saw the valley to the westward
And the dim blue range far thrown.

"Turning, looked he down the valley"
Stretching eastward—saw the new sun
Kiss the world until it quivered
That delighted wakened lay—
For in these days the Great Spirit
Showed himself on slope and hilltop
Wrote his name upon the ledges
Just as God does here today.

"Long that Indian, old and bitter,"
"Looked upon the wondrous landscape,"
"Harkened to dawn's wordless music,"
And the Spirit's mighty word.
In that hour his mood was shattered;
All the old and icy harshness
Seemed to melt and break within him
And new life was roused and stirred.

And he turned to those who watched him
"Smiling in his new found pleasure,"
"Spoke the one great word, 'Tu-jun-ga,'
"That with meaning throbs and lives, "
"Mingles rapture, admiration"
"And the heart's exhilaration,"
"Just as we do when 'delightful'
To the soul expression gives.

"Long the old chief looked about him,"
"Long upon the summit lingered,"
Lived and died he in the shelter
"Of the Green Verdugo Hills,"
"And his spirit mellowed, softened,"
"Millionaire of calm contentment,"
Till his smile was like a mother's
That above her papoose thrills.

"Here he lies, up near Haines Canyon,"
From the grounds of happy hunting
Comes his spirit oft to linger
In the haunts of old delight.
And the ground is still enchanted
Till whoever walks upon it
"Feels the meaning of Tujunga,"
And the word's alluring might.

Author unknown. Poem appeared in a Moon Festival program, dated September 1, 2, 3, 4, 1922.
The Second Annual Moon Festival was held at the Garden of the Moon in Tujunga.

With current political redistricting, in September 2001 Sunland-Tujunga was divided into two separate congressional districts, but the twin communities remain united in spirit and heritage.

Notes

[1] In 1984 and 1985, the intersection of Ventura and Balboa Boulevard in Encino was excavated, revealing an Indian community that dated back to 5,000 B.C.

[2] Leonard and Dale Pitt, *Los Angeles A–Z—an Encyclopedia of the City and County*.

[3] The natural spring and pond are located in Los Encinos Park. Old photographs indicate a large Indian mound (removed in 1945) next to the Garnier House.

[4] John R. Johnson, "The Indians of Mission San Fernando," *Mission San Fernando Rey de España, 1797–1997—A Bicentennial Tribute* (Historical Society of Southern California, 1997), 249.

[5] Horace Bell, *Reminiscences of a Ranger—Early Times in Southern California (1851–1854)* (Norman: University of Oklahoma Press, 1881, 2nd Edition 1999), 35–36.

[6] "Tujunga was Tuyunga in 1796," *The Record-Ledger Newspaper* (May 21, 1953), Historical and Progress Edition. Bolton Hall Museum Archives.

[7] Donna Larson, Docent Director, *Bolton Hall Museum Docent Handbook* (1985).

[8] Horace Bell, op. cit.

[9] Joan M. Jensen and Gloria Ricci Lothrop, *California Women: A History* (San Francisco: Boyd & Fraser, 1987), 8.

[10] Jack Forbes, "The Tongva of Tujunga to 1801," Appendix II, Abstract, *Archaeological Investigations of the Big Tujunga Site* (Los Angeles: University of California, 1966 [LAN-167]).

[11] Gloria Ricci Lothrop, "Father Serra," Letter to the Editor, *Los Angeles Times* (September 8, 1997).

[12] Edwin Walker, *Five Prehistoric Archeological Sites in Los Angeles County, California* (Los Angeles: Southwest Museum, 1951).

[13] A. L. Kroeber, *Handbook of the Indians of California* (Washington, 1925).

[14] Leonard and Dale Pitt, op. cit.

[15] Richard Toyon's presentation to the Historical Society of Crescenta Valley (October 18, 2003).

[16] Donna Larson, op. cit.

[17] Mabel Hatch, *The Green Verdugo Hills—A Chronicle of Sunland-Tujunga, Calif. And how it grew* (Tujunga, California, 1952).

[18] "The Origin of the Name Tujunga—Local Organizations Might Take Part in Settling of the Matter," *The Record-Ledger Newspaper* (April 10, 1924).

[19] "Tujunga Gains Early National Recognition," *The Record-Ledger Newspaper* (undated). Bolton Hall Museum Clippings File.

[20] Jimmie Smith passed away in Tujunga in 1957. His portable traveling organ was returned to the Kiwanis organization and subsequently lost. His wife died in 1961 in Salt Lake City, Utah.

[21] "Change of Street Names Generated Consternation Among Old Timers," *The Record-Ledger Newspaper* (September 12, 1968).

[22] Donna Larson, loc. cit.

[23] Chan Livingston Memoirs. Bolton Hall Museum.

[24] Ibid.

[25] Ibid.

"Best Little Town in the U.S.A."
by "Singing" Jimmie Smith

If you want to get a home and you want to settle down,
Just take a look at our hometown,
It's up above the fog where the skies are blue,
And we'll be there to welcome you,
Tujunga is the name, don't forget,
Tujunga is the town—you bet—you bet,
T-U-J-U-N-G-A—it's the best little town in the U.S.A.

Nella Terry and her sagebrush family. San Ysidro Street (Valmont) in Tujunga. Despite cactus and calluses, most women pioneers appeared happy, c. 1918.

Oh! To Be a Happy Little Lander

There once was a time, long before Garrison Keillor made *Lake Wobegon* famous, when a small colony existed in the foothills of the San Gabriel Mountains, where all the colonists were happy and their children were all healthy and above average. The Little Lands Colony, or Los Terrenitos, was just such a mythical place in print. Photographs of happy Little Lands folk, engaged in work or gardening in the picturesque Vale of Monte Vista, appeared weekly in newspapers and agriculture and tourist magazines throughout southern California and the United States. Real estate promoter and the "Prince of Prose," Marshall V. Hartranft published three magazines: two about the fruit industry and one, *The Western Empire*, that afforded him an opportunity to extol the virtues of living in one of the Little Lands Colonies.[1]

William Ellsworth Smythe, founder of the Little Lands Colonies, also wrote many books and pamphlets about irrigation and his agrarian colonies, literature that was rich with hyperbole.[2] In one of M. V. Hartranft's pamphlets, he tells of a woman who arrived from Kansas and, upon seeing the lush gardens in the colony exclaimed, "Sakes alive, don't that look like the Holy Land!"[3]

The question is, were all the Little Landers happy, healthy, and prosperous? It would not be until the tenth anniversary of the colony in 1923 that the printed recollections of Zoe Gilbert and Mabel Hatch divulged their early disappointment in the Little Lands experience. Although the early colonists endured much by today's standards, there was little criticism of the colony among themselves. Whatever discouraging thoughts they may have had, they kept them to themselves. Much was observed and little was spoken. Their sense of humor about their shared predicaments gave them a certain buoyancy of spirit. They all agreed that the place was called "The Little Lands," because after all the rocks were removed from their properties, there was "little land" left.

Locals would tell stories of hardships and the inventive ways in which the colonists coped with the rocky soil for the next fifty years. It was reported that a woman almost eighty years of age, "A woman of education and refinement and used to the comforts and conveniences of life in her eastern home, tied a trunk rope to her turkey roaster and hauled cobblestones off her little plot of ground, built a stone wall of them and then told the story with much zest and flourish in a poem."[4]

Even Hartranft's Home Extension Association made jest of the many rocks and stones by referring to them in promotional literature as "free building material." When Dr. Edwin Spates (1875–1953) and his wife Leah came to Tujunga in 1912, M. V. Hartranft gave them a tour. Dr. Spates complained about the rocky landscape, so Hartranft cleverly placed his hand across the bridge of Dr. Spates' nose and instructed the doctor to look at the lovely view above his hand. They were so impressed with this view that they bought ten acres on the spot. Dr. Spates returned to Chicago, sold his

FOUNDING SISTERS

A Few of Tujunga's Happy, Healthy Children

MRS. A. V. HOLMES

"I am a happy Little Lander. We have a half acre and have been here ten months. We find our condition here a great deal more desirable than in the city. Although in this community but a short time we already have considerable to show for our labor. This community life is just what we wanted. With one-half acre under intensive cultivation in this fertile spot, two people have about all they can attend to. We will specialize in chickens, ducks and winter vegetables. To all those who are tired of the struggle with city conditions I can recommend the City of the Little Lands as a veritable harbor of refuge."
MRS. A. V. HOLMES.

* * * *

(*above*) In this March 15, 1923, *Record-Ledger* photograph, "A Few of Tujunga's Happy, Healthy Children" (*left to right, top row*) Audrey Isabel Harvey, Donald Richard Masser, Robert Blake, (*center row*) Betty Gale, out for a stroll, (*circle*) Antine, Jack and Sally Fischer, Gladys Gale, (*bottom row*) Lily Fischer in foreground, a naked Lila Begue and Annie Rittenour sitting on wall. A young Laura Theobald is to the left of group photos.

(*left*) Mrs. A.V. Holmes attests to the fact that she is a "Happy Little Lander." "Many Answer Last Call to Join Little Landers." *Los Angeles Times* (May 29, 1914).

Since I have moved to California,
I have no desire to go to heaven.
—*Margaret Collier Graham*

practice, and quickly returned to Tujunga. He became so enamored with the area that he never stopped praising it.[5] Although his sanitarium, at the corner of Foothill Boulevard and Plainview, had many patients, he would derive his primary income from the invention of an herbal laxative tablet made for humans and the occasional animal. His story of the mule that ate one of his famous pills would make for many laughs at club meetings.

Tujunga has always been known as the "Home of Health." The blending of geography and geology had created an atmospheric condition known to purge the air of contaminants.

> The San Gabriels are of granite. The stone has a high capacity for storing heat from the sun, which, since the range parallels the sun's course, beats against the south slopes from morning to night. After sundown, ordinarily the worst time for the asthmatic because irritants in the atmosphere settle with the cooling air, the heated granite keeps the air warmed and rising, pulling out any mischief-makers it may hold. The updraft along the San Gabriels is so pronounced that an asthmatic's attack artificially induced here may clear up in 20 minutes. Elsewhere, the attack may hang on for three days.[6]

Twelve hundred feet higher than coastal and lower valley towns, Tujunga became known as the highest, driest, and healthiest semi-arid town in the United States.

At the turn of the twentieth century, the world was waging a war against a bacterial infection, tuberculosis (*the white plague*), that was the second leading cause of death. Doctors realized they were seeing twice as many cases in women as in men, because urban working women—dressmakers, stenographers, factory workers, and clerks—worked indoors under crowded conditions; the outdoor occupations that were plentiful for men did not exist for women. There were few options if the disease struck: ignore the symptoms and carry on as long as you could, infecting everyone around you; stay in bed with family members nursing you; or go to a sanitarium for cleaner air. In 1902, Barlow Sanitarium was built by Dr. W. Jarvis Barlow on 25 acres of land adjacent to Elysian Park in Chavez Ravine in Los Angeles. It was used for indigent tubercular patients and to isolate patients during periodic smallpox epidemics.

By 1926, there were 350 tubercular citizens in Tujunga.[7] In the twenties and thirties, rest homes and sanitariums dotted the landscape.[8] There were many miraculous healings of arthritis, asthma, and the symptoms of tuberculosis. Anna Adam, John Steven McGroarty, and Mary Phillips's husband, Ray, became walking testaments to the healing power of the area. They celebrated their return to health in unique and imaginative ways. When Victor Boesen wrote his article for *Coronet Magazine* in 1952, the entire world learned of Tujunga's healing power. "Thousands of sufferers have flocked to Tujunga and found relief overnight."[9] As far away as Europe, physicians advised their patients of the health-imparting attributes of this unique environment. It was estimated that the town's population of 30,000 (in 1952) had 7,000 asthmatic inhabitants. "At the town of Sunland, 1,400 feet above sea level, the boy was breathing easier. At Tujunga, another 300 feet higher, he was breathing normally again."[10] The 300 feet made the difference!

Tujunga proved to be one of the finest natural sanitariums in the world. The curative effect of Tujunga's climate was not exaggerated and would contribute to saving many lives, or at least making their last days bearable. It was said that there was health in every breath of the clean air that proved to be the elixir of life. However, a real health crisis occurred in 1924, when the entrance to Big Tujunga Canyon was closed in order to prevent the spread of hoof-and-mouth disease. The highly infectious viral disease caused the death of numerous cattle, swine, sheep, goats, deer, and other hoofed animals. Armed state and federal agents manned the closed canyon for most of the year.

The same year saw sections of Los Angeles County

> Here they are rich, though fools esteem them poor;
> They rule a plot which kings should wish to buy;
> The Glory of the eve about their door,
> And all the quiet stars up in their sky.
>
> —*Anon*

Unidentified "Happy Little Landers" at work. "Many Answer Last Call to Join Little Landers." *Los Angeles Times* (May 29, 1914).

Tujunga, Land of Happiness and Contentment

(*top*) Tujunga, Land of Happiness and Contentment. *The Record-Ledger*, March 15, 1925.

(*bottom*) Just a few of M.V. Hartranft's descriptions of "Happy Land" in his "My Hand-made Home in the Hills" brochure, c. 1922.

put under quarantine for pneumonic plague. Bacteria, carried primarily by the fleas on rats, cause this contagious infection. The epidemic of 1924 caused the overnight sale of 40,000 rattraps in Los Angeles. During the outbreak, thirty-one out of thirty-three people infected died in just one week.[11]

If you were broken in body or mind, though the Tujunga Valley called for you. The peace and clean air were recommended for those engaged in intellectual pursuits: writers, artists, and students.[12] To this day the town has a large percentage of writers, poets, and artists. The peace and beauty of nature continues to inspire the artistic talents of many.

In 1900, the average life expectancy of a woman was approximately forty-five years. If you were a woman who lived in Tujunga and survived the many road accidents, you would live well into your eighties or nineties. The average age of the women profiled in this book was eigfhty-eight years, almost twice the national average. Yes, clean air made the difference.

"The town Tujunga grew apace during 1914. The cooperative store burned and was rebuilt. It is believed by some that the fire was set to cover a robbery attempt. The contents were valued at $4,000, only half of which was covered by insurance. The store resumed operations in a large tent until another building could be constructed."[13] Several colonists suggested the arson-caused fire was made to destroy the long list of people in debt.

In the first year, it was realized that the excess produce from each plot was not sufficient to trade or sell. The only colonists that could be considered successful were the chicken ranchers, Marie Frish and Anna Souto. Years later, as acreage was sold off, the original colonists did make a profit. But the concept of a family of four successfully living off of this acreage did not materialize. But they all considered themselves rich, as in spirit.

Westerly view of 4,000-acre tract of Rancho Tejunga, c. 1904. *Courtesy of Viola Carlson.*

Notes

[1] *The Western Empire* was a rural monthly publication that sold for fifty cents a year. M. V. Hartranft described his magazine as "a home paper—fit for any home and devoted to the interests of Suburban and Rural Home life in California, where mere existence is counted in perpetual pleasure."

[2] Smythe's first social agricultural experiment was in New Plymouth, Idaho; his first Little Lands Colony was in San Ysidro, near San Diego, California (1908); his second Little Lands Colony was in Tujunga. See Chapter 2 herein.

[3] M. V. Hartranft, "Official Announcement of the Home Extension Colonies," California Home Extension Association (undated).

[4] "History, Development of Tujunga Valley," *The Record-Ledger of the Verdugo Hills*, February 1929.

[5] "Dr. Edwin Spates, Tujunga Resident Since 1912, Taken by Death Monday," *The Record-Ledger* (December 3, 1953).

[6] Victor Boesen, "California's Cure Town for Asthmatics," *Coronet Magazine*, October 1952, pp. 140–144.

[7] Los Angeles County Health Department statistic. When Bolton Hall became Tujunga's City Hall in 1925, a well-baby clinic and county nurse were housed there.

[8] In 1938, Sunair Home for Asthmatic Children opened at 7754 McGroarty Street, Tujunga. The facility had two infirmaries, a large dormitory, dining facilities, medical laboratory, library, swimming pool, park and a recreation area. It was closed in 1985.

[9] Victor Boesen, op. cit.

[10] Ibid.

[11] Edward Marriott, *Plague—A Story of Science, Rivalry, and the Scourge That Won't Go Away* (New York: Metropolitan Books, 2002), p. 227.

[12] "Tujunga Valley's Healthfulness Known Far and Wide—Cures Asthma, Hay Fever, Benefits Bronchial, Pulmonary Ailments," *The Record-Ledger of the Foothills*, February 1929.

[13] Sarah R. Lombard, *Rancho Tujunga: a History of Sunland/Tujunga, California* (Burbank, California: The Bridge Publishing, 1990), 45.

The Edenization of Tujunga

"And the Lord God planted a garden eastward in Eden; and there he put the man whom he had formed." Genesis, chapter 2:8. John Muir envisioned nature as a pathway to religion. Charles Lummis, editor and publisher of the magazines *Land of Sunshine* and *Out West*, said that "the lands of the sun, expanded the soul." Edward James Wickson, in his 1913 book entitled *The California Vegetables in Garden and Field*, promoted small to medium vegetable gardens and the rotation of crops. The planting of flowers and trees was encouraged to turn ordinary plots of land into "gardens of earthly delights." In southern California, land was connected to social reform. "The creation of sustainable environments were an important goal of reformers. Social and environment salvation would follow small scale farms."[1] At the early part of the twentieth century, in a time of California myth-making, gardens and social reform went hand-in-hand. The mined gold of the southland was water. In a land of either monsoons or meager rains, irrigation was necessary to turn the land into a Garden of Eden.

In the 1860s, the state of California experienced a severe drought that brought an end to its lucrative cattle business. The days of sheepherding and cattle raising vanished as a way of life. In 1872, another severe drought devastated the land. Later in 1876 and through 1877, the combination of the drought and dry winds left crops burned in the fields. With the addition of a smallpox epidemic in the Los Angeles area, grazing ranges, ranches, and streams all dried up and the thousands of barren hills were covered with the carcasses of sheep and cattle. There was very little green to be seen on the horizon.[2] By the early 1900s, the frontier gold seekers and prospectors had also stepped into the pages of history.

For Los Angeles there was simply not enough water to sustain the growing population. Before the turn of the twentieth century, the locals often said that "The Los Angeles River was so dry most of the time, coyotes had to carry canteens to cross it."

By 1913, when the towns of Eagle Rock, Montrose, and Tujunga appeared on maps, artesian well water was harnessed for drinking and crop irrigation. When the water demands of the Southland began to grow at a tremendous rate, it was Los Angeles's chief engineer, William Mulholland, who would create deliverance. After a bitter struggle, he channeled the water of the Owens River in November 1913 and delivered it south to the San Fernando Valley via a 233-mile long aqueduct. Within ten years, Los Angeles desperately needed more water. It took $260 million in bonds to bring the water of the Colorado River to rescue the southland.

From the 1860s to the late 1930s, California became linked to Australia. They both realized that the soil damage from mining, sheep ranching, and giant wheat fields must be repaired, and new crops planted. The palm and eucalyptus trees that dot the southland today were Australian immigrants. The Monterey pine tree was exchanged for Australia's palm and eucalyptus trees and their ladybug beetles.[3] In 1912, the United States Forest Service planted a nursery of 20,000 eucalyptus trees in the Little Tujunga Canyon, west of Big Tujunga Canyon.[4] Today, more than 48,000 palm trees grace the Southland landscape and have become an icon for sunny California. Pepper trees also became a prominent feature of nineteenth-century California. The Brazilian jacaranda tree joined the list of imported trees that masqueraded as native flora of California.

M. V. Hartranft planted hundreds of eucalyptus trees on the hills behind his Lazy Lonesome Ranch in Sunland and various areas throughout Tujunga. He became interested in soil conservation and was an early advocate of check dams used in the mountain canyons to retard the flow of water after heavy rains, thereby preventing soil erosion. He also advocated the planting of fire-resistant trees in the area. He dearly loved the mountains and the land. John Whelan, museum director at Bolton Hall Museum, said, "I have seen this man actually lie down in the field and hug the earth in pure ecstasy."[5]

Before 1892, homesteaders and land squatters had populated the Big Tujunga Canyon and hillsides. On December 20, 1892, the San Gabriel Timber Reserve was created and renamed the Angeles National Forest in 1908. It was the first reserve in California and the second in the nation.[6] California was known as the state with the highest native plant population. By February of each year, the hillsides of Tujunga were covered in buckhorn, a shrub that reaches eight to ten feet in

Marshall V. Hartranft's porch and his thoughts on Sunland-Tujunga's semi-tropical climate, c. 1910.

height and is covered with tiny white flowers. In March, the hills took on a purple hue when the wild lilac bloomed. In the 1920s, the Tujunga Women's Club rallied to have a wild lilac shrub in every garden of Tujunga. Hundreds of plants were distributed with no cost to the gardener.

In April, May, and June, the canyons along the streams of the Big Tujunga Canyon were abloom with the wildflowers so common to the southern California canyon landscape. This area, deemed semi-arid, grew prickly phlox, yarrow, greasewood, western wild flowers, wild clematis, peonies, and starflowers. In June, the abundance of yuccas, sometimes known as Spanish bayonet or the Lord's candle, dotted the washes, canyons, and hillsides of the Sunland-Tujunga area. The mighty and exotic yucca best represented the natural beauty of the area. M. V. Hartranft took advantage of the fabulous scenery when he took prospective land buyers on a "swoon trip," a three-mile motor trip along McGroarty Drive in Tujunga and Sunland, where he described local chaparral as "California Lilac."[7] It would not be until the mid-thirties, when prominent horticulturalist Theodore Payne would come to Tujunga and plead the cause for the preservation of wildflowers and native plants, that a sanctuary was set aside for each.[8]

When the Begue family planted grapes in lower Tujunga (50 acres in 1882), others followed suit. The Fehlhabers (50 acres); the Zitto brothers, Victor and John (67 acres); and the Petrotta family (17 acres) all

The southeast corner of Commerce and Foothill Boulevard as it appeared in 1913.
This was the scene that greeted Mabel Hatch and her family when they arrived in the Colony.

planted vineyards that produced delicious table grapes and some bottled wine.[9] Tujunga did not have a commercial winery; the closest winery was located on Dunsmore Avenue in La Crescenta, where the "Old Heritage" wine was produced. When Congress ratified the Eighteenth Amendment to the Constitution prohibiting the production and consumption of liquor (1919–1933), the flow of wine continued in Tujunga, hidden from view. Following World War I, young and old threw caution to the wind, enjoying "bathtub gin," home-brew beer, and bootleg whiskey in speakeasies in Los Angeles and a few places in Tujunga. The Begue barn on Tujunga Canyon Boulevard and the Ardizone residence on Mt. Gleason Avenue became popular places for locals and lawmen from all over the state. Even today, residents recall when a still blew up in the mouth of the Big Tujunga Canyon. No Women's Christian Temperance Union (WCTU) meetings were held in Tujunga and the only local woman of record to be a member and "White Ribboner" was the highly-educated Nora Millspaugh.[10] Although Tujunga residents were restricted from buying liquor legally until the Eighteenth Amendment was repealed in 1933, there were many clever ways that alcohol consumption could be disguised. There was a much-advertised *Vinol*, a so-called iron tonic that was made by local grape growers. Sales were brisk until Dr. James Doran, a commissioner of prohibition, came from Washington, D.C., to explain to Californians the legality of producing beverages like wine or iron tonic from grapes. He said it was not illegal to manufacture fruit juices or cider for "home use," as long as they were "not intoxicating."

Occasionally, stills were found by federal agents in the hills or washes of Tujunga, but there were always ways for the citizens to obtain "bootleg booze." California and the nation may have gone dry with the Volsted Act of 1920, but Tujunga remained rather wet.

Even though Tujunga soil was not as fertile as neighboring Sunland—in fact it was not much more than crushed granite mixed with sand and a little silt—by 1916 walnuts and prize quince were being grown. Flowers from Tujunga gardens were winning awards at the Glendale Free Flower Show, and avocados were also being harvested. On September 12, 1916, all the organizations in town contributed to the first Harvest Home Festival. By this time, the Adams Olive Cannery in Sunland was processing 150 tons of olives each year, and by 1917, Tujunga oranges were making their way back east. With diligent labor, oranges, lemons, plums, apricots, figs, peaches, blackberries, and strawberries joined the list. By 1920, grapes were bringing in a return of $400 per acre. In 1923, canned apricots and three boxcar loads of ripe olives were shipped to England. The Adams Olive Cannery employed forty-five people, most of whom were women.[11]

M. V. Hartranft, never a man to miss an opportunity to promote Tujunga, set up large displays of fresh fruits and vegetables in his real estate office to show perspective land buyers what the soil was capable of producing. He often took them to view the more successful gardens in town. Visitors delighted in Dr. Virginia Smith's banana tree, cotton plants, and other exotic plants.

Poultry, goat, and rabbit farms were considered the most successful in the area. Fresh eggs were always considered a "cash crop" and many a housewife had a secret stash of egg money for emergencies. The myth of their farms providing large amounts of excess crops for sale or barter had totally faded by 1917. Realistically, the plots were too small to provide produce for a family of four and excess to barter with neighbors.

> Forget what you've heard about green thumbs:
> A gardener's greatest asset is a fertile
> Imagination. How else could we envision Eden
> In a single seed or Paradise in a clay pot?

The No-Mistake Way

The experience of many thousand families who have moved from other States to California argues emphatically to homeseekers, who are unacquainted with this State to first get a safe anchorage on a small piece of garden land near one of our growing cities, thereupon to practice and learn and become experienced Californians.

The genial climate, providing fruits and vegetables every month in the year, and the comfortable, tho' inexpensive California bungalow home, saves the big expense sustained by homeseekers who move into the hotels or rooming-houses of the large cities. By locating at first near any of our growing cities, one has the safety valve of employment near at hand during all the early days of his experience in a new region, and the advantage of profit taking from his suburban homesite when he feels equipped in experience to move to the interior and larger farming areas.

Working in your own garden and poultry yard, conferring with neighbors and learning through their experiences, will ripen the practical knowledge so necessary to success; and upon such experience good judgment will be based, to guide you in any future move in California you may decide upon.

Such a home place near Los Angeles is always salable because of the thousands of new homeseekers coming in each year, and is always exchangeable at a premium for ranch property in any part of the State. If selection of the suburban home is made carefully, the constantly broadening values with the city's growth makes a profit for the seller. Getting paid a profit for having occupied a piece of ground near a large city is much better than paying out board bills or house rent.

Having provided yourself a job working for yourself, selling your products to your best home market, i. e., your own stomach, you are then in position to listen and learn and later to acquire more extensive holdings or to embark in some commercial enterprise.

THE WESTERN EMPIRE

*A Home Paper-Fit for any Home
Devoted to the Interests of Suburban and
Rural Home Life in California
where mere existence is counted perpetual Pleasure*

Ground Floor, Chamber of Commerce Building
Los Angeles, California
Telephones: Home 60433; Main 762

(*above*) M.V. Hartranft standing next to a tobacco plant at the Fitzgerald Ranch in the Seven Hills area of Tujunga, c. 1911.

(*right*) Little Landers and Big-landers were encouraged to do their gardening in hot houses and cloth houses. *The Los Angeles Times* (1914).

Bee-keeping, hothouse gardening, poultry, pigeons and taking in boarders, in a veritable vacation land—of such is the Little Landers Mountain Village. "And this is the life!"

What kind of a living are you making, anyhow?

Come up here on the frequent auto stages and talk it over with these folks. Don't make the common error of going off to some lonely spot to garden or raise poultry. You can suffer more from soul starvation than from your stomach. It isn't difficult to get something to eat from a little land, but it is a difficult thing to get a social life and neighbors that is a superior substitute to the gayeties of city life.

Don't make the common error of thinking you have to go to some flat, level river bottom land to get garden results. The Big-landers can beat you on an open field cultivation. To make any money, you must assist this kindly nature in California and do your gardening in hothouses or clothhouses. And you have got to know how to do it—but it's worth learning.

Not over three out of one hundred of you can become successful big-landers, but we can make little landers of you. We've got to change some of your ideas first, however. If you are young and still anticipating the day when you will strike an oil well or a gold mine, you are not of the temperament for little landers. If you want to live the real California life, in a real California way, and live it in the valley that happy people have had to designate as "the Little Yosemite," then come see us. The most prosperous nations of the earth are Little Landers, all of them. America will be when she learns the lesson of the City of the Littlelands. Individuals perish at the art — but only from social isolation. Looking at the nations of Littlelanders, we find the people grouped. And our mountain village is grouped. You reach Los Angeles in one hour's auto stage ride, but around about you is the club life, the church life, the commercial program for community welfare, and the widely renowned Colonial and Junior Dancing clubs. Come spend a Thursday evening at the Colonial, in the great stone clubhouse.

One and three room cabins and bungalows to rent, $7.50 to $15 per month.

One hour auto stages from Hotel Lille, 534 South Hill street, at 9:15 a. m., also 1:15 and 5:30 p. m., Sundays and holidays. Sixteen miles round trip 75c. Little Landers weekly magazine, four weeks for 10 cents. Address Little Landers' Agency, Littlelands P. O., Cal.—Advertisement.

THE EDENIZATION OF TUJUNGA

Rain—the sweetest music to the California ear.
—*Theodore Van Dyke, 1890*

When Tujunga became an incorporated city on May 1, 1925, the sun-loving zinnia became its official flower, chosen by the Tujunga Women's Garden Club. This cheerful and undemanding member of the daisy family grows best in hot weather and comes in all colors except blue.[12] Its growing requirements made it well suited for the climate of Tujunga.

The residents of Tujunga never failed to marvel at the transformation of their rocky, barren land into a true Garden of Eden. Their unusual or extra-large produce always made the front page of the local newspaper, *The Record-Ledger*. Motorists often stopped, delighted at the view of the majestic yucca, the extraordinary century plant, the brief beauty of the night-blooming cirrus, or the incredible produce from the gardens, vineyards, and orchards.

M. V. Hartranft, who once owned a produce market until it failed in 1893, was often heard to recite this jingle, "To grow crops to sell, is to speculate like hell, but to grow crops to eat, keeps you standing on both feet." He began to establish colonies of gardeners and small farmers on virgin California land. People with small financial means could buy into his suburban farm colonies and then hope it would turn into their very own Garden of Eden.

"What is wanted is a form of country life that shall bring the people reasonably close to the great towns, both for market and social advantages; that shall give them near and numerous neighbors; that shall permit of the organization of a rich, up-to-date social and intellectual life—full, elevating, and satisfying."[13] John Whelan, first Museum Director at Bolton Hall Museum, said, "Smythe's urgent message caught the attention of many who yearned for the independence and security they believed a small piece of agricultural land would bring, and their enthusiastic state-wide response produced a social movement that was to be known as Little Landers."

The early settlers always hoped that good fortune would smile on them. After all, the Southland was always known as the land of sunshine and second chances.

Notes

[1] Margaretta J. Darnall, "Review of *True Gardens of the Gods*," *California Historian* (Summer 2001): 33.

[2] Robert Glass Cleland, *The Cattle on a Thousand Hills* (San Marino: Huntington Library, 1951), 142.

[3] Ian Tyrrell, *True Gardens of the Gods: California—Australian Environmental Reform 1860–1930* (Berkley and Los Angeles: University of California Press, 1999), 12.

[4] By 1907, there were 100 species of eucalyptus trees in California. Blue Gum Canyon in Tujunga is still on the map. The eucalyptus trees produced hardwood for wagons, carriages, agricultural implements, and building materials. They were also used for medicinal applications and as windbreaks, shade trees and to beautify the area. The trees were generally thought to clean the air; because they absorbed large amounts of water, they could drain swampland, destroying the habitat of the mosquito and ending malaria in California, which had reached its peak here in the 1880s. By 1912, the love affair with the eucalyptus tree was over and it became known as the "Australian weed." It didn't help that the tree litter proved to be a fire hazard. Robert LeRoy Santos, "The Eucalyptus of California," *Southern California Quarterly* 80, no. 2 (Summer 1998): 105–114.

[5] Donna Larson, "Hartranft-Smythe-Harris," *Docent Handbook for Bolton Hall Museum*, 88–91.

[6] Sarah R. Lombard, *Rancho Tujunga—a History of Sunland/Tujunga, California* (Burbank, California: The Bridge Publishers, 1990), 25.

[7] "Flora, Wild Life Abound," *The Record-Ledger* (July 24, 1958).

FOUNDING SISTERS

THE EDENIZATION OF TUJUNGA

(*above*) Ensign Woodruff and his wife, Mary, were able to turn the rocky soil into a prosperous bean field, c. 1915.

(*opposite, top*) Skyline Drive was sixteen miles long, winding along the crest of the Verdugo Mountains from Brand Park in Glendale to Sunland, c. 1924. *Courtesy of the Los Angeles Public Library.*

(*opposite, bottom*) A few of the many eucalyptus trees M.V. Hartranft planted on the ridge of the Green Verdugo Mountains, overlooking Tujunga, c. 1916. *From the personal collection of Lee Brown, Adventures in Postcards, Sunland, California.*

[8]"Thomas Paine Pleads Cause of Wild Flowers," *The Record-Ledger of the Verdugo Hills*, 1934.
[9]Charles Miller, "He Grew Grapes in Tujunga," *True Grit, The Record-Ledger* (March 26, 1986).
[10]In the 1880s, the Los Angeles chapter of the WCTU was formed to campaign for the total abstinence of alcohol, total prohibition, more drinking water fountains, less medicine containing alcohol, and many other social issues. In 1906, Los Angeles hosted the thirty-second national convention for the group.
[11]Sarah R. Lombard, *Rancho Tujunga—a History of Sunland/Tujunga, California*, 52.

[12]Zinnias are native to the southcentral United States, Mexico, and Argentina. They were grown by the Aztecs and are said to have flourished in Montezuma's gardens in the early sixteenth century. The United States didn't begin to appreciate the zinnia until the nineteenth century. The plant was named for Johann Zinn, a German doctor who died in 1759. "All About Zinnias," *Rebecca's Garden Magazine* (June/July 2000): 18–22.
[13]Donna Larson, "Hartranft-Smythe-Harris," *Docent Handbook for Bolton Hall Museum.*

119

FOUNDING SISTERS

Tujunga *Wrinkles* that Aid Economy—

Crafted at Tujunga

LIVING amid surroundings that inspires the spirit of invention, the Tujunga Folks have created many helpful devices; chief among which may be mentioned the Tujunga Interlocking home-made Roofing Tile; Tujunga Roofing Composition; Tujunga Fire-Faggot Binder; and the Tujunga Solar Fruit and Vegetable Dryer.

The Interlocking Tile is the creation of Mr. Halflinger. By means of a simple home-made machine, he has produced a flat, handsome-colored tile that is unusually distinctive, weatherproof, and economical. This tiling can be manufactured by anyone in your own Tujunga backyard.

Tujunga Roofing Composition is the invention of Mr. George Harris. It is weatherproof and fire-proof; does not crack, and is applied like stucco. At a distance it looks like tile, but in reality it makes a one-piece reinforced concrete roofing.

To Mr. Loyd, the Tujunga Community is indebted for the Fire-Faggot Binder—an ingenious contraption that bundles twigs, branches, leaves and tree refuse into a compact fire ration. Until you have witnessed and felt the cheery heat instantly created by these synthetic logs in your fire-place, you can't appreciate the esteem in which we hold Loyd's machine.

And then there's the Solar Dehydrator, here illustrated—another Tujunga home-made device that renders matchless assistance to kitchen pantries. The glass concentrates the heat and forces the rapid sun-curing of figs, grapes into raisins, apricots, prunes, sugar corn, beans, and other gustatory tid-bits. The glass covering keeps the evening moisture from retarding the sun-curing process and as a result we have pantry shelves loaded with good things to eat—almost *without cost*, and beyond price.

For Further Particulars Address

California Home Extension Assoc

M. V. HARTRANFT, Pres.

> Every week we went to town meeting. It was held in the club house [*sic*] and we all lighted our kerosene lanterns and trudged up the hill. We were weary in mind and body. Running behind a plow and throwing out rocks only to find when you go back over the field to plant your walnut trees you have to dig the holes with a pick, is neither refreshing nor encouraging, furthermore, you take so much stone out of the hole, there isn't enough earth to plant the tree. But we went to town meeting.
>
> —Mabel Hatch on the condition of Tujunga soil, *The Green Verdugo Hills* (1956)

120

THE EDENIZATION OF TUJUNGA

(*left*) M.V. Hartranft and John Steven McGroarty, both members of the State Forestry Board, advocated the reforestation of bottomland. The *Los Angeles Times* front page (November 15, 1943).

(*below, left*) Blue denim overalls were perfect for farming and rock removal. Helen Florkowski and Walt Babulski. *The Record-Ledger*, c. 1926.

(*below*) The ideal happy gardener in "her home-in-a-garden." Illustration from William E. Smythe's City Homes on Country Lanes—Philosophy and Practice of the Home-in-a-Garden, c. 1921. *Courtesy of the MacMillan Company, New York.*

(*opposite, top*) Looking east to Tujunga from the entrance of the Tujunga Canyon Wash. The yucca, more than any other plant, symbolized the natural beauty of the area.

(*opposite, bottom*) Tujunga's Solar Dehydrator was a boon to the small-scale farmer. Pantry shelves remained full as Tujunga was known as a land of sunshine, c. 1922.

DOWNTOWN LOS ANGELES RAINFALL
Los Angeles annual rainfall compiled at the National Weather Service Station, located on the campus of the University of Southern California. Time period: 1886–1912.*

Year	Rainfall
1886	16.72 inches
1887	16.02 inches
1888	20.82 inches
1889	33.26 inches
1890	12.69 inches
1891	12.84 inches
1892	18.72 inches
1893	21.96 inches
1894	7.51 inches
1895	12.55 inches
1896	11.80 inches
1897	14.28 inches
1898	4.83 inches
1899	8.69 inches
1900	11.30 inches
1901	11.96 inches
1902	13.12 inches
1903	14.77 inches
1904	11.88 inches
1905	19.19 inches
1906	21.46 inches
1907	15.30 inches
1908	13.74 inches
1909	23.92 inches
1910	4.89 inches
1911	17.85 inches
1912	9.78 inches

Los Angeles Times.

TUJUNGA RAINFALL
Tujunga rainfall compiled by local resident W. E. Magee, an observer for the United States Weather Bureau. Time period: January 1 through December 3.*

Year	Rainfall
1913	27.17 inches
1914	33.65 inches
1915	27.05 inches
1916	29.92 inches
1917	18.45 inches
1918	23.86 inches
1919	18.58 inches
1920	18.60 inches
1921	37.51 inches
1922	25.25 inches
1923	9.81 inches
1924	11.61 inches
1925	16.22 inches
1926	30.45 inches

The Record-Ledger.

Everyone talks about the weather, but no one does anything about it.
—*Charles Dudley Warner (1897)*

Earth, Wind, and Fire
Facing the Elements

The majority of early Tujunga settlers presumed their climate had always been semi-arid, with few trees and little plant life. From the Ice Age until the mid 1800s, the southern California coastal lowlands were lush and tropical. Even at the higher elevations in the Big Tujunga Canyon, lush stands of maidenhair fern and large areas of live oak, sycamore, alder, and cottonwood trees flourished. The Tongva Indians of the area lived in a rich ecosystem that teemed with rabbit, deer, wolves, bears, and antelope.

The waters from the Pacoima, Little Tujunga, and Big Tujunga Canyons all emptied into and formed the Los Angeles River. The banks were at one time verdant with vegetation. Waters from the San Gabriel and Santa Monica mountains converged at a point near present day Elysian Park in Los Angeles. Only after heavy winter rains would the waters flow into the Santa Monica Bay. In 1825 a great flood caused the course of the river to flow into the San Pedro Harbor. The majority of that floodwater came from the Big Tujunga Canyon. Mustard plants, indigenous to the "Mighty T," now planted themselves into the greater Los Angeles Basin. After the great flood, all but a few spots of the coastal plain went dry. Venice, Bixby Slough, and Balsa Chica remained wetland marshes. Rarely did a year pass without recorded floods. Fortunately, these floods often replenished the soil and created a more fertile agriculture plain.

As the San Fernando and Monte Vista valleys became populated with settlers, floods and forest fire problems multiplied. After California statehood in 1850, the settlers required building materials and wood to fire the brick kilns in Los Angeles, which denuded the watershed of the area. Water now raced down the decimated slopes and disappeared into the sandy plains. Early explorers said of the San Fernando Valley, "The valley lay before them, carpeted with poppies, lupines, wild mustard and other flowers providing a picture of incredible beauty and charm. The valley floor was covered with grasses, cacti, sage and small shrubs with oaks around the margins, while along the Los Angeles River there were numerous willows."[1]

The drought of the 1860s and the introduction of sheep grazing to the land, stamped out the native grasses and clover before they could seed. By the late 1870s, most of the range grass had been destroyed. As the settlers of Sunland-Tujunga arrived in the early twentieth century, the brush and chaparral were quickly cleared and the all-important ground cover disappeared.

Although the land was subject to severe fires, winds, and flooding, the early pioneers were spared the devastation of earthquakes. Despite the fact that the Monte Vista Valley was laced with the San Andreas, Sierra Madre, and numerous other small-unmapped faults, no severe problems were caused by the many small quakes. Bolton Hall, built by an eastern publisher with no set of blueprints, proved to be seismically sound.[2] The Sunland-Tujunga area was mainly unpopulated at the time of the great Fort Tejon earthquake in 1857 (magnitude 8.3), and the 1925 Santa Barbara earthquake was only slightly felt by residents. When the 1933 Long Beach earthquake struck, it was the stonemasons of Sunland-Tujunga that were the first to offer aid.

Official weather observations began in Los Angeles in 1878. Recorded floods before 1780 came from mission records. Floods that affected the Rancho Tujunga area were in 1770, 1815, 1822, 1825, 1832, 1862, 1884, 1886, and 1889. Simple facts tell the story of this flooding. Every flood experienced in the area always followed a major fire. The first recorded fire was in early September 1896, an exceedingly bad fire year. Strong winds and the driest year recorded since 1876 contributed to a massive fire started by lightning in the Big Tujunga Canyon. It began just above Silas Hoyt's ranch and raged for six weeks, burning over 11,000 acres. Few people were directly affected by the fire, as miners and a few mountain hikers sparsely populated the Canyon.

The fire that early residents would never forget was the one that started in August 1913. With Bolton Hall newly completed, colonists were swarming into the area. While Harry Grosvenor and Gotlieb J. Fisher were clearing brush on property at the north end of Sunset Street (Commerce Avenue), a fire broke out and swept up the hills and mountains, completely out of control, between Haines Canyon and the Big Tujunga Canyon. The fire then turned around and came down Haines Canyon and traveled west to Walnut Avenue (Mt. Gleason Avenue). Desperate citizens with only shovels of sand bravely fought the fire, which raged on for seven days and burned over 4,000 acres.[3]

A cloudburst in November of that year saturated the ground and set the stage for the coming big flood. Heavy rains began on February 20, 1914, and did not let up for three straight days. Sand, rock, and boulders surged down Haines Canyon despite the four hundred check dams that had been put into place. The flooding waters crossed Michigan Avenue (Foothill Boulevard) and deposited up to two feet of debris on the flat ground of St. Estaban Road, where Lydia May Dean resided. She lost her orchard of twenty-two trees and was forced to spend the night on the roof of her house, clutching the family rooster. As the winter of 1915 approached, Lydia pleaded with the Los Angeles County Board of Supervisors to redirect the drainage or, at least, let her come before the board to plead her case. The board's response to her was not recorded nor saved. During the first large flood to hit the Tujunga area, the tent house belonging to librarian Florence Gilmour was carried off. No one was killed or seriously injured but "Mrs. Slusher and Miss Gilmour had to wade in water waist deep on their way to the home of Leo Lang east of Haines Canyon Road, where they were given shelter."[4]

The following year, floods once again menaced the city. In Haines Canyon, a Mr. Thompson recorded an inch of rain every hour for six hours during the heavy winter rains. The years 1919, 1923, and 1925 would record large-scale flooding, but those years pale in comparison to the great floods that would occur in 1934 and 1938.

Despite living in a harsh land, the benefits of clean air and sunny days made life tolerable and sweet to the memory. Settlers soon found out that the coldest Tujunga day beat the harsh winters of Michigan and the eastern coast. As early Sunland pioneer Robert Rowley related,

> An important landmark to old settlers was the summit situated about where Love's Barbecue now stands (Foothill Boulevard and Lowell Avenue). This marked the top of the climb from Tujunga to La Crescenta along a dusty, small trail. As many later day residents have noticed, this point often marks a change in the weather. Ground fogs used to creep up to this point, but rarely came into the valley. We had bright sunshiny weather up here.[5]

The Tujunga pioneer soon learned that its worst enemy was not man but nature itself. Each season had its own set of hazards. Summer often brought the harsh Santa Ana winds and drought conditions. For those hardy souls living in tents and tarpaper shacks, the only refuge would be moving into Bolton Hall with family and pets until the storms subsided. The bell in the tower of Bolton Hall would ring for Sunday service and to alert the colonists of fire and windstorms.[6] To children and family pets, the temporary quarters at the clubhouse were filled with laughter and fun, but often the anguished parents returned to homes that were severely damaged or destroyed. The young trees in Tujunga provided little protection from the harsh winds that swept down the Big Tujunga Canyon. Unchecked summer fires denuded the slopes, causing flooding during winter and early spring months. Homes were fortified and a few had basements, but it would be the old clubhouse that proved to be the ultimate refuge. As Ida McGroarty would learn, not all fires were on the mountain slopes. After losing two homes to fire, she, like most other residents, had a deep respect for its power.

Letters home to family and friends describing Tujunga's beauty, wondrous mountains, majestic yucca, and superb climate became a "call to California." As the years passed, the residents' love affair with Tujunga intensified. Forgotten were the early tears and doubts about their new homeland. During those difficult early years, the sharing of common hardships brought the members of the community together in a bond that would never be broken. They were well aware that "what man proposes, God disposes." Often their fate was decided with the flurry of the wind, the scorching of the sun or the rush of raging water. Their deep love of nature and the freedom the land gave them, made the Tujunga experience the best years of their lives. The endless supply of immigrants to California could be correlated to California's increase in population and the numbers of forest fires and floods.

Notes

[1] *Bolton Hall Museum Docent Handbook*, "Verdant California," Sarah R. Lombard. In a 1915 report, the Los Angeles Board of Engineers reported the watershed of the Big Tujunga Canyon covering 11.32 square miles, the Little Tujunga Canyon covering 18.66 square miles and the Pacoima Canyon covering 30.44 square miles, for a total of 165 square miles covered. With the exception of great flooding, the water was mostly underground in an aquifer, instead of running in streams, after it left the mouth of the canyons.

[2] It would not be until 1994, when the City of Los Angeles completed its seismic retrofit of Bolton Hall Museum, that cracks began to appear.

[3] "First Big Flood Hit Valley in 1913; 7-day Fire Broke Out Same Year," Wallace Morgan, *The Green Verdugo Hills—A Chronicle of Sunland-Tujunga and How It Grew*. The Record-Ledger, 1952.

[4] "Raging Floods Ranked with Fire as Early-Day Enemies," *The Record-Ledger* Historical Edition, September 12, 1968.

[5] "Rowley Recalls Early Days of Sunland-Tujunga," Lucy Colville, *The Record-Ledger*, September 27, 1973.

[6] The bell in Bolton Hall tower was removed by Los Angeles city officials and placed in the Little Red Schoolhouse in Travel Town, located in Griffith Park in Los Angeles. In the mid 1960s, the bell was reported stolen by vandals.

John Speed's 1626 map "America." Note California appears as an island.
Courtesy of the California Historical Society FN-31949.

Silenced Voices

Myth and misunderstanding spring from Tujunga's early days as readily as the yucca bloom on the mountains surrounding the town. Only eighteen years after Christopher Columbus discovered the New World and thirty-two years prior to Juan Rodriguez Cabrillo sailing along the Pacific shore, the word *California* was already in print. The name was invented by writer Garcia Ordoñez de Montalvo. His novel, *Sergas de Esplandián*, appeared in print in Spain in the year 1510.

California, a mythical terrestrial paradise, was an island inhabited by dark-skinned Amazon women. They wore golden armor and breastplates and their pets were griffons, dragon-like monsters that devoured any invading males. The griffons would carry those males high into the air and drop them on the rugged terrain below.

Queen Califa was the most beautiful and powerful of the Amazons. It was in her honor that the kingdom was called *California*. However, by the time California was admitted as a state to the Union, it was represented by a light-skinned woman, the goddess Minerva. In 1957, when the County of Los Angeles adapted their official seal, it would be represented by another light-skinned woman, the goddess Pomona.

The early history of Tujunga's women pioneers was seen from the Anglo-American perspective. As difficult as it was to locate the early written remembrances of those pioneer women, even more obscure were the stories of the lives of the minority women who lived in the Tujunga area before 1960.

Often ignored in the national census, their true numbers may never be known. In 1900, of the 800,000 women that were recorded living west of the Mississippi River, "approximately 4,500 were Chinese, 370 Japanese, 12,000 blacks and 6,000 American Indian."[1]

From 1860 to 1900, California's population grew by only one-third. The failed Mexican land grant system caused a large section of land to pass into the hands of the railroads and land syndicates.

The Southern Pacific Railroad hired hundreds of Chinese laborers to lay track, blast, and dig the 6,975-foot tunnel through the mountains from Newhall into the San Fernando Valley. By 1876, Los Angeles and San Francisco were finally linked by rail. In 1885, the Atchison, Topeka and Santa Fe Railroad came through the deserts of the southwest into Los Angeles. "In 1890 there were 69,382 Chinese men in California and only 3,090 Chinese women."[2] Between 1870 and 1900, most settlements bordering Los Angeles had their own "Chinatowns." Almost all of the Chinese in Los Angeles had arrived from San Francisco and would number 20,000 by 1880. Originally brought in by the larger ranches as cooks and houseboys, they began to branch out into their own businesses: hand laundries,[3] restaurants, curio shops, and vegetable distribution. They contributed to the rapidly rising citrus industry with their excellent aptitude for harvesting.

Throughout the later part of the nineteenth century, 97.29 percent of California women were recorded

FOUNDING SISTERS

Only known photograph of Fernandeño mission woman, date unknown. *Courtesy of San Fernando Mission Historical Society.*

in the "white group" of census records. These records are deceptive since Native American women and Hispanic women were lumped together in the statistics. In 1885, the Mexicans in the Los Angeles area had become a romantic "picturesque element rather than a functional part of the social life and economy of the region."[4]

News of the racially motivated "Chinese massacre" in Los Angeles in 1871 and other violent acts against minorities was reported nationally in newspapers and magazines.[5] It was obvious that there was discord in California's Promised Land. It was important in California "booster" literature and history books that racial problems and the fact that Californians lived on shaky ground be downplayed. It was always pointed out that the southern and mid-western states had floods and tornados. "We have an earthquake now and again to let the people know God's greater than men."[6] Tujungans and southern Californians would be reminded of that when the Santa Barbara earthquake hit on June 29, 1925.

The literature of the day would provide the basis for problems in the Promised Land. "Southern California was the first tropical land where our race has mastered and made itself at home in." In a novel entitled *Hilda Strafford* written by Beatrice Harraden, a character says, "I am rather lazy—somewhat of a Mexican in fact."[7] By 1887 there were approximately 30,000 Mexicans living in Los Angeles and the surrounding communities. Hispanics had declined in power and influence and were now principally seen as sheepherders and ranch hands. A look at Los Angeles from its first day would show much racial diversification. The process of racial stratification would find its birth during the Spanish-American period at the ranchos and missions. As the poorer Mexican immigrants displaced the Indians from their land, the dirty, least desirable jobs, such as the stripping and storing the fat of cattle or tallow, were taken over by the "greasers" (the derogatory name applied to the immigrants).

The dormant conflict between Mexicans and Anglos would wait until the early 1930s to resurface, when a large number of Mexican immigrants would arrive in California only to be deported by train back to Mexico.[8] On February 26, 1931, the La Pacita Raid took place and marked the removal of Mexican nationals from the Los Angeles area. The uniformed I.N.S. agents and plainclothes detectives, with guns and batons, sealed off the tiny park near Olvera Street in downtown Los Angeles and began removing people. Within a week, the "repatriation train" left Los Angeles for Mexico with four hundred nationals on board. At the end of six months, 50,000 Mexicans had been returned to Mexico by ship and rail. This was part of a decade-long national effort to reduce unemployment and welfare rolls.[9] By 1940, more than a million people across the country had been deported. Ethnic tensions between Anglos and Mexicans were heightened after the 1942 "Sleepy Lagoon" murder trial and the 1943 "Zoot Suit" riots in Los Angeles.[10]

While Anglo-American writers and boosters like George Wharton James, Charles Lummis, and John S. McGroarty wrote of a fantasy Hispanic past, the Californios (i.e. General M. G. Vallejo) were busy creating their own positive legacy with the planning and execution of colorful parades and festivals. Their efforts to keep their voices heard was helped by Hubert Howe Bancroft, who recorded over one hundred of their oral histories in his seven-volume *History of California*.[11]

Anglo-American pioneers, when recording their pioneer remembrances, purposely chose to emphasize the savageness of the Indians and their propensity to steal. Their reconstructed reminiscences were used to justify the Anglo-American expansion to the west. Historian Richard White observed that when constructing the new frontier heritage, "everything is inverted and Americans had to transform conquerors into victims."[12] Boosters and writers often sent mixed messages to their readers. While frequently espousing reform for the Indians, their comments were as a double-edged sword. John S. McGroarty, referring to the Franciscan priests, said, "They took an idle race—a useless race that they made useful in the world."[13] By 1937, angered over the treatment of the Indians, McGroarty proposed the abolishment of the Bureau of Indian Affairs (H.J. Resolution 114, January 12, 1937).

Even before the creation of the "Mission Myth," Charles Fletcher Lummis was writing in his publication *Land of Sunshine/Out West* about southern California as the "new Eden of the Saxon home seekers." In 1895, he boasted, "The ignorant, hopelessly un-American type of foreigner which infests and largely controls eastern cities is almost unknown here." These writers wrote of health, pleasure and romantic nostalgia but underneath their words was subtle racial discrimination.

The true vanishing Americans would be the Native Americans who had co-existed with nature in California for ten thousand years. By the 1880s the vanquished Indian survivors were pitied by most arriving Anglo-Americans. When early Tujunga pioneer Franciscoa

In the nineteenth century, California was often symbolized by a woman. This romantic idealization of a woman is by artist Jules Tavernier, c. 1893. *California Historical Society. North Baker Research Library, Kemble Collection*

Begue heard stories from her husband, the forest ranger, she was appalled at the Indians' state. The clothing worn by the Indians in the Chilao Flats area of the San Gabriel Mountains was rags. Franciscoa saved her flour sacks, which her husband took to the Indians by horseback, to help ease their discomfort. Thus, the "Pillsbury squaw" legend was born.

There are no written accounts about the few remaining Fernandeño Indians that lived in the Rancho Tujunga area at the turn of the century. When fourteen-year-old Elsie Ellenberg arrived with her sister and *(left)* The Seal of the County of Los Angeles, designed by Supervisor Kenneth Hahn, was adopted in 1957. Pomona, the goddess of fruit trees and gardens. In her arms is a sheaf of grain, an orange, a lemon, avocado and some grapes.

(below) In 1849 the Great Seal of the State of California was adopted. It was designed by Major Robert Selden Garnett and is located in the office of the Secretary of State. The explanation of the seal as read on October 2, 1849, was: "Around the bevel of the ring are represented thirty-one stars being the number of states of which the union will consist upon admission of California. The foreground figure represents the Goddess Minerva having sprung full-grown from the brain of Jupiter. At her feet crouches a grizzly bear feeding upon clusters from a grape vine. A miner is engaged with a rocker and bowl at his side. In the background above is the Greek motto 'Eureka (I have found it).'"

father in 1912, they built their ranch on Mt. Gleason Avenue (now the western boundary of Tujunga). Elsie saw a few remaining Indians living in a tent on the dirt road leading into the Big Tujunga Canyon.[14] Just eight years earlier, in 1904, Rogério Rocha, one of the last San Fernando Mission Indians, died at the age of 102 years. He was evicted from his home on ex-mission lands; his story illustrates the pathetic ending to the Indians that once flourished in the San Fernando Valley before the turn of the century. As reported in Maurice and Marco Newmark's "Census of the City and County of Los Angeles, California for the year 1850," the Indians in the vicinity of the old Tujunga Village numbered only twelve.[15] From 1769 to 1900, there was a 95 percent reduction of their numbers. By 1900, the majority of Gabrieliños were homeless and poverty-stricken.

The land upon which the San Fernando Mission was built was not owned by the Indians. The Church was a trustee for the benefit of the Indians living there. On June 17, 1846, the San Fernando Mission lands were sold for $14,000 to Don Eulogio de Celis, a Spaniard who lived in Los Angeles. The 121,319 acres were now privately owned by an individual. The real estate transaction specifically stated that "The purchase is bound to maintain the old Indians actually living on it, and to sustain them for the remainder of their days."[16] In 1875, de Celis' son sold the land to ex-state senator Edward Maclay and lawyer G. K. Porter. De Celis was assured the Indians would not be disturbed. In keeping with a century of broken promises, Porter and Maclay filed suit to evict Rogério, his wife, and three women who lived with them. Rogério's father, Germán, was Chumash and his mother, Maria Guadalupe, was born in the ranchero (village) of Tujunga (Tuxuonga).[17] Rogério was the only child of six born to Maria who survived childhood. In 1841, he married Manuela, whose parents had come to the Mission San Fernando from the Lake Piru area. In 1843, his only child, a daughter, was born. By the following year, she had died. The childless Rogério rose to the leadership of the Indians in the vicinity of the mission and became captain or chief. He was an accomplished blacksmith and violinist. He and his wife lived in an *adobe* on his twelve acres of land near the Pacoima creek. His title to the land was based on a 1843 grant given to the Indians by

Mexican general Micheltoreña. Although he paid taxes on the land, it was not patented. He lost his legal fight against eviction by Maclay and Porter in an 1878 court suit. In the winter of 1886, during the middle of a rainstorm, Los Angeles Sheriff William E. Hammel and Morton Aguirre evicted the elderly Indians from their property.[18]

> Though forced to do this disagreeable duty, we regarded it as a hard and cruel thing to take these old people from their home and throw them into the street, unprotected, in the midst of the winter season.
>
> The old women, his tools and household goods, his chickens in sacks and all his movable belongings were tumbled into a wagon (the old man, protesting against his removal, would not be put into the wagon, but followed after), taken some two miles from their home, and thrown out by the roadside, and here lay unprotected from the incessant rain for eight days, during which the old man made his way to Los Angeles, and got permission from the priest to occupy an old shed connected with the Mission Church. In the meantime people passing along carried off baskets, tools, fuel, whatever they chose to take, either as curiosities or for use; their chickens were dead when taken from the sacks, and pounded parched corn was their only food. It was thought by some that the old man must have money hidden about his house, as he had for so many years been an industrious mechanic, and prospecting parties made search for it, digging up the floor of the house, and exploring every possible hiding place. The old wife contracted pneumonia, from which she soon died.[19]

Rogério conducted an impressive and dignified funeral service for his wife at the mission church.

> Not only was Rogério robbed of the land on which even the Mexican government had held him secure; he was not provided for by the ex-State Senator and the Christian lawyer who benefited by the forcible conveyance; nor was he paid for the improvements he had made on the place. Bereft of his wife who died as a direct consequence of the exposure naturally to be expected from an eviction in winter, he has since been dependent on the charity of those who could not afford to give him what their hearts dictated. He removed, after his wife's death, to a tiny patch of land in a wild cañon back in the mountains, a place too poor to be coveted by any white man, even for a theological seminary; and there eked out such an existence as he could in his extreme old age. A man of 84 or 85 at the time of the eviction, he has passed the last eighteen years on land loaned him by a Mexican, and with such slender aid as he could secure from time to time. In 1889 I was appointed U.S. Indian agent to the Mission Indians, and during my term assisted Rogério as well as I could with the miserable pittance allowed by the government to the agent for the sick and indigent of 3000 Indians—about $200 per annum all told! Since then I have called his case to the attention of my successors, and the present incumbent has sent him a few rations. So far as I know, he received about $5 worth in all.

Rogério's death in the spring of 1904 was widely published in newspapers throughout the country. "Those who knew Rocha longest speak of his good traits, his keenness of intellect and kindness of heart. . . . He was a giant in stature and almost a Hercules in strength until recent years, and even a century did not bend his form."[20]

No documentation of oral histories or written memoirs about the early Mexican women who lived in the Rancho Tujunga area is known. The small Mexican population of Tujunga was mainly males employed in agriculture. Many early pioneers fondly remembered the De Silva family, which lived at the corner of Woodard Avenue and Foothill Boulevard in Sunland. They had several children who attended schools in Sunland. The family was highly regarded by the Rowley and Perner families in Sunland.[21]

Marshal V. Hartranft brought in some East Indian men to pave Michigan Avenue. Hilda Livingston's son,

---

> No loose fish enters our quiet bay.
> —*Gertrude Atherton*, Sleeping Fires (1922).

> . . . on the right hand of the Indies . . . an island called California, very near to the Terrestrial Paradise . . . which was peopled . . . their arms full of gold.
> —*Garci Ordonez de Montalvo, 1510*

Chan, remembers going down to Michigan Avenue after dinner to talk to the turbaned Indian men. They lived in tents and seemed exotic, but proved to be very friendly.[22]

The exclusion of non-Anglos from booster writing clearly indicated that the California dream was an Anglo dream. "Racial thought among Anglo-Americans throughout California in 1910s generally defined racial minorities as part of the laboring classes: Mexicans, Punjabi Mexicans, Japanese and Chinese were viewed as 'child like' and needed reform and moral guidance from whites."[23]

The Little Landers Colony in San Ysidro, which had a racial restrictive covenant on land holdings in their by-laws, adopted many of the minorities' agricultural techniques. Those by-laws were later amended to also exclude Orientals and Negroes from owning property in the colony.[24] The Little Landers Colonies had parallel racist sentiments equal to those prevailing in southern California and the nation. Wilber J. Hall, writing for *Sunset Magazine*, declared, "The Indians and Mexicans are not highly satisfactory or efficient farm hands, but they can be had in large bands in the Valley. They work cheaply, and in the end, the planters may employ them profitably."

"Los Angeles of the 1920s and 1930s was a town dominated by whites who made little allowance for racial minorities. Many jurisdictions routinely enforced Jim Crow patterns."[25] The term "Jim Crow" was part of a song performed by "Daddy" Rice, an entertainer with a painted black face in an all-white minstrel show in 1830. The term later became synonymous with segregation and racist laws and actions that deprived African-Americans of their civil rights. California's racial prejudice was fueled by economic, religious, and social considerations. The state's attitude toward Asians greatly influenced the national sentiment against that race in particular. Thus, the Tujunga story would be represented by the stories of "white suburban sisters."

To better comprehend the legal background of discrimination and exclusion laws, we can go back to 1790, when the United States Congress declared that the right of naturalization was restricted to any alien who was a "free white person." Africans, or people of African descent, were eligible for naturalization in 1870. In 1922, the United States Supreme Court, in the case of *Ozawa v. The United States* declared that a Japanese immigrant "was not a free white person." The Japanese would have to wait until 1952, when the McCarren–Walter Act was passed, allowing Asian immigrants to become United States citizens.[26]

From 1907 to 1913, at each California legislative session, "Alien Land Laws" were discussed. Finally in the spring of 1913, the Henry–Webb Alien Land Law was passed. Previously, in 1905, the California Civil Code had been amended to add "Mongolians" and include the Japanese with those prohibited from marrying "white" citizens. In 1920, the 1913 "Alien Land Law" was amended to state that Japanese could not own land or lease land for more than three years. The aim of the amended law was to return the Japanese farm lessee back into a farm laborer.[27] From 1923 to 1926, one-half of California's Japanese farmers returned to Japan with their families. In 1924, the United States Immigration Act abruptly terminated all Japanese immigration to the United States.[28]

The escalating numbers of Japanese immigrants became threatening to most Californians. The use of Japanese farm labor and later tenant farming became crucial to Anglo-Californian landowners and to the economic health of the state. However, the German, French, Italians, and Irish immigrants did not meet with the same harsh social and economic barriers as the Asians.

In 1880, in the southern California area, there were only fifty-eight Japanese residents recorded. In 1900, there were 481 people of Japanese origin and by 1910, 13,068 Japanese. The final count in 1920 indicated there were 25,597 Japanese residents.[29] From farm laborers, the immigrants from Japan progressed to farm owners. Unable to lease their farms for more than three years, they simply sub-leased the land and began to control large amounts of truck farming acreage. As they moved from citrus groves to flower and produce farms, they were replaced by resident and immigrant Mexican labor. Though the Japanese were unable to own land in the Little Landers Colonies, the Anglos who could own land often used the Japanese intensive farming methods extensively. By 1940, the Japanese controlled 90 percent of the truck farms in the San Fernando Valley.[30] The Burbank Land Office recorded 115 ranches owned or leased by Japanese farmers in 1942. Early in the 1930s, the Sunland-Tujunga area welcomed the Heishi, Hideo, Nakayama, Okada, Nawa, and Okudo families, who would join the George Tsumori family. They were well respected and an integral part of the community. Residents were shocked when their neighbors were shipped off to internment camps throughout America during World War II.

In the 1920s, the nation was seen as prosperous but it was one burdened by social conflict, including prohibition, women's suffrage, and the second rise of the

> Exclusion is always dangerous.
> Inclusion is the only safety
> if we are to have a peaceful world.
> —*Pearl S. Buck*, A Bridge for Passing (1962)

(*below*) In M.V. Hartranft's promotional pamphlet, "My Hand Made Home in the Hills," it is pointed out that land could only be sold to Native Americans and white citizens of good reputation, yet no sale of land to a Native American was recorded or remembered, c. 1922.

Things you will want to know about Tujunga
(*Pronounce it "Tu-hoon-ga"*)

Q. Where is Tujunga?
A. A little less than eighteen miles north-east from the city center of Los Angeles; via Tropico, Glendale, Montrose and La Crescenta.

Q. What are the prevailing climatic conditions at Tujunga?
A. Situated on an elevation ranging from 1,600 to 2,000 feet above sea level, the air is light, dry, and bracing. Lying on a high plateau between the Verdugo Hills and the Sierra Madres, Tujunga is effectually screened from fogs and damp sea breezes. Chronic sufferers of asthma find instant relief in this revivifying climate. There is no frost in the winter—and the summer's heat is tempered by the dry air.

Q. Are there any restrictions in force at Tujunga?
A. Yes; although we have purposely kept them few and easy to comply with. Purchase of property is restricted to native Americans, white, and of good reputation. That property purchased shall be used for residential purposes only. That all buildings and their extensions shall be erected at least 20 feet back of front property line. Temporary structures are permitted at a distance of 75 feet back of property line. Reasonable allowances will be made for family poultry stock, vegetable and fruit gardens; except in the week-end oak tree lots of Golondrina Park and along Thousand Oak Drive where live stock of all kinds are prohibited. Family pets, such as bird, cat, and dog, excepted, and cabin plans must be submitted for approval to avoid unsightly structures.

Q. What about water?
A. One of the finest and most complete water systems was installed at Tujunga before the property ever came on the market. Mains were laid on every street without any expense to residents. The Haynes Canyon Water Company, controlling the watershed of Haynes and Blanchard Canyons, operates a $141,000 system having 21 miles of pipes through all the streets of Tujunga, and an auxiliary pumping plant in the floor of the Valley. The watershed which supplies Tujunga is the strongest of all the foothills in Southern California. The Big Tujunga drains an area that extends as far east as Monrovia. The water that falls behind Monrovia, behind Sierra Madre, behind Altadena, behind Pasadena, behind Crescenta, falls back into the far regions of the Big Tujunga and drains out into the basin of the Tujunga Valley. Here the auxiliary pumping plant whenever necessary, guarantees ample supplies of water over all our slopes. With such an enormous source of supply and distributing facilities, the Tujunga Valley is assured all the water—for all time—that any amount of population can use and pay for at reasonable rates.

Q. Have you electricity at Tujunga?
A. Yes; current is available, and connections easily made anywhere in the tract. Special inducements in lower rates are made for those who will use current for heating, kitchen stoves, etc., in addition to lighting.

Q. Are there stores at Tujunga?
A. Yes, some small stores that carry all commodities. Freight busses make regular trips several times a day from the city and will deliver goods bought in the city practically at your doorstep; this being even more convenient than would be possible by trolley.

Q. Any trolley connections?
A. No, the nearest line reaches Crescenta, four miles away. The sentiment of Tujunga property owners seems to be against entry of car lines.

Q. What transportation facilities are there?
A. Bus lines give quick and comfortable service to the city and intermediate points. Five round trips daily leaving Sixth and Los Angeles Streets.

Q. Are there any schools?
A. We have a school in Tujunga, and High School pupils are carried by motor bus to Glendale H. S. and brought home. Plans now under way call for the early erection of a High School at Tujunga.

Q. What kind of soil have you at Tujunga?
A. To merely say it is good would be underestimating it; and to say it is "wonderful" would sound like exaggeration. It ranges from sandy to loam—depending on location. On it is being grown the finest Tokay Grapes in California; the Los Angeles Chamber of Commerce requesting this valley especially to enter this exhibit annually. The finest avocadoes, figs, olives, walnuts, peaches, apricots, and oranges are also met with on every hand in this valley; not to mention the abundance of vegetables of all varieties that are raised here.

Q. Aside from the advantages of living at Tujunga, can purchases of property be considered a sound investment?
A. Most decidedly yes: developments made within the past six years have automatically increased property values, and with the ever increasing number of residents coming in, values are certain to go far higher. Tujunga has advantages that neither Hollywood, Pasadena, or Sierra Madre ever possessed; twenty years ago, nay even fifteen and ten years ago—who could have foreseen the remarkable strides made with the consequent rise in values? Tujunga is distinctly the last big Foothills development along Pasadena-Hollywood lines.

Ku Klux Klan (KKK), also known as "The Hooded Order" or "The Invisible Empire."[31] The KKK of the 1920s and 1930s was different than the national vigilante group of the post–Civil War years. The KKK was reborn in 1915 at Stone Mountain, Georgia. It still abided by hoods, sheets, and cross burnings, but expanded its hatred to include Catholics, Jews, radicals, labor activists, and "wet back" Mexicans. By the late 1920s, the Klan would lay claim to a national membership of over 3 million.[32] They now saw themselves as advocates of moral and political reform. Shortly after the Klan meeting in Georgia, the pro-Klan movie *Birth of a Nation* was released and the Klan experienced a renewed interest and membership increased throughout the land.

Grand Gôblin William S. Coburn aggressively recruited in California and chapters were formed in Los Angeles, Santa Monica, Huntington Park, Long Beach, Glendale, San Pedro, and Anaheim. Throughout the state the Klan ruled by fear and intimidation. Kidnappings, beatings, tar and featherings and lynchings were the order of the day.[33] In Tujunga racism was a reality—racial harmony was never a dream of the Little Landers movement. Most Americans, during the 1920s and 1930s, eagerly forgot the fact that twenty-six of the original forty-four settlers of Los Angeles were of African or mixed ancestry. While black Angelinos were subject to arrest for appearances at the beaches, hotels, diners and restrooms labeled "whites only," it would not be a problem in Tujunga. Unable to own land or be seen in the town after sundown, Tujunga was a white enclave that would later be home to future white supremacists and skinheads. Although an official KKK chapter did not exist in Tujunga, there was a KKK order situated in the San Fernando Valley. Tujunga pioneer Helen Rutherford's grandson would forever remember the site of hooded Klansmen on horseback burning a cross on a hill above Tujunga in the 1930s.[34] Racism would continue to haunt the foothill communities into the twenty-first century.[35] The winds of prejudice blew through Tujunga long before December 7, 1941, and Tujunga would join a nation that still struggles with real solutions to racial problems.

Notes

[1] Cathy Luchetti and Carol Olwell, *Women of the West* (St. George, Utah: Antelope Island Press, 1982), 26.

[2] Doyce Nunis (editor), *Women in the Life of Southern California—An Anthology* (Los Angeles: Historical Society of Southern California, 1966), 56.

[3] Contrary to popular belief, Tujunga never had a Chinese laundry. Author's interview with Tom Theobold, June 14, 2002.

[4] Carey McWilliams, *Southern California: an Island on the Land*, 1946 (Santa Barbara: Peregrine Smith, 1973), 65.

[5] On October 24, 1871, one of the nation's worst race riots took place in Los Angeles. Over 1,000 Angelinos and the police robbed and hanged nineteen Chinese men in Chinatown. In 1895, Pasadena would burn down their Chinese laundry. By the early 1900s, the Japanese would displace the Chinese. They bought the land the Chinese had rented and forced them to move. By the second generation, most of their language and customs were lost. In July 1937, at the Chinese Cemetery in Los Angeles, the graves of 850 people were opened and the remains sent to Hong Kong. Ibid., 94.

[6] Ibid., 201.

[7] Ibid., 64.

[8] For a better understanding of the issue, see *Decade of Betrayal* by Ray-

[8] mond Rodriguez and Francisco Balderama (Albuquerque: University of New Mexico Press, 1995).

[9] "Apology Sought for Latino 'Repatriation' Drive in 30s," *Los Angeles Times* (July 15, 2003).

[10] "Raid: 1931 Roundup Set Tone for Decades of Ethnic Tension," *Los Angeles Times* (February 25, 2001).

[11] David M. Wrobel, *Promised Lands—Promotion, Memory, and the Creation of the American West* (Lawrence: University Press of Kansas, 2002), 124.

[12] Ibid., 178.

[13] Kevin Starr, *Inventing the Dream—California Through the Progressive Era* (New York: Oxford University Press, 1985), 89.

[14] Author's interview with Elsie's daughter-in-law, Caroline Ardizzone, November 1997.

[15] Lawrence C. Jorgensen, *The San Fernando Valley—Past and Present* (Los Angeles: Pacific Rim Research, 1982), 76–77.

[16] Ibid., 271–274.

[17] Ibid., 112.

[18] Charles C. Painter, *The Present Condition of the Mission Indians of California* (Philadelphia: Office of Indian Rights Association, 1887), 7.

[19] Doyce B. Nunis, Jr., ed., *Mission San Fernando, Rey de España, 1797–1997—A Bicentennial Tribute* (Los Angeles: Historical Society of Southern California, 1997), 273.

[20] Painter, *The Present Condition of the Mission Indians of California*, 7.

[21] Author's interview with Myra (Perner) Lighthart, February 17, 2003.

[22] Author's interview with Chancellor Livingston, April 12, 1993.

[23] Tomás Almaguer, *Racial Fault Lines: The Historical Origins of White Supremacy in California* (Berkeley: University of California Press, 1994), 183–213.

[24] Lawrence Lee, "The Little Landers Colony of San Ysidro," *Journal of San Diego History* 21, no. 1 (Winter 1975): 43.

[24] Almaguer, op. cit., 175.

[25] Leonard and Dale Pitt, *Los Angeles A to Z—An Encyclopedia to The City and County*, 413.

[26] Cecilia Rasmussen, "Mother, Sons Overcame Internment, Postwar Racism," *L.A. Then and Now, Los Angeles Times Newspaper* (May 20, 2001).

[27] *California History, The Magazine of the California Historical Society* 73, no. 1 (Spring 1994).

[28] Ibid., Eichiro Azuma, "Japanese Immigrant Farmers and California Alien Land Laws," 14–30.

[29] Roger Daniels, *Coming to America—A History of Immigration and Ethnicity in American Life* (New York: Harpers Perennial, 2nd Edition, 1990), 250.

[30] Jorgensen, op. cit.

[31] The "Hooded Order" first emerged in Tennessee in 1866. Formed as a secret social order by Confederate soldiers, the KKK spread nationally; its first order was to spread white supremacy, then to terrorize blacks and their white supporters. Newell G. Bringhurst, " The Ku Klux Klan in Central California Community: Tulare County During the 1920s and 1930s," *Southern California Quarterly* 82, no. 4: 365.

[32] Pitt, op. cit., 241.

[33] For further information on mob murder and the "Rule of Lawlessness" read: James S. Hirsch, *Riot and Remembrance: The Tulsa Race War and Its Legacy* (Houghton Mifflin, 2002); and Philip Dray, *At the Hands of Persons Unknown: The Lynching of Black America* (Random House, 2002).

[34] Author's interview with Forest Theriot, January 17, 1995. "It was a sight you would never forget."

[35] Ryan Carter, "Local Merchant Wants Hate Crime March," *The Leader Newspaper* (March 15, 2000). In the year 2000, hate crimes greatly increased and constituted a large percentage of crimes reported to the Los Angeles Police Department, Foothill Division.

We must learn to live together as brothers
or perish together as fools.
—*Martin Luther King Jr. speech,
March 22, 1964, St. Louis, Missouri*

Just down the road from the detention center was Hindenburg Park (Crescenta Valley Park) that was used for the large gatherings of the German-American Bund. Once considered a cultural group, they emerged as politically oriented in the late 1930s. *Courtesy of Crescenta Valley Sun.*

A rare photograph of Ku Klux Klan activities in the valley, c. 1930. *The Record-Ledger,* September 27, 1973.

SILENCED VOICES

Tujunga never openly advertised nor displayed any anti-Asian sentiment.
Photograph of a home in Los Angeles, c. 1920s. *Source unknown.*

In this rare advertisement, it is printed that residential property was restricted. Tujunga Telephone Directory, c. 1924.

EARL F. CHAPMAN
Realtor

*RESTRICTED RESIDENCE AND HIGH CLASS
BUSINESS PROPERTY*

OFFICE—First and Michigan, Sunland.
RESIDENCE—First St. and Oak Drive, Sunland.

Phone Sunland 794

FOUNDING SISTERS

(*top*) The Tuna Canyon Detention Center was located south of the Fehlhaber Ranch. It was once a CCC Camp in the 1930s. Photos of the CCC Camp before barbed wire, sentry boxes, and floodlights were added. *El Portal Yearbook, 1940.*

(*bottom*) This 1933 photograph shows the mess hall at CCC Camp No. 902.

(*opposite, top*) Map of Tuna Detention Center dictated to Author by Mabel (Tsumori) Abe, August 18, 1995, c. 2003. *By Sunland resident Martine Prado.*

(*oppsoite, middle*) The Tuna Canyon Temporary Detention Center joined a network of centers throughout the United States. It, along with Sharp Park, held the most prisoners on the West Coast. *Courtesy of Professor Tetsuden Kashima.*

SILENCED VOICES

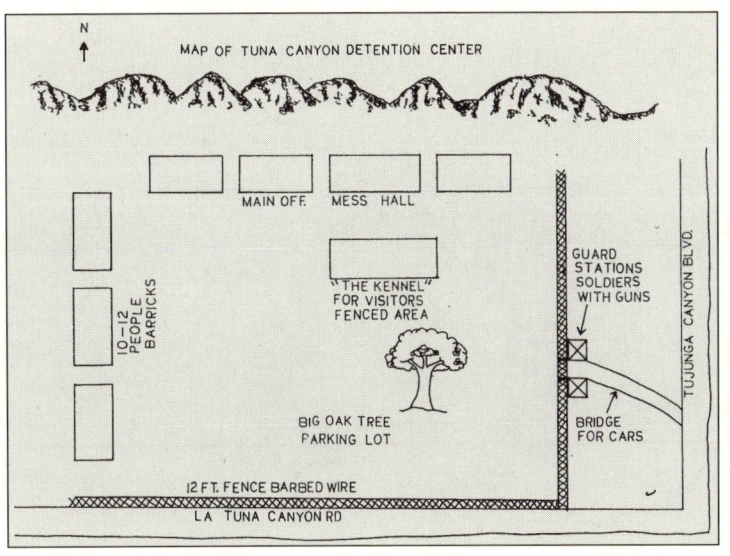

Today (Sunday, March 15, 1942) is the dawn of the CCC Camp of Tujunga which is outside of Los Angeles... we are prohibited to go within 10 feet of the fence, and it is most painful to be cut off from the outside world.
—Diary of Japanese internee Daisho Tana.
The Los Angeles Times, *September 14, 1995.*

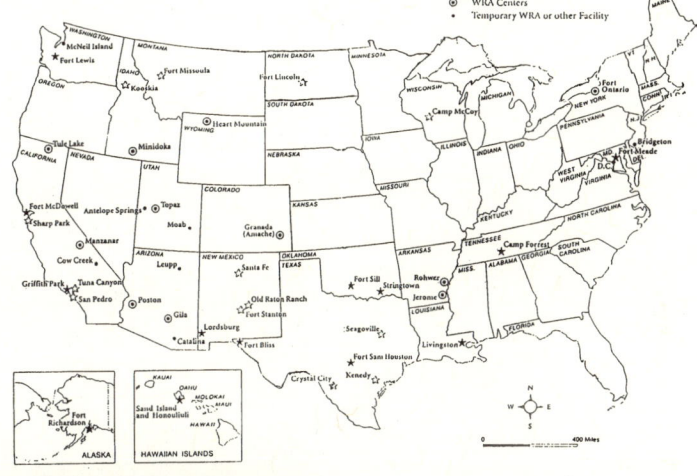

Once home to an internment camp, the site is now the Verdugo Hills Golf Course, c. 2003. *Courtesy of Author.*

FOUNDING SISTERS

> Ordinary lives are extraordinary
> if you really see them.
> —*Agnes De Mille (1905–1993),*
> *American dancer and choreographer*

Portrait of Mabel (Tsumori) Abe, c. 1943. *Courtesy of Carol and Greg Abe.*

Fifty-six years late for their own graduation, Mabel Abe and Gilbert Ceferatt receive their diplomas at Verdugo Hills High School in Tujunga, June 18, 1998. The event made national and international news through CNN, the *Los Angeles Times*, and several newspapers in Japan. *Courtesy of Author.*

SILENCED VOICES

VOL. I, NO. 1   TUJUNGA, CALIFORNIA, SOMEDAY, FEBRUARY 30, 1966   PRICELESS

Wrecker Ledger Learns

Red-Haired Family Moves Into Sunland

The first red-haired family known to have moved into any 9800 block in Sunland is renting a residence there.

In response to repeated rumors, some of them exaggerated greatly from the time we started them, and several inquiries and telephone calls, the WRECKER - LEDGER investigated, and found out that a red-haired family from the Glendale area has indeed taken up residence in Sunland.

The newspaper ascertained from the owners of the property, the J.B. Fussmores, that the property was rented for them by the All-American Realty of Sun Valley, without any information to them as to what color hair the new tenants had.

"The house was rented without our knowledge and without consultation," said the obviously-outraged Mrs. Fussmore.

Artful J. Dodger, broker with the All-American firm, said that he handled the transaction. "From time to time, the All-American Realty Company has enquiries from red-headed people for both rentals and purchases," he said, "which we try to serve. I did so in this case. After all, I'm an All-American boy."

Monday evening the WRECKER - LEDGER was called by a citizen and told: "The Human Relations Council has finally succeeded in getting a colored family into Sunland." After a great deal of natural misunderstanding, the newspaper was able finally to determine what color he meant.

> The present procedure of keeping loyal American citizens in concentration camps on the basis of race for longer than is absolutely necessary is dangerous and repugnant to the principles of our government.
> —*Attorney General Francis Biddle, December 30, 1943*
>
> An "assembly center" was a euphemism for a prison ... so-called "relocation centers" a euphemism for concentration camps.
> —*Supreme Court Justice Owen J. Roberts, December 18, 1944*

In 1966, the *Record-Ledger Newspaper*, in a special "spoof" edition, recorded the first family of color moving into the Sunland-Tujunga area.

141

Women's Voices from A to Z

Photograph of Anna prior to her champion walks, c. 1924.

Anna Negy Adam
1873–1955

Anna Adam was perhaps one of the most colorful women to reside in Tujunga. She literally walked her way into the pages of the town's history.

She was one of the many health seekers that had come to the Little Lands Colony. When forty-year-old Anna first arrived, she weighed over 200 pounds, had a heart condition, and was unable to walk without a cane due to severe arthritis.[1] After a regimen of mud baths, sleeping outdoors year-round, and eating raw vegetables and garlic, she claimed victory over her physical challenges. By 1928, her health had been regained and she embarked on a most remarkable walking adventure.

Anna and her husband, George, were both born in Rumania. They came to the United States in 1903 and, by April 1913, had joined the Little Lands Colony.[2] Her husband advertised himself as "Tujunga's Pioneer Painter and Paperhanger" and Anna was a housewife. They had no children but lavished their love on their dogs, who frequently accompanied George on his round-trip walks to Pasadena.[3] George, Anna, and their dogs lived in a small house at 10235 Silverton Avenue in Tujunga.[4]

Every July 27, Anna's birthday, Anna would celebrate her good health by taking a forty-two-mile round-trip walk to Exposition Park in Los Angeles. By 1938, her weight was down to 130 pounds.[5] She was tan and healthy and even enjoyed walking around town barefoot.[6] She told columnist Daisy Breeden, in an article published in 1938, that she took walks each year "to make sure she wasn't getting soft."[7] After a six-hour walk to Exposition Park, she would arrive by 10 A.M. and turn around for the walk home, which took a little longer as it was uphill. She was often offered a ride home by concerned citizens but she refused all offers as the "walks must be kept honest."[8]

Anna had skills beyond her capacity for long-distance walks. In Rumania, she had learned to carry bundles on her head, some as large as a clothesbasket, while walking.[9]

Every year Anna grew stronger. Her tanned, heavily lined face was well-known throughout the area.[10] The newspapers often covered her yearly walks. She attributed her stamina and good health to walking, eating raw foods and drinking goat's milk and fruit and vegetable juices.[11]

Anna was active in the local Eastern Star, Chapter 445. She attended meetings regularly until the final five weeks before her death.[12] In July 1955, she attended the groundbreaking ceremonies for the Masonic Lodge 592, which was being built on Valmont Avenue in Tujunga.[13] She and her late husband had made substantial contributions to the lodge building fund.

One month after the groundbreaking ceremonies, she won the award for the best costume in Tujunga's yearly Old Timers' Celebration fashion show.[14] This second-annual celebration was a three-day affair that included a parade, pioneer costume contest, and a large outdoor barbecue at Sunland Park.[15]

After the tragic death of her husband, George, from a gunshot wound to the head in 1949, Anna lived alone for six years, tending her garden and taking her famous long walks.[16] For twenty-seven years, she walked to Exposition Park and back home to Tujunga.

Anna Adam left us a triumphant legacy of the woman walker from Tujunga.

Notes

[1] Daisy Breeden, "Facts-Fads and Fancies," *The Free Press*, 1938. Bolton Hall Museum clippings file.

[2] Record of Funeral, December 20, 1955, Bades Mortuary, Tujunga.

[3] "George Adam Finds Walking Dangerous on Arroyo Freeway," *The Record-Ledger* (June 19, 1941).

[4] Interview with Tom Theobald, retired Tujunga postmaster, October 2, 1996.

[5] Breeden, op. cit.

[6] Interview with Esther Van Essen, Eastern Star Member, July 15, 1999.

[7] Breeden, loc. cit.

[8] Breeden, loc. cit.

[9] "Remember When—25 Years Ago, December 1939," *The Record-Ledger* (December 17, 1964).

[10] Interview with Forrest Theriot, former Tujunga resident, May 10, 1997: "She was seen walking about town with her gray hair done in a washer woman style. She had a very tanned, lined face."

[11] Breeden, loc. cit.

[12] "Anna Adams [sic] Succumbs at Tujunga Home," *The Record-Ledger* (December 22, 1955). (Note: in later years, the newspapers often misspelled her name).

[13] "Masonic Earth Movers," photo, *The Record-Ledger* (July 28, 1955).

[14] "Genuine Old Timers," photo, *The Record-Ledger* (August 4, 1955).

[15] "Three Day Old Timers' Celebration." Photo. *The Record-Ledger* (February 2, 1978).

[16] Record of Funeral, November 13, 1949, Bades Mortuary, Tujunga.

> I AM A CALIFORNIAN,
> and we have twice the individuality and originality
> of any people in the United States.
> We always get quite huffy
> when we are spoken of as merely Americans.
> —*Gertrude Atherton, 1898*

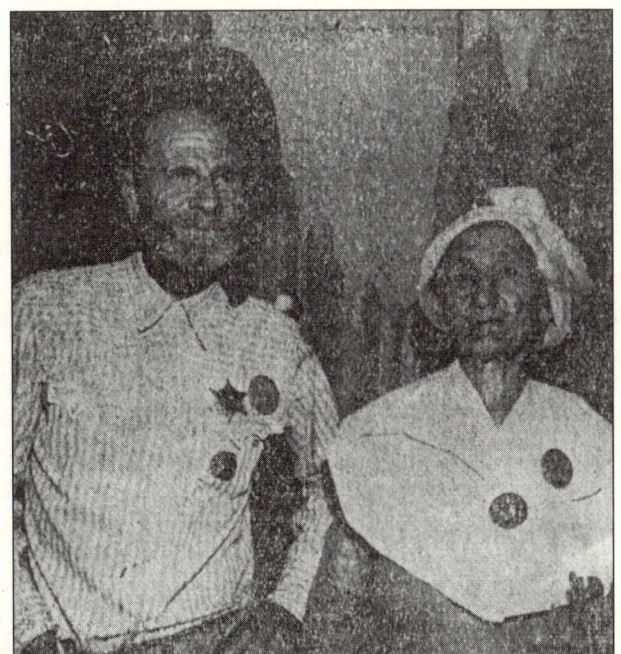

Just three months before her death, Anna wins an award for her costume in "The Old Times" celebration, c. 1955. *The Record-Ledger.*

In July 1955, Anna (*center*), wearing leather moccasins, helps break ground for the new Masonic Lodge 592. *The Record-Ledger.*

Franciscoa (*far left*) at their Haines Canyon cabin, c. 1915.

Franciscoa Begue
1867–1940

The year was 1879 and twelve-year-old Franciscoa had just lost her parents, Marie and Martin Morticorena, to smallpox. She was left alone to raise her nine-year-old sister in the Basque village of Eguie, Spain.[1] Although she and her sister had survived the terrible epidemic, they were left with many scars from the disfiguring disease.

The young girls were alone, and the only solution to their dilemma was to set sail for America to join their three older sisters who had previously left Spain and settled in Los Angeles, where they ran a boarding house.[2] They sailed out of Barcelona on a clipper ship bound for New York. Upon arriving in New York, they again set sail for San Francisco around the treacherous Cape Horn, at the southern tip of South America, noted for its churning waters and violent gale force winds. The voyage was a test of courage for even the most daring seamen. What bravery these two exhibited; with no parents, speaking only Castilian Spanish, they embarked on an arduous six-month voyage. They left their home with three possessions: a change of clothes, a down comforter, and a brass bed warmer.[3]

The story of Franciscoa's courtship and marriage to fellow Basque Philip Eugene Begue is unknown. What is known is that Philip's father, Bertrand, had lost his wife and a daughter to the smallpox epidemic in San Francisco. Bertrand and Philip then came to Los Angeles and opened a butcher shop. Every week, father and son would come to the east section of Tujunga by freight wagon to bring deer, bear, other game, and honey back to their butcher shop.

In 1882, Bertrand, Philip, and Franciscoa arrived in the eastern portion of Rancho Tujunga to settle. Bertrand and Philip bought Lot 46 of Rancho La Cañada and 10.92 additional acres from Victor Beaudry, the mayor of Los Angeles. They paid five dollars per acre, a high price at the time, for the property located on the southern portion of Tujunga Canyon Boulevard (Horse Thief Trail).[4] In addition to the property, Philip bought the water rights to Haines and Blanchard Canyons. They built a dam and reservoir in Haines Canyon in order to pipe water to their orchards and vineyards.[5]

In 1906, the Begues built a wood frame house they named El Descanso Ranch. The home was built on a knoll overlooking the only road leading into Tujunga. That road, Horse Thief Trail, is now Honolulu Avenue and Tujunga Canyon Boulevard. To the rear of their home, high up the mountain, were two silica mines. These mines operated in the 1920s and 1930s as the Crescenta Valley Mining Company.

Also located on their property was an artesian well, some sixty to seventy feet deep, believed to have been used by Sister Elsie, a Sister of Charity who ministered to the local Indians.[6] Sister Elsie's well was dedicated by the Native Sons and Daughters of the Glendale Parlor in 1930 and bears a plaque in its honor. In 1932, the well was incorporated into the grounds of the Tujunga Hotel. Almost directly north of Sister Elsie's well tow-

149

Mary and her husband, J.F. Fitzgerald, under the oaks at their home, c. 1906.

This 1845 map from Walter Colton's book *Deck and Port, or Incidents of a Cruise in the United States Frigate Cypress to California* shows the Cape Horn route from the East Coast to California.

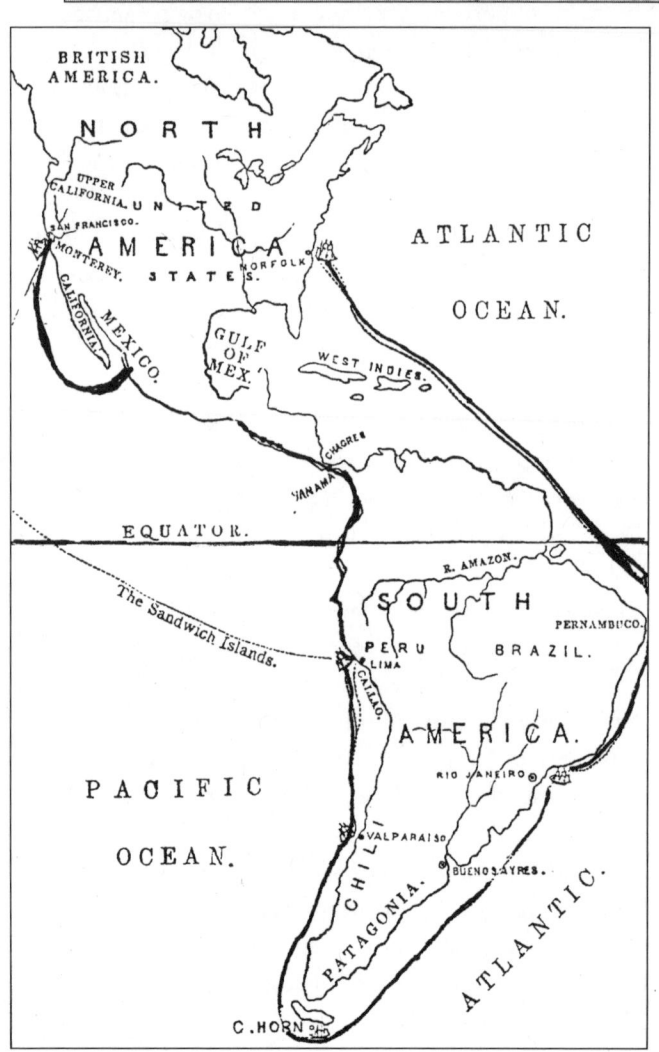

ers a high peak of the Sierra Madre Range that bears the name Sister Elsie's Peak. For many years, the Forestry Department lookout tower, Luken's Lookout, was situated on this peak. The tower was abandoned in 1937.[7]

As did many who arrived after them, the Begues cleared their acreage and started a beekeeping business. When more land was cleared, they planted a vineyard of Tokay, Black Prince, Malaga, Zinfindel and Cornishon grapes and an orchard.[8] They also built a cabin in Haines Canyon. Friends and neighbors would often gather for a few days of resting and hunting at the popular retreat in the hills above the canyon.

In 1917, their wood frame house was torn down and a larger home built on the site. The remodeled home, at 9751 Tujunga Canyon Boulevard, and their wooden barn, built in 1906, are still visible while driving north on Tujunga Canyon Boulevard.[9] It was here at their home, overlooking Horse Thief Trail, that Franciscoa and Philip raised their five children. They had two daughters, Mary Smith Enos and Josephine Begue. Josephine, born breach, was left spastic and confined to a wheelchair. A Mrs. Shaunesy was brought into the household to assist in caring for her. Josephine lived to the age of eighty-five. Mary Smith Enos lived to

FRANCISCOA BEGUE

EL DESCANSO RANCH. (*left to right*) Philip, Jr., Frank, George, Josephine (*seated*), Mary, Bert and a visitor from Oxnard, c. 1906.

just short of her hundredth birthday.[10] Her husband, Dick Smith, helped build Bolton Hall (1913), the McGroarty home (1926), the Mission Playhouse in San Gabriel (1924), and the Cross of San Ysidro, atop the Verdugo Mountains (1923).

The Begues had three sons: Philip, a prominent builder who passed away at the age of fifty-four, Frank, also a building contractor, and Bertrand.

The Begue ranch was always busy. Philip would leave the ranch each morning at four to take the produce to Los Angeles. Franciscoa was absorbed with child rearing, cooking, entertaining friends, and hosting community events. From 1905 to 1908, Philip served as the first contract forest ranger. In the fall, the Indians would gather near Chilao Flats, in the San Gabriel Mountains, to harvest pinion nuts. Franciscoa would save her hundred-pound flour sacks to give to these Indian women for making dresses.

Franciscoa was a renowned cook and did all of her cooking on a wood stove. In 1938, the family bought her an electric stove, but she hated it and returned to her trusty old wood stove. Her grandson described her usual dress as a long skirt with the ever-present apron over it.[11]

The Begue family was noted for their many contributions to the community and their warm hospitality on the ranch. Their property had two large in-ground barbecue pits. Meat would be put in cheesecloth, then in a burlap bag and placed on the hot coals with a heavy iron lid placed over the pit. It took six to eight men just to lift the lid on and off of the pit. In ten to twelve hours the meat would be cooked to perfection.[12]

Every Thanksgiving, the American Legion held their annual turkey shoot on the property.[13] In August 1936, nearly one thousand people attended a barbecue to benefit their church, Our Lady of Lourdes, in Tujunga.[14] In that same year, Philip, Jr., opened Begue's Barbecue at the corner of Foothill and Tujunga Canyon Boulevards. The restaurant seated thirty-two people inside and an additional eighteen in the fountain area.[15] The main attraction at the restaurant was the pit barbecue meat.

FOUNDING SISTERS

Original El Descanso Ranch house. Road in foreground is now Foothill Boulevard, c. 1890s. *Courtesy of Philip Begue III.*

The size of the Begue property would change many times during the course of their ownership. In 1929, the ranch was subdivided and the acreage around Shady Grove Avenue was developed with piped water and sidewalks. During the Depression of the 1930s, most of the property was lost to the City of Los Angeles because of high taxes and street assessments.

In September 1940, Franciscoa passed away at her beloved ranch. Her husband lived just three years after her death.

In 1941, the Spahr family bought the remaining twelve acres of the ranch for $6,500. Included in the price of the property was the old barn, the silica mines, the pool that had once been a reservoir for Haines Canyon water, and a stone well that traces its history to the Verdugo land grant from the king of Spain.[16]

With the passing of the senior Begues and the dismantling of the ranch, a way of early California ranch life disappeared. The legacy of the Begue hospitality lives on in memories even today.

Notes

[1] Record of Funeral, September 13, 1940, Bades Mortuary, Tujunga.
[2] Author's interview with Philip Begue III. July 18, 1999.
[3] Ibid. Franciscoa's bed warmer is in her grandson Philip's possession.
[4] Sarah R. Lombard, *Rancho Tujunga: a History of Sunland/Tujunga, California* (Burbank, Calif.: The Bridge Publishing, 1990), 22.
[5] "Beginnings of the Valley's History as told By One of Tujunga's First Settlers," *The Record-Ledger*, 1924, Bolton Hall Museum clippings file.
[6] Viola Carlson, "Sister Elsie Legend Finally Solved—She was not a Nun," *The Record-Ledger* (July 23, 1959).
[7] Grace Oberdeck, *History of La Crescenta-La Canada Valleys* (Montrose, Calif.: The Ledger, 1938).
[8] Author's interview, July 18, 1999, op. cit.
[9] The Begue barn is now on the Spahr property and was featured on the Sunland-Tujunga Historic Home and Garden Tour, April 19, 1998.
[10] Viola Carlson interview with Mary Smith Enos, July 1982, Bolton Hall Museum, Tujunga.
[11] Author's interview, July 18, 1999, op. cit.
[12] Author's interview with Philip Begue III, September 13, 1999.
[13] "One Hundred Fat Birds for Legion Turkey Shoot," *The Record-Ledger* (November 23, 1922).
[14] "Everybody has Good Times at Church Barbecue," *The Record-Ledger* (August 13, 1936).
[15] "Begue's Barbecue to Open Friday," *The Record-Ledger* (October 8, 1936).
[16] "Begue Barn—Part of Sunland-Tujunga History," *The Record-Ledger* (August 25, 1979).

FRANCISCOA BEGUE

Philip and Franciscoa on porch of Ranch house, c. mid 1930s.

Philip Begue Jr.'s first school, Glorietta, corner of Marcus and Foothill Boulevard, c. early 1900s.
The two-room schoolhouse was razed in 1956 and replaced with a parking lot.
Both photos courtesy of Philip Begue III.

Remodeled Ranch house, c. 1917 *Courtesy of Philip Begue III.*

M. V. Hartranft used the Begue home in his promotional brochure "My Hand-Made Home in the Hills." c. 1920.

Swinging out from the sky-line like the *hanging gardens* of ancient Babylon—

Photograph taken from rear of Begue property.
The dirt road running horizontally through the picture is now Foothill Boulevard.
Big Tujunga, Haines and Blanchard Canyons are in the background, c. 1915. *Courtesy of Philip Begue III.*

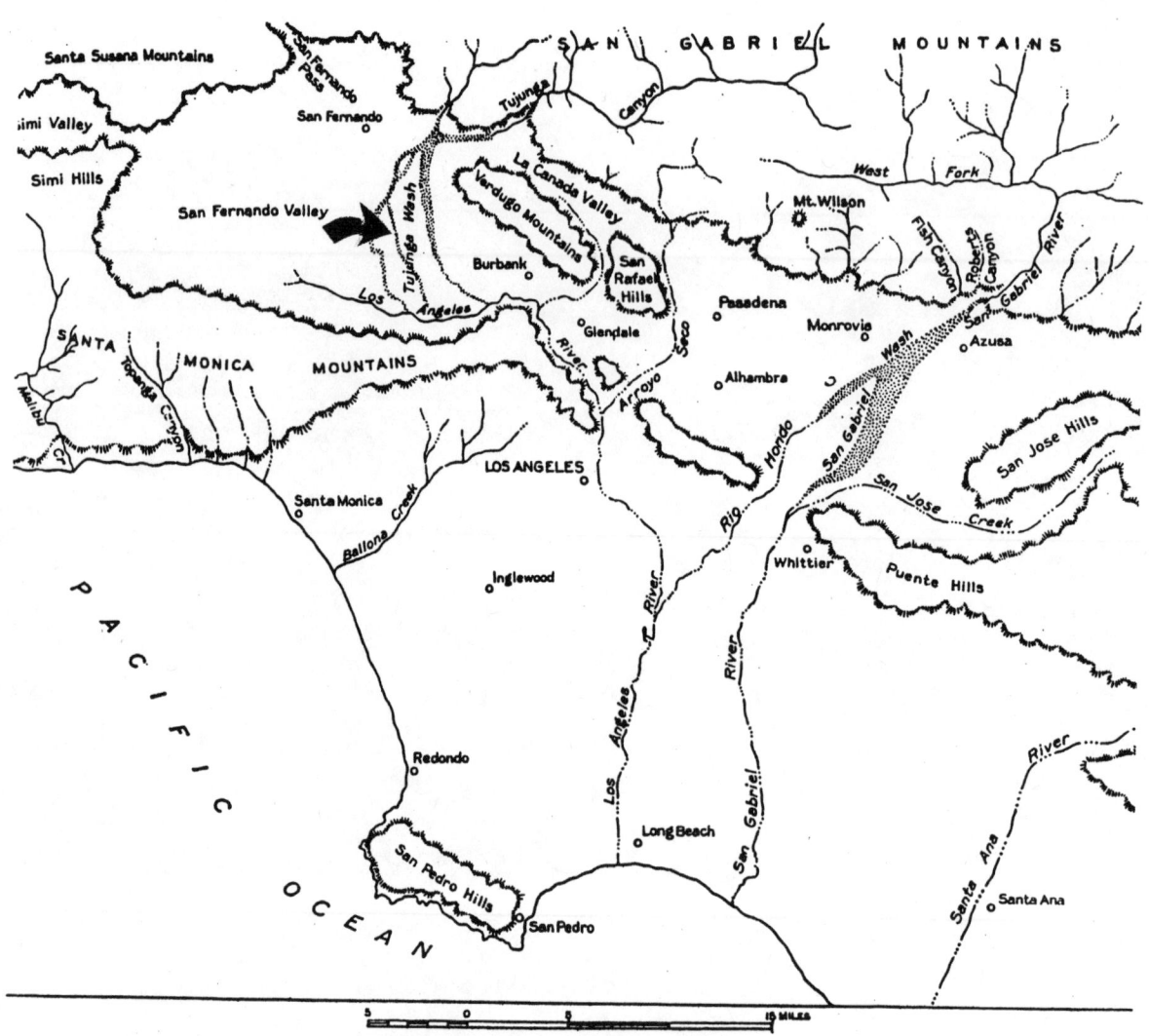

(*above*) This 1938 Department of the Interior, Water Paper no. 796.3 map, shows Tujunga Canyon and the Tujunga Wash. Sketch map of Tujunga and environs.

(*opposite, top*) Postcard of Begue's Barbecue, located at the southwest corner of Foothill Boulevard and Tujunga Canyon Boulevard, c. 1940. *From the personal collection of Lee Brown, Adventures in Postcards, Sunland, California.*

(*opposite, bottom*) Advertisements for Begue's Barbecue. *The Record-Ledger* (October 8, 1936, and December 10, 1936).

FRANCISCOA BEGUE

Announcing

The Opening On

Friday Evening, October 9

Of the New

Begue's Barbecue

Featuring

Noon Luncheons
Evening Dinners
Fountain Service

Try Begue's French Dinners, Served from 5:00 to 9:00 p. m.

A La Carte Service at All Hours
Open from 10:00 a. m. to 1:00 a. m.

Pit Barbecued Meats
Real Broiled Steaks

Foothill Blvd. at Tujunga Canyon Boulevard

DECEMBER 10, 1936

Let Our Chef
"THE KING OF SOUPS"
Serve You His Famous
French Onion Soup, Crab Gumbo, Vienese Potato Soup
Or His "None Better"
CLAM CHOWDER

Your Idea of a Good Meal Is Our Idea

FRIED NOODLE DINNER
With Minced Chicken and Cornfritters Will Delight You

Begue's Barbecue
Tujunga's Bright Spot
Foothill Blvd. at Tujunga Canyon Blvd.

FOUNDING SISTERS

SISTER ELSIE'S WELL.
Foothill Retirement Care Home, 6720 St. Estaban, c. 1999.

(*opposite*) In 1930, the Begues sold a portion of their property. New owners built the Hotel Tujunga with Sister Elsie's Well, located in the center of the patio, "Where Nature waits to help you."

FRANCISCOA BEGUE

Hotel Tujunga is Built Around the Famous Historical "Padre's Well"

Widely Known as a Health Spot

Climatic Conditions Equal to Famous Switzerland Resort, says U. S. Gov't. Report.

Elevation 2000 Ft. Located in the Green Verdugo Hills

BEAUTIFUL PATIO of HOTEL TUJUNGA

HOTEL TUJUNGA ROOM RATES - TUJUNGA, CALIFORNIA

WITHOUT MEALS
COMMUNITY TUB and SHOWER BATH

    Two Dollars ($2.00) per day, single
    Two Fifty ($2.50) per day, double
    Ten Fifty ($10.50) per week, single.
    Fourteen Dollars ($14.00) per week, dbl.

WITHOUT MEALS
PRIVATE TUB and SHOWER BATH

    Three Dollars ($3.00) per day, single
    Four Dollars ($4.00) per day, double
    Seventeen Fifty ($17.50) per week, single
    Twenty Five ($25.00) per week, double

WITH MEALS
COMMUNITY TUB and SHOWER BATH

    Three Fifty ($3.50) per day, single
    Six Fifty ($6.50) per day, double
    Twenty One ($21.00) per week, single
    Thirty Five ($35.00) per week, double

WITH MEALS
PRIVATE TUB and SHOWER BATH

    Five Fifty ($5.50) per day, single
    Nine Dollars ($9.00) per day, double
    Thirty Dollars ($30.00) per week, single
    Fifty Five Dollars ($55.00) per Wk. dbl.

Twin Beds—10% Extra on the above Rates
Children under eight years old—half price of above rates.

VIEW OF ONE OF OUR BED ROOMS

We extend to you and your friends a cordial invitation to visit this beautiful Hotel. This new Hotel Tujunga has been built to assist nature to cure chronical ailments such as, colds, asthma, bronchitis, hay-fever, rheumatism, neuritis and lumbago and similar ailments. Come to Hotel Tujunga—Nature waits to help you—Pleasures abundant Outdoor sports nearby —Hotel Tujunga is only 17 miles from Los Angeles.

Historian Viola Carlson and Don McLean stand above Sunland Park and point to Sister Elsie's Peak in a 1957 photograph. Sister Elsie's Peak was named in a U.S. geological map of 1896 but was later renamed Mt. Lukens, after an early mayor of Pasadena. *The Record-Ledger.*

El Descanso Ranch barn, c. 1979. *The Record-Ledger.*

El Descanso Ranch barn, c. 2000.
In 2001, the ranch was sold to the Korean Church and became "Joyland."
The barn was razed in 2005. *Courtesy of Author.*

Patrick and Catherine with children Robert and Ida May, and "Bobs," the family dog, on the porch of their home in 1924. *Courtesy of Ida May daSilva.*

Catherine Forster Blake
1888–1981

Catherine's was a life devoted to church, family, and community. She was kind hearted and generous to all, including the less fortunate, who often came to her front door on Mountair Avenue. She was known as the sweet lady who served sandwiches to the unemployed and homeless on her front porch.[1]

Catherine Forster was born and grew up in Sharpsburg, Pennsylvania, on the banks of the Allegheny River. The river often overflowed, forcing her family to move their furniture to the top floor of their home. Her father, Christian, born in Germany, was a barber and her mother, Mary, a busy homemaker. She had three sisters—Lillian, Mame, and Marcella—and four brothers—Joseph, Edward, Leo, and Jake.

Always a good student, Catherine excelled in spelling and writing. After graduation from school, she worked as a stenographer and telephone operator in Pittsburgh.

On an early trip to California, to visit her brothers, she met Patrick Blake, a real estate broker who promoted the health benefits of the Tujunga Valley. Major Blake was retired from the United States Army after serving in World War I. By the residents of the Tujunga Valley, he was addressed as Major Blake. In 1909, Catherine's father bought a tract of land opposite Major Blake's home on Cedar Street. He planned to bring his entire family west, but died before the journey began. His widow, Mary, brought her family west by train and became Major Blake's neighbor in 1917. Cedar Street, later to be named Mountair Avenue, was unpaved, strewn with rocks, and home to several of Catherine's brothers. They built their houses of stone close to their mother's home.[2]

On November 25, 1920, Patrick and Catherine were married in Glendale. Her brothers, by now accomplished stonemasons, helped Patrick build their two-bedroom home. Patrick, retired from the United States Army, Cavalry 4th Troop, started his real estate business on Michigan Avenue (Foothill) in 1921. Their property on Cedar Street was large, with an orchard and beautiful garden. Catherine tended the animals—a cow, horse, chickens, and turkeys—and sold eggs. Because her home was in such close proximity to her married brother and sisters, there were many family gatherings and camping trips to the mountains and Big Tujunga Canyon.[3]

Her family was an important part of her life. Her son, Robert, was born in 1921 and her daughter, Ida May, was born in 1924 and named after Catherine's good friend, Ida McGroarty.

Like her mother, Mary Forster, Catherine was a devout Catholic who attended Mass daily. There was no Catholic Church in Tujunga, so Mary set up an alter in her front room and Father Giuseppe (Joseph) Tonello held Mass there.[4] Thus began Our Lady of Lourdes Church. By the early 1920s, the number of parishioners grew too large for the house and a small church was built on Manzanita Drive on land donated by Ida McGroarty. Our Lady of Lourdes Church was later moved to Apperson and Commerce Streets. On September 18, 1924, following a long illness, Mary Forster died in her home on Cedar Street.

163

Despite her responsibilities at home, Catherine was active in the Altar Society. As well as work for the church, the society functioned as a social organization, holding card parties, luncheons, and bake sales. Catherine was fortunate to have excellent health and remained healthy well into her nineties. While in her eighties, she was the chauffeur for her friends, taking them to appointments and shopping. She had a disposition described as happy and peaceful. She didn't travel much, except to visit her family. Catherine's true joy was spending time in her garden, walking to church, and visiting the many friends she made over the years.

In 1952, her daughter, Ida May, married Leon daSilva at Our Lady of Lourdes Church and moved to San Francisco. Seven months later, Catherine's husband, "The Major," passed away in their home. He had just celebrated his eighty-fourth birthday. Catherine lived alone in her home for the next twenty-six years. In 1978, she moved to San Francisco to live out her days with her daughter. Her son, Robert, currently lives in Morro Bay, and her daughter continues to reside in San Francisco. Her niece, Jeraldine Saunders, who grew up in Tujunga, became famous when she authored the book *The Love Boat*, based on her experiences as one of the first women cruise directors.[5]

Catherine Blake was a woman who was characterized by her faith. Hers was a life well lived and devoted to helping others. She truly enjoyed living in Tujunga with its friendly, small town feeling.[6]

Notes

[1] Author's interview with Catherine's daughter, Ida May daSilva, June 20, 2000.

[2] "Tujunga Pioneer Dies at His Home," *The Record-Ledger* (September 4, 1952).

[3] Author's interview, June 20, 2000, op. cit.

[4] Father Tonello (1851–1933) was born in Turin, Italy, and was a member of the Order of Charity (Rosemenians). Ordained in Italy in 1878, he was sent to America and founded an Italian colony near Joliet, Illinois. His work with immigrants drew the attention and admiration of Jane Addams, founder of Hull Settlement Houses. Failing health brought him to California in 1912. His home in the Silverlake district of Los Angeles was a magnet to musicians and artists. An accomplished musician and musical composer, he was a friend of Enrico Caruso, as well as many world leaders. In 1923, he became only the second American priest to receive the honor of knight chaplain, first degree, of the Sacred Military Order of Saint George, with the title of monsignor. Information provided to the Author in a letter, dated January 28, 2004, from Monsignor Francis J. Weber, Archdiocese of Los Angeles Archival Center, Mission Hills, California.

[5] Author's interview with Jeraldine Saunders, September 1997, while cruising the waters off Alaska.

[6] Author's interview with Catherine's granddaughter, Mary daSilva, June 28, 2000.

Forster brothers' home on Mountair Avenue. Our Lady of Lourdes School now stands on this spot, c. 1919.

CATHERINE FORSTER BLAKE

Mary Forster in front of her home, built by her sons, Jake, Leo, Edward, and Joe, c. 1911. *Courtesy of Jeraldine Saunders.*

Marcella, Mary Forster and Catherine Blake (*left to right*) seated in Mary's parlor. Note the flag photograph over the fireplace, c. 1919. *Courtesy of Jeraldine Saunders.*

Mary Forster's home at 10342 Mountair across the street from Catherine's, c. 1924. *Courtesy of Ida May daSilva.*

165

FOUNDING SISTERS

(*left*) Monsignor Joseph Tonello, an Italian priest and musician, held the first service of Our Lady of Lourdes Church on October 17, 1920, in Mary Forster's home, c. 1923. Padre Tonello served until 1925 and passed away in Turin, Italy, in 1936 at the age of 82 years. *Courtesy of Our Lady of Lourdes Church.*

(*below*) Mary Forster's parlor became the first Catholic Church in Tujunga. Her fireplace was the altar, c. 1920. *Courtesy of Our Lady of Lourdes Church.*

(*opposite, top left*) This photograph of Major Blake and Catherine was printed on a wedding calendar, November 25, 1920. *Courtesy of Jeraldine Saunders.*

(*opposite, top right*) A proud Major Blake holds son Robert, c. 1922 *Courtesy of Jeraldine Saunders.*

(*opposite, bottom*) Catherine Blake in 1925. *Courtesy of Jeraldine Saunders.*

166

CATHERINE FORSTER BLAKE

> Have nothing in your houses
> which you do not know to be useful
> or believe to be beautiful.
> —*William Morris, 1880*

FOUNDING SISTERS

Catherine's home had a view of the entire Tujunga Valley. Note the fancy wall, c. 1920. *Courtesy of Ida May daSilva.*

The Blake family; Major Pat, Catherine, Ida and Robert (Lt. Col.), c. 1940s.

(right) 1925 Tujunga Telephone Directory advertisement for Major Blake's realty company.

(below) Major Blake's real estate office on southeast corner of Foothill Boulevard and Mt. Gleason Avenue, c. 1921.

FOUNDING SISTERS

(*left*) Ida May weds Leon daSilva. *The Record-Ledger* (February 28, 1952).

(*below*) Catherine receives a watch from Herb Rostand for winning a contest in the *Record-Ledger*, May 14, 1970.

CATHERINE FORSTER BLAKE

(*right*) On May 3, 1970, Cardinal Manning dedicated the new Our Lady of Lourdes Church at the corner of Tujunga Canyon Boulevard and Apperson Street. *Courtesy of Author.*

(*below*) Under Father Falvey's leadership, the second Our Lady of Lourdes Church was built on Mountair Avenue, at the site of the current lower school playground. Built of stone and wood in the English rural style, it seated 450 persons and served the community from 1941 to 1969.

(*below right*) This 32-foot-high stained glass window depicted the parish's patroness, Our Lady of Lourdes. The window is a memorial to Ida McGroarty. The window from the second Church was installed, along with the bell from the first Church, in the rose garden of the current Church. It was made by the Los Angeles Art Glass Company in 1941. *Courtesy of Our Lady of Lourdes Church..*

Alice at her home on Tujunga Canyon Boulevard,
holding the minutes of the Town Hall meetings and standing
in front of the regulator clock that hung in the post office.

Alice Carr Bolton
1881–1968

Alice Carr Bolton was a simple woman who lived a simple life. She and her father played an important role in the founding of the Little Lands Colony. Fortunately, she was always aware of the importance her father held in the community and she saved his papers, gavel, and Town Hall minutes in order that future generations would understand the development of Tujunga.

The building named Bolton Hall, or "The Clubhouse" as it was known to the colonists, was actually named after an attorney and writer from New York. Bolton Hall (the man, not the building) was a socialist and a founder of "Free Acres" in New Jersey. It was his friendship with the developer, Marshall Hartranft, and the promoter, William Smythe, that produced their inside joke. Bolton Hall never came to California and, therefore, never set foot into the building that bears his name. Alice spent a lifetime explaining that it was a mere coincidence her last name was Bolton. Her short marriage to Courtland Bolton brought much confusion in the later years.

Alice Genevieve Ashby Carr Bolton was born in Brookfield, Massachusetts, on May 18, 1881. She was the daughter of Emma Harrington and Fredrick Mason Ashby.[1] Nothing has been recorded of her life prior to coming to the Little Lands Colony with her father in 1911. Her father was a newspaper publisher in Brookfield and brought Alice to the Little Lands Colony, settling among the rocks and sagebrush of Hartranft's utopian colony. They lived on Greeley Street, named after Horace Greeley who always urged his readers to "go west, young man, go west."

From 1913 to 1915, Alice's father conducted the weekly town meetings, held at night in Bolton Hall. Fellow Little Lander Mabel Hatch recalls in her book, *The Green Verdugo Hills*,

> Every week we went to town meeting. It was held in the Club House and we all lighted our kerosene lanterns and trudged up the hill. We were weary in mind and body. Running behind a plow and throwing out rocks only to find when you go back over the field to plant your walnut trees you have to dig the holes with a pick, is neither refreshing nor encouraging. Furthermore, you take so much stone out of the hole, there isn't enough earth to plant the tree. But we went to town meeting.
>
> There was an old New England schoolmaster, Mr. Fred Ashby, in the colony and he originated the idea of the old time town meeting. He acted as moderator and everyone got up and told his troubles; troubles with rocks, with gophers, with trees that wouldn't grow and goats that wouldn't give milk and pigeons that died of disease and the rocks, always and always the rocks. Then there was the rattlesnake problem. That came in for considerable discussion.
>
> Mr. Ashby usually managed to keep things from getting entirely out of hand, whether it required turning the professor off or adding a whimsical note to a tale of woe to make us smile, or re-stating a problem with such logic and clearness we were made to see it was not beyond solution. Parliamentary law and the gavel settled all disputes and arguments. That was the beginning of government in Tujunga.[2]

Membership Certificate
Little Landers Store, Incorporated
Los Terrenitos, Los Angeles County, California

Certificate No. _____

This is to certify that *Fred M. Ashly* is a member of Little Landers Store, Incorporated, a co-operative business Association, organized under Section No. 653b, Title XX, Part 1, of the Civil Code of the State of California.

This certificate is executed under the authority and by direction of the Board of Directors of said Association. Dated this 23 day of August 1913, at Los Terrenitos, Los Angeles County, California.

Secretary — President

By 1916, the directors and stockholders of the Little Lands Co-operative Store in Tujunga voted to sell the store, its contents and the fixtures. It was considered a failure.

Alice recalled in her memoirs,

> Many issues came up in 1913–1914, as we scarcely had roads, and of course no sidewalks, lights or gas and the mail had to be brought up from La Crescenta by horse and buggy and the carrier brought up the correct time of day. That is when the big clock in the Post Office would be regulated so that all the hillbillies (as we were known) could set their watches and clocks.[3]

In 1914, Alice's father was appointed the first postmaster of Tujunga, holding the office until 1923, when Mrs. Nana Halferty succeeded him. She served until 1929. Prior to 1915, Frank Hall, the rural mail carrier for the La Cañada district, brought all the Tujunga mail "as far as the summit between La Crescenta and Tujunga, and George Buck, one of the earliest real estate dealers in Tujunga, brought the mail back to his office on Foothill Boulevard. The Little Landers gathered at his office and sorted the mail themselves."[4]

It was when the Colony applied for an actual post office that the movement to select a new name began. Most of the colonists disliked Los Terrenitos or Little Lands Colony. Mr. Ashby presided over the spirited meetings, and at one point it was suggested the town be called "Fairy Dell." Mabel Hatch's aunt laughed so loud it was heard all over the hall.[5]

The colony got its official post office on April 15, 1915, and shortly thereafter got a new name, Tujunga. No one seems to recall how the name Tujunga was selected, but later, when the town was thriving, several people claimed authorship.

Because Mr. Ashby's service as town hall moderator was voluntary, Marshall Hartranft gave Mr. Ashby the use of the post office building on the corner of Commerce Street and Valmont. After Mr. Ashby retired, Mr. Hartranft moved the post office building farther down Commerce, next to what was Johnson's Feed Store and is now Admart, and had it stuccoed over as a store.[6] Ashby's store featured post cards by Lamson, drugs and Halferty's homemade candy. As in most small towns, the store and post office were the traditional gathering place and where you could find out the latest news and gossip.

Publisher Wallace Morgan was fond of telling how the post office kept lists of people that left town and gave a forwarding address.[7] A lady named Rossi Gish, a cousin of the actress Lillian Gish (star of *The Birth of a Nation* [1915] and many other films), arrived in town one evening and was at the post office the very next morning. She had just one question: "How do you get out of this h___ hole?" The postal clerk answered her question, but before transportation could arrive to pick her up, she changed her mind and decided to stay. Her musical talents brought much joy to the town and she became a valued member of the community. She was rewarded by having a street in Tujunga named for her.

In November 1928, Alice's beloved father passed away from pneumonia at the age of seventy-three years. He was buried at Forest Lawn, Glendale.[8]

Alice was never very lucky in the marriage department. Her first husband, Joseph Edward Carr, died at the age of thirty-eight years, when their only child Charles was three.[9] Young Charles gave the widowed Alice and her father much delight.

> My father sat in the living room of our home at 127 Greeley Street and opened the midwinter edition of the *Los Angeles Times* for 1916. There were five supplements in color and when he came to the fifth—called *The Earth and Its Fullness*—there was a picture of our little boy—Chuck—Charles Carr. It was a great thrill to us and it was like winning a prize in a contest. Unknown to us—the *Times* photographer had cruised up through the foothills to find a suitable scene for its cover picture and found our boy sitting on the flagstone with two baby goats standing alongside. My father had a much better name for the picture, calling it "The Three Kids".[10]

The photo would remain a prized family possession.

In 1932, Alice's second husband, Courtland Bolton, died after only a few years of marriage. The twice-wid-

---

IN THE VALE OF MONTE VISTA
By Miss Winifred Steen
(Air of "Where the River Shannon Flows.")

There's a dear old spot near Sunland,
I'll always claim for my land;
Where the live oaks and yuccas
Shall ever, ever stand.
It's the land of the Little Landers,
In the Vale of Monte Vista;
In the sunshine or the shadow,
It's the only place for me.

Not a moment I'll be losing;
My home I'll now be choosing
In this vale of shade and sunshine,
There I'll settle down forever,
I'll leave the old place never,
'Tis the land of the Little Landers,
In the Monte Vista Vale.

CHORUS

In the Vale of Monte Vista,
Where the live oaks grow so fair,
Where my heart is, I am going,
To the soft and balmy air
Of the land of the Little Landers,
With its rolling hill and dazzle;
For there's not a country fairer
Than the Monte Vista Vale.

Compliments of the moderator

—Frederick Mason Ashby
Los Terrenitos, Cal.
October 28, 1913

In October 1913, moderator Ashby gave this poem to participants of his town meetings.

(*above*) Early photograph of the post office at Little Lands, c. 1914.

(*left*) "The Postmaster" c. 1920.

(*opposite*) "The Three Kids" c. 1916.

owed Alice lived alone at 10131½ Tujunga Canyon Boulevard. Her son, Charles Carr, had moved away and was living in Ventura, California. Alice's later years were spent confined to her home due to severe arthritis and several falls. When she was seventy-two, she wrote to a doctor, "My New England constitution has done more than anything else to keep me on the road up 'til now." She enjoyed a brief fame when the town and the members of the Little Landers Historical Society joined in the battle to save Bolton Hall from demolition by the City of Los Angeles. She was amused that so many newspaper reporters and people in general assumed Bolton Hall was named for her husband's family.

Alice knew that future generations would want to know about the origins of Tujunga and life in "The Vale of Monte Vista."[11] She donated her father's gavel, the town hall minutes, and the regulator clock to the newly formed Little Landers Historical Society in 1968, just months before her passing.

NOTES

[1] Record of Funeral, November 27, 1968, Bades Mortuary, Tujunga.
[2] Mabel Hatch and Wallace Morgan, *The Green Verdugo Hills—A Chronicle of Sunland-Tujunga, California and How It Grew* (Tujunga, Calif., 1956).
[3] "Facts About Bolton Hall" as recorded by Alice Carr Bolton, December 18, 1962, Bolton Hall Archives.
[4] "Little Landers Sorted First Mail Brought Into Tujunga by Frank Hall," *The Record Ledger Historical Edition*, September 12, 1968.
[5] Hatch, op. cit.
[6] Bolton, op. cit.
[7] Wallace Morgan, "Tujunga's Post Office opened in 1915," *The Record Ledger*. Bolton Hall clippings file.
[8] Record of Funeral, November 8, 1928, Bades Mortuary, Tujunga.
[9] "Long Illness Ends for Joseph E. Carr," *The Record-Ledger*, 1922.
[10] Alice C. Bolton, "My Story," March 1954, Bolton Hall Museum.
[11] Song written by Winifred Steen and given out by her father at a meeting at Bolton Hall on October 28, 1913. The Vale of Monte Vista refers to the Sunland-Tujunga valley.

(*above*) The southwest corner of Commerce and Valmont. By 1927, the post office had moved across the street.

(*below*) Postmaster Ashby (top of photo) holds daily session of "Millionaires Club of Happiness & Contentment." John S. McGroarty made the group famous in his weekly column in the *Los Angeles Times*, c. 1923.

Laura Jessup Bryson
1881–1965

Family legend says that the highlight of Laura's life was dancing with the prince of Wales.[1] Living with husband Carl was almost as exciting. Laura Elizabeth Jessup was born on September 29, 1881, in New York, to Albert and Mary Laura (Farmer) Jessup.[2] Laura's mother was born in Birmingham, England, and her father was born in Keokuk, Iowa. Albert Henry Jessup was a Methodist minister, and Laura's childhood was one of rules and a strict behavior code.

Laura met Carl Bryson in Chicago, Illinois, and married the fun-loving man at Fort Madison, Iowa, on April 21, 1904. The serious-minded Laura and the electrician Carl, with his great sense of humor, would have many adventures while they lived in Costa Rica and Panama.[3]

Daughter Isabel was born in 1907 and daughter Genevieve in 1910. In 1914, the family moved to Panama, where Carl worked on the Panama Canal.[4] While Laura and her family were living in this tropical paradise, her mother passed away in 1915 and her father in 1916.[5] Their time in Central America left their daughters, Isabel and Gene, with a lifetime love of all things tropical. Isabel would later marry a man from Mexico and become a permanent resident of Mexico City, where she taught English.

Shortly after the turn of the century, at the time of her parents' deaths, Carl and Laura bought two lots in Tujunga on Mountair Avenue. They built a small wooden home to be used primarily as a vacation getaway. The Brysons returned to the United States in the early 1920s and lived in Long Beach while Carl was employed by the Los Angeles Water and Power Company. He was forced into an early retirement when he

Laura (wearing black skirt) loved hats. In this 1920 photograph, she appears with an unidentified friend and children.
Courtesy of Barbara Hughes.

179

(*above*) Unidentified workers on the Panama Canal. Carl was fortunate to not be included in the 25,000 workers who lost their lives to tropical disease and accidents. Landslides were frequent during dredging and the installation of forty-six massive lock gates. Undated photograph. *Courtesy of Pat Kerr.*

(*below*) Carl Bryson in a 1919 travel photograph taken in Costa Rica. *Courtesy of Barbara Hughes.*

(*opposite*) Laura and daughters Isabel (*left*) and Genevieve explore the ruins in old Panama. Taken in front of the Tower of San Jerome, c. 1917. *Courtesy of Barbara Hughes.*

was struck with 33,000 volts of electricity (three times the amount used to kill a man in the electric chair). In the late 1930s, because of Carl's accident and retirement, the family took up permanent residence on the two-lot acreage in Tujunga. Laura's new role was caretaker for Carl and the property. Carl succumbed to his injuries on August 2, 1945.[6]

Laura's daughter, Genevieve, returned home to live with her mother following her marriage and divorce to Douglas Roesch. Laura's new role was to keep house and raise her two grandchildren, Roland and Barbara.

Genevieve, "Gene" as they called her, went to work at Lockheed Aircraft Plant during World War II. She was an original "Rosie the Riveter" and joined a labor force of 19 million women who left housework and took on the jobs vacated by the men fighting the war.[7] In 1990, World War II's "Rosies" received their own park, on the site of the former Kaiser Shipyard in Richmond, California. The Rosie the Riveter Memorial stands as a testament to the women who rolled up their sleeves and went to work for their country.

Laura Bryson stood "tall" at 4 feet, 11 inches, but

she was a feisty bundle of energy, sometimes referred to as "dynamite." Along with raising her grandchildren, Laura's later years were filled with volunteer work in community organizations in Tujunga and the PTA in which she attained a life membership. She was a good friend of fellow Tujungan Cora Corrigan (also under 5 feet tall). Together the two ladies battled Los Angeles City Hall to prevent a rock crushing plant from locating at the entrance to Big Tujunga Canyon. Cora and Laura fought hard to preserve the air quality of Tujunga that drew so many health seekers to the area.

Tragedy struck on March 13, 1965, when Laura was getting out of bed. She fell and fractured her left leg. Nine days later, she died of a heart attack.[8] The Bryson home is currently occupied by Laura's granddaughter, Barbara, and her husband, Harry Hughes. Portions of Laura and Carl's wall is still visible on the property. Daughter Genevieve passed away in 1997 at the age of ninety. Her grandson Roland lives in Glendale and Barbara, like her grandmother, is a community activist, past president of the Chamber of Commerce, journalist, and renowned artist. She helped initiate the first "Old Town Street Faire" and the Fourth of July celebration at Verdugo Hills High School, her alma mater. Barbara is a journalist at the local newspaper, *The Record-Ledger* and like Laura, has a deep love of her community and has worked very hard to see her beloved Tujunga revitalized.

Notes

[1] Author's interview with Barbara Hughes, October 16, 1997.

[2] State of California, Certificate of Vital Records, March 26, 1965.

[3] Author's interview with Barbara Hughes. March 22, 2001.

[4] A treaty between the United States and Panama in 1903 gave the United States the right to build the canal. The main work was completed in 1914 and the canal was opened April 15, 1914. A massive landslide closed the canal in 1915–16. Carl was then rehired as an electrician on the project at the wage of one dollar per hour. President Wilson officially opened the canal on July 12, 1920.

[5] Author's interview with Barbara Hughes, March 24, 2001.

[6] State of California, Certificate of Vital Records, August 2, 1945.

[7] Researcher and teacher of women's studies at Cal State–Long Beach, Sherna Gluck interviewed Gene and her fellow "Rosies" for a 45-volume oral history project in 1983. Ms. Gluck contends that the real "Rosies" sowed the seeds for the Women's Movement twenty years later. "Revisiting the Riveting Rosies 40 Years Later," *Los Angeles Times* (March 1983).

[8] State of California, Certificate of Vital Records, March 26, 1965.

FOUNDING SISTERS

In this 1916 photograph, Carl lays the corner stone of the family home at 10818 Mountair.
Courtesy of Barbara Hughes.

(*above*) A proud Laura stands in the doorway of her newly completed weekend home, c. 1920.

(*left*) Laura poses in the driveway of their now permanent home, c. 1930s. *Both photos courtesy of Barbara Hughes.*

(*above*) Researcher Sherna Gluck addresses a group of "Rosies" who worked in the aircraft industry during World War II. "Gene" is seated under the arrow, c. 1983. *Courtesy of Barbara Hughes.*

(*left*) On October 18, 1999, Barbara was honored by the Sunland-Tujunga Business and Professional Women as their 1999 Woman of Achievement. *Courtesy of Author.*

Edna Rising Buck
1854–1916

She was to live just three short years in the Little Landers Colony and was surprised to become the "poster girl" for the House of Little Landers. M. V. Hartranft used photographs of Edna and her house and garden in many newspaper advertisements, throughout the Southland and the United States to extol the virtues of healthy living in the Vale of Monte Vista.

Edna was born in Michigan on February 24, 1854 to Flora and J. G. Rising.[1] Little is known of her life prior to coming to the colony except that she lived on a small farm with her husband, George, and children, Clarence and Edna Belle, in Monarch, Montana.

After a brief visit to their friend Marshall Hartranft's Lazy Lonesome Ranch in 1912, they returned to Montana to sell their farm, happy to leave the harsh winters behind. Their son, Clarence, had already moved to Red Bluff, California. Soon after their move, their grandson Leslie would also come to Tujunga and stay for the next seventy years.

Edna's husband was kept busy selling real estate from his small office on the north side of Marcus and Foothill Boulevard. He was to own acreage in Haines Canyon, on St. Estaban Street and Sunset Avenue (now Commerce Avenue). Not only was he involved in real estate, as Hartranft's agent, he also ventured into the insurance business. George and Edna were active participants in the many social events in the newly formed colony.

Although Edna was suffering from colon cancer, she was able to keep up with her energetic husband. She helped clear the land and planted an extensive vegetable garden and many rose bushes that were enjoyed by all who passed by their cottage.[2] Like numerous older aged Little Landers, Edna's joy was her garden and her grandchildren.

On August 15, 1916, Edna passed away at her cottage and was buried the next day at Forest Lawn Cemetery in Glendale. Her husband would live until 1933, marrying a second wife, Eva.[3]

Both Leslie Buck and Arthur Buck, Edna's grandchildren, stood in front of Bolton Hall the day the cornerstone was laid and would return to the hall many times before their deaths in 1997 and 1999.[4]

Although Edna's time in the colony was brief, she considered it the best part of her life. She explored the neighboring towns and took delight in seeing the Pacific Ocean and the amusements the beach towns provided. She was truly a "happy Little Lander."

Notes

[1] State of California, Certificate of Vital Records, August 16, 1916.
[2] Author's telephone interview with Edna's grandson, Arthur Buck, March 25, 1997. Leslie Buck suffered a debilitating stroke in the early 1980s that left him unable to speak or write.
[3] Record of Funeral, April 19, 1933, Bades Mortuary, Tujunga.
[4] Author's interview, March 25, 1997, op. cit.

(above) Edna and George "over" Long Beach. Photograph was taken in a studio with a canvas backdrop, c. 1912.

(left) George, Edna and daughter, Edna Bell, at the family home near Monarch, Montana, prior to arriving at the Little Lands Colony, c. 1911.

In this 1913 newspaper advertisement, Edna Belle, George, and Edna pose in front of their newly built cottage. Note the young trees.

Edna poses in front of her rose-covered cottage on St. Estaban Street, c. 1915

FOUNDING SISTERS

> The kiss of sun for pardon,
> The song of birds for mirth—
> One is nearer God's heart in a garden
> Than anywhere else on earth.
> —*Dorothy Gurney, 1925*

(*left*) In 1914, the House of Little Landers featured Edna's home in their advertisement with the caption, "2000 feet above Sea-Level at the Rim—Rock Base of High Mountains in the Vale of Monte Vista—in a Balmy Mountain Climate and Location That Only Little Landers and Millionaires Can Afford to Occupy." *The L.A. Express* (June 14, 1914).

(*opposite, top*) George and Edna in their garden, c. 1915.

(*opposite, bottom*) Edna and George attended the Dedication Ball at Bolton Hall on August 16, 1913. The new colony celebrated the completion of the "Clubhouse."

```
                                    Grand March ......................
                                      1. Waltz .......................
 Little Landers                       2. Two-Step ....................
                                      3. Waltz .......................
 Dedication Ball                      4. Quadrille ...................
                                      5. Two-Step ....................
                                        Song.
                                      6. Waltz .......................
  Saturday Evening                    7. Two-Step ....................
  August 16, 1913                     8. Rye Waltz ...................
                                      9. Two-Step ....................
                                     10. Schottische .................
                                     11. Two-Step ....................
                                     12. Waltz .......................
                                        Extras ......................
                                               ......................
                                               ......................
                                               ......................
```

Edna poses with grandson Leslie in front of her cottage on St. Estaban near Marcus. They are sitting on seats wedged between trees.

George pictured in front of his first real estate office located on Foothill Boulevard. *The Record-Ledger.*

EDNA RISING BUCK

(*above*) In this 1925 photograph, the Millionaires Club is on the porch of Rancho Chupa Rosa.

(*left to right*) Wallace Morgan (publisher), Leo Lang (fire warden), M. V. Hartranft (developer), Captain Hatch, Mr. Eby (the man who played the flute), George Buck (the man who played the phonograph) and John S. McGroarty (author).

191

Nana and Nanette share a special moment on a picnic in 1936.
Courtesy of Nan Chapman Matuska.

Nana Mae Chapman
1892–1983

She survived a childhood filled with tragedy and went on to become one of the best known and respected citizens of Tujunga. Her unusual wedding in the clouds made her famous around the world.

Nana Mae MacKenzie was born on July 5, 1892, in Missouri, to R. J. MacKenzie and his wife.[1] Shortly after Nana's birth, her mother died, leaving her to be raised by her father. When she was five years old, the United States Army sent her father to the Philippines to fight in the Spanish-American War. He was killed on duty and his body shipped home. Five-year-old Nana was then sent to Indiana to be raised by a strict aunt and uncle.[2]

Nana's life with her aunt and uncle was not a happy chapter in her long life. She was quite young when she met and married Lloyd Halferty, an accountant. They were blessed with two daughters, Ruth and Doris.

Lloyd's health was fragile due to a case of tuberculosis, so his doctor suggested they move to a warmer and drier climate. As many before and many after, the couple set out for Tujunga in search of health. They came from Indiana in 1920 and bought a house at 10358 Las Lunitas Avenue. After Nana arrived in Tujunga with her sick husband and two girls to look after, it was imperative that she find work. Although Lloyd had begun making candy at home and for a while sold his homemade candy at Zoe Gilbert's store, next to the post office on Commerce Avenue, it was not enough to support the family. Nana went to work at the Tujunga Post Office and in 1923, at the age of thirty-one, she was appointed the third postmaster of Tujunga, the second woman to hold the post (Susan Siegler was the first postmaster from 1914 to 1915; Frederick Ashby was postmaster from 1915 until 1923).

Nana was now the breadwinner of the family and raising two daughters while her husband was still reaching for a return of health. On July 28, 1928, Lloyd passed away from pulmonary problems caused by his tuberculosis. He was just thirty-seven years old.[3]

Two years later, while attending the State Postal Convention in Oakland, California, a very special event happened in Nana's life. On July 19, 1930, she married Roy E. Chapman, a rancher from Oregon. Nana had met Roy earlier at a dance in Los Angeles. The ceremony took place in a tri-motored Fokker airplane, circling Oakland Airport at 2,000 feet. True to her love of everything connected to the post office, she was married by the postmaster of Oakland (also an ordained minister).[4] News of their unique ceremony, the first of its kind in Oakland, appeared in newspapers throughout the United States and overseas. It could be said that Nana went "postal" before the word took on a new meaning.

After a difficult decision whether to live in California or Oregon, Roy and Nana came to Los Angeles and lived in a rental unit. When Nana became pregnant, at the age of forty-one, she returned with Roy to Tujunga and her old home on Las Lunitas Street. Her third daughter, Nanette, was born in 1933. It was a surprise and delight to become a mother again at that

FOUNDING SISTERS

Nana Halferty and Roy Chapman (*left*) are shown boarding the airplane, which carried them to a marriage in the clouds. *The Oakland Tribune* (July 20, 1930) *Courtesy of* The Oakland Tribune.

> When a great adventure is offered—
> you don't refuse it.
> —*Amelia Earhart*

> **ASKS LOCAL PEOPLE TO OBSERVE AIR MAIL DAY**
>
> Mrs. Nana M. Halferty, Tujunga postmaster, asks the people of Tujunga to observe "Air Mail Day" on Tuesday September 20, the day Col. Lindbergh will visit in Los Angeles.
>
> Postal authorities are endeavoring to achieve a new record in volume of air mail on that date in honor of the flyer. Mail going north or east should be sent by air mail if possible if possible.

In this September 1927 article, Nana makes a request of fellow Tujungans.

age. With her work years behind her, she relished the role of wife and mother.

Nana saw many changes in the growth of Tujunga and the post office that had three addresses on Commerce before finally arriving at its current location. In 1922, the Post Office was changed from 4th to 3rd class. In 1926, it became 2nd class, and in 1938, city delivery service was started with one city route and one rural and one part-time route. By 1940, the post office had arrived at a first-class rating. On May 13, 1967, Nana Chapman was an honored guest at the dedication of the new Tujunga Post Office at 10209 Tujunga Canyon Boulevard.

Nana was one of many businesswomen who challenged themselves when faced with an ill or dying husband. Like Lydia M. Dean, Nana just did what circumstances dictated. She was proud to serve as the city's third postmaster from 1923 to 1929.[5] Roy Chapman passed away in 1969, but Nana remained in the family home, where she passed away on April 10, 1983 at the age of ninety-one.[6]

The Record-Ledger photograph of Nana in her later years.

Notes

[1] State of California, Certificate of Vital Records. April 14, 1983.
[2] Author's interview with Nan Matuska, Nana's daughter. September 6, 2000.
[3] Record of Funeral. July 30, 1928. Bades Mortuary, Tujunga.
[4] *Oakland Tribune* (July 20, 1930).
[5] Obituary, *The Record-Ledger* (April 27, 1983).
[6] State of California, Certificate of Death. April 13, 1983.

The lovely Nellie, c. 1910.
Courtesy of Camp Colby Museum.

Ma Colby in her later years, c. 1930s.
Courtesy of Camp Colby Museum.

Nellie Colby
1872–1914

Lillian Colby
1854–1927

Even though a street in Santa Monica bears their name and Colby is on the present-day map of the San Gabriel Mountains, Nellie and Lillian Colby are, perhaps, better known as the "forgotten ladies of the Canyon."

There was a time, though, at the turn of the century, when every traveler passing through the San Gabriel Mountains knew of the Colbys' hospitality. Their ranch was located under the great granite cliffs of Strawberry Peak (elevation 6,164 feet) in Coldwater Canyon. It was accessible by going up the Big Tujunga Canyon or hiking eight miles from Switzer's Camp in the Arroyo Seco.

Nellie and Lillian's story is one of adventure, drama and, ultimately, tragic decline. They survived fires, floods, deep snows, and desolation but, ultimately, the isolation took its toll.

Lillian's husband, Delos, placer-mined along the Big Tujunga Canyon and Wickiup Creek, in the San Gabriel Mountains. In 1889, he discovered a hidden mountain glen with isolated streams, lush ferns, and wild strawberries and became determined to live in this enchanting place. His life in the isolated glen would be far removed from that of a Laramie, Wyoming, saloonkeeper.[1]

Nellie's parents, Lillian and Delos, came to southern California during the real estate boom of the 1880s. The family attempted farming in the Santa Monica area but found real estate a more lucrative business—until the economic crash of 1888–89 left them destitute.

Delos Colby had invested several thousand dollars of his mother's and friends' money into building the Pullman Hotel (later named the Parker House Hotel) on East Fifth Street in downtown Los Angeles. As the investment soured, Delos took his remaining $13.50 and bought food and supplies. He headed up Big Tujunga Canyon to go about the business of gold mining. He built himself a crude cabin and, at one point, was making $10 to $15 a day mining dust and nuggets. In the autumn of 1891, Delos filed a homestead patent for 320 acres and built a small wood cabin. He later added extensive stone walls and walkways and expanded the cabin to two stories.

In 1896, Nellie and Lillian left Los Angeles and joined Delos at the ranch. Being descendants of pioneer Michigan families, Delos and Lillian were well prepared for the gigantic task of clearing the land.[2] They planted an apple orchard, a cherry orchard, and a garden of vegetables, alfalfa, and berries along the stream that flowed through the property. Delos built a reservoir, sawmill, and barn, and also added a kitchen and dining room to the cabin.

Lillian Colby's reputation for good vitals became well known throughout the Southland. Although slight of build, she was muscular and could do the work of two men. Like a true mountain woman, she played the harmonica and smoked a pipe.[3]

Supplies were brought to the ranch by pack mule, either over the range from Acton or up sixteen miles of narrow, crooked trail from the mouth of the Arroyo Seco. Delos and his daughter, Nellie, used donkeys to bring a 600-pound piece of sawmill equipment up the trail. With the weight of the machine continually shifting, this was no easy task.

Just as life was settling down, Delos left his family to find adventure and fortune in the Alaska Klondike gold rush of 1897. He became ill while there and never regained his health. It would be two years before he returned to the ranch. In Delos' absence, Nellie and Lillian did their best to keep the ranch going. Neighbors helped, but it was an impossible task. The girls had plenty of produce—difficult to pack out twenty miles to market—but little money. In order to balance things out, they decided to advertise the ranch as a resort. Colby's soon became a popular stopping place for hikers and prospectors.

The ladies became well known not only for the resort but their heroism as well. Nellie single-handedly brought supplies by mule train, at night, for the firefighters during the forest fire of 1897. Winter was always a challenge for the ladies. One winter, visitors to the ranch were trapped by snow. The ladies shoveled their way through the snow and led the visitors out over the dangerous cliffs. On March 20, 1909, the gas balloon American left Tournament Park in Pasadena, with Captain Mueller and his five passengers aloft for a trip to San Bernardino. An updraft sucked the balloon to 13,000 feet, where the group experienced a horrific storm. Forced to land, the men spent a miserable night in rain and hail in Grotto Canyon near Strawberry Peak. The next day, it snowed heavily. The exhausted and nearly frozen men stumbled into Camp Colby that afternoon. Lillian Colby told the men to strip and gave them each a towel to wear while their clothes dried.

(*above*) The Colbys' home in 1916. Building at far left was Nellie and Lillian's first house. *Courtesy of Camp Colby Museum.*

(*right*) Lillian and Delos in front of their cabin, c. 1916. *Courtesy of Camp Colby Museum.*

(*opposite*) Entrance to Big Tujunga Canyon and the Angeles Forest as viewed in a 1947 Chamber of Commerce brochure.

FOUNDING SISTERS

(*above*) This 1905 photo shows the dirigible on the grounds of the Raymond Hotel in Pasadena. The Colbys' rescue of the 1909 wayward balloon made front-page news throughout the United States.

(*below*) When the exhausted balloonists stumbled upon the Colby Ranch, they thought they were in heaven. (*left to right*) Captain Mueller, Edwen Dobschutz, Nellie Colby, Lane Gilliam, Delos Colby, Lillian "Ma" Colby, Sidney Cray and Richard Halsted. Photograph was taken by balloonist Harold A. Parker, c. 1909. *Courtesy of Mrs. Donald Parker.*

Nellie Colby in front of her remodeled house. Note leaning barn to the right, c. 1914
Courtesy of Camp Colby Museum.

Nellie came forward with hot ginger tea while Lillian cleaned out her cupboards and put a real feast out for the suffering voyagers. Delos told the men it was the worst blizzard in the eighteen years he had been there. On Tuesday morning, after a hearty meal, the men were led out of the canyon, over Josephine Saddle to Switzer's Camp. Two long blasts of the big steam whistle at the Pasadena Power Plant let the town know the men were safe. Tuesday afternoon, the *Pasadena Daily News*, in an extra edition, reported the miraculous tale of survival. The reputation of the Colbys' hospitality spread far and wide. Days later, the balloon's 105-pound gondola was removed from Strawberry Peak (less than a mile from the Colby Ranch) by seven men. Lillian and Nellie forever won the hearts of the six survivors and the Southland.[4]

A visitor to the ranch once described Nellie thus: "Miss Colby was a typical mountaineer, did a man's work, played better poker than her dad and was a top mule packer; she had a voice that would have won a hog calling contest and employed many burro-encouraging adjectives extraordinaire."[5] Despite the colorful description of her persona, it was also said Nellie's beauty attracted many suitors. She eventually married a young man from Los Angeles who, shortly after the marriage, enlisted in the army and left during the Spanish-American War. In 1904, Joe Argay, then a chef at the California Club in Los Angeles, came to the ranch. He fell in love with the beautiful scenery and with Nellie. In 1911, Joe gave up his city job and moved onto the ranch, where he could be with Nellie.

By 1914, Nellie was gravely ill with throat cancer. Her unfaithful husband returned but refused her parents' request that he stay and care for her. He then mysteriously disappeared. It wasn't until 1926 that a possible answer to his disappearance came to light. Joe was out in a field on the ranch when he discovered a skeleton with a bullet hole right between its eyes.[6]

Just prior to Nellie's death, Joe promised to stay on and help her parents with the heavy ranch work. Within four years, her father would pass away, leaving her mother, Lillian, and poor Joe Argay with only memories. Both Nellie and Delos were buried on the property.

The decline in hikers and World War I brought about some economic hardship to the ranch. Joe, alone to do the heavy work, could not keep up. Soon nature reclaimed the orchards and fields. A severe drought finished it off. Today, there are still some surviving apple trees, planted by the Colbys, on the hillside behind the cabins. Lillian, her mind deteriorating from the stress, could take no more hardship.[7] Five years prior to her death, Lillian had been engaged to marry a gold prospector named Tom Clark. A few days before the wedding, to the bewilderment of their friends, the ceremony was called off.[8]

On November 2, 1927, Lillian made the decision to end her loneliness and her life. Friends reported she had been in poor health and very despondent. At 9:00 P.M., the crackling of flames awakened Joe Argay. He ran to Lillian's cabin and tried to enter the inferno. He was burned on the right leg and right side of his face as he attempted to enter her cabin.

Lillian had doused the house with kerosene, locked herself in, lay down on her bed and put a bullet to her head.

Joe called John Opid, proprietor of Opid's Camp five miles away, for help to extinguish the blaze. Forest fire fighters arrived from Barley Flats. The foresters protected the nearby mountains from the spread of the fire.[9] The next day, the front page of the *Pasadena Evening Post* carried the banner "Hill Woman Lights Own Death Pyre" and her photo. The Pasadena *Star-News* was kinder with a front-page column entitled "Death of Mrs. L. Colby is a Mystery."

A funeral was held at the ranch presided over by Rev.

Frank Stevens, then pastor of the Lake Avenue Methodist Church in Pasadena. He had a cabin near Switzer's Camp.[10] At Camp Colby, there is a stone obelisk that holds the marble grave-markers of the three Colbys.

The faithful Joe Argay had been promised the ranch but Lillian died without a will. The property went to her nearest relatives, the Moultons, who lived in Verdugo City. The Moultons sold the property to H. K. Koebig in 1936. Mr. Koebig removed the welcome mat—hikers were not allowed on the property and "No Trespassing" signs were posted. Joe went on to build himself a squatter's cabin off the property. He named his home "The Hermitage," where he lived alongside Strawberry Creek until 1940. Joe was laid to rest in the Colby cemetery near his beloved Nellie.

In 1945, the Colby Ranch was sold to the Methodist Church who now operates it as a year-round recreational retreat. The camp covers 373 acres of land at an elevation of 3,600 feet and can accommodate 195 guests. Its appearance is far different from the Colby's time. The graveside monument is all that stands as a reminder of happier days when the Colbys lived in paradise.

Notes

[1] "A Mountain Gem," *Trails Magazine* 5 (Winter 1938): 11.
[2] Ibid.
[3] Donald L. Parker, *Perilous Voyage of the Balloon American* (Pasadena: self-published, Castle Press, 1993).
[4] Ibid.
[5] John W. Robinson, *The San Gabriels... Southern California Mountain Country* (San Marino: Golden West Books, 1977), 189.
[6] Ibid. p. 190.
[7] "A Mountain Gem," op. cit.
[8] "Hill Woman Lights Own Death Pyre," *Pasadena Evening Star* (November 3, 1927).
[9] Ibid.
[10] "Death of Mrs. L. Colby is Mystery," *Pasadena Star-News* (November 3, 1927).

(*right*) Ma Colby prepares hot tea for the cold and hungry balloonists. Her stove and canned preserves are on exhibit at the Methodist Church Camp Museum. Photograph was taken by balloonist Harold A. Parker on Sunday, March 21, 1909. *Courtesy of Mrs. Donald Parker.*

(*opposite*) Ma Colby and her closest relative, Mrs. Moulton of Verdugo City. *Courtesy of Camp Colby Museum.*

(*right*) Joe Argay—the man who never stopped loving Nellie. *Courtesy of Camp Colby Museum.*

(*below*) The Lonely Joe Argay, c. 1935 *Trails Magazine*, Winter 1937.

(*opposite, top*) This 1914 photograph shows a group climbing Strawberry Peak (6,164 ft.) during the Golden Age of Hiking. *Courtesy of John W. Robinson.*

(*opposite, bottom*) This 1918 photograph shows present-day infirmary and pioneer cabins. *Courtesy of Camp Colby Museum.*

FOUNDING SISTERS

(*clockwise from top*) The cement foundation and stairs are all that remain of Lillian's two-story cabin. *Courtesy of Author.*

Camp Colby's Steven's Hall (dining room) also houses a 10-by-20-foot museum. Inside is Lillian's stove, canned preserves, cooking utensils, farm equipment and a guest logbook. Note Joe's house sign on the wall outside the museum room. *Courtesy of Author.*

Colby's obelisk graveside monument at Camp Colby. *Courtesy of Author.*

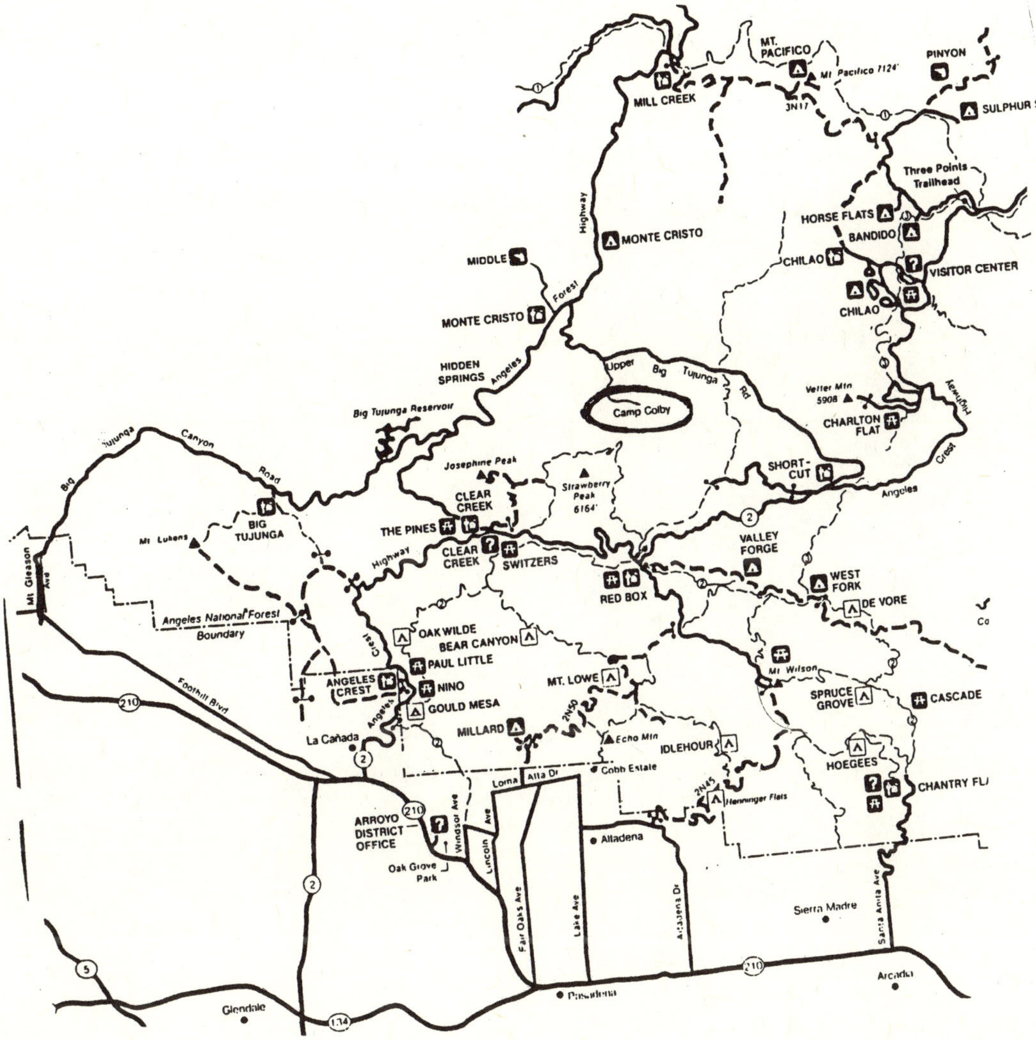

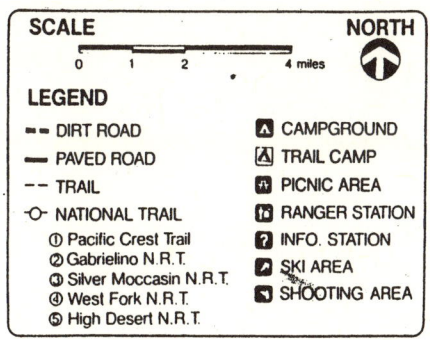

ARROYO SECO RANGER DISTRICT
ANGELES NATIONAL FOREST

In this 1922 photo, Lydia, Darius, and son Charles stand in front of their home at 7037 St. Estaban Street.

Lydia May Dean
1850–1938

Mrs. Lydia Dean, proprietor of Tujunga's Pioneer Store, was proud to state that she was the only great-grandmother in active business life in the Tujunga Valley. At the age of eighty-three years, she finally retired from commercial trade when she sold the family's dry goods store, Dean & Company. The year was 1933 and she would have just five short years to enjoy her garden and family.

The Little Lands Colony once had a co-operative store that burned down after only one year of operation. Arson was the suspected cause. Lydia and her husband, Darius, built their wood-frame store next to the post office and moved in June 1, 1914. Dean & Company quickly became a favorite gathering place for the residents of the colony. The store was small but was said to carry everything from calico to mousetraps.

Little Lander Gladys Maygrove recalls, "Mrs. Dean ran a little dry goods store that was on the same side of the street as the Club House. She and her son, Charlie, managed the tiny shop. Every lady in the community seemed to sew in those days. Material was 10 cents a yard and the *fancy kind* a few cents higher. Mrs. Dean had in stock a very few store made dresses and they sold for 50 cents a piece."[1]

Shopping in Glendale and Los Angeles was an all-day event in the valley's early years. It took a round trip by bus and a long trudge up the hill at the end of an exhausting day. Having a purchase delivered to the house was almost impossible, as most of the downtown merchants had little or no idea where Little Lands Colony or Los Terrenitos was located. Having Dean & Company in town saved time and energy for the work weary colonists.

During her twenty-nine years in business, Lydia missed only two days of work: the day she buried her husband and the day she buried her son in 1923.[2] Every day, in winter and summer, Lydia would walk from her home at 7037 St. Estaban Street to the store and, rain or shine, walked home again at night. She bragged that she hadn't seen a doctor in forty years; however, her health had not always been so robust.

Lydia May, who was born in Adrian, Michigan, had come to Ventura, California, in 1874, suffering from respiratory problems. After four years of California's healthy climate, she returned to Michigan, cured. Lydia married Darius, had two children and returned to California in 1912 to live in Los Angeles. Unhappy with living in the "city," the family moved to the Little Lands Colony in 1913. They were present at the laying of the cornerstone for Bolton Hall on April 12, 1913. This date was always celebrated as the anniversary of the colony. The laying of the cornerstone was an all-day event, a party enjoyed by over two hundred participants. Shortly thereafter, Lydia's daughter married Grant Williams and moved to Glendale.

Life was difficult for the early colonists, their worst enemy being nature and all its wrath. Late into the first year of the colony, an extensive fire denuded the hills. In February 1914, there were heavy rains and massive flooding of the area. Lydia's photograph was taken on the roof of her chicken house, at her home on Los Robles Avenue (St. Estaban).[3] Five feet of mud and silt were washed into her home, and it was weeks before the family could return to the house. Lydia's indignation over the city's lack of disaster and repair assistance is evidenced in her letter, dated October 1, 1915, to the Los Angeles Board of Supervisors[4]:

October 1, 1915

TO THE BOARD OF SUPERVISORS OF LOS ANGELES CO.

Gentlemen:

Two years ago I purchased a home in the Vale of Monte [V]ista at Littlelands [sic], an acre and a third, on which I h[o]ped we would be able to earn our living. In February of 1914 the storm swept the water over the land down into the cellar, and all one night my husband worked out in the swirling raging waters that were carrying rock and sand down the valley, to keep it out of the house. In the morning we found that less than a half an acre of the land and the house was all that was left to us. A small orchard of 22 trees that had just come into bearing, [sic] were all swept away, and only rock and sand was in its place. As soon as we could right ourselves we tried to have the rocks and sand removed, but found we had not money enough to take from two to four feet of rock and sand off the fine black mulch below. Then I took some of the sand and sent it to Prof. Bailey and he returned [an] answer that it would be impossible to grow anything on this soil. Now you can see what a proposition we are up against.

Last winter the storm drain was begun from Haynes [sic] canyon to carry off the water, and after the surveyors were at work, it looked as if we would be able to sell the property for a baisin [sic], or reservoir from which the water could be carried off with the Verdugo waters, and thereby solve the problem. Before it was completed, Mr. Wright and his brother served an injunction on the company and stopped the work. This left the drain within a half mile of our home the opening pointed direct at our house, and at all times a menace to us. During the late rain last spring the water came down with a rush through the ditch, and by the aid of Mr. Hartranft the water was diverted off its course some, and only cut through a corner of our land, but that was right

Lydia (*seated, wearing straw hat with black band*) right of cornerstone, center of photo.
The start of the "Clubhouse." April 12, 1913.

through the garden and swept off much of the good soil, leaving in its place the same silt that is useless for any purpose. I am sending you an imperfect diagram of the run of the ditch so you can see our peril. We offered to sell the place to the county for less than we had ever held it in order to save it as we could not sell it today for enough to cover the mortgage on it let alone what we have paid and expended on the place. Now I have not taken this matter up with any lawyer, as I have not any money to do so with, but think that knowing the circumstances, and also knowing that before the State highway passes over Michigan Blvd. this matter of the storm drain will have to be attended too [sic], also that as your surveyors determined that our land was the lowest point, and the only place for the seepage baisin [sic], from Haynes [sic] Canyon perhaps you would be kind enough to attend to the matter before the winter rains began. If I have not explained matters clearly enough I am willing to come before the board at any time for a further hearing, of questioning. Trusting that you will look into the matter at your earliest convenience, I remain,

Sincerely Yours, Mrs. L. May Dean, Box 23—Littlelands, Calif—

Lydia May was active in many community events, despite her long hours at the family store. She was one of the founding members, in 1913, of the Tujunga Women's Club and its first president. The club had a large variety of activities, including philanthropic ventures, card parties, harvest festivals, luncheons, holiday parties, and fashion shows. In 1924, the Tujunga Women's Club erected their meeting hall on San Ysidro Street behind Bolton Hall. Lydia was a frequent speaker at the club. She had a great love for California and its colorful history.[5] At a luncheon in 1925, she spoke of her life, claiming that she distinctly remembered the election of Abraham Lincoln, both times. Her voice shook as she recalled Lincoln's assassination.[6] She was also deeply concerned about the deterioration of the California missions.

The Tujunga Women's Club made many lasting contributions to the community and Lydia found her club work very satisfying. Throughout the nation, a half-century of progressive changes in women's lives were finding expression in women's club activities and

Dean's Pioneer Store, nestled between the Post Office and Doc Carney's Shoe Store on Commerce, was the Colony's hardware and dry goods depot, c. 1915

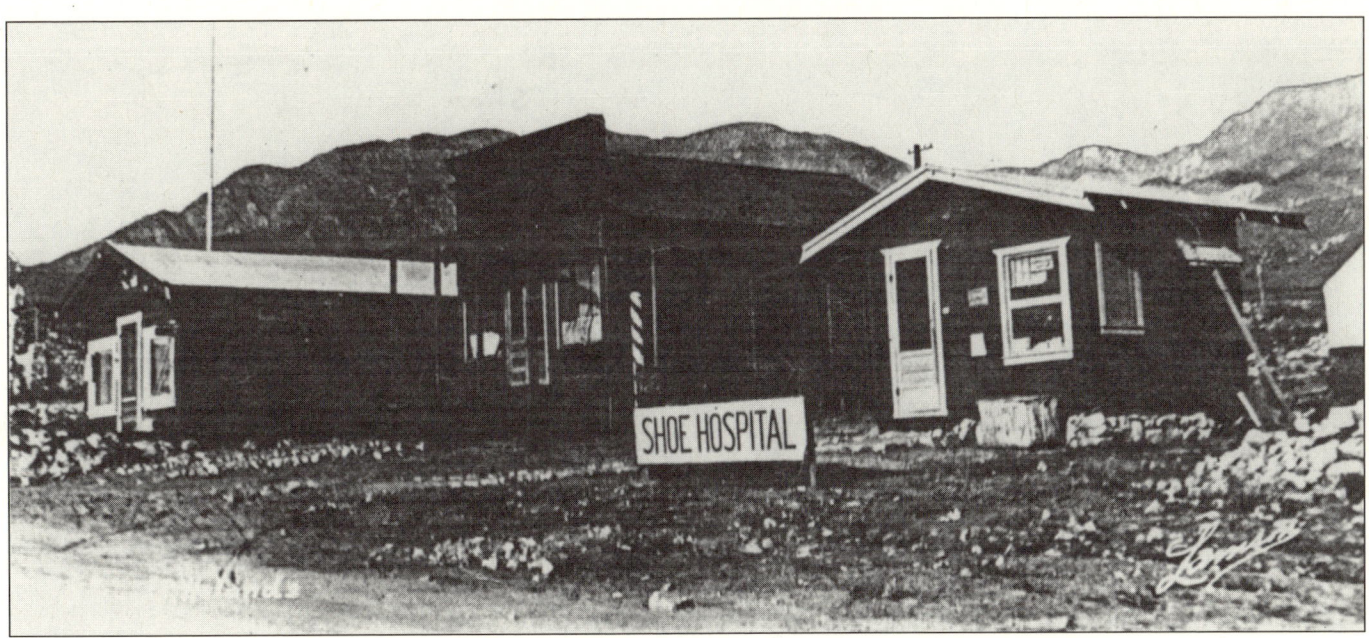

(*above*) 1932 photo of Tujunga Woman's Club at 10121 Samoa Avenue (San Ysidro Street).

(*below*) Groundbreaking, May 2, 1924, for Tujunga Women's Club.
Lydia May Dean, founder, bending over tree, far right.

becoming publicly visible. The "new woman" held the promise for the future. Lydia, like other urban matrons, would share this trend through membership in voluntary associations that would educate the ladies and benefit the community. Greatly influenced by the ideals of Progressivism, Tujunga women sought better welfare for themselves and their children. Usually these women favored Prohibition and avoided racial issues. Their club work, through the State Federation of Women's Clubs, enabled them to help develop a more active and responsible government. It helped transform Tujunga into a modern city, dedicated to better service for its citizens. When other clubs disbanded during World War I, the Tujunga Women's Club carried on and remained active for fifty-four years. In 1967, after the club's meeting hall was razed and an apartment building erected in its place, the club's finances were left to Verdugo Hills High School for a scholarship fund.[7]

The Little Lands Colony was always known as a place where artists and eccentrics flourished. Lydia's son found the truth of this statement after an unusual marriage caused him great anguish.

Charles married Mabel Free, a painter, and they built their home at 6463 Valmont Street. Shortly after their home was completed, Emma Kraft, Mabel's best friend, built her house next to theirs.[8] Emma was an artist who raised purebred Nubian goats. She was a colorful character, fond of driving her goats in her convertible (with the top down) to Exposition Park in Los Angeles. There the goats won many awards and blue ribbons for excellence.[9]

As Mabel and Emma spent more and more time together, Charles saw his marriage dissolve and he eventually divorced Mabel. Now the two artists were free to spend their summers together in Carmel-by-the-Sea.[10] They built a summer home on the Monterey peninsula and painted watercolors of the beautiful area. Mabel often had a "one-man show" of her paintings at the library building in Tujunga.[11] Emma's chauffeured goats brought much amusement to the colony as she motored through town. Tujunga was a town where the unusual was the norm.

Lydia May Dean spent her retirement out of doors, gardening, walking, and visiting the many friends she had made since the birth of the community. In 1938, the community was once again involved in heavy rains and flooding. On March 12 of that year, Lydia passed away just days and blocks away from her good friend, Helen Fehlhaber.

> Never doubt that a small group of thoughtful, committed individuals can change the world, indeed it's the only thing that ever has.
> —*Margaret Mead*

Notes

[1] "Remembrances by Gladys Maygrove Davies."

[2] "Mrs. L. May Dean, Pioneer Merchant to the Tujunga Valley Sells Store to Business Man from Kansas City," *The Record-Ledger* (August 31, 1933).

[3] "Photo Shows What Flood of 1914 Did to Tujunga," *The Record-Ledger* (March 1, 1934).

[4] Letter to Los Angeles Board of Supervisors, October 1, 1915. Bolton Hall Museum Archives.

[5] "Landmarks and History of this District," *The Record-Ledger*, 1923. Bolton Hall Museum.

[6] *The Record-Ledger* (February 19, 1925). Bolton Hall Museum clippings file.

[7] "Tujunga's Women's Club was Active for 54 Years," *The Record-Ledger* (September 12, 1968). Bolton Hall Museum.

[8] Author's interview with Tom Theobald, retired Tujunga Postmaster. June 19, 1997.

[9] "Seven Years Ago This Week," *The Record-Ledger* (October 1929). Bolton Hall Museum clippings file.

[10] *The Record-Ledger*, 1936. Bolton Hall Museum clippings file.

[11] "One-Man Exhibit of Water Colors, Sat. In Library Building," *The Record-Ledger* (May 19, 1934). Bolton Hall Museum.

FOUNDING SISTERS

(*right*) Business card of Lydia's daughter-in-law, Mabel Free and her good friend, Emma Kraft, c. 1920s.

(*below*) Dean's Pioneer Store (*far right*) as it appeared after Lydia's death, c. 1940. *Pen and ink drawing by Forrest Theriot.*

Dean's Pioneer Store
1914 to 1923

All Kinds of Dry Goods and Notions

Hardware and Crockery

Stationery and Hosiery

Don't Forget the Place
308 SUNSET BLVD.
TUJUNGA

Dean & Company

TUJUNGA'S PIONEER STORE

We carry a full line of
HARDWARE, DRY GOODS
KITCHEN UTENSILS
STATIONERY, NOTIONS
TOOLS, GAS STOVES

The patronage we have built up over a long period of years is a proof of the quality of goods we sell.

308 Sunset Blvd.
Tujunga

Phone Sunland 724

214

Helena Peters Fehlhaber
1866–1938

Helena and her husband, Herman, came to the United States from Brunswick, Germany, and settled in Cleveland, Ohio.[1] In 1902, they came to Los Angeles with their young family of five and rented a row house in the industrial part of town, near Boyle Heights.[2] The family hated city living! In May 1906, while the San Francisco earthquake was making news, the Fehlhabers moved again, with their family and grandmother Peters, to a 59-acre ranch in the eastern section of Tujunga, on what is now the southern portion of Tujunga Canyon Boulevard. Their ranch had 759 feet of frontage on the dirt road that became the boulevard. The rear of the property ran to the crest of the west ridge. Today, the Emerald Hills subdivision is located there.[3] Harry Brooks had the property to the north, and to the south was natural forest that became a Civilian Conservation Corps camp in the 1930s.

The Fehlhabers occupied a home built by the Sherer family, who homesteaded the land in 1885. It is considered the earliest home built in the Tujunga Valley, making Helena the earliest recorded mother in the Tujunga Valley.

When they bought the ranch, there were already 2½ acres under cultivation. The Fehlhabers cleared another 45 acres of brush and undergrowth and planted a vineyard of Cornishons (choice table grapes) and Tokay and Malaga grapes for wine. In the early days, there was no system for irrigation, so each young vine had to be hand-watered.[4] The family's water was obtained from a deep spring in the mountains in back of their home.

Life was difficult as the family turned the land into a business but they prospered. Their prosperity was obvious when, in 1911 after selling an acre of land, they bought a Cadillac automobile. The grapes of their vineyards produced tartar, a necessary ingredient in the making of munitions; with the approaching war, it was most profitable. The family also planted peach and other fruit trees and enlarged their home. Helena's mother lived in a cottage nearby and her brother, Emil, lived on a ranch in Saugus.[5] They constructed an extensive glass greenhouse to raise rare tropical and Mediterranean plants. They also added a billiard room for leisure enjoyment.[6] When Prohibition arrived, the billiard room became even more popular. Life was good, but the looming twenties and thirties would test the Fehlhabers' endurance.

To help pay expenses, they leased some of their hillside property to a silica mining company in the 1920s. All of the boys who worked in the mine, ingesting silica particles, would eventually succumb to throat malignancies.[7] The Cadillac was retained but converted into a makeshift truck. Helena and Herman turned the wash area, at the backside of the property, into a shooting range used by the public, local police, and the United States Army. "Ma" Fehlhaber collected money for use of the shooting range and personally picked up the used brass cartridges for cash redemption. She had a room filled with large barrels to hold her recyclable materials.

215

A young Helena and Mother Fehlhaber in her later years, c. 1930s. *Photos courtesy of Edith Fehlhaber Stover*

As the 1920s progressed, the price of grapes began falling. Grapes were difficult to sell at even six dollars per ton by 1931. Their son, Ray, once delivered sixty lugs of choice grapes to a wholesaler in Montrose and came home with just five dollars.[8] The price of silica also fell, and by 1935 the family closed the mine, but not before Ernie suffered a broken leg during a cave-in.

"Ma" and "Pa" refused to be vanquished. They built a roadside fruit stand that became a landmark to motorists in Horse Thief Pass along Tujunga Canyon Boulevard. Fortunately for the Fehlhabers, a large grove of California native live oak trees dominated their ranch, on the west side of Tujunga Canyon Boulevard. Primarily used for family picnics, the Oak Grove was now rented out for fifty cents a day for a family and, later, to large organizations. As use increased, the family added a cement dance floor (doubling as a badminton court), two large barbecue pits (each 4 by 7 feet and four feet deep), several grated stone fireplaces for grilling, picnic tables, benches, counters, and a makeshift bar in the ranch building known as "the garage." The garage was turned into a wine-making area with vats, presses, and barrels, instead of fancy motorcars.

The popularity of the "Oak Grove" increased and by the mid 1930s, under the management of Ray and his wife Irene, many local community groups held their annual picnics there. History was made in the "Grove" when over one thousand employees of the Griffith Construction Company celebrated the completion of their portion of the Pasadena Freeway. Father Falvey and his congregation of Tujunga's Our Lady of Lourdes Church most often used the grounds. In the early 1940s, the church staged many events among the oaks. Small families also enjoyed the "Oak Grove." The Fehlhabers, Houks (Irene's clan), Maiers, and Boettners celebrated life's holidays there. A picnic at the "Oak

Grove" was special, with tables heavily laden with food. For smaller groups, the menu might include game—the ranch was lush with deer, rabbit, quail, doves, etc.—lamb, pork, or domestic fowl. For larger groups, the main course was beef, prepared by the Fehlhaber boys.

On special occasions, Señor Lopez (a true Californio) was called in to perform his magic. Irene's nephew, John Houk, wrote in 1995:

> All night long tended fires heated rock in the bottom of the pits to a white intensity. Then just the right leaves and moisture were added before the beef, shrouded in wet burlap, was put into the pit, and covered with tin and buried with earth. The meat baked and steamed in this environment for precisely the correct amount of time before being unearthed and shared with the waiting and salivating crowd. Oh, paradise! The tender, succulently moist meat, topped off by Senor Lopez's own sauce was a treat not to be forgotten. [9]

During her years on the ranch, Helena cooked on a wood-burning stove. By the mid 1930s, she was happy to have the cooking taken over by her adult children and Señor Lopez. Helena greatly enjoyed music and was content to sit by her phonograph, coincidentally a Brunswick. Both Helena and Herman were college educated. Their home had a large library that included Shakespeare's complete classics. Reading and music were very important to them.[10]

Life was always a battle with "Mother Nature" and the elements, including those man-made. Many times the family ranch was threatened by fire. The most severe was in 1924 when a brush clearance fire along Foothill Boulevard got out of control and sent hot embers to the ridge in back of the ranch. Irene and Ray climbed the ridge and battled the fire through the night. Rattlesnakes were an everyday problem, and Esther and the boys often toted rifles. Their dog, Stubby, would become a true hero when he bit a coiled rattlesnake in order to save George's daughter, Edith. Stubby survived his heroic deed.

Heavy rains and flooding were also a major problem, but never as much as the famous New Year's Eve flood of 1934. For three full days, torrential rains flooded Tujunga, Montrose, and other foothill communities. The damage was extensive and many lives were lost. Boulders the size of cars were carried down slopes. The Verdugo Wash became a raging torrent and the Fehlhabers were marooned for days.[11]

Señor Lopez's Fehlhaber Ranch Barbecue Sauce (a facsimile)
Courtesy of John Houk

1¼ cup chili sauce
2 tbls. dry mustard
1 tbls. grated fresh ginger
2 or more cloves garlic (crushed)
1 small onion
1 cup brown sugar or molasses
1 cup red wine vinegar
6 tbls. Worcestershire Sauce
1 tsp. dry cilantro (crushed)
1 tsp. dry oregano (crushed)
1 tsp. Tabasco Sauce
¼ cup sweet butter
juice of 2 lemons, including pulp
salt to taste

Combine the first eleven ingredients; bring to boil and lower heat to simmer about 15 minutes.

Add the sweet butter and continue to simmer for another couple of minutes. Blend in lemon juice and salt. Let the sauce stand in the refrigerator overnight to allow flavors to blend, strain if desired. Store ready-to-use sauce refrigerated two to three weeks. Makes about 4 cups.

Although Helena's life had been a struggle against the elements—fires, floods, winds, heavy snows, and economic recession—her indomitable spirit made her a survivor. On March 4, 1938, "Ma" died in her home.[12] Helena's death was a shock to her family, as she had been taking care of her husband, recently felled by a stroke. She was ill less than a week before she succumbed to heart and kidney disease.[13] Her death is well-remembered by locals because the heavy March rains caused the Tujunga Canyon Boulevard to be washed out. A new road had to be dug in order to remove her body from the property.

On July 27 of the same year, her husband, Herman, passed away. Their beloved ranch was divided equally between their five children. Eventually, Ray and his wife, Irene, bought out the interests of the other children, making Irene the sole heir. Ernie passed away in 1960, and George Washington Fehlhaber died in 1964. George's daughter, Edith, still lives on a street near the original Fehlhaber home. Esther married Armand Boyer and moved to Paso Robles, California, in 1931. Although the family donated some of their land for the building of Tujunga Canyon Boulevard and they were the first family of record in Tujunga, no street bears their name.

In 1961, 31.8 acres of the ranch were sold to Philip Auswacks and developer Sol Pessin, who turned the acreage into Crystal View Estates. Pessin Development bulldozed the dance platform in January 1968 to make way for 104 new homes.

The Fehlhaber Ranch area was transformed into a lovely 1.2 acre park when Dr. John Houk and his sister, Betty Swanson, donated their portion of land to the City of Los Angeles in 1975.[14] After five years of struggling over funding, the groundbreaking was held June 25, 1980, and the park was dedicated and opened to the community on October 27 of that year. The Verdugo Hills High School band and drill team performed, and Los Angeles Mayor Tom Bradley, Councilman Bob Ronka, Congressman Carlos Moorehead, Mike Antonovich, Assemblyman Pat Nolan, Park Committee Chairperson Gladys Anderson, Recreation and Parks Department Representative James Hadauay, and other dignitaries graced the stage during the dedication ceremony.[15] The Fehlhaber-Houk Park is an ideal place for picnicking, strolling and playing among the oak and birch trees. The Park continues to be enjoyed and stands as a living monument to the early families who shaped the land and conscience of Tujunga.

(*above*) The Fehlhaber Ranch, looking southeast from Foothill Boulevard, sits above Horse Thief Trail, once the path of padres and cattle rustlers, c. 1900. *Courtesy of Edith Fehlhaber Stover.*

(*opposite*) The Fehlhabers picked up their mail at the old Post Office, situated at the corner of La Crescenta Avenue and Foothill Boulevard, in the Plucarp Store. It was also the stage stop for the line that ran from Pasadena through La Cañada to La Crescenta. It was across from the La Crescenta Hotel. The two-horse carriage carried six passengers, c. 1895.

Notes

[1] Over the years, there was much confusion over her actual first name. Her death certificate reads "Helen." Her granddaughter, Edith, reports it was Helena and her great-nephew, Dr. John Houk, reports it was Helene.

[2] Author's interview with John Houk (Ray's nephew). May 3, 2000.

[3] "Old Fehlhaber Ranch," *The Record-Ledger* (June 15, 1961).

[4] "59 Acre Ranch Purchased by Fehlhabers in 1906," *The Record-Ledger* (September 30, 1954).

[5] Author's interview with Edith Fehlhaber Stover. January 21, 2001.

[6] John Houk, "Barbecues at the Fehlhaber Ranch: Remembering When" (1995).

[7] Author's interview, January 21, 2001, op. cit.

[8] Houk, op. cit.

[9] Houk, loc. cit.

[10] Author's interview with Edith Stover (Helena's granddaughter). July 29, 2000.

[11] This Author's parents became engaged that night and were marooned at the Belmont Country Club in La Tuna Canyon, just southwest of the ranch.

[12] Record of Funeral. March 4, 1938. Bades Mortuary, Tujunga.

[13] Author's interview, January 21, 2001, loc. cit.

[14] "Dedication Set for Mini-Park," *The Record-Ledger* (October 16, 1980).

[15] "A Gift for Tujunga," *The Record-Ledger* (October 30, 1980).

Fehlhaber Ranch at time of purchase in 1906.

The original house in 1909 (*left to right*) Esther with dog, Ray, "Ma" and George.

(*above*) Back row is son Ernie. Front row is Herman, Esther, Ray, Helena with George on her lap and Otto.

(*right*) An early photograph of Helena and her children, George, Esther, Raymond and Otto, taken while visiting a friend in Pasadena. *Photos courtesy of Edith Fehlhaber Stover.*

FOUNDING SISTERS

(*above*) Grandmother Peters and grandson, Carlton, c. 1915. *Courtesy of Edith Fehlhaber Stover.*

(*opposite, top*) "The Fehlhaber Bandits" (left to right) Papa Herman, Esther, Emil Peters (Helena's brother), Ernie and Ray, Otto and George (kneeling front row), c. 1916. *The Record-Ledger.*

(*opposite, bottom*) Fehlhaber Family photograph on the porch in 1916 (*top row from the left*) Herman, Helena and George, (*bottom row from the left*) Ray, Ernest, Otto and Esther.

222

FOUNDING SISTERS

(*clockwise from top left*) Photograph taken January 1922, from the Fehlhaber porch during a heavy snow, shows lower Tujunga Canyon Boulevard. *The Record-Ledger.*

Son Otto before leaving for World War I. *Courtesy of Edith Fehlhaber Stover.*

Son George and wife Ruth, with Edith and Sunny, c. 1926. *Courtesy of Edith Fehlhaber Stover.*

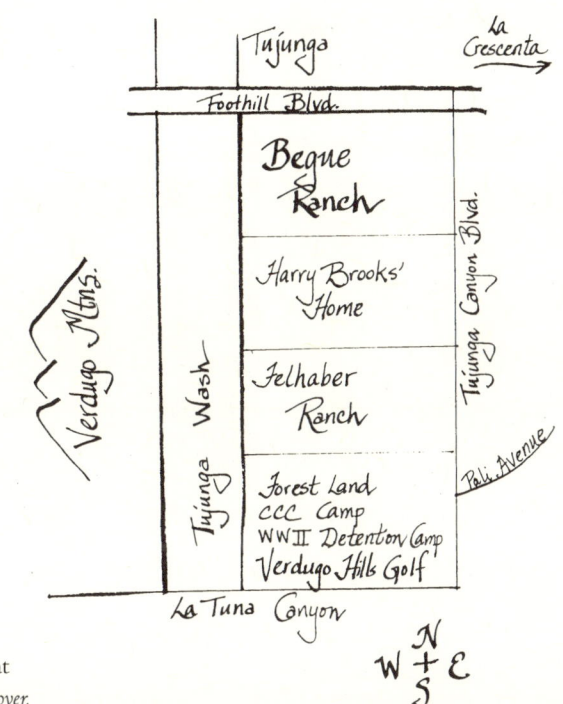

(*right*) Pen and ink drawing of the ranch.
Courtesy of Lyn Hill, La Crescenta.

(*below*) George and Ruth's home on the Fehlhaber Ranch. Daughter Edith was born at the house, c. 1920s. *Courtesy of Edith Fehlhaber Stover.*

(*left*) The interior of the main house. Helena's brother, Emil, built the artistic fireplace, c. 1920s.

(*above*) The Fehlhaber family home. *Photos courtesy of Edith Fehlhaber Stover.*

"Ma" and "Pa" Fehlhaber sit on the porch of
their remodeled home, c. 1930. *Courtesy of Edith Fehlhaber Stover.*

The ranch swimming pool was one of the reservoirs used to store water for the irrigation system.

FOUNDING SISTERS

(*opposite page, top*) The Fehlhaber fruit stand in the mid-1930s at the southern corner of present-day Elmhurst Drive on the west side of Tujunga Canyon Boulevard.

(*middle*) Fehlhaber crate label.

(*bottom*) Rear of fruit stand and entrance to Oak Grove. Road in front of fence is Tujunga Canyon Boulevard.

(*this page, above*) Irene and Ray's house in late 1920s. One of four houses on the property.

(*right*) In 1934, a twelve-inch white cactus bloom drew many tourists to the Fehlhaber ranch, causing a traffic jam. The blossom, a night-blooming cereus (*Trichoncereus Pachinoi*), bloomed for only two nights. Shown here is a surprise cereus bloom from the author's garden. *Courtesy of Author.*

FOUNDING SISTERS

(*left*) Park dedication plaque, October 27, 1980. *Courtesy of Author.*

(*below*) Fehlhaber-Houk Park dedication ceremony October 27, 1980. (*left to right*) Congressman Carlos Moorhead, Superintendent Mike Antonovich, Assemblyman Pat Nolan, Mayor Tom Bradley, Betty Houk Swanson, Wellington Love (representing Senator Newt Russell), Captain John Konstanturos (ex-Foothill Police Station captain), Park Commission chairperson Gladys Anderson and Councilman Bob Ronka. *The Record-Ledger*, "A Gift for Tujunga."

(*opposite page, clockwise from top left*) Ruth Fehlhaber, George's widow, looks over family photographs of the ranch at the dedication ceremony of the park on October 27, 1980, with her grandson, Robert (*left*). *The Record-Ledger.*

John Houk and his sister, Betty Swanson, at dedication of park. October 27, 1980.

Fehlhaber-Houk Park at the corner of Tujunga Canyon Boulevard and Elmhurst. This 1.2 acre park consists of rolling green grass knolls and oak and birch trees. *Courtesy of Author.*

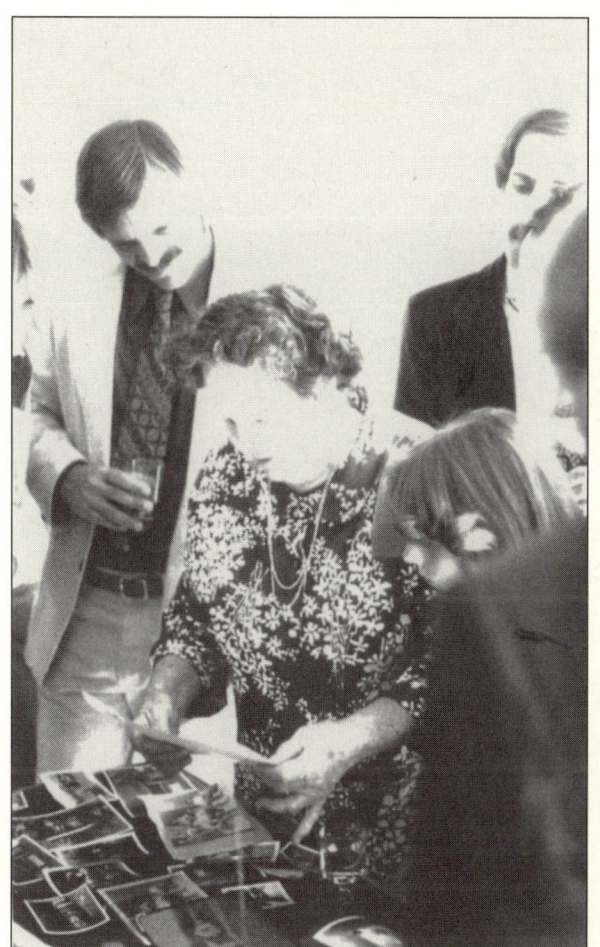

Marie and Anna (seated far left) attend a Garden Club Meeting in Bolton Hall. October 29, 1915.

"The Girls"
Marie Frish
1881–1969

Anna Souto
1883–1969

They were partners in business and life-long companions—the only Little Landers who were ever considered successful.

Marie and Anna worked as domestics in Santa Barbara, at residences across the street from one another. According to Anna, it was no casual meeting that brought the girls together. She had been so homesick and lonely that she prayed for a friend. Marie asked Anna to accompany her to church services and their friendship began.[1] They shared many common interests; both were born in Europe, Anna in the Azores and Marie in Austria, and both loved the outdoors. Marie wanted to raise chickens and Anna liked gardening. It was a friendship made in heaven. Marie had already purchased a half-acre of land, in 1913, on Tujunga Canyon Boulevard in far-off Tujunga, where the Verdugo Hills Hebrew Center once stood. In 1919, the girls purchased the half-acre north and the half-acre south of Marie's property. They brought a builder from Santa Barbara to construct their home.[2]

"There was nothing much but greasewood and sage here in those days," the women recalled, and "rocks—oh, plenty of rocks." Marie started the chicken business with five hundred white leghorn chickens. "We built one chicken house per year and stocked it," she remembered. At the peak of production, they had fifteen hundred chickens.[3] Clearing their 1½-acre plot was a Herculean task. Some of the boulders were larger than Anna, but she rolled the larger rocks to the bottom of the property to use as a base for her wall. She built the wall four feet high, two feet wide and encircled the entire 90-by-70-foot property. Neighborhood children were tempted to walk "the wall that Anna built," but the girls kept a close vigil.

These industrious girls grew most of their own food, fruits and vegetables, and sold eggs and chickens to supplant what they couldn't grow. They also raised feed for their chickens: kale and alfalfa in summer and barley in winter. Anna recalled the Little Lands Colony even had a co-operative store that the settlers owned and operated. If a colonist was lucky enough to have surplus produce, it could be traded for needed staples. Most of the colonists saw their dreams dashed due to the unproductive soil and scarcity of water. While others struggled and gave up, the Frish-Souto chicken business flourished. Their success was due, in part, to their hard work, but also included their courtesy and friendly manner. People enjoyed visiting their ranch, sitting on orange crates on the back porch and chatting with the girls.

There was little entertainment for the girls, but they did enjoy dancing with each other at the weekly dances held at Bolton Hall. Everyone who knew them referred

233

FOUNDING SISTERS

to them as "The Girls"; they were always together, on the street, in the shops, on the bus, and at the dances. They were loved and respected by the town folk and remained life-long companions for fifty years. Marie and Anna lived in a town that prided itself on religious and personal freedoms. However, racial freedoms would remain restricted by real estate policies that lasted until the late 1950s and early 1960s.

In March 1956, the girls sold their business and land and built their final home at 10128 Hillhaven Avenue. On December 23 of that year, ground was broken on their old land for a new Hebrew temple. Famous tree trimmer Slim Vaughan brought down the mighty trees that shaded their old home and the chickens.[4] The girls spent their last twelve years together gardening and taking bus trips to Santa Monica for a day of ocean breezes and fun in the park. Yes, Anna built a small wall of native rock around her new home—old habits die-hard. Marie had a few chickens in the back yard, despite having a market close by.

When Marie passed away on June 30, 1969, Anna was left alone for the first time since meeting Marie all those years ago.[5] Within six months, Anna joined Marie at Glen Haven Memorial Park Cemetery, in Sylmar, where the two now reside, side by side as they had been in life.[6] The chickens are gone, the walls torn down, but the legend of "The Girls" lives on in their inspiring story of courage and devotion to one another and the land of Tujunga.

NOTES

[1] "The Wall That Anna Built," *The Record-Ledger*. Bolton Hall Museum clippings file.

[2] Marie Walsh, "They Remember the Little Landers," *California Farmer* (March 1, 1958).

[3] Ibid.

[4] "Groundbreaking Rites for New VH Hebrew Temple set Dec. 23," *The Record-Ledger* (December 13, 1956).

[5] Record of Funeral. July 3, 1969. Bades Mortuary, Tujunga.

[6] Record of Funeral. January 3, 1970. Bades Mortuary, Tujunga.

"The Girls" send chickens off to Mark Brostoff's Poultry Exchange in La Crescenta, c. 1920s. *The Record-Ledger.*

MARIE FRISH & ANNA SOUTO

(*left*) Marie (*far left*) and Anna cultivate broccoli for their own use, c. 1920s. *The Record-Ledger.*

(*below*) Marie gathers eggs. Often the count was 700 to 800 eggs per day, c. 1920s. *The Record-Ledger.*

Anna single-handedly built this four-foot high wall with boulders from their property. It entirely bordered the 90-by-70-foot property and was known as "The Wall That Anna Built." *The Record-Ledger.*

FOUNDING SISTERS

(*above*) Anna stands in front of her last wall, February 24, 1968.

(*below*) Marie and Anna at their Hillhaven home, March 24, 1968.

Zoe M. Gilbert
1895–1995

One of only three known photographs of Zoe taken in Tujunga. She promised, on her 100th birthday, to be photographed again. Unfortunately, she died four months before she became a centenarian, c. 1926.

She came west to Tujunga in March 1913 and bought one of the first six lots offered in M. V. Hartranft's Little Lands Colony. When she left town in 1926, with no forwarding address, locals assumed she left to pursue her real estate career.[1] In fact, she returned to her birthplace in Kokomo, Indiana, married Lex "Splint" Gilbert in 1913, and returned to Tujunga, where the town knew her as a single lady.[2] In 1950, she and Lex began a car trip west to California to show him her Tujunga. However, a serious auto accident forced them to return to Indiana. Zoe never mentioned her thirteen years in Tujunga to her friends and neighbors in Kokomo. To them she was the happy wife of a corn and soy grower. She carried the secret of those Tujunga years to her grave.[3] To the residents of the colony, she was an astute businesswoman and one of the town's biggest civic boosters.

Zoe was born on September 22, 1895, in Ervin Township of Howard County, Indiana. She was the daughter of Milton and Margaret (Martz) Harpster.[4] Her years on the family farm, with younger sister Beatrice, remain unrecorded.[5]

On March 17, 1923, St. Patrick's Day, the town of Tujunga celebrated their tenth anniversary. Zoe published a narrative, in *The Record-Ledger* newspaper, of the first auto sojourn of Little Landers colonists. Her words capture the awe of the colorful trip at the base of the green Verdugo Mountains and the large number of boulders that would await them.

"The Landing of the Pilgrims"
by Miss Zoe M. Gilbert

Almost equal in importance to the landing of the Pilgrim fathers from the Mayflower was the landing of the first auto load of passengers on the rock-bound hills of Los Terrenitos, as the new townsite was called. On the 17th day of March, 1913, ten years ago, a little party of six left the House of the Little Landers on Figueroa Street, Los Angeles, for a trip to "The Port of Hearts Desire," coming by way of San Fernando Valley. The day was sunny though cool, and a March wind blowing. Not enough, however, to cause discomfort. At Lazy Lonesome Rancho near Sunland, a stop was made for lunch. The surrounding mountains from this location seemed very wonderful, though interest, of course, centered on the distant view of our destination on the gently sloping hillside, with Sister Elsie peak towering above. The ride along the foot of the beautiful Green Verdugos completed the journey. At the end of Sunset Boulevard (Commerce) and Michigan Avenue (Foothill) we landed amid towering boulders, which might be likened unto the Plymouth Rock of old. This was as far as we could be carried by stage. The streets were laid out, some of them partially cleared of the greasewood and wild sage. On foot we slowly wended our way through brush and over stones. At the corner of El Centro (Valmont) and Sunset Boulevard (Commerce) ground was being broken for a large building. We stopped to make inquires and learned that this was to be the civic center, the building to be erected was the community clubhouse in which the native stones would be used; the architect and builder, George Harris. Mexicans with mule teams were plowing the street here. We tramped through the plowed ground as far as Summit Street (Summitrose), then across lots to Pine (Pinewood), down Los Angeles Street (Apperson) and explored a portion of Stevens Way (Hillhaven Avenue). At the end of the pilgrimage five members of our party bought lots that day on Sunset Boulevard between El Centro (Valmont) and Los Angeles (Apperson) Streets. My section was lot 86, one-quarter acre on the east side of the street. The others then selected lots just opposite on the west side. Ben Clark bought the half-acre where J. Bodkin now lives. Dr. And Mrs. S. P. S. Edwards purchased the half-acre now owned by Miss Georgia Shane and J. S. Lewis bought the half-acre adjoining on the south. The sixth member of our party, Frank Zeitler, bought a house and lot in what was then known as the Western Empire tract, about a mile distant. We were delighted with our choice of location and each declared, as everyone else does who buys here, that we had the finest view of all. We took a personal interest in the buying of every lot, commenting on the desirability of each location. Some of the comments made regarding my lot were: "Such a smooth surface," "So few stones," etc. As we plodded our weary way back to the waiting car, and during the return trip to the city, we, who were total strangers to each other at the beginning of the day, talked together in the most neighborly fashion about our future plans.

Mr. Lewis, my neighbor, was one of the first settlers at San Ysidro, the Little Landers colony near San Diego. While the house was being built, I made my home at the Lazy Lonesome, through the courtesy of Mr. And Mrs. M. V. Hartranft. The Earl Sims stage line was running at that time between Sunland and Los Angeles. I came over to the townsite every morning to note progress on the building. Each day I viewed with amazement the immense boulders and rocks that Mike Jones and his gray horse were excavating from my premises. From the number and size of them I thought it likely that my small ranch would be converted into a sunken garden. All of these boulders and stones were used later in the building

Louise and Marshal Hartranft on the porch of their home in Sunland, c. 1920s.

> GILBERT'S GIFT SHOP
> New line of Candlesticks and Book Ends
> Fine Stationery
> Reduction in Prices of All Gifts
> New Year's Greeting to All
> Sunset Boulevard, Tujunga

(*clockwise from top*) In this 1915 photograph, "Aunt" Jennie and "The Parson" are on horseback in front of the Tujunga Post Office, Gilbert's Gift Shop and Mrs. Dean's Pioneer Store. View southeast from the corner of Commerce and Valmont.

Advertisement for Gilbert's Gift Shop, next to the Post Office at 156 South Sunset, c. 1923. *The Record-Ledger.*

In 1923, on the tenth anniversary of the Colony, Zoe penned the lyrics to the first of many Tujunga songs.

In 1918, Tujunga celebrated the end of World War I. Zoe's gift shop is seen in front of the parked car. *The Record-Ledger.*

TUJUNGA

By Zoe Gilbert

(Air: My Bonnie)
Tujunga lies over the mountains,
 Tujunga, not far from the sea,
In the beautiful valley of sunshine—
 O this is the homeland for me.

Chorus
Homeland, homeland, Tujunga the
 homeland for me, for me;
Homeland, homeland, Tujunga the
 homeland for me.

Where canyons lie deep in the shadow
 Of mountains that tower above,
With clear, sparkling streams ever
 flowing—
 Tujunga, the homeland I love.

Chorus

The sky, 'tis so blue o'er the live oaks
 Where the mocking bird sings the
  day long,
When the valley with moonlight is
 gleaming
 We hear the sweet whip-poor-will's
  song.

Chorus

FOUNDING SISTERS

(*clockwise from top left*) April 4, 1926, at the annual Easter Sunrise service.

April 23, 1923, illustration in the *Record-Ledger Newspaper*.

The Cross of San Ysidro, overlooking the Tujunga Valley, c. 1924.

of my fireplace, foundation for the house and walls of the cellar. Dr. Edwards and Mr. Lewis put up tents immediately and lived in them during the summer. Mr. Clark built a small room on his lot to be used later as a workshop. In January of 1914 the name of the town was changed from Los Terrenitos to Little Lands. The following September the post office was established and the name changed to Tujunga.[6]

Zoe would play an active role in the birth and development of the colony and later Tujunga. She was known as a librarian, gift shop owner, post office employee, member of the Board of Trade (later to become the Chamber of Commerce), a Glorietta School trustee[7] and founder and secretary of the San Ysidro Club that erected the Cross of San Ysidro in the green Verdugo Hills.

It was Zoe's work in the San Ysidro Club that would bring her the most satisfaction. The club formed a committee to proceed with erecting a cross in the mountains above Tujunga. Reverend Edgar Pasko headed the committee and, as expected, Zoe was the only woman member. One acre of land around Mt. McGroarty was deeded to the city by M. V. Hartranft and named Pasko Park.

The idea of erecting a large cross on the top of Mount McGroarty, at 2,000 feet, originated with the Millionaires Club of Happiness and Contentment. This group of retired men met daily to discuss life and world events. John Steven McGroarty made them famous in his *Los Angeles Times* column. Developer Marshall Hartranft brought in renowned builder George Harris to build the base for the cross in natural stone. The cross, designed by noted architect Arthur B. Benton of Los Angeles, was made of reinforced concrete.[8]

The first Easter sunrise service on the summit of Mount McGroarty was held April 1, 1923. The cross was blessed by Father Joseph Tonella. Marshall Hartranft gave a speech and named the mountain in honor of poet John Steven McGroarty. The cross was named for San Ysidro, patron saint of agriculture (the plowman saint). He was not a saint of the Catholic Church, but, according to Mr. McGroarty, was a peasant of Spanish and Jewish extraction. McGroarty said, "We pray to God to let San Ysidro watch over our little homes and protect them and those that dwell in them."[9]

Zoe was responsible for getting the cross illuminated the following year. It cost two hundred dollars to light the cross nightly for the first year. This proved to be too expensive, so the lighting was modified to just two weeks before Easter and two weeks before Christmas each year. In 1937, the Easter services became the responsibility of the Tujunga Kiwanis Club. To date, the Easter services have been moved on only two occasions, due to inclement weather. This Tujunga landmark is still clearly seen in the Tujunga and San Fernando Valleys. Perhaps no other icon, with the exception of the yucca plant, most represents the little colony of small homes that grew into a thriving city.

Zoe's later years, on her 180-acre farm eight miles west of Kokomo, Indiana, were happy ones. Her neighbors, both in Kokomo and Ridgeway, remember her as an honest and outspoken woman who enjoyed crocheting, cooking, canning, and her numerous activities at the Judson Baptist Church. After the death of her husband Lex in 1968, Zoe remained on the family farm and was active until her death in 1995.

Tujunga is indebted to this early Little Lander for authoring "The Tujunga Song" and her narrative, "The Landing of the Pilgrims." Fortunately, she was aware that the events taking place were of historical significance. Zoe will always be remembered for her civic work and as Tujunga's woman pioneer with a pen.

Notes

[1] "Miss Gilbert to Devote Her Time to Real Estate," *The Record Ledger* (April 19, 1926).

[2] "Gilbert Rites," *The Kokomo Tribune* (March 21, 1968).

[3] Letter, dated August 20, 2002, to the author from Marjorie and Harold Eller, who eventually inherited the Gilbert's farm and two bedroom Bedford stone home. The Ellers had farmed the land for twenty-nine years.

[4] Twelfth Census of the United States. Schedule No. 1. Population, June 4, 1900, Howard County, Ervin Township.

[5] "Zoe Gilbert Obituary," unnamed magazine, May 1995, pg. 128. Provided by Howard County Historical Society.

[6] "The Landing of the Pilgrims," *The Record Ledger* (April 5, 1923).

[7] "School Trustees are on the Job," *The Record of the Verdugo Hills* (September 23, 1921).

[8] Famed Los Angeles architect Arthur Burnett Benton (1858–1927), who designed the Cross of San Ysidro on Mt. McGroarty, would also rebuild the McGroarty home when it burned down in 1923.

[9] "Hold First Sunrise Easter Service High Above a Sea of Fog," *The Record of the Verdugo Hills* (April 5, 1923).

FOUNDING SISTERS

Zoe M. Gilbert (*seated far left*) at table for a Tujunga Valley Realty Board luncheon on the patio of M. V. Hartranft's Lazy Lonesome Ranch. May 16, 1925.

Marie Huber Hansen
1891–1993

As weddings go, there was nothing to compare it to. The twenty-eight guests would keep memories of that remarkable day, April 27, 1920, for the remainder of their lives.

The wedding guests met at the mouth of the Big Tujunga Canyon at 8:00 A.M., coming in motor cars from various points in and around Los Angeles. It was a perfect day and all who know Southern California appreciate the beauty of an early morning drive, especially in the mountains.

Awaiting us were three-seated buckboards, a big old fashioned tally-ho and extra riding horses, and great was everyone's joy to see coming Dr. Hansen's mother, over eighty years old, full of enthusiasm for the ride up the mountain that made more than one of the younger ladies timid. It was a happy, merry party of warm friends on the way to the most beautiful and unique wedding they had ever attended. The buckboards led the way followed by the four-horse tally-ho and riding horses.

Dr. Hansen had engaged a bugler, who sat beside the driver and the hills resounded with bugle notes at different stages of the journey.

The merry party was thrilled with the beauty and novelty of the occasion and joyous anticipation of Marie's wedding, and one of them told one of Dr. Hansen's famous stories, how there was a prehistoric horse that once roamed these mountains who had short legs on one side of his body and long legs on the other to conform with the hill and mountain sides.

Almost there, the king-pin on the tally-ho broke and they all had to climb out. The maid-of-honor and her escort, who were serving as outriders, occasionally dashed ahead and this was one of the times when they were out of sight and hearing. Miss Mann, one of the bridesmaids, offered to go for help (all the men being occupied with fixing the tally-ho) and she plunged across the stream boots and all.

The outriders were returning to us once more and met the volunteer after she had made two of the stream crossings, and were able to rush ahead to Dr. Hansen's stables for a new king-pin. Fortunately, only the end of the pin had broken and the men were able to fix it before assistance reached them. They were along their way when buckboards and a swift rider came dashing to the rescue. Everything was all right and all proceeded on their way; twenty-one times that rushing mountain stream was forded, water often above the hubs of the wheels.

Arriving within hearing distance of the cabin, the bugler announced our coming.

Presently we came to the level meadowy [*sic*] stretch in which the Doctor's fine stone and log cabin was located. Here the rest of the party was awaiting us, including Mrs. Huber, Marie and Dr. Hansen. How the bugle blew! How glad and happy were we in our meeting. We were invited to rest a bit and refresh ourselves with a glass of cool milk. Then all mounted horses to ride to the Grotto, three miles more up the "High Trail," cut out of solid rock seventy-five feet above the stream.

An hour's ride brought us to the Grotto, fringed with maidenhair ferns and a most suitable place for the marriage of these mountain lovers.

Mr. Hodgin, the Unitarian clergyman, immediately took his place on an island strip just wide enough for him to sit his horse comfortably. The maid-of-honor and the bridesmaids, all carrying wild flower bouquets, took the conventional position in front of the guests who formed a semicircle just behind them as in a church. Everyone sat his horse

With his collie, lawyer and good friend F. E. Davis is driving "three seater," with Marie and Homer on horseback in Big Tujunga Canyon, c. 1920s.

and the same hush and expectancy prevailed as in the most conventional church wedding.

The bride's brother went back a little way to apprise us of the approach of the bridal party and when he announced their coming all softly sang the "Bridal Chorus" from Lohengrin.

Quite the opposite from the slow solemn procession at a church was the dashy splash of the waters as the bride, groom and bride's mother rode rapidly to their places in front of the minister.

After the singing of the wedding march, a moment of silence, then Mr. Hodgin's beautiful impressive ceremony, never to be forgotten. At its conclusion, Dr. and Mrs. Hansen skillfully guided their wonderful horses in and out among their guests receiving congratulations, then spurred their horses and rode swiftly ahead of the rest of the party to the cabin.

A delicious wedding breakfast was served under the trees, the guests sitting around a long table tastefully decorated with mountain flowers and bountifully supplied with all the delicacies of a wedding repast.[1]

Charlotte did not mention that Dr. Hansen, not owning enough horses for the entire party to ride, had to rent several from a local movie studio. One rented horse was trained to lie down immediately when touched in a particular spot. When a female guest touched this horse on the shoulder with her heel, the horse immediately lay down in the middle of the stream. The rider then had to wade to the closest bank, remount the horse and continue on her way to the wedding, completely drenched.[2] The wedding that took place just this side of paradise was in fact up the mighty Big Tujunga Canyon, three miles past the site of the present dam, where caves abounded in lush maidenhair fern.[3]

After Marie and Homer were married in the cave on horseback with lush ferns as a bower, the wedding party returned to Hansen's Lodge for a wedding breakfast. Some of the horses took advantage of the inexperienced riders and set off at a run. As they neared the lodge, one horse stopped abruptly, sending the rider head first into a sand bank.[4] The marriage that took place in the fern grotto that day, between the 48-year-old Homer and the 28-year-old Marie, was a true love story and would last forty years. The couple had four children, Homer Jr., Albert, Mary, and Maude. Unfor-

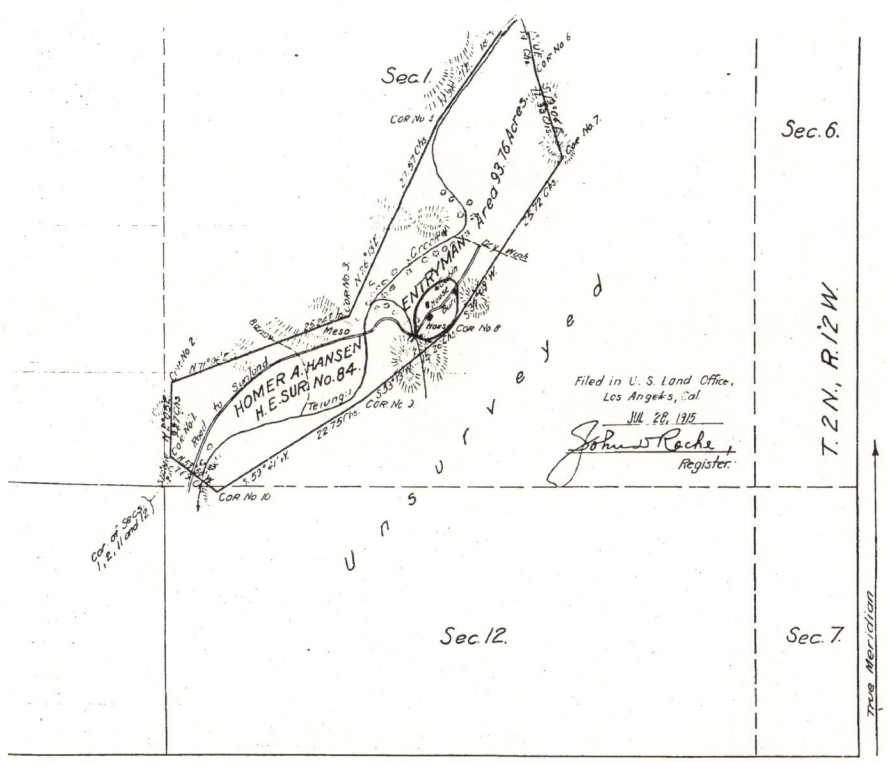

Plat Map of Homer Hansen's 93-acre homestead. Filed in Land Office July 28, 1915.

The first cabin on Hansen property in Big Tujunga Canyon, c. 1918. *Trails Magazine*, 1938.

FOUNDING SISTERS

(*left*) Homer's friend and neighbor, the legendary Silas Hoyt. Homer would inherit Silas' horse, Beelzebub (Prince of the Devils). Photo date unknown. *Trails Magazine*, Winter 1938.

(*below*) The original Silas Hoyt cabin, built in 1890. The eccentric old man nearly lost his sight from wood smoke and overgrown eyebrows. Dr. Hansen saved his eyesight. In 1912, Hoyt left the canyon to be cared for by his daughter. He died in 1925 at the age of 97 years.

tunately the wedding cave did not survive; it was destroyed when the dam was built in 1931.

Who was Marie Adeline Huber of Taunton, Massachusetts? We know she was the daughter of Berthold and Maude (Convers) Huber. Her father had immigrated to America from the Black Forest area of Germany. He became famous for his invention of the two-color printing press. After his death, Marie, her mother Maude, and her brother and sister moved to California. There they purchased land in Hollywood and in the new town of Owensmouth, in the San Fernando Valley.

Before the Hubers arrived in California, Maude and Marie traveled together to Ecuador and the Hawaiian Islands. Family history tells us that Maude and Marie camped on the beach at Waikiki on the island of Oahu.[5] However, details of Marie's childhood education are not recorded, except that she became a nurse before marrying Dr. Hansen. Camera shy her entire life, few photographs of Marie exist. Her story after 1920 would be forever linked to the life of her husband and it would be exciting and disheartening, yet never dull.

Homer Hansen was born in Logan, Ohio, in 1872, the son of John and Mary (McBroom) Hansen. Homer's parents were of fine character; his father, John, fought in the Civil War at the Battle of Shiloh. After graduating from Logan High School, Homer spent one year traveling on foot and horseback through the southwestern and Pacific Coast states.[6] He said, "My introduction to the Big Tujunga Canyon came in the summer of 1892, when as a young hobo in my teens, I was seeing America first and crossed the continent on blind baggage and freight trains."[7] After Homer's big adventure, he settled down and attended Rush Medical College in Chicago, graduating in medicine and surgery. Following graduation, he moved to Columbus, Nebraska, where he would practice medicine for the next nine years. While there, he was briefly married and remained a life-long friend to his ex-father-in-law. In 1901, he traveled abroad and spent six months in Berlin as an assistant to the famous Dr. Landau, surgeon to the kaiser and his family. On Homer's return to America, he resumed his medical practice in Nebraska. He was soon forced to abandon his medical career due to severe inflammatory rheumatism. Given one year to live, Homer decided to return to California and spend his dying days in the majestic Big Tujunga Canyon. With casts on both legs, he journeyed on horseback up the canyon. For the first few weeks, he lived on the banks of the river with "pockets full of parched corn for food." After one year of sunshine, fresh air, and complete relaxation, Homer left the canyon a healed man.

In 1904, he returned to the canyon with a friend from New York, Cecil Campbell. "He made the trip on horseback into the Canyon, going from Pasadena by way of the Arroyo Seco to Oakwilde, by the Dark Canyon–Vasquez Canyon Trail to Silas Hoyt's Ranch, stopping the first night at the old Ybarra Ranch."[8] After this trip, he became determined to own a piece of this paradise. "From 1904 to 1920, he devoted himself to the development of the San Fernando Valley. During this time, he became well recognized and accepted by the society of Los Angeles."[9] His friends ran the gamut from the down-and-out to the likes of Clarence Darrow, Senator Flint, John S. McGroarty, Parson James Wornum, and "Aunt" Jenny Wornum. In 1909, Homer filed a homestead patent for 93 acres in the Big Tujunga Canyon. By 1910, he had built a small rustic log cabin on his property. Far from the stress of the city, his health completely returned. When he finished the arduous task of building a road to his property from the Hoyt Ranch, he began to envision, along with his brother Charles, a water and electric power plant project. The brothers formed The Tujunga Water and Power Company and bought fourteen miles of the riverbanks in the Big Tujunga Canyon. Their property reached from the point where the Big Tujunga River left the Angeles National Forest and extended south out into the San Fernando Valley. This land was later subdivided and became Hansen Heights (Shadow Hills) and Tejunga Terrace (Lake View Terrace). His company controlled the water, the dam, and the reservoir sites above these subdivisions. Among his many business activities, Homer organized a bank and trust company in Searchlight and Caliente, Nevada. The ex-governor of Massachusetts was one of his partners.

Throughout the next twenty years, Dr. Hansen would file many lawsuits over property and water rights. As early as 1880, the City of Los Angeles was claim-

> **Hansen's Ranch Lodge**
> **Big Tujunga Canyon**
> (30 miles from Los Angeles)
>
> **Rates—American Plan**
>
> Single . . . . $6.75 Per day
> Double (2 in Room) . . . . . $5.75 Each
>
> **Weekly**
>
> Single . . . . $40 Per week
> Double . . . . $35 Per week
>
> Children under 12 years Half Rate. Special rates for parties. Banquets and Dinner Parties by reservation.
>
> A Beautiful All-Year Recreational Spot—Not a Sanitarium.
>
> Swimming, Horseback Riding, Hiking, Cabins
>
> Reached by auto via Sunland, through Walnut Drive and Big Tujunga Canyon.
>
> **P. O. Address—Tujunga Box 5**
>
> Phone: Sterling 9933 F1-3
>
> **Elizabeth and J. A. Schiller,
> Proprietors**

A travel brochure for Hansen's Ranch Lodge.

ing pueblo rights, as successor to rights granted by Spain and Mexico, to all water in the Big Tujunga Canyon. Los Angeles water claims had been upheld in court in several lawsuits prior to 1895. As always, there was either too much or too little water, and who owned it would be a question that remained unanswered for half a century.

By 1907, Dr. Hansen had divested himself of his bank and trust companies in Nevada and bought acreage in the western portion of Rancho Tejunga and platted the subdivisions of Tejunga Terrace (Lakeview Terrace) and Hansen Heights (Shadow Hills). In 1917, he built a large two-story lodge on his property. The lodge, located just south of the present Big Tujunga Dam, had a dining room that could seat 125 guests, a large swimming pool, and riding stables. Dr. Hansen's company, now the Tujunga Water and Power Company, applied to build a dam above his Lodge, but the Los Angeles Board of Supervisors opposed the idea of a private company interfering with their own plans to build a dam.

At no time did the Hansen family live in Hansen's lodge. They lived in a magnificent two-story home built of natural stone and wood on a knoll they nicknamed "The Mt. of Olives." The family had a Chinese cook-housekeeper, horses for the children, extensive gardens, and an uninterrupted view of the San Fernando Valley. Life on their mountaintop was paradise. Within twenty years, their land would be confiscated and under water.

In 1925, over 1,000 people visited Hansen's Lodge in one weekend. The hospitality of the Lodge became renowned throughout the Southland, with many famous visitors including movie stars, authors, and politicians. The famous criminal attorney Clarence Darrow became so enamored with the tranquility of the sylvan setting that he spent most of his weekends there during his two-year stay in California. Senator Frank P. Flint and the Los Angeles Board of Supervisors were frequent guests. The lodge became so popular that Homer brought Elizabeth and J. A. Schiller from Wyoming to manage it. By 1928, well over 3,000 visitors were recorded as entering the canyon during the Fourth of July weekend.

Life in the canyon has always been at the complete mercy of Mother Nature. The story of Hansen's lodge parallels the story of the canyon—creation, destruction, and rebirth. The original lodge was completely destroyed by a flood in 1926. More than twenty-eight inches of rain fell that year, with almost fourteen inches in April alone. There were freak storms in July and August when the mountains were covered with snow. In spite of all the unpredictable weather problems, Dr. Hansen remained undaunted and rebuilt the lodge.

The first thirty-five years of the twentieth century were considered the years of the "Great Hiking Era." The weekends in the canyon provided much relief from city living with enthusiastic visitors climbing the fire trails, dirt roads and their favorite, Sister Elsie's Peak.[10] In 1920, Sister Elsie's Peak afforded panoramic views that stretched all the way to the Pacific Ocean. Hiking clubs and locals, including Stella Wieman, enjoyed reaching the 5,074-foot peak. Moonlight hikes became popular with the Sierra Club and local hikers. Trips into the canyon became so popular that by 1923 a ranger station was removed from a location near Sunland Park to Mt. Gleason Avenue (Walnut Avenue) at the entrance of the canyon to facilitate the issuing of camping permits.

In 1926, the United States government won a lawsuit that cancelled the dam rights of Dr. Homer Hansen and the Tujunga Water and Power Company. The suit stated that insufficient work had been done over a forty-year period. By 1928, the residents of Sunland-Tujunga, who had approved $600,000 for a large dam above Hansen's lodge on April 1, 1924, now called for several smaller check dams be built. The concept of one large dam won out over the requested check dams. A site about one-half mile above the lodge was selected. The construction of the dam was to start in 1929, but was delayed by additional surveys ordered by the Board of Supervisors. Dr. Hansen asked the county for $90,000 for a right-of-way across the eighty acres of land he owned in the canyon, but the Forest Service granted the county an easement to the dam site through their property. After a hard fight against the county's condemnation proceedings, Dr. Hansen finally acquiesced and sold his property. In 1930, the Board of Supervisors purchased the Hansen homestead to be used for the dam site for $85,000. On July 25 of that year, the Big Tujunga Dam's construction finally commenced. In 1931, the Big Tujunga Dam was completed three months ahead of schedule. When finished, the dam formed a lake 1½ miles long and 240 feet deep. On May 27 of that year, the dam was dedicated at a luncheon and was christened with a bottle of lemonade. By 1933, Hansen's Lodge had been converted into a Civil Conservation Corps (C.C.C.) camp. They built a new road from the mouth of the canyon to the dam site. Twelve campsites were built along the road, with concrete stoves and tables. The c.c.c. camp had 117 men stationed at the old Hansen's lodge. During the Depression, the camp became a boon for the jobless men of the valley. On November 22, 1933, a fire that began in La Crescenta burned its way over to Mt. Lukens (Sister Elsie's Peak) and devastated over 1,000 acres of brush. The torrential rains, which began a week later and continued through the New Year, caused heavy

During the 1920s, Hansen's Ranch Lodge, complete with stables and swimming pool, was home to celebrities and vacationers.

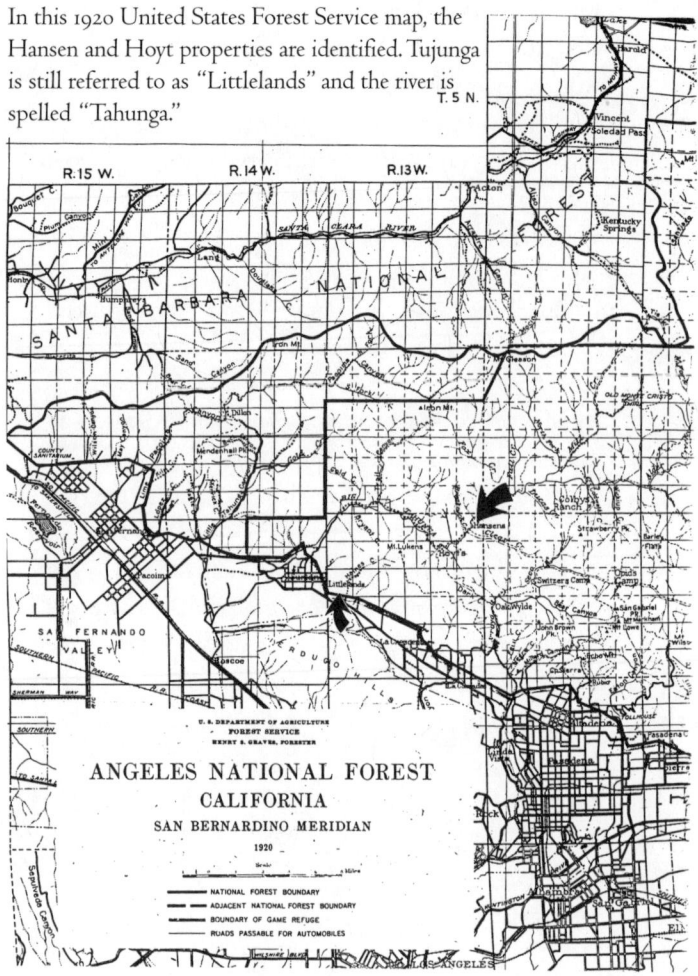

In this 1920 United States Forest Service map, the Hansen and Hoyt properties are identified. Tujunga is still referred to as "Littlelands" and the river is spelled "Tahunga."

flooding in the foothill communities and extensive damage in Montrose and Glendale. Hundreds of homes were destroyed and forty-five people died in the "Great Montrose Flood."

In 1937, work began on Hansen Dam, situated southwest of the entrance to Big Tujunga Canyon. The county spent $600,000 for the right-of-way and the dam site. The Guy F. Atkinson Company won the contract to build the dam with a bid of $5,688,418. By the time it was completed, the cost had soared to $13 million.

During March 1938, rains of biblical proportions once again poured into the valley. Hansen's lodge, now the c.c.c. camp, was completely destroyed. With the exception of the great stone fireplace, the lodge disappeared into history. In 1968 and 1969, when the Big Tujunga Dam was cleaned, the final traces of the lodge were destroyed. The dam that had been built in 1931 above the lodge failed to protect it. When heavy rains filled the dam to capacity in 1938, the gates were opened and water roared down the canyon. This 15-feet-high wall of water killed a c.c.c. camp worker, destroyed 447 cabins in the San Gabriels and most of the cabins in the "Big T," severely damaged Wildwood Lodge, and left hundreds of residents and visitors marooned.[11] All bridges were also destroyed and the fern cave in which Marie and Dr. Homer were married was completely lost. The heavy rains forever changed the confluence of the river and the landscape of the canyon. By June of that year, eight miles of road had been repaired and visitors were once again enjoying the canyon.

Condemnation proceedings were now initiated for the 700 acres needed for Hansen Dam. The cost of the dam was increased to $11,303,454. After a work strike, the job was started again. Two workmen were killed from falls off the dam structure. The newly-formed debris basin served 147 square miles of watershed area. The dam now made it possible for suburban growth in the San Fernando Valley. The 1,500-acre site had three large picnic areas and Holiday Lake, where people could enjoy swimming, boating and fishing. The lake was closed to the public in 1982, when it became filled with silt and sediment. It reopened in 1997, much smaller than its original size. The Hansen Dam site has a golf course and riding stables to further increase the community's enjoyment.[12]

On August 17, 1940, with an estimated crowd of five hundred valley residents and guests gathered atop the newly built dam, considered the largest earth-filled dam in the world, for an afternoon dinner and the dedication, Marie and Homer Hansen took center stage. Many dignitaries spoke and a flood of oratory was released,

but it was the ruddy-faced, old gentleman in a white linen suit who stole the show with about 60 seconds worth of simple talk. Dr. Homer Hansen, who made his home atop the little knoll where the dam got its name, put his fellow speakers to shame with a few well chosen and un-rehearsed words,

MARIE HUBER HANSEN

(*top*) The mounted wedding party, April 27, 1920. *Courtesy of Maude Ann (Hansen) Taylor.*

(*above*) Marie sits on her new husband Homer's lap on her wedding day, April 27, 1920. *Courtesy of Maude Ann (Hansen) Taylor.*

(*right*) Marie preserved this piece of maidenhair fern taken from the grotto in Big Tujunga Canyon, which was the scene of her marriage to Homer, c. 1920.

FOUNDING SISTERS

(*top*) The Big Tujunga Canyon after the flood of 1926.

(*bottom*) The two-story lodge was destroyed by a flood in 1926, rebuilt and destroyed again by the Big Flood of 1938.

"I came here to this spot 21 years ago," the elderly San Fernando pioneer said, "and built a home of rocks and logs on top of the little knoll, where my bride and I settled down to raise a family of four. We liked the spot—it was an ideal home, and then one day the army engineers came along with tests and borings, and the next thing I knew, this mighty dam was standing where our home had been. My family and I are proud and humble to have this mighty structure bear our name.[13]

It was noted by the press that there was a "marked scarcity of representatives from the City Councils and Chambers of Commerce of the honored guests to be presented to the crowd, only about 10 percent were present. Maybe it was the heat."[14]

Dr. Hansen, a positive thinker, was not a man to live in the past or dwell on his legal and financial problems. One of his favorite expressions was "Of all the sad words of tongue or pen, the saddest of these, 'it might have been.'" Son-in-law Lawrence Tollenaere best described the Hansen's life from 1920 to 1940; "It was filled with family happiness, fame, fortune, financial collapse, misfortunes of health, great undertakings, financial recovery and public acclaim."[15] Homer Hansen "successfully prosecuted legal suits against the City of Los Angeles, which were carried and won in the California State Supreme Court. During the great financial crash of 1929, he was heard to say in a tower of rage to the head of one of the great financial institutions, 'You can destroy me financially but you cannot dent my courage.'"[16] Deeply religious, he was able, at the age of 80 years, to sing for two hours, without repetition or interruption, the church songs he had sung in his youth. His faith truly sustained him.

In 1940, Homer liked to say he was in retirement, but in fact built a new family home called "the Wilderness Ranch" in the Tehachapi Mountains. Homer and Marie moved into their two-story ranch home in 1945. The home and stables were in an isolated canyon in the northern Mojave Desert, Cache Creek Park in Jawbone Canyon. Life again became idyllic. The Hansen children and grandchildren would inherit Marie and Homer's love of nature and devotion to the land.

On November 25, 1960, Homer Alfred Hansen suffered a massive heart attack and passed away at his home.[17] After his funeral, Dr. Hansen's family buried him at the highest place on his Wilderness Ranch. It was the place he wanted with a view of his favorite land. His family and friends carried his coffin up the moun-

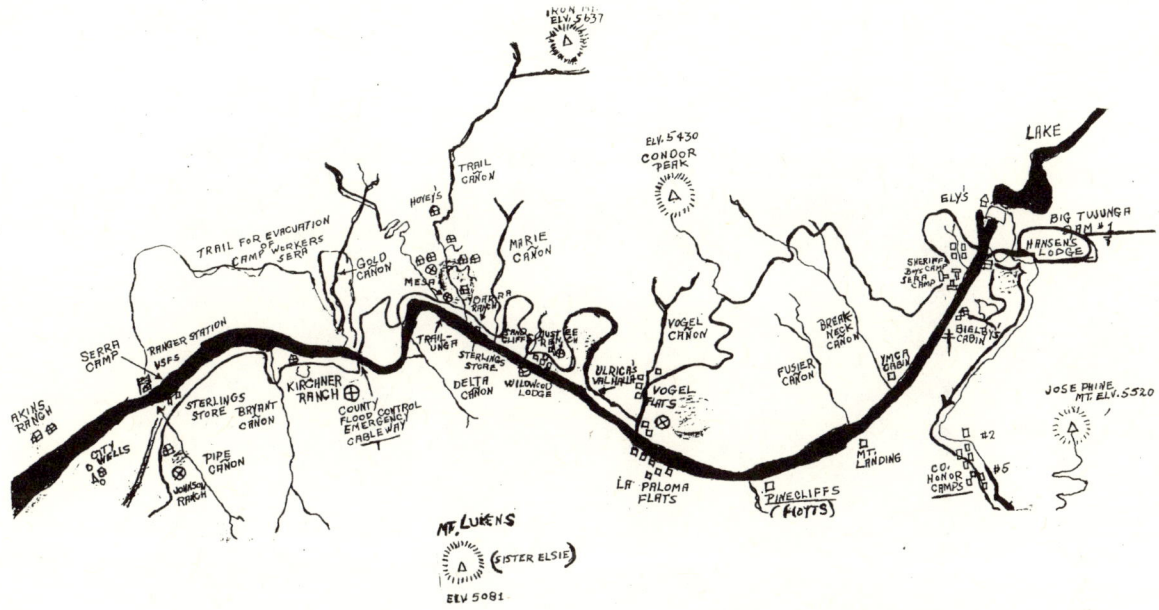

In this 1938 hand-drawn Big Tujunga Flood Map, the site of Hansen's Lodge is just east of the Big Tujunga Canyon and below the Big Tujunga Dam No. 1. Note Marie Cañon, below Iron Mt. *Map by Harry Pulfer.*

tain and two years later made a journey to the site and placed a bronze plaque at the grave. It reads: "Homer Alfred Hansen, 1872–1960. He was an inspiration to his family and friends."[18] His beloved Marie died at her apartment in South Pasadena on August 24, 1993, at the age of 101 years.[19] The family traveled by horseback up the mountain to scatter Marie's ashes where Homer had been left some thirty-three years before. The earth that Marie so dearly loved reclaimed her.[20]

On September 30, 2003, Homer Junior passed away. Once again, the family traveled by horseback to scatter another Hansen family member's ashes on the mountaintop in Cache Creek Park. Homer Junior, like his parents, was wedded to the earth.[21]

Notes

[1] Charlotte Boutwell, "The Wedding 1920," *Dr. Homer A. Hansen* (self-published, 1964), 47.

[2] Marie Hansen as told to Sarah Lombard in a February 1974 visit to her home in South Pasadena, *The Record-Ledger* (February 21, 1974).

[3] *National Geographic Magazine* (May 1925) called the Fern Cave the finest growth of maidenhair fern in the world.

[4] Marie Hansen, op. cit.

[5] Author's interview with Marie's daughter, Maude Ann Taylor, and granddaughter, Jacqueline, May 23, 2002.

[6] John Steven McGroarty, *Los Angeles: From the Mountains to the Sea* (1921), 607.

[7] Ibid.

[8] "The Mountain League of Southern California," *Trails Magazine* 5, no. 1 (Winter 1938): 8–9.

[9] Lawrence R. Tollenaere, *Dr. Homer A. Hansen* (1964), 51.

[10] In 1920, surveyor Donald McLain produced a new forest map. Sister Elsie's Peak, appearing on maps as early as 1875, now became Mt. Lukens, in honor of Theodore P. Lukens, who was responsible for the Forestry Nursery at Henninger Flats, as well as the reforestation, with thousands of trees, of the San Gabriels. The fire lookout tower on the mountain was removed in 1934.

[11] John W. Robinson, *The San Gabriels—The Mountain Country from Soledad Canyon to Lytle Creek* (Arcadia, Calif.: Big Santa Anita Historical Society, rev. ed. 1995).

[12] *The Los Angeles Times* (November 1, 1997).

[13] Tollenaere, op. cit.

[14] *The San Fernando Sun* (August 20, 1940).

[15] Tollenaere, loc. cit.

[16] Ibid.

[17] California Death Records, Kern County, November 25, 1960.

[18] Tollenaere, loc. cit., p. 64.

[19] California Death Records, Los Angeles, August 24, 1993.

[20] Author's interview with Marie's daughter, Maude Ann Taylor and granddaughter, Jacqueline, May 23, 2002.

[21] Author's interview with Marie's daughter, Maude Ann Taylor, January 7, 2003.

FOUNDING SISTERS

An unidentified group under the Tujunga Canyon Dam No. 1, c. 1933.

MARIE HUBER HANSEN

The great flood of 1938 forever erased Hansen's Lodge from the Big Tujunga Canyon.

FOUNDING SISTERS

(*above*) The Hansen family attended the dinner and dedication of the $13 million dam on August 17, 1940. *The Los Angeles Times.*

(*opposite, top*) In 1948, the Federal Government leased the 1,500-acre Hansen Dam Park to Los Angeles City Parks and Recreation Department for forty years. The Park offered picnic areas, boating, golf on an 18-hole course, a merry-go-round and train rides for the youngsters. *The Record-Ledger.*

(*opposite, bottom*) An aerial view of the newly built Hansen Dam, designed to control the turbulent flood waters of the Big and Little Tujunga Canyons. The 10,509-feet-long structure would be a lasting monument to the Hansen family.

Holiday Lake and recreation area was 130 acres. When it closed in 1982, it had shrunk to 80 acres. When it reopened to the public in 1999, it was a 9-acre boating and fishing pond, c. 1950.

MARIE HUBER HANSEN

Marie presents a line drawing of the western portion of the Tujunga Rancho to Sarah Lombard. Camera-shy Marie had to be coaxed into having her photograph taken, c. 1974. *The Record-Ledger.*

Mabel relaxes in front of the home she and her father built in 1913 at 10205 Tujunga Canyon Boulevard. Her home was located on the site of the present Tujunga Post Office. *The Record-Ledger.*

Mabel Louise Hatch
1880–1957

Mabel joined the ranks of such literary ladies of Tujunga as Zoe Gilbert, Frances Parcher, and Beth Pasko when she penned a humorous and honest account of her arrival at the Little Lands Colony in 1913. Her written story first appeared in the *Record-Ledger* on March 17, 1923, during the celebration of the town's 10th anniversary.

In 1952, Mabel co-published, with Wallace Morgan, a green-covered booklet entitled *The Green Verdugo Hills—a Chronicle of Sunland-Tujunga, Calif. And how it grew*. It sold for one dollar. She published the booklet in a desperate attempt to obtain funds to help preserve the Verdugo Hills Cemetery. For thirty-two years, Mabel was the overseer for the operations of the Hills of Peace Cemetery, created in 1922 when Parson Wornum was laid to rest there. Mabel passed away in 1957 and her cremated remains were interred in the lava rock wall encircling the Hatch Family plot, high on Pioneer Hill, in the Verdugo Hills Cemetery. Two x's carved into the wall indicate the location of her burial.[1]

As her story attests, she was there from the birth of the colony:

"The Little Landers"
by Mabel Hatch

We stepped off the train, my father and I, at the dingy old Los Angeles station, the day before Thanksgiving, 1913.

I think it was during the second day after our arrival that my aunt ushered us into a hall where Mr. William E. Smythe, a silver tongued orator in a frock coat, was telling the story of the Little Lands, with pictures thrown on a large white screen to prove his points.

I looked round at the people in the audience. Next to me was a woman of fifty or so, perhaps more, with a tired, lined face but with the look of a fearful eagerness in her pale eyes. Her hands were smooth and well kept. She was a stenographer or office worker or maybe a teacher, I guessed. I noticed how tightly she clutched her bag, a worn, black leather affair, and every now and then her free hand wandered to the front of her blouse to be sure the chamois bag was still there.

Next to her were a heavy, red faced farmer and his frail, frightened looking wife. He had a chamois bag, too, sewed to his shirt and tied with a string around his neck for extra security. You could see the dirty tape above his collar, and he too reached every now and then to be sure it was there.

The there were small businessmen who had developed asthma, and asthmatic wives and children, and they were looking for climate; there were widows striking out on their own after a long life of taking orders; there were spinsters, oh lots and lots of spinsters, who had been stenographers and book-keepers and file clerks and teachers for more years than they wanted to remember.

There were bachelors too, mostly old but some middle aged, who had just begun to realize they would be old someday and decided they better fasten onto something after the roving life. There were all sorts, but a few things they had in common; mostly they were middle age or older, though some had young sons and daughters with them. But almost every one of them had somehow taken a beating from life and now, with a last throw, looked and hoped so eagerly for a new chance.

Reluctantly, I turned from the people to the lecture. There was the picture of a sort of tent house on the screen. It was filled with luxuriantly growing vegetables. There were tomato vines climbing to the roof and a pretty girl pulling the

261

ripe fruit: there were lettuce and onions and radishes and dozens more looking good enough to eat. All you had to do, the speaker said, was to bring a trowel and a sack of cement (there were rocks and sand on the property, he promised, and in all these forty years, as far as I know, no one has risen to refute him in that), and you could build your own house.

Before you started you were to drop a few seeds in the virgin soil of your back yard and in no time at all you would be picking vegetables for your dinner. To complete the picture you were to buy a goat for milk, a few chickens and pigeons for meat and the three together would fertilize the soil when it was no longer virgin.

As soon as you got a small cellar dug you could plant some mushrooms and by the time you had the roof on your house, they'd be adding to your food supply.

There would be a cooperative store, the speaker said, owned and operated by the settlers, where you could trade any excess of your produce for salt and sugar, and there would be a community marketing system which would provide trucks to pick up anything you had to market and would deliver the coffee and calico. Oh, it was all very perfect!

There would even be retired people in all the arts and professions among the colonists—professors ready to advise on all growing problems, plumbers who would plumb for you if you didn't want to tackle that job yourself, builders who would give a hand with getting the frame of your house up and the roof on, musicians and actors who would entertain in the big new "Club House" to be dedicated in a few days!

Looking back over these nearly forty years, I can still see those eager, tired, flushed faces!

And so with colors flying and hopes held high, we followed the real estate salesmen to their automobiles, and descended upon, or rather ascended to, the stony foothill that is now Tujunga.

There were no paved streets then. Even what is now Foothill and was then Michigan Blvd., but familiarly called the Highway, was just a dirt road. Our cars approached the site from the East, taking what is now Honolulu and going beyond the site to double back and so approach it from below.

Just west of Sunland, on the little crest there, we stopped to look up the valley. There was no question about it; it was a gorgeous view, the warm, sunny little valley lying between the mountains and the Verdugo Hills. Of course, to eyes born to the lush, cosy [sic] landscape of southern Michigan, it seemed a bit austere, but it did have its own sort of beauty and we were all ready to admire it.

It was a little harder to hang onto your enthusiasm when we arrived and got out of the cars and took a close look at the rocks and the sage brush. The sun had begun to be pretty hot by that time.

But, my aunt, who had been completely sold by the view, scraped up a little soil from between the stones and squeezed

(*opposite*) In this 1916 photograph, "Bird's Acre" and the Hatch family home are seen on the bend of Tujunga Canyon Boulevard.

(*above*) Mabel and her father erected the cloth house seen to the left of Aunt Cora's house. In the nursery, they raised vegetables and plants by seed to get a jump-start on spring. Winds destroyed the structure, but a lath house replaced it. *The Record-Ledger.*

it in her hand and it stuck together and she said that meant it had lots of humos [*sic*] in it.

We stood on the edge of the acre and a quarter on which my aunt had taken an option for us and looked. My father was nearly 70 then. He was completely different from most of the other settlers. He had been very active in both business and politics but, like many of them he had suffered losses and tragedies and after a long illness had looked to a friendlier climate where he could make a garden and find peace.

What he saw looked neither friendly nor peaceful. It was about the roughest, toughest looking piece of land I EVER saw.

Well, we decided to think it over and went back to the hotel. The next day the salesman took us out again, this time to the dedication of the "Club House," later the City Hall. It was a small and rather pathetic group who stood around and saw the flag raising, but somehow as it fluttered to the top, our hopes went with it. The good old Stars and Stripes that was the same in Michigan or in this strange new country. It was familiar and reassuring and gave us a feeling of security.

Anyway, we bought it, the acre and a quarter, influenced more, I think, by the fact we were stuck with it than anything else, and father hired a flock of laborers and two or three teams of mules and began trying to plow and take the stones out. Father and I ran along after the plow, rolling the stones to the sidelines when they weren't too big.

It was new work for both of us, but there was none of the powerful automotive equipment then that there is now to do such work so, round and round, we went over and over the acre and a quarter, and always there were stones and more stones. Finally father decided to consentrate [*sic*] on his garden spot and let the front of the lot go till later for a complete destoning [*sic*].

We got our little shack built, but by that time the "deep yellow sunshine" had become a burning yellow and not nearly so friendly. How it did beat down on that little flat paper roof! And we found there were deprivations we hadn't exactly counted on, because I, for one, didn't know there was any place in the world where you did not have street lights, ice, gas to cook with and mail delivered at your door. Those things I supposed were just basic and existed everywhere. I think to some of the others it was the same. But we learned. HOW we learned!

Every week we went to town meeting. It was held in the Club House and we all lighted our kerosene lanterns and trudged up the hill. We were weary in mind and body. Running behind a plow and throwing out rocks only to find when you go back over the field to plant your walnut trees you have to dig the holes with a pick, is neither refreshing nor encouraging., Furthermore, you take so much stone out of one hole, there isn't enough earth to plant the tree. But we went to town meeting.[2]

263

(*left*) Tujunga's original insurance agency, Hatch & Clemens, was established by Leo L. Lang as the first agency in the Little Lands Colony. Mabel purchased it in 1924 and in 1942 combined it with the law firm of Homer Martin and Bower. In 1946, Neil Clemens purchased an interest. Sunland-Tujunga Chamber of Commerce pamphlet.

(*below*) Mabel ran these ads for her business in 1926 in the *Record-Ledger Newspaper*.

EMPLOYERS OF LABOR, ATTENTION!

Assembly Bill No. 205 was passed at the last session of the legislature and went into effect July 24th, 1925. It provides that on or after that date anyone hiring employees subject to the California Compensation law will be obliged to secure a workman' Compensation policy or file a $20,000 bond. Failure to do either of these things constitutes a midemeanor on the part of an employer for which he will be subject to a fine of not more than $500.00 or imprisonment of not more than six months, or both.

Do not delay taking out this insurance—WE SELL IT!

MABEL L. HATCH

The Lang Insurance Agency   Tujunga Valley Bank Building   Tujunga, California

---

Little is known of Mabel's life prior to her coming to the Little Lands Colony. When she arrived in the colony, she was thirty-three years old and her father, Hiram, was seventy years old. Her father had been a captain in the Civil War and was the former warden of the Michigan State Penitentiary. Hiram and Mabel came to Tujunga as a result of Marshall V. Hartranft's Western Empire Land Promotion advertisements, seeking a friendlier climate and a peaceful retirement for Hiram. His wife, Sarah, had died many years before. After much difficulty, Mabel and Hiram built their stone and wood cottage at 10205 Tujunga Canyon Boulevard, then called Monte Vista Boulevard, next to his sister Cora Belle Linaberry's home.[3] The small but attractive cottage was featured in Hartranft's promotional brochure on the Little Lands Colony, and Mabel lived in this home with her nephew, Ashley, until just three years prior to her death. Hiram's sister, Cora Belle, had arrived in the colony first and built a little Cape Cod cottage that, because of her love of nature, she named "Bird's Acre."[4]

Hiram passed away in 1922 and was the second person buried at the Hills of Peace Cemetery. Mabel's brother, Henry F. Hatch, a brigadier general in the United States Army, passed away in New York of a cerebral hemorrhage in January 1937. His body was shipped back to California and, with much fanfare and pomp, he was buried in the Hatch family plot at the Hills of Peace Cemetery, now known as the Verdugo Hills Cemetery.[5]

Hilda Livingston's son, Chancellor ("Chan"), wrote in his memoirs in 1977:

> A Miss Hatch, a maiden lady, after Bolton Hall was completed, devoted her time and talents to supervising and arranging the social events for the young folks as well as the seniors. She was usually assisted by two other ladies. One was a retired drama teacher and the other a qualified dance instructor. A Mr. Maygrove, a former bandleader with the British Army, with his wife and two daughters, Gladys and Dorothy, provided the music for dancing programs. Miss Hatch challenged the obstacles to raise money for the purchase of curtains, chairs, tables, floor wax, kitchen hardware and costumes for the local amateur plays.
>
> Now remember the average scale of wages for a full days work was two dollars. Schoolboys made one dollar per day clearing brush, stacking rock or picking fruit. With the ratio of approximately five boys to one girl, Miss Hatch put in operation a box lunch auction. She knew full well that a dancing boy would gamble on a box to be assured of two or three dances with the girl. One other silent agreement was that he could escort her home by foot or horse cart.[6]

The years from 1911 to 1915 were when Tujunga experienced the transformation from the horse-drawn wagon to the Model T Ford. After spending fifty cents to buy Miss Hatch's auctioned lunch boxes, young men found that the girls didn't want to go home from the Saturday night dances at Bolton Hall in a horse-drawn wagon. The schoolboys paid half a day's wage to dance with the girls at Bolton Hall. Some of the young men cursed Miss Hatch for costing them money, but the adults approved of her ingenuity to raise maintenance funds for Bolton Hall.

Mabel, who remained single, became a valued member of the community. For years she was a successful businesswoman, running her own insurance agency from various locations in Tujunga. She was active in many of the organizations, but her most successful work was preserving the town's cemetery.

Without a husband or children to raise, Mabel turned her energies to rescuing cats and dogs that needed help. She became a voice for the voiceless. Despite her diabetes and deteriorating health, she continued her efforts to protect the cemetery and the abandoned animals in town.

In June 1955, Mabel wrote a letter to the *Record-Ledger*, showing her disgust over the deterioration of the Hills of Peace Cemetery:

> "Hills of Peace Restoration is Urged by Mabel Hatch"
>
> The annual Memorial Day rites at the cemetery were not held this year because of the accumulated rubbish on the Parsons Trail approach to the cemetery.
>
> Text of Miss Hatch's letter follows:
>
> "Sirs:
>
> Yes, I know of a condition I think should be corrected, here in the Sunland-Tujunga area.
>
> In 1922 M. V. Hartranft gave four and a half acres of rolling foothill land to the community for a cemetery. He deeded it to an association to hold for the community and had the association incorporated. It is secure in its title and can never be abandoned.
>
> A number of the very old timers are buried there—men and women who dug the rocks and endured the heat and the deprivations of the early days—back when the going was REALLY hard—soldiers, sailors, preachers, builders and just plain folks with stout hearts.
>
> Only the money taken in for graves has been available and it is not enough to make even the simple improvements desirable. I suggest the community these people built gather 'round and make the heights where they lie the beautiful memorial that it should be.
>
> The Veterans of Foreign Wars have put forth a valiant effort to make the improvements the little cemetery needs but everywhere they have met indifference and even destructive vandalism.
>
> It needs more than willing hands and strong backs. It needs a little money—not much—and a real community effort to make it, not only a beautiful memorial to the early men

and women, but an inspiring cemetery for the present community. It could be a beauty spot of which the area would be very proud.

The name has been changed to 'Hills of Peace' cemetery. If you will drive up there I believe you will think it is appropriate.

Old Timers' Week is just ahead. Wouldn't a real effort to correct the neglect of the little cemetery be in order?

Very sincerely,
Mabel L. Hatch[7]

One year before her death, Mabel had to have her leg amputated due to the complications of diabetes. Undaunted, she appeared before the Sunland-Tujunga Chamber of Commerce to gain their assurance that they would keep an eye on her cemetery and promise to keep it maintained.[8] Sadly, that promise was not kept and the quaint hillside cemetery fell into ruin.

When Mabel passed away on August 27, 1957, at her home on Parr Avenue in Sunland, the *Record-Ledger* recorded her passing on the front page with a description of her funeral rites. All the businesses in town closed so that employers and employees could pay a final tribute to "this quiet little woman with a delightful sense of humor and an intrepid strength of character that marked the Little Landers."[9]

Notes

[1] Sunland resident Jack Wollard finally solved the mystery of Mabel's burial during a brush clearing session at Verdugo Hills Cemetery, May 5, 2002.

[2] Mabel Hatch, *The Green Verdugo Hills—A Chronicle of Sunland-Tujunga, Calif. And how it grew* (Tujunga, California, 1952).

[3] Record of Funeral. August 27, 1957. Bades Mortuary, Tujunga.

[4] Hatch, op. cit.

[5] Martha McKee, "Buried at Hills of Peace Cemetery" (February 7, 1968). Bolton Hall Museum Archives.

[6] Speech of Col. Chancellor E. Livingston at Bolton Hall on May 7, 1977. Bolton Hall Museum Archives.

[7] "Hills of Peace Restoration is Urged by Mabel Hatch," *The Record-Ledger* (June 9, 1955).

[8] Author's interview with Marjorie Johnson (Marjorie bought Bird's Acre Cottage in 1942 and became Mabel's next door neighbor and best friend). November 20, 1993.

[9] "Last Rites Set for S-T Pioneer, Mabel Hatch," *The Record-Ledger* (August 29, 1957).

(*opposite, left*) In this 1953 photograph, Mabel poses with Wallace Morgan, founder of the *Record-Ledger Newspaper*, as they prepare the first annual "Historical and Progress" edition for the *Record-Ledger*.

(*opposite, right*) Mabel sitting at home in a chair made by inmates of a Manila prison. The chair was a gift from her brother, Brig. General Henry J. Hatch. Photograph was taken in the early 1950s. *The Record-Ledger.*

(*above*) Mabel and family were buried on the hill to the right of Verdugo Hills Cemetery sign. *Courtesy of Author.*

(*right*) Headstone of Mabel's father, buried in Verdugo Hills Cemetery on October 12, 1922. *Courtesy of Author.*

An early photograph of Alice before her move to California, c. 1900.

Alice Grant Lamson
1877–1964

With the exception of Ida and John McGroarty, the Lamsons, both passionately committed to their profession of photography, were considered the most widely traveled couple to live in Tujunga. From the first day of Alice's marriage to Harry, on October 4, 1899, in Boston, Massachusetts, the exciting life he led became Alice's. Harry's father and grandfather were famous photographers in Portland, Maine. The Lamson family came to America from Essex, England, in 1635.[1]

Alice Grant was born in Searsport, Maine, on May 5, 1877, to Martha Pendleton and Henry Grant.[2] She was the youngest of six children. Little is recorded of her early years. We do know that when she was in her early twenties, she went to work for Joseph H. Lamson Sr. in his photography studio. While working there, Alice became an expert photo retoucher and photo colorist. Her boss and future father-in-law traveled and took scenic photographs from Maine to Florida. The senior Lamson also traveled to Cuba and South America in search of new vistas to capture with his cameras. Alice found life in the Lamson studio exhilarating. The walls of the studio were hung with portraits of the famous and not-so-famous. Henry Wordsworth Longfellow, the poet, commented that he preferred Lamson's photographs of himself above all others.[3]

In 1901, Alice's father-in-law passed away. Alice and Harry continued their work at the family studio but eventually closed it down. The couple then moved to Jamaica, where they were hired to photograph sugar plantations for the owners. They made a dynamic duo, with Harry photographing the scenery and Alice expertly hand-coloring the photographs.

After their stay in Jamaica, they traveled to Europe. Prior to World War I, they took photos in France, Switzerland, Germany, and Norway. Often they would go on bicycle tours, taking photographs for tourists.[4] Harry became a student of languages, learning French, German, Spanish, and Italian. Alice and Harry shared a love of music and they collected opera scores to play on their grand piano.

In 1912, they moved to the West Coast and set up a photography studio in downtown Los Angeles. Although they were moderately successful despite much competition, they were unhappy about having to rent space and work so hard to stretch their dollars. By chance, they met Marshall V. Hartranft, who told them about his new "Little Lands Colony" in Los Terrenitos. Harry said he was one of the first to succumb to developer Hartranft's slogan, "An Acre and a Living."

Early in 1913, Alice and Harry moved to the Little Lands Colony and pitched a tent on their lot at 139 East Greeley Avenue. They would live and work here for the remainder of their lives.

In a 1922 promotional booklet entitled "My Hand-Made Home in the Hills," Hartranft showcased their home and let Harry write about his home building experience:

> Here we decided to make our home and build it; although it meant giving up my business. That is where you will be

269

(*above*) "We bought our land, pitched a tent and started to work." Note the lean-to (*right of tent*) used for cooking, c. 1913.

(*opposite*) Alice and Harry stand on the patio Alice built for sixty cents worth of cement, c. 1914.

better off than we were, because transportation facilities have become so perfected since then that you can reach the city now daily, quickly and easily.

With an amount pitifully small, less than the average present-day monthly salary, we came out and started home building. What we achieved in building you can see before your eyes. Although we ran into what appeared to be insurmountable obstacles, we worked them out—slowly and not without some little difficulty—but we wouldn't take *thousands* for the pleasures our experiences have brought us.

Harrison, take my word for it—neither you nor anyone will ever know until they have had that happy experience, building for yourself with your own hands, to see the building for yourself with your own hands; to see the *Dream Home* you have planned slowly taking shape by your own creation.

My wife and I with very little outside help, and at small cost, built this entire home ourselves. Night after night, we were so tired from the unaccustomed toil that we could barely stay awake long enough to have our evening meal—but the work never hurt us a bit, and the next day always found us on the job with increased strength, fresher faculties and deeper inspiration for our task.

Our home has been completed, the land cleared and our trees are bearing larger crops every year. From time to time I get some professional work to do, and while my income is not by any means to be compared with what I earned in the city—we have more money. Of every dollar I bring in, ninety cents stays in our pockets.

Mrs. Lamson is not a robust woman, and yet she built that handsome stone terrace outside without any help or expense. The French glass windows in this room we made ourselves from the old photo negative glasses which I had accumulated in years of photographic work. We did our own wiring, shingling, covering of walls; practically everything. Quite a number of women as well as men have come up here and put up a good portion of their homes.[5]

The majority of other city dwellers had constructed simple shelters that they tried to modify with trees and flowers. Being artists, the Lamsons could not build just any structure. They chose a lot with a large live oak tree in the front yard and built their home to the back of the tree. Neither of them had ever done any rough carpentry work, but they built their artistic home and studio with very little outside help. In the studio, they used eucalyptus poles for the rafters, shakes for the sides, and washed photographic plates for the many small panes of the casement windows. Heavy purple drapes lined the large studio to regulate the sun-drenched room.[6] The residence was of equal artistic merit. To the other early settlers, the Lamson home represented a courageous stand for gracious living and they passed by the home as often as they could.

Marshall Hartranft made Harry the official photographer for the colony. For many years he and Alice were the only professional photographers in the valley. They loved photographing the mountains, the colony in various stages of development, the people, and the festivals and gatherings of all kinds. It was an exciting time, to see the births of the town cemetery, the Cross of San Ysidro, various churches and the schools.

After having the Lamson home used in Hartranft's land sales pitch and showcased on the tours, Harry decided to sell real estate, cashing in on his popularity. He was also chosen to be the official photographer for John Steven McGroarty.

While Harry photographed the town and its people, Alice was working hard at her career of expert color retouching. Her fame grew and she became well known throughout the United States. Because of her unique skills, she was employed by the Willard Art Photography Studio in Palm Springs, California. Mr. Willard would send her his famous desert photographs; Alice would hand-color them and send them back to Palm Springs by mail. When Alice was asked why she had no children, she replied, "There wasn't time for children with our busy careers." In her spare time, Alice was also an accountant.[7]

During World War I, Harry went to Washington, D.C., to work in the War Department. Alice continued with her career at home. After Harry's return from Washington, D.C., the couple enjoyed traveling throughout California and photographing such scenic spots as Catalina Island, Yosemite, and many beaches and deserts.

In 1939, Harry started the successful town camera club at "Campy" Shires Photo Shop in Sunland. It was here that the Lamsons met Ray Brunke, a fellow pho-

tographer. Ray would later inherit Alice's 1936 Nash automobile, Harry's cameras, and several thousand photographs, glass negatives, and prints. Shortly after the beginning of World War II, Alice and Harry retired from their active careers, taking just an occasional photo for friends. They spent their time enjoying their home, special cactus garden, and the many friends they made throughout the years. Ray Brunke remembered Alice as a very lady-like, warm, and congenial person. Both she and Harry retained their New England accents long after their arrival in California.

On May 6, 1962, Alice's eighty-fifth birthday, her husband died of lung cancer. She was a devoted wife who cared for him at home until he passed away. Alice would live less than two more years in the family home. After

FOUNDING SISTERS

Early photograph of Lamson Studio.
They lived and worked here for the rest of their lives, c. 1923.

she took a fall on her front steps, Alice lived in a convalescent hospital in Sunland until she, too, passed away, on April 7, 1964.

The Lamsons were a gifted pair whose photographs documented the growth of the colony and the emergence of Tujunga.[8] In 1966, Ray Brunke donated the Lamson photo collection to Bolton Hall Museum, making Tujunga one of the best-documented towns in southern California.

The Lamson home is long gone, the distant relatives silenced, but the photographic legacy they left of Sunland-Tujunga and their "Little Yosemite Valley" lives on.

Notes

[1] "Lamson Genealogy, An Undated History from a Lamson Family Member." Bolton Hall Museum clippings file.

[2] Record of Funeral. April 7, 1964. Bades Mortuary, Tujunga.

[3] Author's interview with Sunland resident Ray Brunke, the Lamson's unofficial "adopted" son. February 10, 1996.

[4] "Pioneer Builds Home in Tujunga," *Los Angeles Times—Valley Edition* (October 25, 1950).

[5] "My Hand-Made Home in the Hills," California Home Extension Association promotion pamphlet. c. 1919.

[6] Ray Brunke lecture, docent class, Bolton Hall Museum (November 1, 2003).

[7] Author's interview, February 10, 1996, op. cit.

[8] "Joseph Lamson Made a Unique Record of Community's Origin," *The Record-Ledger* (July 28, 1955).

ALICE GRANT LAMSON

(*right*) Alice sits beside her piano in the newly built home, c. 1915.

(*below*) The Lamson home to the left of their studio, c. 1926.

273

FOUNDING SISTERS

(*left*) Alice appears in her garden, wearing an afternoon tea dress (her dress was donated to Bolton Hall Museum), c. 1926.

(*below*) The Lamson's home was the pride of the colony. Their love of books and music is much in evidence in this interior photograph of their home, c. 1915.

(*above*) Alice enjoyed working out of doors near her studio, c. 1920s.

(*right*) The Lamson campsite on the desert in early 1930s. Note the graffiti on the rocks to the right.

(*below*) Alice and Harry's "adopted" son, Ray Brunke, presents the Lamson photograph collection to Martha Houk, Museum Director, at Bolton Hall Museum, c. 1996. *Courtesy of Author.*

Jennie in Pittsburgh, before heading west in search of good health, c. 1890. *Courtesy of Wilma Martin.*

Jennie Lichtenthaler
1862–1927

Jennie Elizabeth Winters was born in Titusville, Pennsylvania, to Martha Plummer and John Winters, on September 12, 1862.[1] Titusville became famous in 1859 when Edwin L. Drake completed the drilling of the first commercial oil well. The town's population was just four hundred people at the time of the first oil strike. Soon after the oil boom began, the town swelled to thousands as wildcatters came with their dreams.

At one point during Jennie's childhood, she survived a case of tuberculosis that left her weak, thin and sickly throughout her life. At an early age, she married W. D. Lichtenthaler, and on November 14, 1889, her only child, James, was born.[2] This sickly seventeen-year-old girl now had a baby to care for.

In 1907, with Jennie's weakened health, her doctor insisted she move to a warm, dry climate. Jennie's husband insisted she stay with him in Pittsburgh, Pennsylvania, where they made their home.

Her course of action was clear to her, a matter of life or death. It was a most difficult decision for Jennie, but she decided to meet her fate in California. With a heavy heart, she said good-bye to her husband and eighteen-year-old son, James, and boarded a train for the West.[3]

After an arduous trip, sitting on a wooden bench in the train, Jennie arrived in the desert town of Lancaster, California. For the next thirteen years, this independent woman would operate a successful bakery and restaurant there.

Her neighbors and granddaughters remember her as a strict, religious woman. Each day she would open her Bible and randomly pick a verse to guide her day. She considered the Bible to be her best friend and often wrote letters using Biblical dialogue and references:[4]

> For him who must run and yet would read, and particularly for her who at seventeen has already begun to run, these commands and promises of Holy Writ are gathered and grouped by one who, while running has felt the need. Dear James, This (Bible) is truly a wonderful book. It has been a wonderful help to me. Very precious to me. This book has helped me deeply and it will help you. Love, Mother.[5]

Jennie's parents had raised hunting dogs in Titusville and she would retain a love for dogs throughout her life. She was also described as always wearing black and having a luxurious head of red hair.

Two years after Jennie arrived in Lancaster, her son, James, and his fiancée, Pauline, traveled by train to visit her. Jennie would not allow an unmarried couple under her roof and insisted that James and Pauline be married at the train station. James and Pauline had two daughters, Ruth and Wilma. Ruth would go on to become mayor of Bunker, Missouri and Wilma married Homer Martin, who practiced law in Tujunga for fifty years. His office was at 9945 Commerce Avenue. Ruth now lives in Myrtle Beach, South Carolina, and Wilma lives in the state of Washington.

In 1920, Jennie moved to Tujunga and lived on Mountain View Avenue (Beckett Street). After she completed building her small wooden cottage, she planted a very nice garden. Much like Anna Adam, Jennie felt her diet of raw vegetables and goat's milk would restore her health. Although she worked very hard, she remained weak. After a mere seven years in Tujunga, she passed away at home from chronic kidney disease on September 7, 1927.[6]

Her husband, W. D., would remarry a widow with five children. Her son, James, found employment as chauffeur for John Steven McGroarty, and Jennie's granddaughters attended Glendale High School.

Jennie was typical of those who moved to Tujunga in search of better health. Like so many that followed her, it would be her last chance at a healthier life. Jennie's strength of character and independent spirit defined the pioneering women in Tujunga.

Notes

[1] State of California, Certificate of Vital Records. September 8, 1927.
[2] Author's interview with Wilma Martin, Jennie's granddaughter. June 26, 2000.
[3] Author's interview with Ruth Stanton Jordan, Jennie's granddaughter. February 17, 1998.
[4] Ibid.
[5] Letter written to James. Undated. Courtesy of Ruth Stanton Jordan. March 1998.
[6] Jennie's elaborate black dress and cape were donated to Bolton Hall Museum by her granddaughter, Ruth Stanton Jordan, March 21, 1998.

> I am not afraid of storms
> for I am learning how to sail my ship.
> —*Louisa May Alcott*

W. D., James, and Jennie in Pittsburgh.
Note the size of their dog, c. 1891. *Courtesy of Wilma Martin.*

Lichtenthaler's Ice Cream Parlor and little store in Lancaster, California, c. 1907.
Courtesy of Ruth Stanton Jordan.

Jennie's simple home on Mountain View Avenue (now Beckett Street).
Note the lush reed-like growth of plants, indicative of underground
water flow below Haines Canyon, c. 1920. *Courtesy of Forrest Theriot.*

Cora Belle (*left*) stands next to good friends
Myra Osgood and Alice Lamson, c. 1930.

Cora Belle Linaberry
1859–1945

History does not record her initial reaction when she arrived in the Little Lands Colony in 1913. The newly widowed Cora Belle Linaberry left Michigan and was one of the first colonists to help establish the colony. She had a Cape Cod cottage constructed that, because of her love for wild birds, she named "Bird's Acre."[1] Bird's Acre was built on a dusty dirt road called South Monte Vista Boulevard. Shortly after her arrival, Cora Belle's brother, Hiram Hatch, and his daughter, Mabel, arrived and built their home next to Bird's Acre.

Cora Belle made herself a valuable member of the fledgling colony by playing the piano for community dances at Bolton Hall and baking for community picnics and festivals.

Her home was located at 10213 Tujunga Canyon Boulevard, where the Tujunga post office parking lot is now located.[2] The lush grounds surrounding Bird's Acre and her many avian friends made her home a show place for many years. In 1936, she entered a sample of her exotic pineapple-guava fruit in the Los Angeles County Fair at Pomona and won second place.[3]

From 1936 through 1941, the childless Cora Belle shared her home with Myra Osgood, the office manager of the Haines Canyon Water Company.[4] In 1942, she sold her home to Marjorie and Stanley Johnson. In the early 1990s, the Johnson family donated the wrought iron Bird's Acre sign, photographs of the home, and Mabel Hatch's traveling trunk to Bolton Hall Museum.

Cora Belle spent the last few years of her life residing at 10143 Mountair Avenue in Tujunga. She was cremated and buried at Forest Lawn Cemetery in Glendale.[5]

Like many of the other colonists, Cora Belle took pride in performing a bit of magic, transforming the barren rocky land into a small tropical paradise.

Notes
[1] Mabel Hatch, "The Green Verdugo Hills—a Chronicle of Sunland-Tujunga, Calif. And how it grew," *The Record-Ledger*, 1953.
[2] Author's interview with Ruth Marjorie Johnson. November 20, 1995.
[3] "Local Exhibit of Pineapple-Guavas Wins 2nd Premium," *The Record-Ledger* (October 29, 1936).
[4] Author's interview with Tom Theobold, retired Tujunga postmaster. October 9, 1993.
[5] Record of Funeral. September 16, 1945. Bades Mortuary, Tujunga.

FOUNDING SISTERS

Cora (*right*) and good friend Myra Osgood on an outing in the Big Tujunga Canyon, c. 1930s

"Birds Acre" photograph taken in 1913. Newly staked eucalyptus trees grew to 70 feet.
Snow came early that year. *Courtesy of Stan Johnson.*

By 1923, Birds Acre was almost hidden from view.

Birds Acre in the 1930s.

On June 30, 1950, Hilda and Jim celebrated their sixtieth wedding anniversary.
Courtesy of Philip Livingston.

Hilda Esco Livingston
1863–1958

Hilda Esco was born on a Christmas evening in a small town in Finland, near the Arctic Circle. Her earliest memories were of the Laps (the indigenous dwellers of Lapin Land) coming into her town with their herds of reindeer. She spoke little of her childhood, but remembered her father training trotting teams of horses during the long harsh winters. "She always compared Santa's reindeer with those she had seen the Laps drive when she was a small girl."[1] In 1885, at the age of twelve years, this daughter of Finland came to America with her parents and brothers. They settled in Red Wing, a small town in Michigan, on the Mississippi River.[2]

When Hilda was in her twenties, she left Red Wing for Fort Buford, North Dakota, near the Montana border. She worked for a general's wife at the fort. While there, she met and fell in love with James Henry Livingston. Her husband-to-be was a brilliant linguist who spoke and understood five American Indian tribal languages, and served with the 15th Infantry Regiment of the United States Army. Hilda would marry into a family that had come to America from Scotland in 1742. The early Livingstons had lived on 250 acres that were part of the Peter Stuyvesant land grant in New York.[3] Jim was born in Petersburg, New York, in 1865, on Livingston land that bordered Vermont and Massachusetts.[4] On July 30, 1890, Jim and Hilda were married in St. Paul, Minnesota.

After their marriage, Hilda and Jim moved to Cincinnati, Ohio, where Jim worked for the Cincinnati and Ohio Railroad.[5] Their son, William, was born there in 1892, and a second son, Chancellor, was born in 1896 at Fort Sheridan, just outside of Chicago, Illinois. Jim had left his job with the railroad and secretly reenlisted in the Army. Hilda was not pleased with his decision, as it would leave her alone with the boys. Jim was called to Cuba to fight in the Spanish-American War and served as a scout for Teddy Roosevelt.[6] He was wounded there and, after suffering a bout of malaria, Jim retired from the Army in 1907. He received an Army pension for the remainder of his life.

Lured to California by work as manager of the Pacific Electric Railway Company, which served Glendale and Montrose, in 1909 the Livingston family boarded a tourist train, bound from Ohio to Los Angeles. Tourist trains did not pull freight cars. They were designated for passengers only and, although the cars had sleeping spaces, they did not have dining facilities. Hilda had packed a large wicker hamper of food for her family. The trip was arduous, as the family had to sit on wooden benches for the entire journey.

Upon their arrival in California, the family lived in Glendale until a meeting with Marshall Hartranft changed their fate. In December 1910, the Livingstons were invited to spend the night at Hartranft's Lazy Lonesome Ranch in Monte Vista (Sunland). Jim never forgot the beautiful sight of the mountains and the rocky hillsides bathed in the glow of that December night's full moon. The land looked barren and so isolated, but Marshall assured Jim that in ten years there would be electricity and many homes in a new community. The Zachau home's lone light was the only sign of man on those barren slopes. Jim and Hilda were so impressed with the scenery that they purchased five acres in Glorietta Heights, the Western Empire Little Lands sub-division. They were excited about being part of building a new community. Jim checked out the water supply in Haines Canyon and found it sufficient to supply his newly acquired property.

In January 1911, the family moved into a housekeeping tent on their property on Hill Street (Hillrose Street).[7] The Livingston men began to clear the heavy mountain growth from their newly acquired land. The month they moved into the tent, the area experienced the worst freeze in twenty years. All the fruit and crops were destroyed. Hilda's childhood, spent near the Arctic Circle, enabled her to endure that harsh winter. Fresh water for the household and washing had to be hand-carried in a bucket from three-fourths of a mile away. Family meals were cooked on a wood-burning stove and lanterns were used to illuminate the night. The only sounds to disturb the quiet nights were the singing of the coyotes.[8] Every two weeks the family made the all-day trip to either Glendale or San Fernando for a fresh supply of groceries. Rabbits and freshly caught trout supplemented their diet.

Hilda lived in an all-male household and a world ruled by men, but she was definitely the one who ruled her own roost. This strong-willed woman was too busy living life to record her experiences, but her son, Chan, recalled, "We lived in a tent infested with red ants. The big red ants came out of the virgin brush along with tarantulas, scorpions and snakes. I remember how my mother accepted and adjusted to the situation. Surely, upon her death, God gave her recognition for her stability and courage."[9]

The Livingston property was part of Hartranft's Western Empire Little Lands subdivision, the area east and west of Mt. Gleason and extending to the mountains on the south. "Hilda had only six other families for neighbors: Ardizone, Rowley, Zachau, Begue, Zitto, Fehlhaber and Forster. The Rowley family sold their homesteaded property in the Seven Hills area, just northeast of the Livingstons, and moved to Sunland."[10] The J.T. Fitzgerald family, who owned the Los Angeles Music Company, bought the Rowley property and would use the large ranch house as their weekend get-away.[11]

In 1910, there were just two dirt roads leading into town. Sons Chancellor and William went to Glendale High School by riding their horses to the Tujunga Depot, where they caught Earl Sims's stage (a 1908 Cadillac) for the bumpy ride south. The paying passengers and the girls sat inside, while the boys stood on the running boards and hung on for dear life.

History does not record how Hilda felt about tent living but, in July 1911, her stone home was completed and the family moved into permanent quarters. Hilda's backyard had two stone walls, running parallel to each other. This design was meant to keep the rattlesnakes out of the yard.[12]

One of the big events of Hilda's life in the Little Lands was the opening of the "Clubhouse," Bolton Hall, in August 1913. Son Chan would become a member of the Maygrove's Monte Vista Band, which would play for many dances and social events there. While Hilda was home doing more than her share of housework and cooking, her husband would join a group of six other men who called themselves "The Millionaires Club of Happiness and Contentment." They met each afternoon, under the shade oak at the southeast corner of Foothill (Michigan) and Commerce (Sunset) to discuss politics, life, and the latest news of the colony. Chan recalls,

> On this particular day, after arriving home from school, coupled with completing my daily chores of bringing in the cooking-stove wood and the house water needs, my mother instructed me to "hitch the horse to the cart and drive up the hill and bring your father home. He is up there with those other six windjammers worrying about the troubles and complaints of those Eastern City lot buyers. Tell him to get home and do some worrying about milking the cow, she has been mooing for the last half hour to be milked."[13]

Jim Livingston was hired by Marshall Hartranft to complete a water delivery system from Haines Canyon. Hartranft also appointed a four-man council, consisting of Jim, Ed Forester, Leo Lang, Harry Zachau,

Fort Buford, North Dakota, where Hilda met Jim.
Courtesy of the Fort Buford website, www.fortbuford.com.

Fort Buford (1866–1895) was established as a military post, guarding the trails and serving as a supply depot. It is best remembered as the site where the Hunkpapa Sioux leader, Sitting Bull, surrendered in 1881. Its last fifteen years as a working post, it served to protect the survey and construction crews of the Great Northern Railway. *Map courtesy of www.cr.nps.gov.*

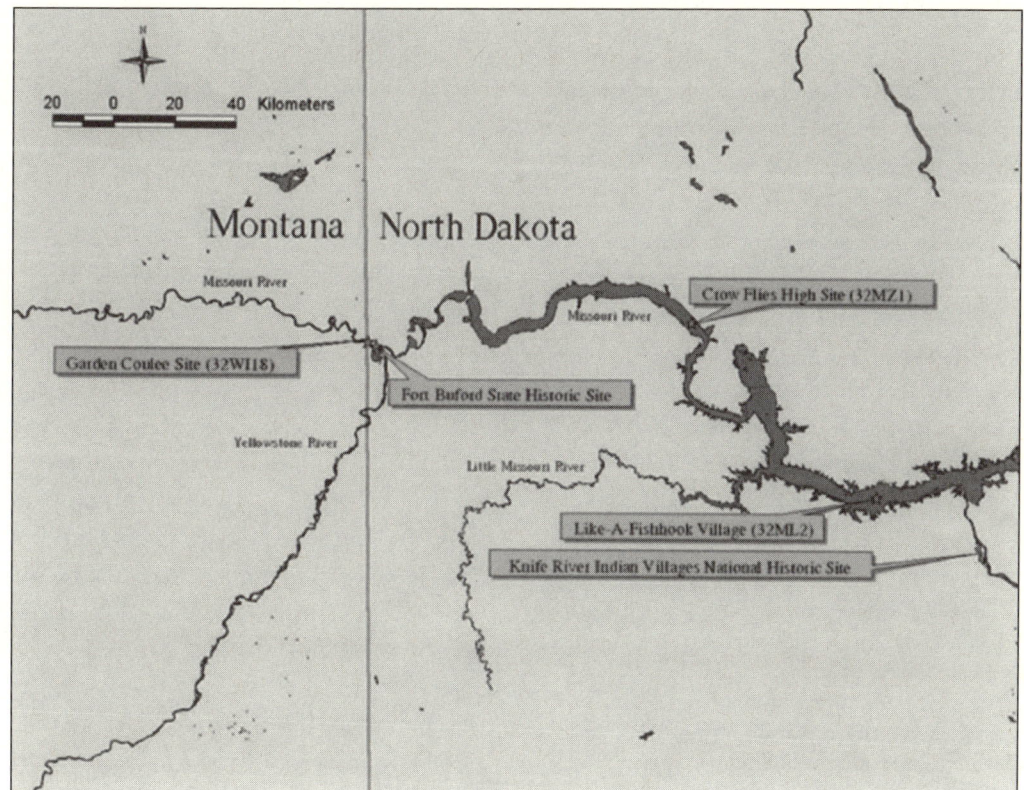

(*above*) The Livingston home was completed in 1911. Standing (left to right) is Pearl Livingston (Hilda's daughter-in-law), Pearl's children Ray and Bob, Hilda and Jim, c. 1918.

(*opposite*) Looking north on Commerce Avenue (Sunset). Note the J.T. Fitzgerald Ranch on the hill above Sunset (arrow indicates Livingston home), c. 1916.

and Gotlieb Fisher, to survey and mark out lots and streets. These landowners, on Hartranft's payroll, helped convert upper Tujunga from heavy, untouched mountain growth to the present-day community of Tujunga. Many new arrivals in town contracted with Jim to have rock houses and walls constructed.

Eighteen months before the start of World War I, Chan Livingston enlisted in the United States Navy. He got his father to sign the enlistment papers, as he knew his mother would not want him to leave home.[14] Chan spent four years in the Navy and returned home to work with his father as a stonemason. He quickly became disenchanted with civilian life and enlisted in the United States Army, where he remained for twenty-eight years. Both sons, Chan and Bill, would go on to important careers in the Armed Services and, like their father, enjoyed writing about the early days when their parents were pioneers and the town of Tujunga was born.

In 1928, the Livingston family moved to El Centro, California, where they attempted to run a dairy farm on forty acres. Chan and Bill became active in the building business and stayed away from the dairy farm as much as possible. After two years, the bankers won the battle and Jim and Hilda returned to Tujunga. They moved into a new stone-and-wood cottage in 1922. Jim built the home at 10429 Tujunga Canyon Boulevard and they named it "Bonnie Brae."[15] Jim and Hilda, both early risers, would sit on their porch and watch the sun come up over their beloved "Green Verdugo Hills." In the evening they would again sit side by side on their porch and view the grandeur of the sunset, when golden light shone atop the rosy granite mountain peaks. Gone were the scorching rays of the sun, giving way to the silhouette of the pine and yucca covered mountains.

Once again, they became active in the affairs of the community. They were considered one of the founders of the old Boulevard Christian Church on Foothill

Boulevard. On July 30, 1950, they celebrated their sixtieth wedding anniversary at the church. Their sons and many family members and friends joined them for this joyous celebration. Just over a year later, the greatest heartache of Hilda's life happened when her son Bill, coming home to visit his parents, was killed in an automobile accident Thanksgiving Day 1951.

Hilda and Jim, considered the earliest pioneers residing in the community, were pleased to participate in the Chamber of Commerce Old Timers' Week each year. The outgoing Jim loved to tell and write stories of his days as an Indian interpreter and the early days of Tujunga, when his mule team helped clear the land. The very quiet Hilda did not record her memories and did not talk about those early pioneer days when she was the First Lady of the Foothills.

In 1954, Jim passed away at the age of ninety-two years. After a long day spent in his garden, he succumbed to a heart attack and died at home that night. In 1958, Hilda passed away at the Mt. Gleason Sanitarium in Tujunga after suffering a stroke at the age of ninety-four years. She was ill only three days.[16]

When son Chan retired from military life in 1957, he moved his family into "Bonnie Brae," where they would remain until 1980. On July 24, 1995, Colonel Chancellor Livingston passed away in La Crescenta at the age of ninety-eight years.[17] It is fortunate that the Livingston men recorded the early days of their beloved town; their names live on in print.[18] Hilda was happy to keep her memories to herself. They were rich and full of adventure and perseverance.

Notes

[1] Letter to Author from Hilda's grandson, Philip Livingston, dated September 16, 2000.

[2] "Mrs. Livingston Tujunga Pioneer—Services Today," *The Record-Ledger* (June 26, 1958).

[3] Chan Livingston Geneology Notes (March 1986). Bolton Hall Museum Archives.

[4] *The National Atlas with Descriptions* (Philadelphia: O.W. Gray and Son, 1879). Petersburg is now known as Grafton, New York.

[5] "James Livingston, Pioneer of Tujunga, Dies at Home," *The Record-Ledger* (1954).

[6] Author's telephone interview with Bob Livingston (William's son). October 13, 2000.

[7] The remodeled house still stands on Hillrose Street, across from Verdugo Hills High School athletic field.

[8] "Jim Livingston's Planning 59th Wedding Anniversary—Review Life in Tujunga Since 1910," *The Record-Ledger* (1949). Bolton Hall Museum clippings file.

Hilda's son Chancellor (*left*) with good friend Howard Smothers, c. 1920.

[9]Undated letter from Chan Livingston to friend Tom Theobald. Bolton Hall Museum clippings file.

[10]Author's interview, October 13, 2000, op. cit.

[11]The J.T. Fitzgerald ranch, on the hill at the north end of Commerce Avenue (Sunset), would be sold to Laura Glassey, who opened Elysia Nudist Park. She was arrested in 1939 and her home, for those seeking "air baths," was closed. Cecilia Rasmussen, *L.A. Unconventional— The Men and Women Who Did L.A. Their Way* (*Los Angeles Times*, 1998).

[12]Author's telephone interview with Bob Livingston. October 13, 2000.

[13]Chan Livingston, "Seven Millionaires of Contentment," 1986. Bolton Hall Museum Archives.

[14]Philip Livingston letter, dated March 13, 1997, to Author.

[15]"Bonnie Brae" has had a major facelift but still stands, now behind a high wooden fence. The once-panoramic view is gone.

[16]State of California, Certificate of Vital Records. June 23, 1958.

[17]Col. Chan was in the Army for twenty-six years and the Navy for four years. The Author attended his burial at Forest Lawn, Glendale, on July 30, 1995. United States Army and Navy personnel presented a twenty-one-gun salute to Colonel Livingston.

[18]Hilda's granddaughter Nancy passed away in the winter of 1995 in St. Croix. Hilda's grandson Philip lives with his family in Texas and is a renowned western writer of team penning and horsemanship of all varieties. Grandson Bill is a retired radio announcer and lives in Laguna Hills, California. Both grandsons attended the Colonel's graveside service and the reception at Bolton Hall Museum.

Women were encouraged to do their part in the war.
Courtesy of West Point Museum Art Collection, United States Military Academy.

FOUNDING SISTERS

The J.T. Fitzgerald Ranch in the Seven Hills area, near the Livingston and Zachau homes, c. 1918.

Interior view of Hilda's neighbor's home, the J.T. Fitzgerald Ranch in Seven Hills.
Mr. Fitzgerald owned the Fitzgerald Music Company, which later became the Southern California Music Company.
The ranch was the family's weekend get-away residence, c. 1920. *The Record-Ledger.*

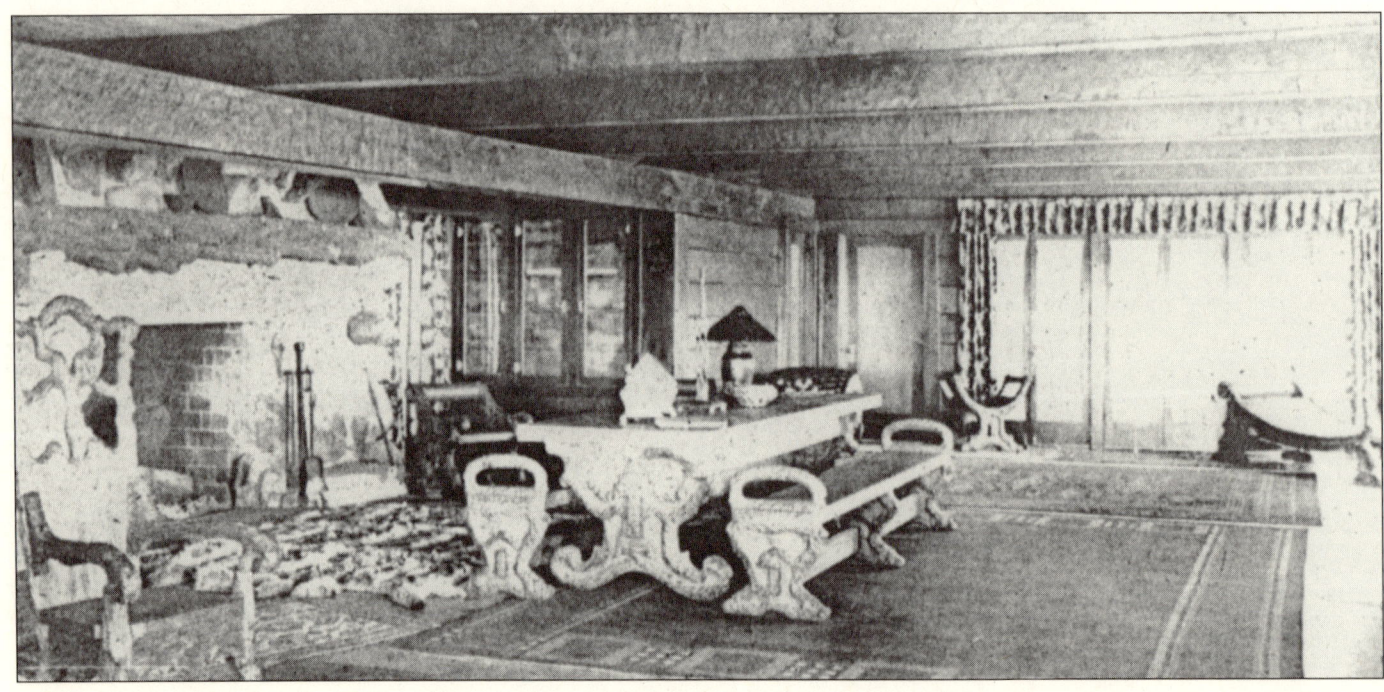

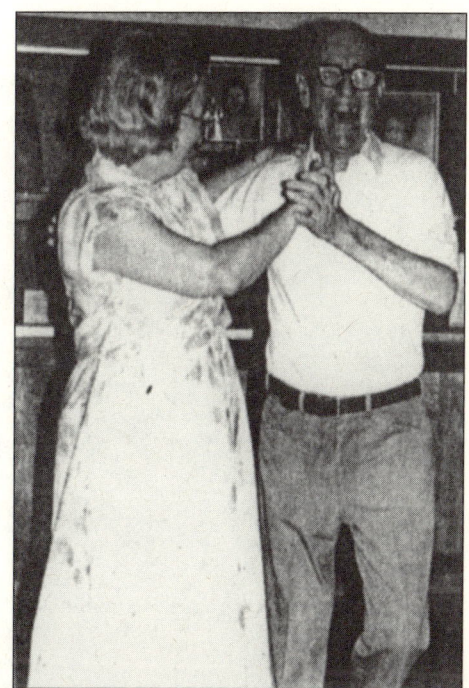

(*right*) In 1980, when Bolton Hall reopened as a history museum, Chan danced with historian Viola Carlson. *The Record-Ledger.*

(*below*) The chimney is gone, the rock front covered in siding, yet the Livingston's home survives into the twenty-first century. *Courtesy of Author.*

Earliest known photo of Ida McGroarty, c. 1885.
Courtesy of McGroarty Cultural Arts Center.

Ida Lubrecht McGroarty

1866–1940

She was engaged to John Steven McGroarty at the age of nineteen and, after a five-year courtship, finally married the man who was destined to travel the world, serve two terms in Congress, run for president of the United States, become the third poet laureate of California, author the famous *The Mission Play*, complete a forty-year career as a writer for the *Los Angeles Times*, and become Tujunga's most famous citizen.[1] Ida's life was one of devotion to her husband and to his career. When she became his wife, she became his helpmate and constant companion for close to fifty years.

Ida Caroline Lubrecht was born June 15, 1866, in Hazelton, Pennsylvania. Her parents, Mary Louise (Kreyscher) and Christian Lubrecht, were born in Germany and immigrated to the United States after their marriage.[2] The story of Ida's childhood in Pennsylvania is perhaps lost to time. We do know she had two brothers, William and Louis, who would remain close to her throughout her life. We also know she attended the State Teacher's College at Millersville, Pennsylvania. After graduating in 1885, Ida taught school in the area for five years.

When Ida met John Steven McGroarty, her fate was sealed and her life forever tied to her husband's story. She became devoted to John and was an asset to him in his many careers. Her lifetime pride in his accomplishments led her to collect and preserve his many press clippings, letters, and editorials. She called the numerous scrapbooks "The Happy Books."[3]

John McGroarty was born the last of twelve children to Mary (McGenty) and Hugh Montgomery McGroarty of Donegal, Ireland. John was born in Luzerne County, Pennsylvania, on August 20, 1862. This charismatic man was proud of his heritage and, like many charming Irishmen, was gifted with a "silver tongue." John Steven was a sickly child and spent a good deal of his childhood housebound in the mining township. He had respiratory problems and asthma. During one of his many convalescences, he wrote a poem that was published in *The Boston Pilot*. He was just ten years old at the time. After completing his education, he was certified to teach at the age of sixteen. He taught for three years and then abandoned the profession for journalism. He fulfilled his apprenticeship and rose to the position of managing editor of the *Wilkes-Barre Evening Leader*.[4] At the age of twenty-one, John was elected justice of the peace. A few years later, he won the election for county treasurer on the Democratic ticket. At last, he had a job that paid well. This enabled him to marry his longtime friend, Ida, in 1890.

Margaret McHale, McGroarty's niece, recalled Ida's wedding on November 19, 1890:

> I remember the wedding very well. It was held in the evening, in Mrs. McGroarty's home. With my father, mother, and the pastor of the church my uncle attended, we went by train to Wilkes-Barre, only a few miles away. My uncle had just been elected Treasurer of Lucern [*sic*] County, Pennsylvania, and I imagine a great many of his campaign friends were there, together with his family. He was the last of twelve children,

and his sisters were loath to give him to another woman. My grandfather was also in attendance, but my grandmother had been dead several years. During the campaign he managed a little courting on the side. He even found time to write poems to his Princess, as he called Ida Lubrecht then.[5]

The newlyweds lived in the Lubrecht home in Wilkes-Barre for the first year of their marriage. After John's term as treasurer, he was admitted to the Pennsylvania Bar in 1892 and practiced law for the next three years.

In 1896, John accepted a job as legal advisor to fellow Irishman Marcus Daly, "The Copper King," so Ida and John headed west to Butte, Montana, a land of open spaces and staunch individuals.[6] Marcus Daly had bought a mine in Montana for $10,000, which turned into the famous Anaconda Copper Mine.[7] In 1890, he built a 42-room Queen Anne-style Victorian residence in Hamilton, Montana, in the Bitterroot Valley.[8] Ida and John lived nearby in a two-story home, and Ida occupied her time by renting out her home to boarders. In a four-year period, her guest book registered two hundred visitors. Every day she would cook breakfast and send the miners off to work with pail lunches. The guests in her home stayed for various lengths of time, but the monthly boarding fee was $30.[9] This independent businesswoman brought her skills of cooking and entertaining into a cash-earning occupation. Ida's reputation as an excellent cook and hostess would magnify as the years passed. Even later, when she and John had help in the home, she preferred to do the cooking.

The McGroartys stayed in Butte until Marcus Daly passed away in 1900. They packed up and moved to Mexico, where John was involved in another mining venture. During the year they spent there, the mine failed and the McGroartys moved back to the United States, traveling throughout the Southwest. Eventually, they settled in Seattle, but because of John's respiratory problems, they left and arrived in Los Angeles in 1901. John was exhausted and suffering from asthma. Too ill to work, he stayed in the hotel in downtown Los Angeles while Ida went to work at the Hamburger's Department Store (now known as Macy's). Prior to coming to Los Angeles, they lost their entire savings of $35,000 on an investment in a pear orchard operation

> There is no life that doesn't contribute to history.
> —Dorest West

296

IDA LUBRECHT MCGROARTY

(*right*) A newly married Ida at the age of 25 years, c. 1891. *Courtesy of McGroarty Cultural Arts Center.*

(*opposite*) Ida's job at Hamburger Department Store, on Eighth Street between Broadway and Hill, would help the family's finances until John obtained work at the *Los Angeles Times*. *From Author's collection.*

in the San Joaquin Valley in central California. With few finances, John was forced to sell books door-to-door. However, the resourceful Ida was able to present her husband with a gift of $800.

Eager to get back into journalism, after his many failed business ventures, John arranged an interview with Harrison Gray Otis, owner of the *Los Angeles Times*. Mr. Otis, a friend of John's uncle, was favorably impressed with the charming and witty Irishman. John was hired and thus began a forty-year career with the premier newspaper of Los Angeles. For the next fifteen years, he would serve as chief editorial writer and often used his editorials to express his lofty idealism.

In 1910, Frank Miller, owner of the Glenwood Mission Inn in Riverside, California, had traveled to Germany and became enthralled with the *Passion Play* staged in Oberammergau. He returned home and asked John to take a leave of absence from his duties at the newspaper and write a pageant play that would tell the colorful story of early California and mission life. John did just that, and he and Ida moved into the inn.

It was during this two-year stay at the Mission Inn that the issue of women's suffrage became the hot topic of conversation and action throughout California. Ida's viewpoint on the subject was never recorded and her side of the issue is erased by time. Her husband was one of fifty prominent men who formed the Men's League Opposed to the Extension of Suffrage to Women. This prestigious group was organized in Los Angeles and included such notables as Captain William Banning (San Pedro), George S. Patton, Sr. (San Marino senator), Frank Flint (La Cañada), and the attorneys O'Melveny and Graves. John's old employer, the *Los Angeles Times*, was one of the few California newspapers to openly oppose the right of women to vote. On October 11, 1911, the Eighth Amendment to the California State Constitution passed in Los Angeles with a 15,000 to 13,000 vote, passing statewide by 3,587 votes. California became the sixth state to extend the voting franchise to women. The *Los Angeles Times* quickly reversed its position on the issue; it was an election year for mayor of Los Angeles and the vote was in two months. The mayoral race pitted socialist Job Harriman against George Alexander. More than 82,000 women registered in Los Angeles and almost 90 percent voted in that December election. The *Los Angeles Times* and the Committee of Fifty praised the ladies who saved the city from Job Harriman and administration by a Socialist Party.

297

Ida and John moved into Frank Miller's Glenwood Mission Inn in Riverside while John wrote "The Mission Play." In this 1903 photograph, President Theodore Roosevelt replants two of the original naval orange trees in the courtyard of the inn. *Courtesy of Riverside Municipal Museum.*

When John finished *The Mission Play*, Mr. Miller wanted it to be staged at his Mission Inn, but with a cast of over one hundred people and animals, it would be impossible. A new playhouse was built across the road from the San Gabriel Mission on seven acres of land. The play finally made its debut on April 29, 1912. For the first two years, the playhouse struggled to keep its doors open. In 1915, after two California expositions (in San Francisco and San Diego), the playhouse would draw crowds of eastern visitors to one of the "must see" tourist attractions of Southern California.[10]

When tourists came to the playhouse, they could spend an extra ten cents and see "The Old Grapevine," the original grapevine planted in California in 1775 by the Franciscans. By 1915, the grapevine trunk had a diameter of 8.9 feet and the vine covered 12,000 square feet, providing a ton of fruit annually. Near this "mother" vine was a café where tourists could dine in an adobe structure that was claimed to be Ramona's birthplace.[11] In 1926, the original playhouse was replaced by a larger concrete building that seated 1,492 people. This was a great improvement over the original building that shook every time the train passed nearby—the noise forced the actors to hold their pose until the locomotive had passed and they could resume speaking. At Ida's suggestion, the new playhouse had a west patio that contained miniature replicas of the twenty-one California missions. The display of miniature missions was to evoke an impression of the original El Camino Real.

By 1916, *The Mission Play* was so successful that Ida and John took the entire cast on tour. They played in

Reno, Nevada; Salt Lake City, Utah; St. Louis and Kansas City, Missouri; Omaha, Nebraska; and Chicago, Illinois. The farther east they traveled, the less interest there was in Father Serra and the California mission story.[12] In Chicago, the touring company became stranded, unable to pay their fare back to California. As a favor to the McGroartys, the Southern Pacific Railroad brought the entire cast home. Eventually, John repaid the railroad but was embarrassed by the failure and $40,000 debt. The whole event so shattered the nerves of Ida that she suffered a serious breakdown.[13] There would be even more disappointment in store for Ida after her return to California. The building of her home would greatly test her resolve.

"The Mission Play," back in California, went on to become successful with over 3,186 performances in a twenty-one year period (1912–1932) with 2.5 million people viewing the spectacular play. The audiences included European royalty, politicians, tourists from all forty-eight states, and thousands of schoolchildren. During the Depression, the play ceased operations but was briefly revived in the early 1940s.

Ten years after the birth of *The Mission Play*, John Steven decided to build the twenty-second Franciscan mission, to be named San Juan Evanglista, on his Manzanita Park property in Tujunga.[14] The mission was to be used by people of all faiths and the building was to be accomplished by one hundred California Native Indians from the various Indian reservations. The work was to be done under the supervision of Franciscan priests, following the construction methods used during the building of the twenty-one other missions. Material for the adobe walls and red tile roof were to be obtained from the Verdugo Mountains and timbers for the huge cross and roof were to come from Big Tujunga Canyon. There were elaborate plans for the dedication that included priests in ornate vestments, Indians in tribal garments, a company of Spanish cav-

---

"Just California"
by J. S. McGroarty

'Twixt the seas and the deserts,
  'Twixt the wastes and the waves,
Between the sands of buried lands
  And ocean's coral caves,
It lies not East nor West,
  But like a scroll unfurled,
Where the hand of God hath hung it,
  Down the middle of the world.

Days rise that gleam in glory,
  Days die with sunset's breeze,
While from Cathay that was of old,
  Sail countless argosies;
Morns break again in splendor
  O'er the giant, new-born West,
But of all the lands God fashioned,
  'Tis this land is the best.

It lies where God hath spread it,
  In the gladness of His eyes,
Like a flame of jeweled tapestry
  Beneath His shining skies;
With the green of woven meadows
  And the hills in golden chains,
The light of leaping rivers,
  And the flash of poppied plains.

Sun and dews that kiss it,
  Balmy winds that blow,
The stars in clustered diadems
  Upon its peaks of snow;
The mighty mountains o'er it,
  Below the white seas swirled—
Just California stretching down
  The middle of the world.

FOUNDING SISTERS

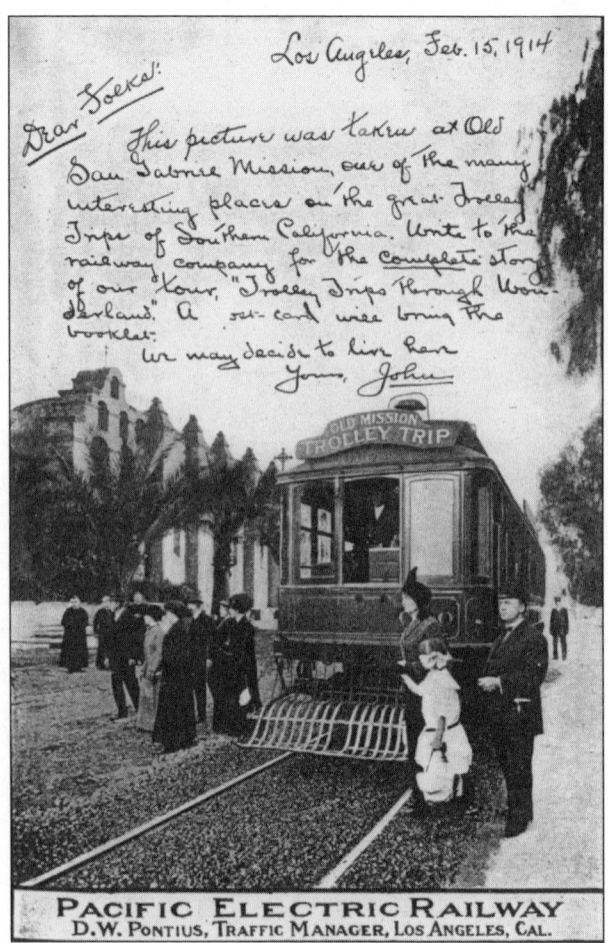

(*left*) One of the great "Trolley Trips" was to see the San Gabriel Mission and "The Mission Play." c. 1914. *Courtesy of Sunset Publishing Corporation.*

(*below*) In the McGroarty Library stands a First Place silver cup, awarded to John McGroarty for his City of San Gabriel's Mission Play Float. In the January 1, 1922, Tournament of Roses Parade, the float was graced by Native Americans and descendents of early California Spanish families. *Courtesy of McGroarty Cultural Arts Center.*

alry, dressed in the uniforms of the mission period, and possibly a detachment of soldiers from Ft. McArthur, a 500-voice choir, a company of trumpeters and a cannon salute.[15] McGroarty expected a crowd of 100,000 people to attend the dedication ceremony in June 1922. People accepted his idea, but the money was not forthcoming. Consequently, McGroarty's dream would not be a reality.[16] Ida's thoughts and comments on the San Juan Evanglista project, to be built in front of her home, were not recorded.

John was quite the storyteller. This was evident to all those present at the raising of the great white cross of San Ysidro atop Mt. McGroarty in the spring of 1923, when John told the story of Ysidro. As legend has it, Ysidro was a Spanish Jew who worked the fields of a landowner in Spain.

> John McGroarty told one of the legends of San Ysidro, substantially as follows:
> "One day, as Ysidro was plowing in the field of his employer, some children came running to tell him that a poor widow woman in the neighborhood was in distress because some dogs had chased her goat away and she was unable to find it. With no hesitation, Ysidro left his oxen standing in the furrow and set out to find the goat. But when the farmer heard what Ysidro was doing, he vowed it was time to stop this sort of nonsense and teach Ysidro to mind the business he was paid for. So the farmer started to the field, stopping on the way to cut a stout rod from the hedge row, swearing to himself that a good beating was the best way to teach his servant where his duty lay. But as the farmer came to a gap in the hedge through which he could see his field, he stopped—his eyes bulged, his mouth fell open, his jaw stuck, and the rod fell to the ground. For there before him were the oxen, walking steadily along the furrow and beside the plow stood a tall figure all clothed in white.
> "For, said Mr. McGroarty, God had sent one of His angels to do Ysidro's work while Ysidro was on his errand of mercy."[17]

Because of this vision, Ysidro's saintliness was celebrated and he became the patron saint of agriculture.

In the early 1920s, John wrote advertising copy for Marshall V. Hartranft. Intrigued by his own copy, John and Ida came as guests and spent the night on the covered porch at Hartranft's Lazy Lonesome Ranch in Sunland. It was the first time in memory John was able to sleep through the night and they decided to build their dream cottage in Tujunga. They built the home in 1921 on the hillside of the Verdugo Mountains. Nestled snugly against the slope, the home would last less than twenty-four hours after completion. The wooden structure was completely engulfed in flames and burned to the ground.[18] Undaunted, they rebuilt their house. On December 6, 1923, the McGroartys invited all the Southland to attend the housewarming party. That Saturday afternoon and evening saw over 1,000 people attend the reception. The following morning at eight o'clock, Ida went to light the kitchen stove. A leak in the kerosene supply line, located outside the house, ignited and the room was engulfed in flames. All of their household goods and clothing were burned. Fortunately, John and Ida's mother Mary were in his "poet's studio" above the main house. The studio contained John's books and manuscripts, which were saved. Ida led her houseguests, Dr. and Mrs. Carney of New York, from the blaze. The two small garden hoses could not save the house and the $20,000 home was razed, but Ida's spirit remained strong.

> "That was a wonderful time we had yesterday—we had that, anyway, didn't we?" he (John) said. "But I'm such a lot of trouble to my friends." Mrs. McGroarty as always was full of courage and resource. Among the pieces of furniture carried down to the roadside were a score or more of chairs borrowed for Saturday's reception. From among these Mrs. McGroarty selected her own belongings—her sewing machine, a grass rocking chair, some white enameled breakfast chairs, a teakettle and half a box of red apples. "We will take these to the upper cabin," she (Ida) said, "I am going to do house-keeping up there." Somebody picked up an old leather traveling bag from the heep [sic] of rescued furni-

---

When I come here to California I am not in the West: I am west of the West. It is just California.
—From the speech delivered at Ventura, May 9, 1903, by President Theodore Roosevelt

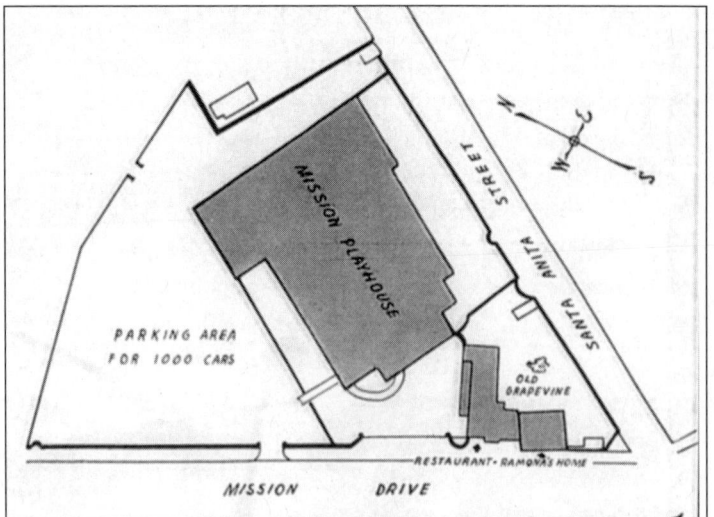

(*above*) Map of the Mission Playhouse, the Old Grapevine Restaurant and Ramona's house. Mission Playhouse brochure, c. 1930s.

(*right*) Cover of "The Mission Play" brochure, c. 1930. The overly romantic and sentimental play helped advance the "Mission Myth." *Both courtesy of McGroarty Cultural Arts Center.*

ture. "Oh yes," said Mrs. McGroarty, "that is my silver from the last fire; I want to save that." So the neighbors carried the sewing machine, the grass rocker, the teakettle, the half-box of red apples and the bag of burned silverware to the upper cabin—the one to which Mr. McGroarty refers as "My little high house in the chaparral"—a little, brown, wooden house under the shadow of the cross of San Ysidro.[19]

By May 1924, the third home was ready for occupation. No formal reception was held and the neighbors made the McGroartys promise to have the fire department on hand for the small informal gathering. This large, fourteen-room home with the a roof was made of local river rock and given the name Rancho Chupa Rosa.[20] The new home, located at 7570 McGroarty Terrace, was built to last by the Forrester brothers, Jake and Ed, of Mountair Avenue in Tujunga. The large downstairs parlor, 20 by 40 feet, had a sweeping view of the Green Verdugo Hills and the Sunland-Tujunga Valley. Next to the parlor was the formal dining room that was often used to stage small plays. The McGroartys and Ida's mother Mary (Mother Lu) lived upstairs. The upper level contained John's library, a small living room, Ida's suite, John's Spartan bedroom, and Ida's mother's complete apartment. Ida served Mother Lu all of her meals upstairs. She was devoted to her demanding mother and was truly happy to be able to care for her. John and Ida were seldom alone, and Mother Lu was a strong force in the home. John once remarked, "Two women in one house, it just doesn't work; two generals."[21]

Ida's home life was always busy and stimulating with a constant parade of politicians, priests, actors, students, travelers, and friends visiting. She shared her love of history with those who visited by prominently displaying her large collection of Indian baskets throughout their home. The 1930s were rich and full for the McGroartys at Rancho Chupa Rosa. Ida often entertained for charities and the Los Angeles Women's Breakfast Club and had fundraisers for the Los Angeles School for Crippled Children. John was busy giving speeches and writing his weekly column, "Seen From the Green Verdugo Hills," for the *Los Angeles Times*. It was a humorous commentary on events of the day and local people (never identified by name). Through the column, Southland residents were made aware of Tujunga and its colorful characters. It was often said that he put Tujunga on the map.

In 1930, John and Ida traveled to Spain and Italy. While in Spain, John was honored with the decoration of knight commander of the Order of Isabella by King Alfonso XIII, in tribute of his contribution to Spanish tradition in the southern California area. Ida studied the clothing of Spain and brought back many ideas for the costumes she designed for *The Mission Play*. The couple also traveled to the city of Petra, Father Junipero Serra's hometown on the Spanish island of Majorca. After visiting Madrid and Barcelona, they sailed to Genoa, Italy, aboard the *Franca Fassio*. During their tour of Italy, they had an audience with Pope Pius XI, who made John a knight of the Order of St. Gregory. Ida, although born into a Lutheran home, was attending an Episcopal church at that time.

In 1934, at the age of 72 years, John shocked his friends by entering the political arena. A Democrat, John beat the Republican incumbent congressman, Rep. William Evans, to become the Congressional representative from the Eleventh District.[22] The charming and witty John Steven McGroarty drew a great deal of publicity in Washington, D.C., because of his support of the Townsend Plan.[23]

While in Washington, John continued to write his weekly column, now entitled "Seen From the Capital Dome." Though his Townsend Plan was defeated, he was effective in bringing to light the plight of the Indians on reservations and the abuses of the Bureau of Indian Affairs. Ida kept herself busy by entertaining the Washington crowd. After serving two terms, John voluntarily retired and headed back to Tujunga and his beloved Rancho Chupa Rosa. In an effort to bring the Townsend Plan to the attention of the Democratic Convention of 1936, John became a candidate for president of the United States. Never a serious candidate, he returned to California to unsuccessfully run for secretary of state.

Ida and John left Washington in May but toured New England and Montana before arriving home in August 1936. Tujunga welcomed the return of their poet and his wife at a big picnic in Sunland Park and an endless round of parties. At the age of 76 years, John went back to writing. He was, after all, a poet, not a politician, and was happy to be home in his adopted State of California. He

The Mission Playhouse in San Gabriel was across the street from the San Gabriel Mission and seated 1,492 people. Mission Playhouse brochure, c. 1928. *Courtesy of McGroarty Cultural Arts Center.*

FOUNDING SISTERS

(*above*) Photograph of the newly built Mission Playhouse, c. 1930s.

(*left*) An early photograph of John Steven McGroarty, prior to his coming to California, c. 1899. *Courtesy of McGroarty Cultural Arts Center.*

(*opposite*) Just a few of the 115 cast members in front of the Mission Playhouse in San Gabriel, c. 1930s.

resumed his title as "Sage of the Verdugos" and Ida resumed her philanthropic responsibilities. By 1939, she was forced to withdraw from public duties due to health problems. As her breast cancer advanced, she became bedridden the last seven months of her life. John didn't want Ida in a hospital, so he hired round-the-clock nurses to care for his beloved companion. Although this created financial hardship, she was able to remain at Rancho Chupa Rosa. On May 14, 1940, the front page of the *Los Angeles Times* reported, "McGroarty's Wife Dies," at home on May 13. Her 92-year-old mother and husband John were at her bedside. Before her death, she converted to Catholicism. Her High Requiem Mass was held at Our Lady of Lourdes Church, located on land she had donated. After services conducted by Father Falvey, close friends and relatives left the church and walked up the hill to Rancho Chupa Rosa. Private services were conducted there with her mother, brother William from Montana, and brother Louis from San Gabriel. John was deeply stricken by her death, for she had been his constant companion since she was nineteen years of age.

Ill and with failing eyesight, John would spend the next four years at home being attended to by his niece, Margaret McHale. One year before his death, Ida's mother Mary died, July 21, 1943, at the age of 95 years. At the time, she was living at Mrs. Flower's home on Mountair Avenue in Tujunga. As John's health deteriorated, Harry Chandler, owner of the *Los Angeles Times* and lifelong friend, insisted he be hospitalized. The famed poet John Steven McGroarty died on August 7, 1944. Mr. Chandler paid for his large, lavish funeral.[24]

Margaret McHale inherited Rancho Chupa Rosa upon John's death. Frances Muir Pomroy campaigned for six years and served twelve hundred signatures and the endorsements of seventy-two civic organizations on a petition to the City of Los Angeles to acquire the rancho as a historical monument and a meeting place for civic and cultural groups.[25] In 1953, the Department of Parks and Recreation for the City of Los Angeles purchased the huge home and twelve acres of surrounding land for $30,000.

Ida McGroarty will always be remembered as the wife of John Steven McGroarty. No history of California would be complete without mention of him. Ida's name has been all but forgotten by most citizens of southern California. The charm and wit of her husband overshadowed the accomplishments of the reserved Ida, but she will always be remembered by the pioneers of Tujunga for her philanthropic work, hospitality, entertaining skills, and costume design expertise. She was the woman who kept John Steven's feet on the ground.

John Steven and his "Teddy Roosevelt" grin, c. 1934.

Notes

[1] John Steven McGroarty served as the third poet laureate of California from 1933 through 1944. The first poet laureate was Dr. Henry Meade Bland, 1929–1931, followed by Ina Donna Coolbrith, 1915–1928.

[2] Record of Funeral. May 13, 1940. Cunningham and O'Connor Mortuary, Los Angeles, California.

[3] "The Happy Books" and the bulk of the McGroarty papers were removed from the McGroarty Cultural Arts Center by docent director Donna Larson and historian Viola Carlson and sent to the archives of the San Fernando Mission.

[4] Sister Mary Eleanor Craggs, "The Career of John Steven McGroarty 1862–1944," Thesis for the Degree of Master of Arts (February 1958) 3. Catholic University of America, Pacific Coast Branch, San Rafael, California.

[5] Margaret McHale, "John Steven McGroarty," paper delivered before a meeting of the California Federation of Chaparral Poets (October 10, 1955).

[6] Marcus Daly left Ireland at the age of fifteen and joined fellow Irish miners in Butte, Montana, for the "Irish Klondike."

[7] In 1914, Anaconda began buying foreign mining companies. By 1929, it owned the largest copper mine in Chile. Anaconda Company is one of the largest American mining companies, producing copper, aluminum, silver and uranium. Since 1977, it has been a subsidiary of Atlantic Richfield Company and its corporate headquarters in Denver, Colorado.

[8] After Mrs. Daly's death in 1941, the mansion was boarded up until 1987. It is now a national historic site and owned by the state of Montana. Tours are given 11:00 A.M. to 4:00 P.M., daily.

[9] Viola Carlson, "John Steven McGroarty—One of the Last Complete Journalists," talk given to the Huntington Westerners Group (January 24, 1981), 6.

[10] A trip to Southern California would not be complete without a visit to *The Mission Play*, Cawston's Ostrich Farm in South Pasadena, scenic Mt. Lowe, the pleasure city of Venice, and the resorts of Redondo Beach and Long Beach.

[11] Helen Hunt Jackson's (1830–1885) *Ramona* (1884) was a fictitious character based, perhaps, on a Cahuilla Indian woman Ramona Lubo, who resided near Palm Springs.

[12] Craggs, op. cit., p. 27.

[13] Ibid., p. 32.

[14] "Historic Scenes to Mark Building of New Mission," *Glendale Daily Press* (March 3, 1921).

[15] "New Mission to Be Built in Tujunga," *The Record-Ledger of the Verdugo Hills* (March 15, 1923).

[16] Sarah R. Lombard, *Rancho Tujunga—a History of Sunland/Tujunga, California* (Burbank, Calif.: The Bridge Publishers, 1990) p. 73.

[17] Wallace M. Morgan, "The Green Verdugo Hills—a Chronicle of Sunland-Tujunga, Calif. And how it grew," *The Record-Ledger*, 1953.

[18] "McGroarty Residence Destroyed," *Glendale Evening News* (December 26, 1922).

[19] "Fire Destroys New McGroarty Home," *The Record-Ledger of the Verdugo Hills* (December 13, 1923).

[20] Rancho Chupa Rosa was named for the chuparosa plant (*Beloperone californica*). This almost leafless, grayish-green shrub grows to a height of five feet. It is abundant in red tubular flowers and nectar favored by hummingbirds. In Spanish, the name chuparosa means "sucking rose." Growing at an altitude of 2,500 feet or less, its habitat ranges from the northern and western edges of the Colorado Desert to Lower California and Sonora. It blooms from March through June.

[21] Viola Carlson interview with Ann Ralser (McGroarty's secretary), May 30, 1974, Oxnard Shores, California.

[22] *The Los Angeles Times* (April 4, 1934).

[23] Dr. Francis E. Townsend (1867–1960) was a retired physician from Long Beach, California, who devised a monthly pension plan for the elderly (a precursor to the Social Security Act introduced by Franklin D. Roosevelt in 1935) after he saw three elderly women going through garbage pails for scraps of food.

[24] John was buried alongside his beloved wife and his mother-in-law at Calvary Cemetery in East Los Angeles. They are in front of All Souls Chapel, near such Catholic dignitaries as Cardinal Timothy Manning.

[25] Frances Muir Pomroy (1902–1986), writer, historian, and president of the San Fernando Historical Society, was responsible for the saving of a legacy. In 1970, Rancho Chupa Rosa became Los Angeles Historical Landmark #63. Frances' daughter Helen Pomroy Sullivan lives in New Jersey. Information about Frances was provided by local historian Elva Meline in a letter to the Author, dated April 25, 2001, and a telephone call to author from Helen Pomroy Sullivan on May 9, 2001.

This 1927 photograph shows the oaks of Manzanita Park, donated for the town's enjoyment by John S. McGroarty.

FOUNDING SISTERS

(*right*) The McGroarty home nestled in the Green Verdugo Hills, above Manzanita Park, c. 1922.

(*below*) John's little wooden studio just above the main house, c. 1921. *Courtesy of McGroarty Cultural Arts Center.*

(*below*) Ida sitting on the porch of the McGroarty's first home. This photograph was featured in M.V. Hartranft's 1920 brochure "My Homemade Home." Note the wooden roof and dense chaparral.

308

IDA LUBRECHT MCGROARTY

Looking northwest to Sunland from John's studio, c. 1922.
Harry Lamson was the McGroarty's official photographer.

Unidentified man surveys the still smoldering house as firemen (*left*)
continue to douse the fire, c. 1923. *Courtesy of the Los Angeles Public Library.*

Invites All the Neighbors To House Warming

Dec. 3, 1923, San Gabriel, California.

To the Editor of the Record-Ledger:

May I ask you to state through the columns of your paper that Mrs. McGroarty and myself would like all the neighbors in the green Verdugo Hills, the Tujunga Valley and all the way down to Montrose, and even farther than that, to do us the honor to come and see our new house and have a cup of tea and a cookie with us next Saturday afternoon, December 8, between 2:00 and 5:00 o'clock.

We want all the neighbors, whether we are personally acquainted with them or not, to please come and help us start the new house off in a happy way. And we can think of no happier way to start a new home than to have our neighbors pay us a visit.

If we were to attempt to personally invite the folks of the Verdugo Hills it would be a big task, and we might forget somebody. So, we thought that by putting a piece in your paper that everybody would know it and everybody would come; and this is their invitation.

We want to get the sounds of the neighbors' friendly voices into the new walls and to have their good wishes for the peace and prosperity and happiness of the new rooftree.

Thanking you in advance for the courtesy of the space that you will give this letter in your paper, believe me to be

Faithfully yours,

JOHN STEVEN McGROARTY.

(opposite, top left) In this newspaper invitation, John and Ida invite the town to celebrate the completion of house #2. Within twenty-four hours after the party, the house burned to the ground. *The Record-Ledger.*

(opposite, top right) The rebuilt house #2 that burned to the ground when Ida lit the kerosene stove, c. 1923. *Courtesy of the Los Angeles Public Library.*

(opposite, bottom) Under the shadow of the Cross of San Ysidro, Rancho Chupa Rosa #3 with the tile roof, c. 1926.

(above) House #3, with a tile roof, was built to last, c. 1940s. *Courtesy of McGroarty Cultural Arts Center.*

FOUNDING SISTERS

Our Lady of Lourdes first church building was located on Valaho Drive, on land donated by Ida McGroarty. It was a simple 40-by-60-foot chapel and served the community from 1921 to 1941.

The first Our Lady of Lourdes Church was designed by Leon Tosi and dedicated on December 18, 1921.

Twenty-five local families, led by John Steven McGroarty, founded the first Our Lady of Lourdes Church, c. 1921.
Both courtesy of Our Lady of Lourdes Church.

(*opposite, top*) John and Ida enjoyed the magnificent view of Monte Vista Valley from their parlor. It was also used to entertain, hold receptions and as a stage for performing small plays, c. 1939. *Courtesy of McGroarty Cultural Arts Center.*

(*opposite, bottom*) In the summer of 1936, Ida and John returned to Tujunga from Washington, D.C. Their return was celebrated in Sunland Park. Father Falvey (*seated far right*) was their priest and campaign chairman.

(*right*) Ida and John on their porch in 1939. The couple was married almost 50 years. *Courtesy of McGroarty Cultural Arts Center.*

(*below*) In death, as in life, Ida shared double billing with her husband. Calvary Cemetery, East Los Angeles. *Courtesy of Author.*

The musical Maygrove family: (*left to right*) Gladys, Gertrude (at the piano), Constance (Bing), R. Walter and Dorothy. Photograph taken in their home, the early part of 1914.

A WOMAN CANNOT DIRECTLY CHOOSE HER CIRCUMSTANCES,
but she can choose her thoughts,
and so indirectly, yet surely,
shape her circumstances.
As a woman thinketh in her heart, so is she.
—*Dorothy Hulst*

Gladys Maygrove Davis
1903–1985

When Marshall V. Hartranft created the Little Lands Colony, he wanted it to be more than a place of retirees, farmers, and ranchers. He envisioned a community of artists and men and women of culture. He recruited R. Walter Maygrove and his wife, Gertrude, to come to the colony and create a community band. He wanted the residents of Sunland and Tujunga to join together, at Bolton Hall, for concerts, parades, and community dances.[1]

When the Maygrove family arrived in the Little Lands Colony in 1913, the area was thick with sagebrush, rocks, snakes, scorpions, and too many tarantulas.

> We had an acre of ground with a two room wooden house for a home. No gas, no electricity, no water piped into the house and an outdoor bathroom. My mother cooked on an oil stove and did the family washing outside in a big tub. We had to have water from a little hydrant in front of the house. When bath time came, it was a scramble to see which one of us kids would get the tub first, as we couldn't have water for each (person's) bath.[2]

This was indeed rugged country for a family used to city living. Gladys remembered her father telling them, "'We are moving back to God's country.' Like all good wives at that time, the wife went where the husband said they were going. So we all moved bag and baggage. My father was the piano player at the old Pantages Theater in Hollywood."[3]

R. Walter and Gertrude were born in England; both came from impressive musical backgrounds. R. Walter had studied music in Malta and became the queen's bandmaster when he was sixteen years old. He was one of fourteen children, all of whom had notable music careers. The family of R. Walter had originally come from Italy and carried the surname of D'Nana. While in London, Rudolph Walter changed his name to Maygrove.

While very little is known of Gertrude's early years, we do know she graduated from college and was a fine musician in her own right. In the late 1890s, the Maygroves were married in England and then set sail for America. Their daughter, Dorothy, was born on board the ship and was given the middle name Columbia, in honor of that year's sailing race winner. In 1899, R. Walter, Gertrude, and Dorothy arrived in New York City.[4]

R. Walter became a solo clarinetist in Lampe's Band in Buffalo, New York. After two years there, the family moved to Niagara Falls, New York, where R. Walter took the position of bandmaster for the United States National Guard. They spent six years in upstate New York before moving to Chattanooga, Tennessee. It was there that R. Walter became the orchestra director for the Orpheum Theater. By 1910, the family had moved to Los Angeles and was spending the summer months on Santa Catalina Island. R. Walter was the music arranger for Porter's Catalina Island Marine Band.[5] He also played the clarinet and piano for the dances held in the ballroom on the island. Gladys would often comment on how safe Tujunga was in those early years. In a letter to the editor of the *Record-Ledger*, Gladys wrote,

FOUNDING SISTERS

The 1914 *Los Angeles Tribune* article on "The Baby Orchestra," consisting of Nadine Bratton on cello, Gladys Maygrove on horn, Mamie Tom on violin, and "Bing" Maygrove on drums, brought the girls fame throughout the Southland, c. 1914.

Even though I live in San Diego I have just finished reading the Police Blotter in the Record-Ledger. When my family lived in Tujunga we would take a three-month vacation every summer, due to the fact my dad R. Walter Maygrove played in the Catalina Island Band. We packed our bags and off we would go to the island. We never locked our doors, in fact we didn't have a lock on the doors—either of them! We enjoyed ourselves all summer without a worry or care. After arriving home after the three month engagement our little home was just as we had left it. The piano and other items of value were still in place, just as we had left them.

Not even so much as a pot or pan had been stolen. Our old Model T Ford was parked in front of the house on the gravel road with the tires still intact, and our neighbors were three acres away from us. Tujunga did not have a police force at that time, let alone a jail. How times have changed! So time marches on—That was sixty years ago dear friends, and this isn't a fairy tale but the truth.[6]

By the time each of Gertrude and R. Walter's daughters was four years old, they had been taught to read music and play the piano, the coronet, and the drums. The Maygrove family arrived in the Little Lands Colony in 1914 and, as M. V. Hartranft requested, immediately formed the Monte Vista Band.

It was formed from raw material, men who knew little or nothing about music. On Monday evenings we had band practice in the old Glorietta school house for anyone that was interested in joining. I remember my dad telling me to take any of the men aside that were interested in learning to play the trumpet, and I was to teach them fingering on the instrument and also teach the scale and the basic fundamentals of music. My sister Dorothy would take another group aside and do the same thing. She was a fine pianist, piccolo and flute player. I was only eleven years old at the time, but I had played in public many times and had been playing the trumpet for seven years. After many Monday nights of hard work and practice, our band began to shape up, so well that we were soon playing in public for affairs given in the Monte Vista Park in Sunland. This led to marching in parades in Los Angeles. One parade I remember so very well was the Prohibition Parade and the band marched the length of Broadway in Los Angeles, our "boys" managed well, due to the fact they had already been put thru [*sic*] the paces of marching around the dirt roads near the school house. And so, the Monte Vista Valley Band was started by my father. I remember well the band concerts under the big oak trees in Sunland Park, trees every place and people would drive in from Los Angeles with their picnic baskets and the "kids" could run and play to their hearts content. The family named Eagler had the ice cream stand across from the park. They served pop, ice cream and candy. The wooden platform was built around the trunk of a very large tree providing shade with a few benches sitting here and there. It was called the stand. Many Western Movies were "shot" in this area during the early years. The lovely natural beauty of the great outdoors made a perfect setting for this type of picture. I remember so well the excitement at one particular time when we heard that William Desmond and company would be shooting a picture in Sunland. I am sure the "kids" gathered from miles around just to watch. What a thrill it was for some of us when we were able to sit in a circle with a bunch of the cow boy [sic] extras and drink coffee with them. In fact when our mothers found out about it, they were not happy, and we were told—"I don't want you hanging around with a bunch of dirty shirts."

Bolton Hall was the one and only place large enough to hold all the activities of the valley. My mother, dad, eldest sister and I played for Saturday night dances held in the Hall. School plays, business meetings, box socials, the Ladies Club and also Church took place in this lovely old building. In those days, the hardwood floors were smooth and shiny, the interior had no plaster on the walls, just big boulders showing on the inside and a huge fireplace that was a conversation piece in itself. Dorothy played the piano, my dad on violin, my mother on drums and me on trumpet. Only square dances were held at that time and once in a while a waltz or a very new foxtrot would be "thrown in" for a change.

A tall stately lady with gray hair did the calling, her name was Mrs. Woodruff. How well I remember her booming voice. We had no mikes in those days, but with her loud, clear voice one was not needed. People came from all over the valley to attend those dances. They came in horse and buggies, or by old Model T Fords, or they just walked the great distance. I remember how much my father was paid for the dance job. Exactly five dollars for four hours of working with a four piece orchestra. As kids we were not paid for playing for the dances. My dad had told us he was giving us the benefit of his experience in teaching us "dance work" and that was enough.[7]

Besides the weekly dances, residents could go to La Crescenta once a month to see a movie at the old La Crescenta schoolhouse.

My sister and I used to walk the distance from Tujunga to La Crescenta on the dirt road, better known as Rabbit Gulch, and Dorothy would carry a revolver to protect us—not from two legged wolves but just in case we came across a coyote or bob cat that might be hungry.[8]

Hayrides were also a very popular pastime.

The hay rides we went on with a big flat top truck drawn by horses! Elmer Adams or maybe it would be Paul Lancaster would pick up the party with a picnic lunch packed by each of us. We would scramble into the loose hay piled

In 1915, Bing and Gladys were bridesmaids at LuLu Barkley's wedding, held at Bolton Hall. It was the social event of the year.

high and settle in for the ride. Much laughing and singing all the way. Sometimes it would be dusk before returning. Someone might bring along a "home made" ukulele, we made these from a cigar box of wood, attached four rubber bands for the strings stretched the length of the box and held with tacks. The neck of the "ukulele" would be made from a piece of straight wood. Very crude workmanship but it answered the purpose, and they were fun to make.

I remember the time Grace Greenfield and I sneaked through the Petrotta grape vineyard and went in swimming in the Begues [sic] swimming reservoir—I got a good licking on returning home for not asking permission to go! Another place for swimming was the Old Doc Spates reservoir. Dr. Spates at that time had a sanitarium between Little Lands and Sunland. Many people would go to the sanitarium to rest or for health reasons from Los Angeles or surrounding cities. The high dry climate seemed to do wonders for people suffering from asthma and other bronchial dis-orders [sic].

Dorothy, Gertrude, Bing, and Gladys (*left to right*) stand in the newly planted garden at home on San Ysidro Street (Samoa Avenue) in back of Bolton Hall, c. 1915

The climate in Tujunga was ideal for people suffering from (a)sthma and the dreadful (t)uberculosis. We had seen many brought to this mountain area on stretchers and in a very short time we would see them up and around. The dry clean air seemed to do wonders for their ailments.

Many of the children living in Sunland attended the school in Tujunga. Some rode horseback others walked the distance on the old gravel road. We had no play equipment to use at recess time, our time was spent playing cow boy [*sic*] and Indians using the huge boulders that seemed to surround the old school house as our "hideouts." This natural beauty was great to play in.

My father gave up the music work in Los Angeles and devoted full time to his many pupils in Tujunga and Sunland. It was at this time he bought a Model T Ford. This was a much needed piece of equipment both in his work and in transporting our instruments back and forth to the Bolton Hall where we played for the dances. We lived on San Ysidro Street and it was quite a chore "hauling" drums, violin, trumpet, and whatever over the dirt roads.

Then there was the time the George Osborn family and our family making ten people in all went to San Diego in 1915 to see the Exposition. Mr. Osborn was in the trucking business in Little Lands so he furnished the transportation which happened to be a Vim truck with wooden benches put in the back for us to sit on. What a ride! We left Little Lands at three in the morning arriving in San Diego ten hours later. The roads were dirt and full of chuck holes. We had to go through every little beach town along the coast, and I mean the towns were little! Mrs. Osborn and my mother had packed a big basket of food to eat on the way. I don't remember seeing any restaurants, and if we had I'm sure our parents could not afford to feed that many people in a restaurant.

Like everyone else we had chickens, and it was necessary to keep a lantern burning all night by the chicken coop to keep the coyotes and bob cats away, from stealing the chickens. Once a week, a little open air market was held on the steps of Bolton Hall. The ladies brought everything from fresh eggs, vegetables, home made baked bread, pies, or cakes, anything they could sell or trade for something they might need. For weeks I took an old red rooster down to "market," but no one wanted him. I couldn't even give him away, so each week I took my mean rooster back home with me.[9]

I can recall most of the merchants on Main Street (Commerce Avenue). A Mrs. Dean had a little dry goods store and always a little dress of some kind hanging in her little

Gertrude and Gladys sitting on a wall they built on their property, c. 1918.

window. The price of the dresses were always the same—50 cents! I can remember wanting a dress I saw hanging in her window one day, it had a big sailor collar on it and after much begging my mother purchased it for me. My mother made all of my clothes and my sisters!

Ward Walling had the store across from Mrs. Dean's shop. He sold groceries and once a week he would have "fresh meat" come in. He would give us a couple of big bones with meat on them for our dogs and also throw in a handful of liver for my cats. He also sold the oil we had to use for cooking in our three burner stove.

Mr. Carney, better known as Doc Carney had his little shoe repair shop near Mrs. Dean's store. A kind person with many professions. First and foremost he was the "Shoe Repair man on Commerce avenue." He was also the part time minister, and one of the trustees on the school board, and in a pinch his shoe shop was an "emergency first aid center." This brings vividly to my mind the time I was pushing my little sister Bing in a wheel barrow. The roads were rough and bumpy, so to make a long story short, as I was trying to run with my "passenger" she fell out of the wheel barrow, almost biting off the tip of her tongue! My mother heard the screams and came running. Bings [sic] mouth was full of blood and tears. My poor Mother gathered up the injured party and half running and walking too off for Doc Carney!! We had no phones in those days and we lived at the end of San Ysidro Street—now Samoa ave. with a bath towel draped across my sisters [sic] mouth we reached the shoe repair shop. Doc Carney was repairing a pair of boots. He gave one look at my sister—wiped his dirty hands on his leather apron and proceeded to take over. He "stuffed" what looked like the insides of her tongue back in place, put a clamp or some such thing over the ripped tongue and told her in quite a matter of fact way—"Keep your mouth shut"—No antiseptics, no washing of the hands, he just got busy. To this day Bing still has the scar but it healed beautifully, and didn't cost a cent!!

Another time I felt a headache coming on, possibly from reading too much music, anyway Mr. H. V. Hartranfts [sic] was there. He came over to me and said he could help my headache. With his forefinger and thumb he pinched gently in the corners of my eyes and held it for a few seconds, then repeated the same. Whatever it did my headache was relieved. We didn't carry such a thing as a headache pill in our purse in those days, and my mother didn't have her "smelling salts" with her for me to use! I wonder how many

FOUNDING SISTERS

Gladys took this photograph of her mother, Gertrude, and sister Dorothy.
Sister Bing stands at the window. Dogs Bruce, and Nemo, join the group, c. 1914.

The Maygrove home in January 1916. Four inches of snow fell,
a rare sight for the Little Lands Colony. Note the extension on the rear of the home.

remember the old smelling salts bottles. It usually came in a small green bottle and was so strong ones eyes would water after taking a sniff. Another old fashioned remedy like a slab of hot bacon rind placed on our chest for a cold! And in the summer time, always a big pitcher of Cream of Tartar to "clear the blood."[10]

Nearby was the post office with Mr. Ashby as postmaster and Zoe Gilbert as his clerk.

Way down the street on Commerce and Foothill, where the Garden of the Moon was located, and popular in the 20s, stood a little soft drink stand in its stead. This was owned and run by Mr. And Mrs. Wilson. They had two children Alec and Olive Wilson. My mother and Mrs. Wilson were very good friends due to the fact they were both from England. When Mr. Wilson died he left a wife and two children without any insurance of any kind. My mother did something about it. She put on her big apron and started out walking all over the countryside collecting as much money as she could from the people living in the valley. Her apron was full of change and some bills, when she had finished she took her apron off and "dumped" the contents into Mrs. Wilsons [sic] lap.[11]

It was a time when neighbors and friends nurtured and supported each other. This network of friends gave the pioneers the strength to endure the everyday hardships. Such closeness was celebrated.

One night we had a dreadful storm, little houses were blown over and chicken coups all over the place. About five families and we were included packed what we could and we even took our dogs and we all stayed in Bolton Hall for two nights. The rain and wind raging like mad. When it was over it looked like a cyclone had struck our little community. These were exciting time for the "kids" but not so for our parents. I remember Bolton Hall as the biggest building in Tujunga. It stood alone with its boulders and gravel. Not a bit of greenery anyplace. No shrubs and no trees, it stood there like a sentinel watching over the countryside. In one corner of the building inside was the little public library. At the other end was the huge fireplace. Church and Sunday school was also held in this lovely old building. I loved it and still do.[12]

Gertrude Maygrove's life with R. Walter would be less than the ideal. R. Walter was a strict vegetarian and an even stricter disciplinarian. He removed Dorothy from school in the eighth grade so that she could stay home and practice her music, and eventually fell in love with one of his music students and left his family. He moved to Honolulu, Hawaii, where he married another woman with two children. In the early 1920s, Gladys and her mother moved to Los Angeles. Gladys obtained work at the Hellman Bank in the downtown area as a courier. She would deliver, on foot, documents to other banks. Her long walks in Tujunga helped prepare her for her job. When Gladys left the bank, she had advanced to head teller.

Although Gertrude had lost her husband to another woman, she did not dwell on her misfortune. She went on with her life but never remarried. Gladys' love for her mother was such a strong bond that not even her mother's death in the 1950s could break it. R. Walter died on February 19, 1928, in Honolulu, a place he dearly loved. Gladys would later meet her father's second wife and her two stepsisters. Older sister Dorothy died at 50 years of age from breast cancer. The youngest sister Constance, "Bing," the comedienne of the family, lived until 1995.

Outside of the Little Lands Colony, Gladys became well known to many in the Los Angeles area. In 1914, she joined her younger sister, Bing, and two other talented young ladies to form "The Baby Orchestra." Her father continued to teach music to the schoolchildren of Tujunga. When Gladys was in her early teens, she, Grace Greenfield, and sister Dorothy formed a vaudeville act known as the "Musical Maygroves." Their group sang, played the ocarina, coronet, and trombone, and danced in theaters throughout the Southland.[13] After a few years of performing, the group split-up and Gladys joined a few different all-girl bands. In 1930, she married Bill Buckland and they had two children, Bill and Patti. Eventually, after her divorce from Bill, Gladys moved to San Diego, where she organized her own dance band under the name "The Gladys Buckland Combo."[14] During World War II, her band entertained the soldiers at the local U.S.O. When the war ended, she and the band toured the United States for nearly twenty years. She formed her own group, called "Laddie and her Rhythm Rogues," with four men and later married her bass player, Clarence Davis. Bing also moved to the San

FOUNDING SISTERS

Diego area and the two women played duets for the local clubs.

In 1961, Gladys experienced the greatest heartache of her life when her thirty-year-old son, Bill Buckland, was killed in an automobile accident while coming home to visit the family for Thanksgiving. Almost as accomplished a poet as she was a musician, Gladys in 1969 published a booklet entitled *My Bill*. It was a collection of her poems inspired by her son's passing.

Gladys and Bing would return with their family many times to Bolton Hall. They dearly loved the clubhouse and considered their time in Tujunga the happiest of their lives. When Gladys was eighty-two years old, she was still sitting in on music sessions held at her home in San Diego. She said she did it for her own amusement, reciting a musician's motto: "an unworked lip turns to jelly." Strong-willed Gladys would tell her daughter Patti, "Every day, wake up, make your bed, do the dishes, put your make-up on and get ready for the day."

On July 5, 1985, Gladys passed away at her home. Her husband, Clarence, and daughter, Patti, were with her. Attending her funeral were childhood chums Chan Livingston, Leslie Buck, and docent director of Bolton Hall Donna Larson. Gladys' first visit to Bolton Hall was in 1913 and her last was on April 13, 1985.[15] This vivacious musician, with the sparkling green eyes, never stopped loving Bolton Hall and her childhood home of Tujunga.

Notes

[1] Donna Larson, Docent Director, *Bolton Hall Museum Docent Handbook* (1984).

[2] Gladys Maygrove Davis, "The Way It Was," undated. Bolton Hall Museum Archives.

[3] Gladys Maygrove Davis, "Tujunga—Sixty Years Ago," (1976). Bolton Hall Museum Archives.

[4] Author's telephone interview with Patti Davis Arbuckle (Gladys' daughter). February 25, 2001.

[5] Author's telephone interview with Patricia Moore, Santa Catalina Historical Society. March 4, 2001.

[6] Gladys Maygrove Davis, Letter to the Editor of the *Record-Ledger Newspaper* (November 22, 1973).

[7] Gladys Maygrove Davis, "I Lived in the Little Lands," *The Record-Ledger Newspaper* (July 1, 1972).

[8] Ibid.

[9] "The Way It Was," op. cit.

[10] "Tujunga—Sixty Years Ago," op. cit.

[11] Ibid.

[12] Gladys Maygrove Davis, "Early Resident Recalls When There Were 200 Residents," *The Record-Ledger Newspaper* (April 20, 1985).

[13] The ocarina is a simple wind instrument that looks like a yam with finger holes in it and a projecting mouthpiece. According to family legend, R Walter Maygrove ordered a large shipment of ocarinas from Italy for use by his young music students. The instruments were sent to the United States aboard the *Titanic* and sank with her on April 15, 1912. The story of the lost shipment of ocarinas was told for years after.

[14] "The Way It Was," loc. cit.

[15] Donna Larson, op. cit., 1985, Vol. 3, No. 2.

This 1918 photograph shows Gladys, as a young woman, with her trumpet.

GLADYS MAYGROVE DAVIS

(*above*) Sunday afternoon band concerts drew heavy crowds to Monte Vista Park (Sunland Park). Standing (*left to right*): Bill Lancaster, Ed Forrester, Clark Lippincott, Elmer Adams, Cecil Percy, Paul Johnson. Middle row: Dorothy Maygrove, Bob Freeman, Ernie Tomalson, Bert Spenser, Joseph Forrester, Rowland Percy, Alf Blumfield. Front row: Paul Lancaster, Addison Wells, Gertrude Maygrove, Leslie Percy, Walter Maygrove and Gladys Maygrove (*seated*), c. 1915.

(*below*) The family's Monte Vista Band in front of the fireplace in Bolton Hall. Gladys in the front row, sister Dorothy in the second row and father Walter in the back row (*right*) wearing hat, c. 1915.

FOUNDING SISTERS

(*left*) "The Musical Maygroves" (*left to right*) Grace Greenfield, Dorothy and Gladys Maygrove. Note all three girls are playing the ocarina, c. 1917.

(*below*) Gladys, with platinum hair, poses with her band, "Laddie and the Rhythm Rogues." The handsome band member on far right, Clarence Davis, would later be Gladys's husband.

GLADYS MAYGROVE DAVIS

(*right*) Undated photograph of an adult Gladys with her horn.

(*below*) The Maygrove sisters, on a return visit to Bolton Hall Museum in 1976, standing in front of the massive fireplace where their band once played. (*left to right*) Clarence Davis, Gladys Maygrove Davis, Leslie Buck, Dorothy Rowley McCollum, John McCollum and Bing Maygrove Crawford, c. 1981. *The Record-Ledger.*

Nora took these photographs of herself, c. 1890s.

Nora Herrick Millspaugh
1857–1950

Nora often saw life through the lens of her camera. She had a lifelong love of photography and never grew tired of taking photographs of family members, friends, schoolchildren, and the many foreign cities she visited.

Nora was born on September 18, 1857, to Frances Goodell and Sidney Herrick. When she was three years old, her father, holding the rank of captain, left the family to fight in the Civil War. Little is known of her childhood in her birthplace of Three Rivers, Michigan.[1] She was married to Jacob Millspaugh, but by the time she came to California in 1890 she was a widow with no children. Nora lived in Los Angeles, where she was a kindergarten teacher in the public school system.[2]

Nora was one of the first seventeen people to buy lots in Los Terrenitos, in the big land sale of 1913. She was fifty-seven years old at the time and planning for her retirement. She and her friend, Zoe Gilbert, bought land at the same time. Zoe had given Nora a copy of *A Little Land and a Living* by New York attorney and socialist Mr. Bolton Hall (for whom the clubhouse was named). It was said that the people who came to settle in the Little Lands Colony were older and more educated than the early residents of Sunland.[3] Although her permanent home was in Los Angeles, Nora spent most of her weekends and summers in Tujunga, her adopted home. Always the teacher, she told the town's residents she would teach them all to play tennis if they would just build her a tennis court next to Bolton Hall. In 1922, townspeople found clay up in the surrounding mountains and built Nora her tennis court on the south side of the clubhouse. It was the first court to be built in Tujunga. Nora knew no limitations of age and could often be seen on the court teaching her eager pupils the artful game of tennis.[4]

In 1923, Nora built a double duplex on her property at 137 North Sunset Boulevard (10337 Commerce Avenue). One duplex was rented, and Nora used the other duplex as a weekend getaway from Los Angeles and its hectic life. When Nora passed away in 1950, the property was left to her niece, Winifred Millspaugh. After a few years, the property was sold to Arthur and Martha McKee, early members of the Little Lands Historical Society.

Martha McKee remembers Nora fondly:

> Nora did a lot of dancing down there at Bolton Hall. She was a nice lady. She often met people on the bus and, if they didn't have a job, she would hire them to do some work for her. Consequently, the duplexes on her property were constantly being added to. The front duplex, where Nora lived, burned down a few years ago. The two-story back duplex (still on site) had around seven roof levels and at one time was rather Chinese in appearance, having two outside stairways.[5]

Nora was fortunate to be endowed with robust health and a zest for living. At the age of seventy-seven years, this independent lady embarked on a seven-month trip around the world—by herself! Armed with letters of introduction from friends in Los Angeles, she gained entrance into schools in many countries, including

Japan, Denmark, England, France, and Italy. Visits to Washington, D.C. (which she said was the greatest city in the world), New York, Boston, Vermont, and Michigan concluded her enjoyable tour. In August 1934, when she returned to Tujunga, Nora held a party to recount her overseas adventures to her many friends.[6]

Civic-minded Nora was active in the Tujunga Women's Club, the Women's Auxiliary of the Ascension Episcopal Church, and the Pasadena WCTU (Women's Christian Temperance Union). She was always concerned about the welfare of soldiers and sailors and visited the veterans' hospital frequently.

Three days prior to her death, Nora drove her friends to Pomona. They found her in perfect health and, as usual, full of fun and life.[7] Nora passed away in her sleep of a heart attack. She requested that she be cremated and her ashes were shipped back to Michigan to reside in the Herrick family plot in Three Rivers.

Although, in the beginning, she resided part-time in Tujunga, at the time of her death she had become a full-time, well-loved citizen of Tujunga.

Notes

[1] Record of Funeral. July 30, 1950. Bades Mortuary, Tujunga.
[2] "Nora Millspaugh Passes Away," *The Record-Ledger* (September 3, 1950).
[3] *Docent Handbook*. Bolton Hall Museum.
[4] Ibid.
[5] "Mrs. Millspaugh Entertains Friends in New Home," *The Record-Ledger* (November 29, 1923).
[6] "Mrs. Nora Millspaugh Relates Experiences of European Trip," *The Record-Ledger* (August 30, 1934).
[7] *The Record-Ledger*, September 3, 1950, op. cit.

(*left*) Nora having a chat with Nora. Millspaugh family album, c. 1900.

(*above*) This photograph was taken of Nora when she was 18 years of age, c. 1875.

(*right*) Of this picture Nora said, "Mother holding her own yarn." Nora's experiment in taking double photographs.

(*below, left*) Nora, at her home in Los Angeles, offers a candy to one of her pupils.

(*below, right*) Nora in her later years, c. 1948.

Captain Mingay, in front of Twin Oaks,
the Tujunga home he shared with Emma, c. 1940.

Emma Mingay
1846–1924

When she arrived in Tujunga in 1921, she had already been an invalid for years. She was confined to her home, at 421 East Michigan Avenue (6847 Foothill Boulevard), and never was able to regain her health or experience the beauty of her surroundings. On March 4, 1924, she transitioned from this world while at home with her husband and her only child, Leta.[1] A large number of Emma's friends and family traveled from Tujunga to the Kiefer and Eyerick Chapel in Glendale to attend her funeral. She was buried at Grandview Cemetery in Glendale. It would be twenty-three long years before her husband would take his place beside her.

Emma was born in New York on August 14, 1846. Her childhood story and subsequent meeting with Henry are lost to time. Emma's husband, Henry, was born in England, but his family moved to New York when he was three years old.

When the Civil War began, Henry enlisted in Company D of the 69th New York Voluntary Infantry. It was the only regiment of the Army that carried over after the conclusion of the war.[2] Emma's and Henry's only child, Leta, was born in New York in 1870. After the war, Captain Mingay, his wife, and daughter moved to Colorado, where he became the publisher of *The Canon City Clipper* and *The Florence Tribune* newspapers. Leaving their publishing years behind them, the family moved to Glendale in 1914 and resided on Elk Street. As a Glendale resident, the captain became very active in community and civic affairs. Although his life as a soldier was over, "He had the honor of being one of the first members of the Grand Army of the Republic, formed after the Civil War. He commanded posts in Pennsylvania, Ryan, New York, Canon City, Colorado, Monrovia and N.P. Banks in Glendale."[3] His lifetime avocation became speaking on the Civil War and the importance of maintaining a patriotic spirit. Being one of the few surviving Civil War veterans in California, the captain was in great demand as a speaker in schools, for community groups, veterans' celebrations, and annual appearances in Glendale's Memorial Day Parade. Although completely blind in his later years, he remained active in Glendale and Tujunga, where he resided.[4] The old soldier became a beloved member of the foothill communities.

Before his death, the captain had one last hurrah. At the age of 98 years, he married again. His bride, Aimee Hennessey, was thirty years his junior. When friends of the couple spotted them at the marriage license bureau, the captain told them they would be marrying the following month, in May. The couple then quietly left the building and went straight to St. Bellarmine's Church in Burbank, where they were married with just the required witnesses. Their marriage culminated a twelve-year friendship that the captain said "had gradually blossomed into love."[5] Sometimes affairs of the heart remain a mystery. His bride was vice-president of the Amanda Jane Norton Tent, a Glendale women's group that was formed to aid "The Boys in Blue" and their dependent loved ones.[6] The newlyweds moved from Tujunga to her vine-covered cottage at 616 North Adams Street in Glendale. Two years later, on December 3, the captain celebrated his 100th birthday. He was feted by Glendale civic groups at Glendale's Patriotic Hall. He was the last surviving soldier of his unit and the last surviving member of Glendale's N.P. Banks Post of the G.A.R. Tujunga was forced to share their beloved "old soldier." On April 5, 1947, the captain fell and broke his hip while posing for a photograph. After a short stay, he died at Sawtelle Veteran's Administration Hospital in Los Angeles. He was survived by his daughter, Leta Perry, three grandchildren, and eight great-grandchildren.[7]

So impressed were Walt Disney and the City of Burbank with Captain Mingay that they designated May 30, 1944, as Captain Henry M. Mingay Day. The City of Burbank also named an elementary school, at Allen and Maple Avenue, after him. Leta resided at her father's home in Tujunga until her death in 1955. While her father was alive, she frequently accompanied him to his many public appearances and his annual visits to schools in Tujunga, Burbank and Glendale.

Glendale, Burbank, and Tujunga would claim Captain Mingay as their own, while Emma left no footprints upon the history of Tujunga.

Notes

[1] "Death Ends Long Illness of Mrs. Emma Mingay," *The Record-Ledger* (March 6, 1924).

[2] "Capt. H. M. Mingay, 100, G.A.R. Veteran Dies," *The Record-Ledger* (undated).

[3] "Still Standing—Building Holds Special Place for Those Who Dedicated Their Lives Fighting for Country," *The Glendale News Press*, May 26, 1997.

[4] Sunland resident, Myra (Perner) Lightheart fondly remembered the old soldier at schools, the Fourth of July parades, and veterans' ceremonies at the Verdugo Hills Cemetery.

[5] "Captain Mingay, 98, Takes Bride 30 Years His Junior," *The Record-Ledger* (undated).

[6] "Still Standing . . ." op. cit. Amanda Norton was the daughter of an early minister of the First Methodist Church of Glendale.

[7] "Last Honors Slated for Capt. Mingay," *Glendale News Press* (undated).

The small wooden building at 902 South Glendale Avenue was where Glendale's Civil War Veterans of N.P. Banks Post 170, Tenet 18 met. It was built in 1892. *The Glendale News Press.*

CIVIL WAR VETERAN HAS SUMMER GARDEN IN WINTER

Captain Henry M. Mingay has found health and youth in his Tujunga home where he has made vegetables and flowers bloom about him by gardening intensively on his property at 421 east Michigan avenue. Captain Mingay is a civil war veteran, and American flags always designate the Mingay property. Captain Mingay has been farming his lots four years, and now even in February, his list of home grown vegetables reads like a summer rather than a mid-winter garden. New potatoes, beets, turnips, carrots, onions, peppers, both green and red, and yellow tomatoes are ripe in this garden, and new peas and cabbage will soon be ready for the table. Even the strawberry bed, which was set out only two months ago, is trying to do its bit, and has fruit to be seen snuggled among the green leaves. Captain Mingay points with pride to his tobacco which is blooming a second time this season. Tobacco is a very tender plant, but on account of the mildness of this season, it has had this remarkable growth. It is of the Burley variety and Captain Mingay had a great many leaves from his one plant, which were vailable for use. Tujunga soil is as desirable for growing vegetables and flowers as Tujunga scenery is beautiful, the captain states.

(*left*) In this 1926 article, Captain Mingay finds health and youth in his garden. *The Record-Ledger.*

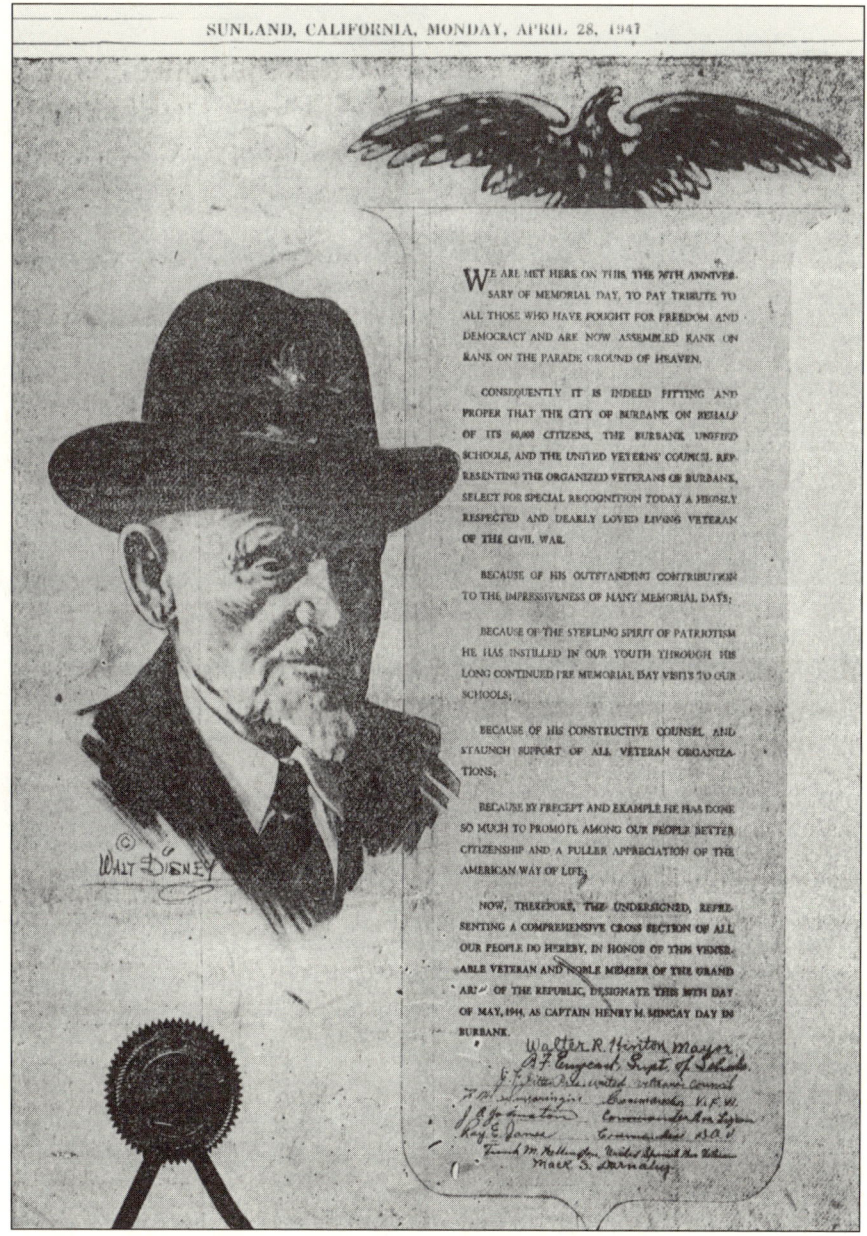

(*above*) The only known photograph of Flora Morgan.

(*right*) Businesswoman Bertha Morgan. *Both courtesy of Maude Therese (Morgan) Farrar.*

Flora Morgan
1868–1931

Bertha Morgan
1882–1959

There was a time, in the history of Tujunga, when the town was inundated with people named Morgan. Morgans outnumbered all other surnames, even Smiths. To put an end to the confusion, the following verse was offered:

> There was two-story Morgan,
> There was publisher Morgan,
> There was nurseryman Morgan,
> There was city clerk Morgan.[1]

The "city clerk Morgan" was Bertha A. Morgan, the only woman to hold public office during the City of Tujunga's seven year (1925–1932) history. She was city clerk for the entire seven years and acted positively on all matters without reference to formal council procedures. These facts point out her broad authority to deal with many duties, which would have normally belonged to other city officials or departments, and her correspondence supports the breadth of her duties and responsibilities.[2] All this hard work and dependability entitled Bertha to a paycheck of $25 a month. Bertha and her mother, Flora Morgan, typified some of the astute businesswomen of the early days in Tujunga.

Flora Melissa Lamb was born in Greensboro, North Carolina, on May 18, 1868, to Abner Lamb and Melissa (Pickett) Lamb. The details of Flora's childhood are unknown, but we do know that she and her husband, William Morgan, came to California in 1890 with their three children Bertha, James, and Hattie. The family came to Los Angeles for the economic opportunities afforded to William, who was a storekeeper and game warden. Unhappy with urban living, they bought acreage on Hillhaven Road in Tujunga and hired local men to build a two-story ranch home of fieldstone and wood. In 1908, Flora and Bill moved into their spacious twelve-room house, called Oak Glen Ranch. A large vegetable garden was planted, along with walnut and fruit trees. The remainder of the acreage was planted in grape vines. Well water was stored in large wooden barrels on the slope to the rear of the property. A lath house, aviary, and walnut shed joined the other buildings. The large patio, on the back of the home, became the scene of many parties and barbeques. Long after the parties concluded, when the night was still, Flora's guinea hens could be heard over the entire valley.[3]

"During the school year, the lady teachers stayed with us—usually two at a time—the young men, often destined for overseas duty, found them very attractive. They enjoyed square dancing in our living room and singing war songs around the piano. Great fun for all of us. We seldom went to other homes: other people came to ours."[4]

FLORA M. MORGAN

wishes to announce to her friends and neighbors that her home place known as The Oak Glen Ranch on the Hillhaven road is now being subdivided into most desirable lots.

This subdivision is most ideally located, being in the Green Verdugo Hills, one block from the business center, overlooking our beautiful Tujunga valley.

Lots $197 and up
$10 Cash — $10 Monthly
OAK GLEN RANCH INC.
Telephone Sunland 142   Tujunga, California

Flora Morgan ran this advertisement in 1928, when she subdivided and sold part of the large Oak Glen Ranch. *The Record-Ledger.*

Flora's hobbies included gardening, sewing, and quilt-making. She was sociable, but not one to be gone from home much. She was especially friendly with four older ladies who needed her care and assistance.

After twenty-three years of living in this rural Eden, the widowed Flora passed away on November 24, 1931, at home.[5] Although she suffered from asthma early in her life, during her stay in Tujunga she was relatively healthy. It was after a brief battle with cancer that she succumbed.

Because of her concern for the elderly women of her town, a group of local women formed a club to raise funds for a "Flora Morgan Home for the Aged." It was a difficult job to raise funds during the Depression years and the club eventually disbanded. The plans for the home were shelved and the money raised was donated to the Tujunga Women's Club. A hiking trail in the Verdugo Mountains was named in Flora's honor and is still seen on today's maps of Tujunga.

Flora's daughter, Bertha, was born in Salina, Kansas, in 1882. She was raised, with her siblings, in Los Angeles and in 1905 graduated from a business school downtown. She married Henry Batz; their son William was born in 1906. Her daughter, Maude Therese, arrived in 1910. When her children were young, Bertha and Henry divorced. Because Henry threatened to take their son from her, Bertha had Flora adopt the two children. Years later, Bertha was able to adopt her children back.[6] Bertha and the children moved into the house at Oak Glen Ranch. The independent divorcee took back her maiden name, Morgan, and began selling real estate. After a few years, Bertha set up her own home in Tujunga. Along with her real estate career and raising two children, Bertha was active in the local chapter of the Eastern Star.

By 1919, Tujunga was experiencing a real estate boom, and Bertha was about to become one of the key players in the short-lived history of the newly incorporated city. Over one thousand lots were sold in a very short time at prices ranging from $300 to $450. Ten dollars down and $10 a month were the accepted terms. M. V. Hartranft seemed to have a knack for knowing the right time to launch another sales campaign. A display of locally-grown fruits and vegetables at his Tujunga real estate office helped to convince prospective buyers that "almost anything would grow here, even bananas."[7]

By the early 1920s, Tujunga's population was estimated to be 3,000 people, an increase of 300 percent. In the first five months of 1923, the tenth anniversary of the colony, it was recorded that 13,499 people had made the round trip by bus from the House of Little Landers on Figueroa Street in Los Angeles to Tujunga. M. V. Hartranft had ten double-decker buses running the route in the morning and nine in the afternoon. Each bus held fifty-three passengers.[8]

At an election on April 21, 1925, the citizens voted to have their colony become a city of the sixth class. Eight hundred and eleven votes were cast: 457 in favor of incorporation and 354 opposed. Tujunga was officially incorporated on May 1, 1925, and Bertha was a witness to this most important phase of Tujunga's history. The incorporation made the City of Tujunga a legal entity and gave residents the right to act as a body through elected leaders, enter into contracts, incur debt, adopt and enforce ordinances, and control the future development of their city. John Russell was the first mayor of the town and Bertha Morgan was elected city clerk. Bolton Hall, "The Clubhouse," became City Hall and Bertha was in her office there every day from nine o'clock in the morning until one o'clock in the afternoon. After closing her clerk's office, she would rush to her real estate office on Foothill Boulevard.

Bolton Hall took on a new look as the City Hall sign went up over the main entrance and a two-man jail cell was added to the rear of the building. The jail cells had been purchased from the City of Glendale for the sum of $1.

Bertha became an integral part of City Hall and her responsibilities were many. She was extremely busy; her new job included maintaining all records dealing with the city's financial matters, the reports of the County Health Department Clinic (in the City Hall building), and all general correspondence. She was also responsible for typing the minutes of the city's weekly night council meetings; purchasing supplies; maintaining the ordinance files; and keeping the records for all building permits, dog licenses, map files, and police, fire, and election records.[9] Bertha never expressed concern that she was the only female elected official. All the other officers and officials had great respect for her personally and for her proficient business skills.

A fire that erupted on November 12, 1933, in La Crescenta raced west to Tujunga and Sister Elsie's Peak and burned over 5,550 acres of brush, altering the terrain and Bertha Morgan's plans for her daughter's wedding.

[The] wild fires burned off all the vegetation including the very old stands of pine trees on the San Gabriel Mountains on the north side of our valley. The burning continued through most of November, causing great consternation in the U.S. Forestry service because a heavy rainy season had been predicted. President Roosevelt then assigned the Civilian Conservation Corps. the job of building check dams in all of the fire ravaged canyons in order to prevent flooding. These dams had to be built in great haste so they would be ready before the rainy season started. Prior to New Years Eve it had been raining off and on for about two weeks, so all of the check dams were now full of water. We slowly learned all details of what had occurred. There was an official United States Weather Bureau Station up at Opid's Camp, which is up in the mountains just a short distance from our house as the crow flies. They had just received a new rain gauge and the weatherman stationed there was checking his new gauge against his old gauge for accuracy. At nine minutes after midnight both gauges reported over one inch of rain falling in one minute!! This was a new world's record for rainfall and it appeared in the Guinness Book of World's Records for many years thereafter! When this deluge hit it poured down into the debris basins in the canyons. Since they were all already full of water, they began breaking and as a result a wall of water, debris and boulders between 35 to 40 feet high would shoot out of each canyon and devastate the areas below. A family just above our house suddenly had a wall of water crash through their picture window and their living room was filled with rabbit hutches with

The Morgan's wood and stone Oak Glen Ranch farmhouse was nestled in a rural setting. During the 1940s, the home and property were used for the West Coast Boys School. On April 27, 1997, it was featured in the Sunland-Tujunga Historic Home Tour. *Pen and ink drawing by Forrest Theriot.*

FOUNDING SISTERS

Miss Lerchen and her class at Glorietta School.
Bertha's son William (Batz) Morgan is far left, front row, c. 1914.

Bertha stands in front of City Hall with the Tujunga Police Force.
(*left to right*) Earl Brunner, Johnny Lambert, Officer Ulrich, c. 1926.

In 1925, Bolton Hall took on a new look.
Note the sign "Tujunga City Hall" over the main entrance.
From the personal collection of Lee Brown, Adventures in Postcards, Sunland, California.

live rabbits in them! A 58 ton boulder was deposited in the middle of Foothill Boulevard and could only be removed by dynamiting it![10]

This was the fire that precipitated the great flood of New Year's Eve and New Year's Day 1934 that locals will long remember.

With so much of the mountain ground cover burned in the November fire, the heavy rains that started in December culminated New Year's evening when eleven inches of rain fell. Bertha's daughter, Maude Therese, had planned to marry William A. Farrar at St. Luke's of the Mountain Church in La Crescenta on New Year's afternoon. All roads leading in and out of Tujunga were completely flooded, and the only route into the city was through Hollywood.[11] Maude Therese and her bridegroom, both recent graduates of the University of Southern California, were married January 1, 1934, at 10:30 A.M. in front of the big stone fireplace at Oak Glen Ranch. Only the guests coming through the Hollywood route were able to attend. Even the groom's parents couldn't make the ceremony. Two weeks later, they held a reception so that all the invited guests could attend.

After Tujunga was annexed to Los Angeles in 1932, Bertha continued to work as secretary to the deputy police chief of Los Angeles. In 1937, she married longtime friend William Harrington. After retiring, the now-widowed Bertha left California in 1947. She moved to a little cottage on Maude and William's property in Oregon, facing the Rogue River. Bertha suffered a stroke in 1958 and passed away in 1959. She is buried in Grants Pass, Oregon.[12] Maude Therese now lives with her daughter and son-in-law in Ashland, Oregon.

Bertha Morgan leaves a legacy of a loving mother, successful businesswoman, and the only female elected official in the history of the City of Tujunga.

Notes

[1] Verse retold to Author by Tom Theobald (retired Tujunga postmaster). April 16, 2001.

[2] Jack Kilfoil, "Records Inventory—City of Tujunga 1925–1932," *City of Tujunga Records* (Compiled by the students from California State College, Dominguez Hills, 1975).

[3] Author's interview with Tom Theobald, June 13, 1994.

[4] Letter to Author from Maude Therese (Morgan) Farrar, dated March 9, 2001.

[5] Record of Funeral. November 27, 1931. Bades Mortuary, Tujunga.

[6] Letter to Author from Maude Therese (Morgan) Farrar, dated April 5, 2001.

[7] Sarah R. Lombard, *Rancho Tujunga—a History of Sunland/Tujunga, California* (Burbank, Calif.: The Bridge Publishers, 1990), 66.

[8] Ibid. 81.

[9] Author's telephone interview with John J. Jones, archivist for the City of Los Angeles, June 1, 2001. Bertha's records are contained in seven 13-by-15-inch boxes in the Los Angeles Archive Center.

[10] Letter, dated January 8, 2004, from survivor Charles Bausback to Historical Society of Crescenta Valley.

[11] "Maude Therese Morgan Weds William A. Farrar," *The Record-Ledger* (January 5, 1934).

[12] Letter to Author, March 9, 2001, op. cit.

Tujunga's Official Family taken in front of the first Tujunga Fire Station located east of Bolton Hall on Valmont: (*front row, left to right*) Councilman John O.B. Bodkin, W.T. Hamilton, Sheridan H. Smith, Mrs. Bertha Morgan, city clerk, Mayor E.A. Miller, City Treasurer John W. Russel, City Attorney C.W. Byrer and (*standing, left to right*) Chief of Police Earl Bruhner, Motorcycle Officer John Lambert, Fireman George Llewellyn, Fire Chief Harry Rice, Call Fireman Bert Davis and (*inset*) Councilman C.E. Stauter. *The Record-Ledger* (February 1929)

Tujunga's City Hall during the snowy winter of 1926. Note the sign over the main door.

Aim high and consider yourself
capable of great things.
—*Elbert Hubbard, 1914*

The collapse of the Seventh Day Adventist Church at the corner of Foothill Boulevard and Rosemont Avenue in La Crescenta. The boulders, loosed by the New Year's flood of 1934, can still be seen today in Montrose.

Although Tujunga roads were blocked, gas and water lines broken, cabins destroyed, and a CCC camp worker in Haines Canyon killed, the city of Montrose took the brunt of the flooding with a loss of forty-four lives.

(*top*) The Flood of 1934 Memorial Plaque stands on a base of stones, four feet high that contains a time capsule. *Courtesy of the Author.*

(*bottom*) Historian Art Cobery at the January 1, 2004, dedication of the plaque, placed by the Crescenta Valley Historical Society, at the corner of Rosemont Avenue and Fairlawn in La Crescenta to commemorate the twelve people who lost their lives at the American Legion Hall when a mud and debris flow ravished the building. *Courtesy of Art Cobery.*

An early photograph of Frances Raymond Morgan.
Courtesy of Stuart M. Parcher.

Frances Raymond Morgan
1867–1959

Frances Morgan Parcher
1903–1970

The Raymond family can be traced back to Richard Raymond, who emigrated from England in 1634 to settle in the Massachusetts Bay Colony. There, he was a successful merchant sea captain.[1] Frances' grandfather, Israel Raymond, made his first trip to California in 1850 as vice president of the Pacific Mail Company. In 1863, he brought his family west to live in San Francisco. While on his first trip to Yosemite Valley, he realized the importance of preserving the area for future generations. Israel was appointed to the first Yosemite Commission and served on the board until his death in 1887.

Frances Howard Raymond was born in San Francisco on April 5, 1867. She was the oldest of four children born to George and Mary (Hatch) Raymond. Her parents were married on December 27, 1865, in Stockton, California.

Little is known of Frances's childhood but her parents purchased property at the Miramonte Colony in the San Joaquin Valley, located in the northern section of Kern County, California.

In 1890, Frances met Wallace Morgan: "My wife and I met on a sagebrush desert one rainy day in the early spring of 1890. It was love at first sight with me, but it was some time later before she began to realize what a super-duper guy I was."[2] Wallace had arrived in California the previous December by train from Irving, Kansas. He settled in Miramonte and spent a few months working in a raisin vineyard in Rosedale. Wallace's three brothers and sister, Alma Florence, along with her husband, Reverend William Henry Wieman, and their children, came to Miramonte in 1891.

Wallace, whose family could also be traced back to the Massachusetts Bay Colony, and Frances were married February 16, 1896. The following year, Frances's father, George, deeded his Miramonte property to her.

The Morgans tried farming and cattle raising on their homesteaded property, but in 1902, they gave up dry farming and moved to Delano, California. For a mere $635, they were able to purchase the *Delano Record Weekly* newspaper. They spent the next year learning the newspaper business and were able to put out the weekly paper with no outside assistance.[3]

In 1903, Frances was expecting a baby, and she and Wallace moved to Bakersfield, the county seat, just thirty miles to the south. Wallace became a reporter for the *Bakersfield Morning Echo*. Their daughter, also named Frances, was born September 13, 1903. Wallace then became the chief editor of the newspaper.

Years passed uneventfully and in 1911, the Morgans decided to move to Hartranft's Little Lands Colony. Frances had become disenchanted with the now-prosperous agriculture, rail, and oil town of Bakersfield and its political fighting. They purchased eight shares of stock (bonds) for $20 each. The bonds were issued in Frances's name, perhaps indicating it was her decision to leave Bakersfield. The following year, they converted their bonds into a down payment on lots 33 and 34 of tract 1406 in the Little Lands Colony. The lots contained 4.18 acres of land and were located on Marcus Lane just south of Los Robles Avenue (St. Estaban Street).

In 1913, Wallace's sister, Alma Wieman, bought property on El Centro (Valmont). Wallace, with the help of Alma's five sons, built his sister a two-story home at the corner of Valmont and Pinewood. It was constructed in four months and the Wieman family occupied the home in 1916.

Though they had left Bakersfield, Wallace was appointed city manager of the town in 1914. A broken-hearted Frances left Tujunga and returned to Bakersfield with their eleven-year-old daughter. They lived at 2026 Twenty First Street, and Frances planted an extensive vegetable and flower garden. She now put to use her talent for writing and authored a children's story entitled "Fidelo, a Fairy Play For Children," an outline for a short movie, and several children's poems.

In 1917, her husband's position as Bakersfield city manager expired and they at last returned to Tujunga, where they would build their own home and start a weekly newspaper. Their daughter, Frances, began attending Glendale High School.

When Wallace and Frances were fifty-two years old, they founded *The Record of the Verdugo Hills* newspaper. It was September 11, 1920, when they began publishing the weekly paper from a small wooden building next to Dean's Pioneer Store on Sunset Boulevard. Its office was a room seven feet by nine, with a kitchen table and chair. From the start, Frances was a full partner with her husband and became the visible symbol of the newspaper. She was the general manager and made the office a popular gathering place.

Looking north on Commerce Boulevard in 1918. The curved road on left is Tujunga Canyon Boulevard.
The dirt road in front is Foothill Boulevard (Michigan Avenue). "X" marks the spot of future *Record-Ledger Newspaper* building.
Note the oak tree where Frances worked from her table and chair.

Although the Morgans were anxious to build a home on Marcus Lane, their top priority was the construction of an office for their newspaper. For several months before the building was completed, Frances sat at a table under a live oak tree, at the corner of Greeley and Sunset, where a circle of boulders was arranged as seating for guests. In that shady and sometimes chilly location, Frances accepted subscriptions and advertising while her husband wrote editorials, news stories and worked on the building's construction.

After the completion of their building in 1922, they began construction of their home on Marcus Lane. Frances's love of nature is revealed in her account "We Went Fifty-Fifty With Nature," detailing her plans for the garden:

> When we bought our three-acre place in the green hills of Southern California we came for the first time in close contact with Nature undefiled and in the rough, if anything so lovely could be so designated.

The oak-clad canyon, steeply banked by native shrubbery and wild flowers, lays as it had lain for a century, untouched by axe or saw; and the narrow trails among the leaves and grasses knew only the small feet of cottontail, squirrel or deer. Quail slipped quietly through the brush, and the trees were full of the chatter of birds and the flutter of their wings. In the Spring, sweeps of color, blue of nemophila and larkspur, the pink of Chinese Houses and Farewell to Spring, and the orange of escholtzia dotted the level delta at the mouth of the canyon. On the hillside climbing pentstemen, honeysuckle, clematis and wild cucumber vine festooned the limbs of the scrub with graceful loops and banners.

We loved it, all of it, just as it stood. And right there we began to run into trouble. It was evident that we could not live under a tree indefinitely, delightful though we found camping in the open. Beauty crowded us on every side, but there seemed no available site for a house without removing some of that beauty. Either a favorite tree already occupied the place planned for an inglenook, or a moss-covered rock lay directly in the middle of the proposed living room.

By 1924, the *Record-Ledger Newspaper* building was complete.
Note street lamps only on west side of Sunset (Commerce Avenue).

FOUNDING SISTERS

(*above left*) 1925 advertisement in the *Record-Ledger* for the newspaper.

(*above right*) A 1923 masthead of the *Record-Ledger*.

(*left*) 1924 *Record-Ledger* masthead showing the Morgans and Carroll Parcher as publishers.

(*below*) The office of the *Record-Ledger* was completed in 1922 at the corner of Commerce and Greeley. The second story was added in 1952. It was the first concrete building in Tujunga. *The Record-Ledger.*

Finally a site was selected that only needed the removal of one small sapling to give us sufficient room to build—so we thought. The Mister put up his forms, poured his cement and laid the hearthstone in the ingle. At this point the Missus made the disconcerting discovery that when completed, the breakfast room as planned would have a thrifty live oak in the corner cupboard.

What to do? Already the breakfast room was full small. But the tree was fine and straight and tall, one of the family, too. Could we chop down one of the family? No question about it. After a wakeful night we picked up our tools, moved down the hill and laid another foundation that wound skillfully in and out among the trees.

In landscaping our garden we began by laying out beds and borders on conventional lines, but we soon found that Mother Nature did not entirely approve our ideas, gathered for the most part from alluring and optimistic catalogues. She nipped here and burned elsewhere, and disciplined us so soundly that at last we dried the tears of disillusion and frustration and meekly followed where she led.

Now we have no garden, but a charming bit of woodsy canyon-and-hillside where the Silver Moon grows rampant over the tree-tops, where fragrant honeysuckle lies like a carpet over the scrub oaks; where native cherry, glossy and clean as holly, mingles with yellow jasmine and perennial pea vine; and where sage and mint, fern-leaved yarrow, mimulus, cascara and smoke-tree combine with brook, bridal wreath, lavender, perennial phlox and coreopsis to make a border unsurpassed.

Beneath the tall live oaks, shaded by their plumy branches from the too direct rays of the sun, ferns flourish in the deep leafmold; and coral bells, on hair-like stems, lilies, begonias, golden gleam, violets and cyclamen dot the green background with bits of color. Rosy nicotiana, opening its blossoms in the late afternoon, scents the air with delicious perfume as we rest on the broad terrace for a well-deserved cup of tea.

Their home consisted of a large living room with a stone fireplace, a small dining room, and a kitchen on the main floor. On the second floor were two large bedrooms, each with a private bath. The lower portion of the front of the house was made with local stone and had a large concrete terrace. Wallace left a hole in the stone fence where they could place a plaque that would read, "We'll stay a little while in the wilderness, then we'll all go Home." The Morgans named their plot of land Elfin Woods and lived in their original house for the next forty years.

In November 1922, they consolidated their newspaper with Carroll Parcher's publication, *Crescenta Valley Ledger of Montrose*. Thus, the *Record-Ledger* was born. The combined publication covered the entire east valley, from Sunland to La Cañada. The paper became recognized as one of the outstanding weekly newspapers in southern California. Carroll and Wallace would remain co-publishers until the paper was sold to Robert Oliver in 1937.

Two years after the merger of their newspapers, the Morgan family merged with the Parcher family. Carroll Parcher and the Morgan's daughter Frances were married on November 8, 1924, at Elfin Woods. The couple had attended Glendale High School and graduated together in the class of 1921. The informal wedding, with 150 guests, took place under live oaks on the property and joined two Tujunga pioneer families.[4]

In 1935, Wallace Morgan retired. At a reception in his honor at the American Legion Hall on December 25, 1935, he acknowledged the importance of his wife's contribution in the early days of their newspaper. Because they started on a shoestring, outside employment for Wallace was necessary. Frances remained in the office every day, writing much of the news, soliciting advertising and doing a large part of the work necessary to publish the paper each Thursday.

After the merger of the *Record* and the *Ledger*, Frances was able to spend more time in her splendid garden at Elfin Woods and enjoy time with her grandchildren, Margaret Ann, Stuart Michael, and Janice Mary.

In 1943, at the age of 75, Wallace began a four-year project. Doing most of the work himself, he built a new home on Marcus Lane. They called the new home Honeymoon Cottage. Once their new hillside home was completed, daughter Frances, Carroll, and their three children left their own home on Samoa and moved into the original Morgan house. In 1946, Frances and Wallace celebrated their fiftieth wedding anniversary at a surprise party given them by their daughter and son-in-law.[5]

Frances surprised her family in 1952 when, at the age of 84, she learned to type. In all of her years at the family newspaper, she had written her stories in long hand. She left her family many typed practice sheets, which showed her to be strong of mind and spirit. One such sheet reads,

> Dad made me laugh this morning. He said there was nothing the matter with us but hardening of the arteries, softening of the brain, and general disintegration of muscular system. And there is more truth than fiction in that. If one is not ill, the gradual disintegration of the body need not be too unpleasant. We like to think so, anyway and certainly there can be no harm in the hope of a fuller life than the one we live on this earth now.

In March 1958, Frances fell in her home, broke her hip and was left bedridden. On August 23, 1958, Wallace Morgan passed away in his daughter's home. He was ninety years old.[6] The following year, Frances passed away on November 11 at Glendale Sanitarium and Hospital. She was ninety-two years old.[7] Her later years were spent enjoying her home, garden, and family, and she left a legacy as the intelligent, witty partner of the founding editor of the *Record-Ledger* newspaper.[8]

The Morgans' daughter, Frances, passed away February 4, 1970, at the early age of sixty-six years, following a long illness. She was active in the musical and cultural activities of Glendale, her new home since 1958.[9] Family friend Richard M. Nixon before he became president of the United States, said to Carroll Parcher, "Your wife always makes me feel better. She has something good to say about everyone." The same could be said for her mother.[10]

Notes

[1] Stuart A. Parcher, "Frances Howard (Raymond) Morgan—a Biographical Sketch" (April 2000).

[2] "Wallace Morgans Celebrate Golden Wedding," *Glendale News Press* (February 1946).

[3] Parcher, op. cit.

[4] "Miss F. Morgan Becomes Bride at her Home—Carroll W. Parcher Weds Dainty Daughter of His Partner," *Glendale News Press* (November 10, 1924).

[5] The Parcher home on Samoa Avenue was featured in the 1994 Historic Home and Garden Tour. The house and garden remain in its original state in the year 2001.

[6] Record of Funeral. August 23, 1958. Bades Mortuary, Tujunga.

[7] Record of Funeral. November 11, 1959. Bades Mortuary, Tujunga.

[8] "Mrs. Morgan Dies; Tujunga Pioneer," *Glendale News Press* (November 13, 1959).

[9] "Daughter of Record-Ledger Founder Dies in Glendale Hospital," *Glendale News Press* (February 6, 1970).

[10] Carroll Parcher, "The Lady of the House Leaves Happy Memories," *Glendale News Press* (undated). Bolton Hall Museum Archives.

(*right*) Frances Morgan in the early 1920s. *Courtesy of Stuart M. Parcher.*

Every Issue Is Full of Interest

THE people of the Tujunga valley look forward to every issue of the Record-Ledger, because each number is full of things that interest local people. Features of The Paper are:

PERSONAL ITEMS

CLUB AND LODGE NEWS

THE KITCHEN CABINET

EDITORIALS

SOCIETY

CITY GOVERNMENT NEWS

CITY PRINTING

CARTOON

WEEKLY FASHION HINT

BILL THE BARBER

COMPLETE NEWS OF THE TUJUNGA VALLEY

Frances Morgan's School
OF
Social and Aesthetic
DANCING
TUJUNGA AND LA CRESCENTA

Girls' Aesthetic Class, Saturday, 9:30 A. M.
At La Crescenta School Auditorium

Baby Class in Aesthetic and Folk Dancing, Friday, 3:30 P. M., at Tujunga Studio

STUDIOS
La Crescenta School Auditorium
Tujunga, Live Oak Lane near S. Marshall St.
For folder and further information phone Sunland 233

An explanatory folder will be gladly sent on request
Address, P. O. Box 1, Tujunga, Calif.

(*above*) 1923 Tujunga telephone directory advertisement for daughter Frances M. Morgan's School of Dance.

A young Frances Morgan Parcher and her children, Stuart and Margaret Ann Parcher (Faulkner), c. 1932. *Courtesy of Stuart M. Parcher.*

(*right*) Photograph taken at the Morgan home at 9229 Marcus Lane. Adults (*left to right*) Huston Smith (husband of Eleanor Kendra Wieman Smith), Wallace Morgan, Frances Morgan, daughter Frances. Children (*left to right*) Karen, Gail and Robin Smith, c. 1950s.

(*below*) Frances and Wallace in front of their fireplace at Marcus Lane in Tujunga, c. 1946. *The Glendale News Press.* Both courtesy of Stuart M. Parcher.

Myra, in center of photograph, facing her companion, Cora Belle (*right*), on an outing with Alice Lamson (*left*).

Myra Osgood
1864–1941

No story of Tujunga would be complete without the inclusion of the Haines Canyon Water Company and Myra Osgood, its chief accountant and manager. Originally the water rights of Haines and Blanchard Canyons were purchased by Phil Begue, Sr., in 1882. In 1910, M. V. Hartranft and the Western Empire Suburban Homes Association purchased the rights from Mr. Begue and, in the early 1920s, formed the Haines Canyon Water Company.

Myra was born in Blue Hill, Maine, on August 19, 1864, and came directly to Tujunga in 1913. Myra's first job with the colony was manager of the Little Landers co-operative store. After an arson-induced fire destroyed the co-operative the first year, she left the colony and moved to Los Angeles.[1] Her stay in Los Angeles was short lived, and Myra returned to Tujunga to work as the office manager for the Haines Canyon Water Company (later to become the American States Water Company). Her position with the water company and many commitments to community activities made her well known. Scores of residents remembered her open-handed generosity and kind acts.

This hard-working businesswoman lived with her friend Cora Belle Linaberry, at Bird's Acre. In 1935, Myra was forced to retire due to ill health. Because of the water company's high regard for her, she was paid a full salary while retired.

Her last few years were difficult due to her failing health, so her sister, Lillian, came from Walliston, Massachusetts, to help Cora Belle care for Myra. Days before her death, she was moved to the Glendale Sanatarium, where she passed away on December 16, 1941, of pneumonia and arteriosclerosis.[2] She was cremated and buried in Forest Lawn, Glendale. Four years later, her trusted friend and companion, Cora Belle, would reside next to her.

Myra, a simple and unassuming woman, wanted no service and no flowers, but the town that so dearly respected and loved her wouldn't hear of it.[3] Bades Mortuary overflowed with flowers and friends as the town said good-bye to the gracious Myra, an original Little Lander.

Notes
[1] "Miss Osgood, Tujunga Pioneer, Answers Last Call," *The Record-Ledger* (December 18, 1941).

[2] Record of Funeral. December 16, 1941. Bades Mortuary, Tujunga.

[3] "Old Time Friends Gather at Service for Miss Osgood," *The Record-Ledger* (December 20, 1941).

This wood frame building, at 10064 Commerce Avenue, housed the offices of the Haines Canyon Water Company, c. 1930s. *The Record-Ledger.*

The wooden Haines Canyon Water Company building in August of 2000. It was the earliest building on Commerce to survive into the new millennium. *Courtesy of Author.*

Nannie McBride Parcher
1859–1941

When Nannie Parcher died in 1941, residents of Glendale and Tujunga each claimed her as their own. Extremely friendly and with a sincere interest in the welfare of others, Nannie became well known in the Tujunga area as a benefactor to the sick and less fortunate. Her neighbor and poet laureate of California, John Steven McGroarty, delivered the eulogy at her funeral. She had lived a long, full, and active life. Though the widow of Glendale's first mayor and the mother of the publisher of the *Record-Ledger* newspaper and future mayor of Glendale, she is best remembered as a person of deep compassion for her fellow man.

Nannie was one of five children born to Jane Ann (Titus) and John McBride. She was born on February 28, 1859, in Sharon, Pennsylvania.[1] The famous town of Titusville, home of Jennie Lichtenthaler, was just fifty-five miles northeast of the McBride family farm. Nannie spent her early childhood on the farm, where she became an expert horsewoman. At the age of sixteen, she was requested to take an exam for a teaching position in the Pennsylvania public schools. Upon passing the exam with high honors, she became one of the youngest teachers in her state.[2] After a few years of teaching, she changed professions to physical therapy, then known as scientific massage.[3]

Nannie moved to Minneapolis, Minnesota, where she met and married Wilmont Parcher on June 30, 1892. Wilmont had previously been married to Ada Eudora Wyman. After fifteen years of marriage and no children, Ada died of diabetes on May 16, 1890. When Nannie married Wilmont, she was thirty-three years old and he was forty-five years old. The details of their courtship are unknown, but her marriage was report-

A young Nannie in Minneapolis, c. 1890s.
Courtesy of Stuart M. Parcher.

Frances Morgan and Carroll W. Parcher, c. 1920s. *Courtesy of Stuart M. Parcher.*

(*opposite*) Nannie and Wilmont visiting the Begue cabin in Haines Canyon, May of 1915.

ed in a Minneapolis newspaper as being a quiet and intimate wedding, attended by a few friends, at the home of Mr. and Mrs. C. C. Jackson. The home was gaily decorated with palm fronds and lots of pink roses.

Her new husband was born in Waterbury, Vermont. At the age of seven years, Wilmont had moved to the forests and prairies of Minnesota. His boyhood was spent on his family's farm in the northern part of the state and he lived later in logging camps. His jobs were many and varied: clerk in a country store, manufacturer of carriages, and horse broker.[4]

After just a little more than a year of marriage, the couple moved west to live in Los Angeles. They began their journey on October 4, 1893, aboard the Minneapolis and St. Louis Railway, in one of the quite famous Phillip's excursion cars. Wilmont wrote, "Our hampers were filled with the good things of life, the car was clean and cool, the berths were well supplied with bedding, the sheets were changed every morning and the car kept in general tidy condition by the obliging porter."[5] Their route took them to Kansas City, where six other excursion cars were added to their train. Their journey continued to Denver, where they changed trains to the Rio Grande Railroad and continued south to Pueblo, Colorado. They proceeded over the Rockies to Salt Lake City, on to Sacramento, California and south through the San Joaquin Valley to Los Angeles.

In 1900, the Parchers were living at 3211 Vermont Avenue in the city of Los Angeles. Nannie became a homemaker and accomplished crochet worker, making table coverings and bedspreads. By the beginning of the twentieth century (1901), they had moved to another small house near the campus of the University of Southern California. In October of that year, the Parchers bought a ten-acre farm on Glendale Avenue and Maple Street in the city of Glendale, for $3,250. They were now strawberry growers. On September 13, 1903, Nannie gave birth to her only child, a son named Carroll Wilmont Parcher. That year, Nannie was forty-four years old and her husband was fifty-six years old.

Wilmont turned out to be better suited to business than to ranching and, in 1904, became the president and general manager of the Tropico-Glendale Berry Growers Association. In 1906, the citizens of Glendale voted in favor of incorporation and Wilmont became the first mayor of Glendale. He was re-elected in 1908 for another four-year term, but resigned after three and one-half years.

Wilmont's health was failing, due to asthma and bronchitis, so he moved alone to Tujunga and lived in a 9-by-10-feet flat board cabin on San Ysidro Street. "During his time there he wrote to his son from Tujunga: "How nice that Mama has a 'dear boy' at home with her now that I am gone. And I wonder sometimes if I'll ever live at home again, especially not if we live in Glendale. I fear not, for it seems impossible for me to live there." Another of Wilmont's notes from Tujunga to Carroll at home in Glendale paints a rather barren picture of his surroundings: "My Dear Boy: You would think this was the funniest place you ever saw. Little houses, plenty of rocks and picturesque scenery. It is a good place to rest all right. No picture shows or anything to distract one. Well my dear I am feeling better—breathe so much better. If you and Mama were only here. I am going for a walk now. Be a good boy and don't forget I love you. Dad."[6]

The high, dry climate revived Wilmont's health and, in 1916, he moved Nannie and fourteen-year-old Carroll to live with him. His enthusiasm for the colony grew, and in 1917 he wrote a letter describing Little Lands and his rudimentary living conditions while he was alone there. The letter was published in a Glendale newspaper on January 23, 1917:

"Little Lands"

The question is often asked where is Little Lands? If those asking the question could have been here for the last ten days or so they probably would have said it is within about thirteen miles of Alaska. With rain and sleet and snow in the air for days, and the wind coming through the old Tujunga at something less than forty miles an hour, it certainly did not tax one's imagination to a straining point to really believe they were in Alaska.

Yet we find Little Lands (now called Tujunga) is only about twenty miles north of Los Angeles.... The question is often asked also, What gave it its name of Little Lands? The tenderfoot possibly could not give a more logical and better answer than that after diligent labor of blasting and digging out of the rocks and stone, you find "little land." One almost stands in wonder and awe at the immensity of the rocks and concludes that here is where the Good Lord finished up the world with an over supply of rocks on hand—and desirous of completing the work in seven days, said "we'll just dump the whole lot right here."

... At an elevation of 2,000 feet, with the pure air, pure water and scenery unsurpassed in the world, the invalid and tourist cannot help but find health and rest, and with it pleasure that they are domiciled in such a beautiful niche of God's universe.

The writer desires right here to speak of one feature of the health-giving properties of this beautiful of mountain homes, and that is for asthma. Having contracted asthma something over a year ago, after suffering months with it, I came to Little Lands where I found almost immediate relief.

FOUNDING SISTERS

(*top*) A young Carroll Parcher in 1929. *The Record-Ledger* (February 1929).

(*bottom*) Wilmont's death made the front page of Frances' son's newspaper. *The Record-Ledger* (September 9, 1926).

After feeling I could go back to my home in Glendale I tried it, but in a few hours I was again overcome with it and returned to Little Lands where I soon got relief again. Have tried it three times now, each time with the same results. . . .

There is a great lack of accommodation for people who have to come here, therefore, I feel confident should some enterprising citizen build and run a hotel-sanatorium and advertise it as a No-As-Ma hotel-sanatorium they would do well here and add a blessing to mankind and a good name for Little Lands.

My friends, perhaps, will be interested to know that I am running a one-man deluxe apartment, i.e. batching it. I am doing my part in reducing the high cost of living in this simple life. Bah on pampered aristocracy! When you can get all the "comforts of home" in a 9 x 10 board cabin, kitchen, living room, sun parlor, sleeping room and bathroom all in one. . . . Washing of my undershirt once a week and hanging my blankets out to air and with a supply of tin can products for the inner man, what more could a man ask for?

Little Lands is comprised of some five or six hundred people. . . . No one here has a special patent on any one industry, for apparently each one knows how to do most anything from raising chickens to building houses, stone walls, etc.[7]

Nannie was never an active clubwoman, but during World War I she became involved in the newly formed Red Cross. She served as the first president of the Verdugo Hills chapter of the Red Cross, an auxiliary chapter of Pasadena. When the United States entered the war in 1917, a sewing unit was established at Bolton Hall. At weekly meetings, the ladies sewed and knitted items for the war effort. John Steven McGroarty and other volunteers then drove these items to the Pasadena chapter.[8]

Both Nannie and Wilmont became active in Tujunga community affairs. Wilmont became director of the Tujunga Board of Trade (now Sunland-Tujunga Chamber of Commerce) and president of the Tujunga Board of School Trusties. He also joined the "Millionaires Club" that was now meeting on the steps of the post office or in the rear of Mrs. Dean's Pioneer Store. Publisher Wallace Morgan, father of Frances Parcher (Carroll's wife), was a member of the club as well. Though Wilmont's attacks of illness later forced him to withdraw from all public work, his advice was still sought.

Nannie and Carroll were bedside as Wilmont struggled to stay alive until his granddaughter was born. He wanted to take her for a walk around the block. Wilmnot's granddaughter, Margaret Ann Parcher, was born to Mrs. Frances Parcher on August 24, 1926. At the age of seventy-nine, Wilmont died on September 4, 1926. Wilmont's time in Little Lands was short, but it was marked by his love for his little cabin and the friendly people who became his neighbors.

Nannie Parcher remained in Tujunga, at 361 San Ysidro Road, until 1930, when she moved to Montrose. In her later years, she moved again to Glendale, sharing a residence at 539 East Elk Street with her dear friend, Mrs. Carrie Hilding. After this final move, most of her time was devoted to her crochet work, which she distributed to her many friends. She continued to keep her mind active and read the newspapers daily for local, national and international stories. On July 24, 1941, Nannie died at home after a lengthy illness. The long and active life of Tujunga and Glendale's "good neighbor" came to an end.[9]

Her son, Carroll (1903–1992), wrote:

I think the word which best characterizes Mother's life is DEVOTION. With her devotion was more than a figure of speech it was a way of life. I thought of her constant and untiring concern for friends, whether in high or low places, whether in sickness or in health, whether in poverty or plenty, and of the times I have seen her set out, laden with food fresh from her kitchen, bound for the home of someone less fortunate—or return in the dawn after having spent the night at the bedside of a neighbor whose hold on the slender thread of life she had helped to keep secure during the long watches. I know there was a great joy last night in that far, still place among the stars. Because Mother was there.[10]

NOTES

[1] Sharon is in Mercer County in western Pennsylvania on the Ohio state line. Stuart M. Parcher, "Wilmont and Nannie (McBride) Parcher—a Biographical Sketch," (Maryland, November 2000).

[2] Carroll Parcher, "In my opinion—Because mother was there," *Glendale News Press* (May 12, 1979).

[3] "Mrs. Parcher, Pioneer Resident is Called to Rest," *Record-Ledger of Verdugo Hills* (July 31, 1941).

[4] Stuart Parcher, op. cit.

[5] "Wilmont Parcher," *The Record-Ledger* (1926). Bolton Hall Museum clippings file.

[6] Stuart Parcher, op. cit.

[7] Donna Larson, Docent Director, *Bolton Hall Museum Docent Handbook* (1984).

[8] "Sunland-Tujunga Red Cross District Formed in 1918 as Pasadena Auxiliary," *The Record-Ledger* (May 21,1953).

[9] "Pioneer Resident Hears Final Call," *Glendale News Press* (July 25, 1941).

[10] Stuart Parcher, loc. cit.

In 1924, the library at Bolton Hall was moved to 7212 Valmont Street.
Beth served for many years as librarian at the Tujunga Branch Library.
In 1952, the library moved to its current location on Foothill Boulevard.
The old library building is now being used as a rental unit.

Beth Pasko
1894–1947

Beth Pasko was only fifty-three years old at the time of her death. Tragedy struck in 1947 when Beth lost control of her motor-ette (electric cart). The brakes of the cart failed and Beth careened down Valmont Street, crashing into a garage building at Valmont and Foothill Boulevard. By four o'clock that Saturday afternoon, she succumbed to shock from a fractured skull, broken nose, and broken leg.[1]

Her untimely death shocked the community and left many adults and children in mourning. Camera-shy Beth had few photographs taken of her and no known photograph of her remains. She lived on Valmont, worked on Valmont, and died on Valmont. The slopes of Tujunga, her home since the age of three years, were finally the cause of her death. Shocked and saddened, the community turned out in whole: men, women, and children came for a service in the Tujunga Community Church of which her father had been the first pastor.

> As the days pass, one realizes more what a widespread influence this quiet unassuming charming little woman had in the community, especially over the children, who adored her. During her sixteen years as librarian of the Tujunga Library, she was always ready to help her readers make their selections. She was always patient with those who were difficult, even when she herself was so crippled with arthritis that she could scarcely rise from the chair.
>
> For the past twelve years she conducted a vacation reading club for the children, which not only developed a love of reading in the children but helped improve their grades at school. While she was waiting for the ambulance on Saturday, so painfully injured, her thoughts were of the children who would be disappointed because the opening of the reading club would have to be postponed. She expressed her regret to some children standing by.[2]

Beth was born on May 19, 1894, in Rochester, New York, to Mattie Bryan and Edgar W. Pasko.[3] At the age of three years, she came to Tujunga with her mother and father and older sister, Ruth. Her father was in poor health and, though he had been a medical doctor, he had engaged in literary work, publishing and editing newspapers in New York and Cincinnati. With his health failing, he sought refuge in Tujunga. After moving his family, he was called to the ministry and preached the Gospel for thirty-two years.[4]

Beth attended Los Angeles High School on Fort Moore Hill and graduated from library school in 1916.[5] The library school was conducted on the top three floors of the Metropolitan Building at Fifth Street and Broadway in downtown Los Angeles. Ione Barber, a fellow classmate, had this to say about the school: "The class, which included some quite distinguished individuals, met in a building on the roof and the famous bindery of Elmo Reavis was in another building alongside. Mr. Reavis, a big, jovial, kindly man, taught each of us how to bind two books."[6] After several years of intensive training, Beth took the Civil Service exam and became part of the City of Los Angeles's library staff. Because of her love of children, she became the children's librarian. Just as her career was advancing, so was her crippling arthritis. She worked part-time as a librarian for the Southern California Edison Company and the Palo Alto and Santa Monica Libraries. Her periods of work were interspersed with periods of ill health. It was a great day for the community when she became librarian at the Tujunga Branch Library, located at 7216 Valmont Street, just north of her family home. Her sister, Ruth, said, "Her whole being was engrossed in her library work... dominated by a conviction of the need of service to mankind."[7]

Ruth graduated from the University of Southern California in 1912 and became a leader in youth organizations, including a Camp Fire Girls group at the Los Angeles YMCA. In 1917, Ruth was forced by ill health to undergo sanatorium care. The Pasko family built a cottage on their property at 7341 Valmont, so that Ruth could continue her convalescence at home and regain her health. In 1923, Ruth joined Miss Agnes MacFie at her art studio/residence at 10227 Tujunga Canyon Boulevard. At that time, Beth and her parents enlarged the Pasko family home. Ruth and her new business partner operated the Potpourri Jar Gift Shop on Commerce. The shop featured gifts from foreign countries and works of local artists. The successful shop had to be closed in 1934 when Miss MacFie's health failed. Ruth and Miss MacFie moved to Morro Bay to join the art colony where Ruth's work was shown in local exhibits and throughout California.[8]

On December 6, 1930, Beth's beloved

This photo of Beth's father, Reverend Edgar W. Pasko, appeared in the *Record-Ledger*, February 1929.

father, Edgar, passed away from a coronary embolism at the age of 69 years.[9] The entire community grieved the passing of the recently retired pastor of the Tujunga Community Methodist Church. Beth told fellow librarian Ione Barber, "It was my father, not McGroarty, who established the Easter Sunrise service on the hill above town, which was then called Mt. Pasko. Later, because of the greater fame of McGroarty, it became Mt. McGroarty." Beth felt the mountain should have her father's name, not the second name of Mt. McGroarty.[10] In 1931, the generous developer Marshal V. Hartranft donated land around Mt. McGroarty to be named Pasko Park, in honor of the Reverend Edgar Pasko.[11]

It was now Beth and her mother who resided at their Valmont home. In 1936, when the *Record-Ledger* society columnist, Esther Warner, took a leave of absence following a serious surgery, Beth took over her column entitled "Town Topics."[12]

In 1945, Beth organized a small group of local poets who met once a month at her home for reading and

Los Angeles High School opened in 1873 at Pound Cake Hill (Temple & Broadway) but was moved to Fort Moore Hill and remodeled in 1891. Beth attended high school here before Library School, c. 1893.

self-criticism of poetry. After her death in 1947, the group was renamed "The Writer's Rendezvous" with poet Arnold Davidson, chairman.

After Beth's unexpected death, her mother, Mattie, closed up the family home and moved to Morro Bay to join Ruth and Miss MacFie. Mattie lived with her artist daughter until 1956. Ruth, the last of her family, passed away one year later in 1957.

"Beth Pasko is a living challenge to all of us. Within the limitations of a station library and of constant physical suffering, she did a fully professional job, as a librarian and as a human being. She easily won the respect and the affection of her community. Beth's candle shone briefly but brightly. As one Tujungan says, 'She leaves behind her wonderful example of patience in suffering and gentleness with others.'"[13]

Notes

[1] "Community Mourns Death of Beth Pasko," *The Record-Ledger* (June 26, 1947).
[2] Ibid.
[3] Record of Funeral. June 25, 1947. Bades Mortuary, Tujunga.
[4] "Rev. Pasko to Teach Bible Class," *The Record-Ledger* (February 28, 1924).
[5] "In Memorium—Beth L. Pasko," *The Broadcaster* (September 1947) p. 4.
[6] "Parson Pasko," two-page biography of Beth, written by Ione Barber, fellow student, Tujunga resident, and lifelong friend. Bolton Hall Museum clippings file.
[7] *The Record-Ledger*, February 28, 1924, op. cit.
[8] "Ruth Pasko, Well Known Here, Dies at Age 68 Following Illness," *The Record-Ledger* (November 21, 1957).
[9] Record of Funeral. December 6, 1930. Bades Mortuary, Tujunga.
[10] "Parson Pasko," op. cit.
[11] Tujunga City Council Resolution No. 254, dated August 5, 1931, accepts the property and the conditions and directs its registration.
[12] "Miss Beth Pasko Now On Staff of Record-Ledger," *The Record-Ledger*, 1936. Bolton Hall clippings file.
[13] "In Memorium," op. cit.

Pasko Park surrounding the Cross of San Ysidro in the Verdugo Mountains.

> It's not the years in your life that count.
> It's the life in your years.
> —*Abraham Lincoln*

THURSDAY, DECEMBER 24, 1936

TOWN TOPICS

By BETH L. PASKO

This columnist wishes a MERRY CHRISTMAS to everyone.

George R. Gruenthal has finished a new home at 10422 Mountair.

Mr. and Mrs. J. Rich are entertaining friends and relatives over Christmas with their niece, Mrs. Marjorie Wilson, and family, at Wilmington.

Howard L. Miller of Glendale has bought the house at 9546 Inspiration Way and has rebuilt and remodeled it, so that he expects to give a good housewarming.

The POTPOURRI JAR

{ MONTE VISTA AT EL CENTRO }

GIFTS

Just a tiny place this is, tucked away in the hills, but packed to the brim with unusual importations from all over the world, each with its story behind it; stories of brown-skinned men sitting cross legged in the dust fashioning exquisite bits of silver, or lumbering elephants piling the logs as they come down the river; stories of linen-smocked men carefully cutting crystal so that the fires flash brilliantly, or stamping heavy silks with gay colors for Potpourri Jar customers. And of course there is Ragged Robin Potpourri, spicy and alluring in fragrance, encased in quaint Aztec pottery boxes or ornate Canton China boxes. Then the many odd and delicious things to eat—Red Pepper Jam, Ju Jube Preserves, thick, juicy wedges of Candied Grape Fruit Peeling, and other rarities, add to the charm and the gift variety to be found.

Mail orders promptly filled. Price lists submitted.
Wholesale and Retail

(above) *The Record-Ledger* advertisement for Ruth and Agnes' shop, "The Potpourri Jar," c. 1929.

Community Mourns Death Of Beth Pasko

The entire community is deeply saddened this week over the death of Miss Beth Pasko, who was fatally injured Saturday morning when her motor-ette got out of control when the brakes failed to hold and smashed into a garage building at Valmont and Foothill. She passed away at 3:55 that afternoon from shock from her injuries of a fractured skull, broken nose and broken leg.

Funeral services were conducted at 11 o'clock yesterday morning at the Tujunga Community Methodist church with Rev. Oscar Newby, pastor of the church, officiating. Interment was at Inglewood Cemetery.

As the days pass one realizes more what a widespread influence this quiet, unassuming, charming little woman had in the community, especially over the children, who adored her. During her sixteen years as librarian of the Tujunga library she was always ready to help her readers make their selections always patient with those who were difficult, even when she herself was so crippled with arthritis that she could scarcely rise from her chair. For the past twelve years she conducted a vacation reading club for the children, which not only developed a love of reading in the children but helped improve their reading grades at school. While she was waiting for the ambulance on Saturday, so painfully injured, her thoughts were of the children who would be disappointed because the opening of the reading club would have to be postponed. She expressed her regret to some children standing by.

Miss Pasko also organized the Tujunga Poetry Club, and was its leader. She wrote very beautiful poetry, much of which has

Mary with the first "litter" of tortoises born at Castle Hi-Yan-Ka.
The tortoise family would eventually grow to 115.

Mary Phillips
1865–1952

There was a time, in the early history of Tujunga, when motorists driving east along Foothill Boulevard would spot a thirty-five-foot stone tower and castle nestled in the Verdugo Hills.[1] Ray and Mary Phillips's castle and tower aroused much curiosity of passing motorists. The Phillips came to Tujunga to build their mountain retreat in 1920.[2]

Mary Johanna Taft was born August 16, 1865, in Georgetown, Michigan, to Moses Taft and Sarah Darling Baldwin. Mary's childhood was filled with geographic diversification and much sorrow. Her mother, Sarah, married Moses Taft on October 24, 1860, in East Greenwich, Rhode Island. The following year, Sarah gave birth to her first child, David, in Burrillville, Rhode Island. During a stagecoach accident a large trunk struck them both, severely injuring David as well as his mother. David never walked or talked again and died at the age of four years. The accident left Sarah with a severe spinal deformity. Mary's brother, Frank, was born in 1863 at the time her father was conscripted into the Civil War's Union Army. The family returned to Michigan at the war's end. Three years later, her sister Lydia was born in Covington, Nebraska, near Sioux City, Iowa. When Mary was twelve years old, in 1877, her parents separated after a bitter quarrel. They never divorced, but Sarah took her three children to Iowa to live. Moses would go on to have several other wives. He would occasionally write and visit his children, but did not remain a major presence in their lives. Moses Taft died at the age of 69 years on July 22, 1901, due to extreme heat exhaustion. It was reported that many people and animals died that same day from the severe heat. Moses's body would not be discovered for another week, when a neighbor came to visit. Sarah passed away in 1928 at the age of 94 years and is buried in South Dakota.[3]

At the age of 28 years, Mary Taft married Raymond S. Phillips in Sioux City, Iowa, on October 19, 1893. Ray's occupation was listed as a bicycle salesman. Little is known about his health, but it is reported that when he and Mary arrived in Tujunga in 1920, Ray was in a wheelchair and partially paralyzed. Miraculously, after a few years in Tujunga, his health improved so much that he was able to single-handedly build their dream home, named "Castle Hi-Yan-Ka." Using native stone, the 62-year-old Ray built a small one-bedroom guest house, a two-bedroom, two-story main house, grottos, patios, walks, and a magnificent thirty-five-foot observation tower that locals soon named the "Turtle Tower."[4] This round stone edifice provided Mary and Ray a sweeping view of Tujunga and the majestic San Gabriel Mountains and a place to fly the American flag every day. Neighbors and locals marveled as Ray produced one structure after another. Ray and Mary became an inspiration to residents of all ages.

In their main house, the kitchen and dining room were paneled in pine boards. The windows opened so that Mary's winged friends (the local birds) could enter and dine on her kitchen table. The ever-resourceful Ray used wooden fruit crates to create the shingled ceiling in the living room. He used Model A parts to shore up the grottos. Running boards were used for walls and other car parts framed the hand-dug grottos.[5] They planted the grounds of their castle with local and rare cactus plants, adding to the charm of their cherished haven.

In 1927, when they stopped building, Ray and Mary opened their property to the public as a wildlife sanctuary for Mary's tortoises, birds, and other game. Deer, foxes, badgers, raccoons, possums, eagles, and snakes greeted the 100,000 visitors that signed Mary's guest book. The picturesque picnic grounds were opened to schools, churches, fraternal organizations, and private groups.

The childless "Uncle" Ray and "Aunt" Mary opened their castle and grounds each year to the graduating class of Tujunga's Pinewood Elementary School. The students and teachers delighted in the picnics there.[6] The Phillips' warm hospitality was known not only by local residents and the neighbors but also, eventually, by citizens around the world.

Once word got out about how well Mary cared for her tortoises, people began bringing unwanted tortoises to the sanctuary. Fortunately, the local Safeway Market donated their discarded lettuce and produce for the cause. It was said that Mary put her "herd" to bed in individual wooden stalls in her basement.[7]

Until the beginning of World War II, when travel was curtailed due to rationing of gasoline and tires, the sanctuary was opened every weekend to visitors. As the Phillips entered their seventies, they were no longer able to maintain their property and were forced to sell their dream castle. Mary passed away at the age of 87 years on December 17, 1952, in Tujunga. She was buried in Los Angeles. Alone, with no one to care for him, Ray returned to Bettendorf, Iowa, where he died in 1957 at the age of 92 years.

The observation tower of their "castle" is gone now, owing to earthquakes, but the cottage, the main house, the grottos and exotic gardens survive into the millennium. As the current owner restores the grounds of Castle Hi-Yan-Ka, small porcelain turtles are being unearthed. They are the only reminder that Mary and her "herd" once lived in a castle in a magical spot in Tujunga.

Looking north from the Phillips property. Valaho Road is in the foreground, c. 1923.

(*above*) View of main house and observation tower built in 1927. Small stone structure at left is a grotto. Building with Hi-Yan-Ka sign is an open-air patio.

(*right*) Ray stands next to the famous Turtle Tower. *Courtesy of Forrest Theriot.*

Notes

[1] "Wild Life Welcomed at 'Castle' in Hills," *San Fernando Valley Times* (January 22, 1947).

[2] Ansel Kickbush, *Sunland-Tujunga California Pictorial 1952–1953* (Tujunga, John Barclay).

[3] Family history provided on http://www.rootsweb.com by Kathryn Louise Taft. Information obtained from Moses's Bible and other family letters and papers.

[4] Their guest house was featured on the April 2000, Sunland-Tujunga Historic Home Tour.

[5] Author's interview with current owner of the castle. November 28, 2000.

[6] Author's interview with Forrest Theriot, who attended the Pinewood Elementary School graduation party at the castle in 1928. September 17, 1997.

[7] Sarah R. Lombard, *Rancho Tujunga: a History of Sunland-Tujunga, California* (Burbank, Calif.: The Bridge Publishing, 1990).

FOUNDING SISTERS

Yuletide Greeting cards often featured their castle and the famous "Turtle Tower." c. 1926. *Courtesy of Forrest Theriot.*

Ray and Mary celebrate their fiftieth wedding anniversary, c. 1943.
Courtesy of Forrest Theriot.

Helen Magdelina in her later years, c. 1930s.
Courtesy of Forrest Theriot.

Helen Magdalina Rutherford
1865–1940

The shiny black, open-topped, two-cylinder Buick approached Helen and her sister, Alice Jones. It was a hot summer afternoon and the ladies had just disembarked from the Pacific Electric Car in Montrose. They were on an important mission—to find some property to purchase in the high and dry climate of Tujunga. Having no idea the distance from Montrose to the Little Lands Colony, they set out to walk the remaining distance. When the handsome stranger offered them a ride, they were more than grateful. The ladies were by now hot and tired and realized the road west contained only sagebrush and more dust. Marshall Valentine Hartranft told them he knew the route and would be happy to give them a ride to his colony.[1]

Helen Magdelina Jones was born just two weeks after the assassination of President Abraham Lincoln, in April 1865. Helen's father, David G. Jones, had immigrated to eastern Pennsylvania from Ystradgunlais, South Wales. There he joined the thousands of Welsh and Irish men working the Pennsylvania coal mines. Helen's mother, Marsena Peters, had married David, then twenty-three, on February 16, 1854. Helen was the sixth of the eleven children born of this union. The birthplaces of the Jones siblings marked the western migration of the family. The first children were born in Carbon Canyon, East Pennsylvania, very close to the birthplaces of Jennie Lichtenthaler and John Steven McGroarty. The seventh through tenth children were born in Warren County, Missouri. The eleventh child was born in 1871 in Kansas.

Little is recorded of Helen's childhood. She married Robert Owen Rutherford at the parsonage in Tecumseh, Kansas, on February 4, 1891. Her first child, Alice, would arrive ten months later. In 1893, Helen's father died and she and Robert Owen took her mother and daughter Alice with them west, by train, to Yuba Township near Marysville, California. Family records indicate they leased a ranch there in 1898. By 1910, the family moved south to Anaheim, California. Helen and Robert were blessed with six children: Alice, Florence, Francis, Constance, Lyman, and Robert.

For the next twenty-five years she would spend her time bearing children, tending livestock of all sorts, and working in the family's small lemon orchard in Tujunga. Helen's lemon crop was sold to the Sunkist Co-operative in San Fernando.

In 1917, Helen took her twenty-five-year-old daughter, Florence, on an extensive train trip east to Kansas, Missouri, Pennsylvania, Washington, D.C., and New York. The ladies spent their time leisurely, posing for many photographs in front of famous buildings. However, Helen soon grew concerned when Florence became severely fatigued as they journeyed. Upon their return to Los Angeles, Florence was diagnosed with tuberculosis.

In 1918, Helen, Robert, Marsena and the ailing Florence purchased a three-room house in Tujunga at 301 Mountain View Avenue (now Beckett Street) from Mrs. W. O. Troutin. Like close neighbor Jennie Lichtenthaler, they were in search of a health cure. Unfortunately, Flo-

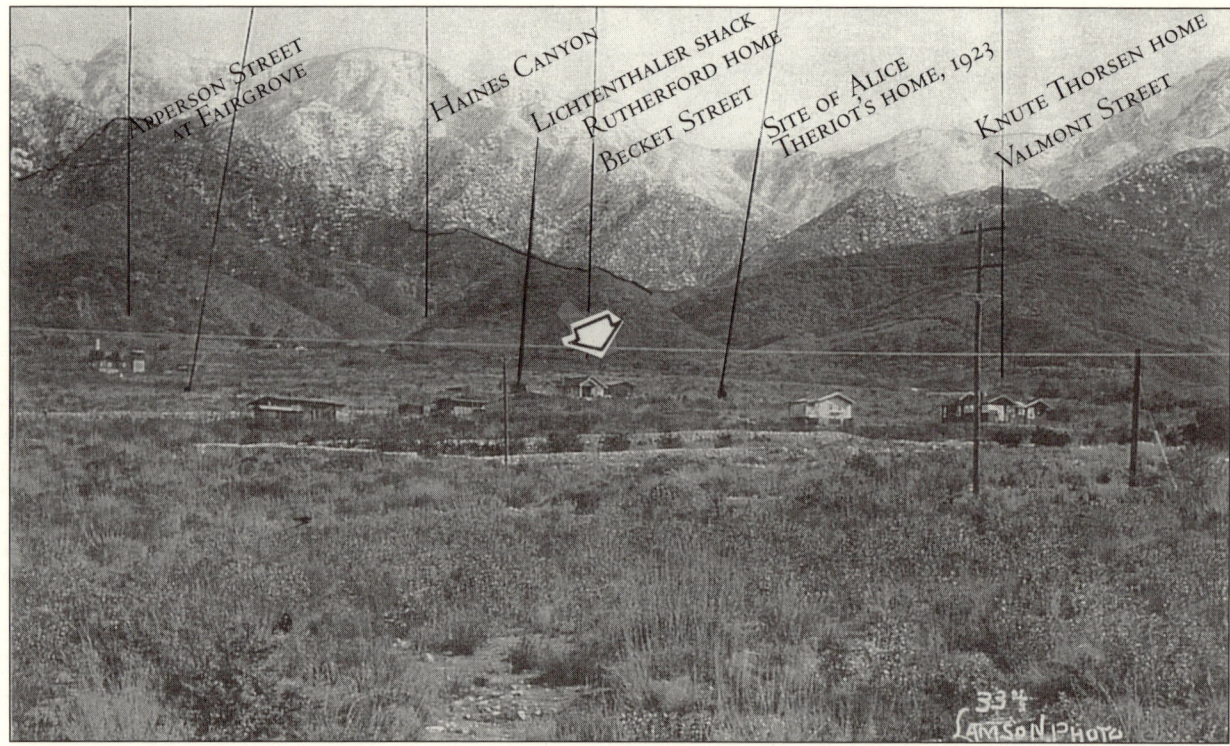

The Rutherford home on Beckett Street. Lot in front of home would become the site of the Theriot home in 1923. Note Jennie Lichtenthaler's cottage to the right of Rutherford home. An arrow marks the spot of the future Pinewood Elementary School on Valmont. The large home to the far right of Rutherford's was the home of Knute and Thelma Thorsen. *Courtesy of Forrest Theriot.*

rence never did experience a return of good health and succumbed to her illness three years after their arrival in Tujunga. Marsena died in 1926, at the age of ninety-one years.

Helen (Nellie to her family) became very involved in the community's many civic activities and enjoyed numerous events at Bolton Hall. A pioneer environmentalist, Helen became alarmed when she saw the habitat of the desert tortoise being destroyed by developers. She turned her energies into conservation of the land and took on the surrogate mothering of many tortoises. "When she settled in the rock strewn delta land of the Haines Canyon alluvial fan flow, the desert tortoises were plentiful. Land developers had somehow with mule power, cleared the great boulders from certain properties and deposited them on smaller sites. These granite boulders made a natural shelter for the tortoises to dig under and lay their eggs."[2] Daughter Alice and son-in-law Terrance Theriot raised a dozen of Helen's tortoises. Eventually, in the 1960s, the reptiles were donated to the Los Angeles Zoo.

Helen also raised goats and chickens to supplement the family income. Her sister Alice married Harry Gusten, who owned Gusten Hardware Store at 3060 South Main Street in downtown Los Angeles. Helen's husband worked at the store and, to be closer to work, he rented a room in downtown Los Angeles during the week and came home on the weekends. With extra rooms in her home, Helen was able to raise Alice's son Robert in her house until he graduated from high school. On occasion, other Theriot clan members roomed with Helen when they were having repairs done to their own homes. Robert Owen died in 1933 and the hardware store closed in 1936.

In 1923, Alice, her husband, who was a lumberman and orchardist, and children, Forrest and Elizabeth moved to Tujunga and lived in a little cabin on El Centro (Valmont), just east of Haines Canyon. They stayed in the cabin while their five-room bungalow was being built on the Rutherford property on Mt. View Avenue (Beckett Street). "They cleared the scrub brush and tons of rock and granite boulders to reveal the fertile, rich sandy soil, ideal for a bounty of grapes, berries and a variety of fruit trees as well as chickens, geese, rabbits, tortoises, dogs, cats and goats."[3] The home remains in the Theriot family, with grandson Warren living there surrounded by seedless lemon trees and a grape vine planted by Robert Owen.

Family photographs show the homes of Jennie Lichtenthaler and Mr. And Mrs. Knute Thorsen near the Rutherford property. The Thorsens resided at 7018 Valmont Street and would become close friends to the Rutherford and Theriot clans. Knute had been a chief cook on an Atlantic sailing vessel. In later years, he became a chef at Clifton's Cafeteria in downtown Los Angeles.[4] Mr. And Mrs. Thorsen and their children, Knute, Norman, George, and Thelma, would visit the family weekly and bring spirited conversation about politics and life to enliven the atmosphere.

Although she appeared to have a serious nature, grandson Forrest remembers Helen as a jovial woman with a hearty laugh. She enjoyed reading and had an extensive library. Always interested in politics, she became friends with Judge Breidt of Tujunga. In 1935, being fond of travel, Helen drove back to Kansas and Missouri with daughter Constance.

After she became bedridden, Helen lived with her daughter Alice for a year before she passed away in 1940 at the age of seventy-five years. An early conservationist and orchardist, the land still bears Helen's footprints.

Notes

[1] Letter to Author, dated October 14, 1998, from Helen's grandson, Forrest Theriot.

[2] Forrest Theriot, *A Copy of the Jones Family Records*, page 3, undated.

[3] Forrest Theriot, *Pioneer Property Purchased by Grandson*, Christmas Newsletter sent to Author in 1998. Helen's great-grandson Warren Theriot purchased the family home. The house was lovingly restored and still retains the charm of its early California bungalow style. Helen's daughter, Alice Theriot lived to the age of 94 and her husband, Terrance to the age of 97.

[4] Letter from Forrest Theriot to Author, dated November 8, 1999.

Helen "Nellie" Rutherford with youngest child Robert on her lap and daughter Florence at their Anaheim ranch, c. 1910.
Courtesy of Forrest Theriot.

FOUNDING SISTERS

(*left*) Helen's daughter, Florence Laura, with family goat and father, Robert Owen Rutherford. Large two-story home in rear of photograph at Apperson and Fairgrove Avenue. Note the year-old lemon trees behind them, c. 1919. *Courtesy of Forrest Theriot.*

(*below*) The beautiful Florence at her Tujunga home, just a year before her passing, c. 1920. *Courtesy of Forrest Theriot.*

(*bottom*) Helen sold her lemon crop to the San Fernando Fruit Growers Association. It was the valley's oldest citrus packinghouse, operating from 1902 to 1951. *Courtesy of San Fernando Valley Historical Society.*

(*right*) A rare event, the town covered in snow. The Knute Thorsen residence on far right with chicken shed in rear. View to the south from Alice Theriot's residence, c. 1923.

(*below*) Helen, her husband Robert Owen and his brother William, of Kansas City, Missouri, in the Rutherford orchard, c. 1931. *Both courtesy of Forrest Theriot.*

Graduation portrait of Virginia Tenney Smith.
The only known photograph of Dr. Smith, c. 1888.
Courtesy of Boston University School of Medicine.

Virginia Tenney Smith
1860–1949

On a daily basis, people motor by the stone castle on Tujunga Canyon Boulevard, next to the Tujunga post office, unaware it was once the home of Tujunga's first woman doctor. Life in Tujunga was far different when Dr. Virginia Smith purchased the Blarney Castle in 1921.[1] Tujunga Canyon (Monte Vista) was just a dirt road with few houses. No tall trees or buildings hampered the panoramic view of the San Fernando Valley. Memories of Dr. Smith, a physician and surgeon, have long faded from Tujunga's history. However, her home, the Blarney Castle, has become a Tujunga landmark.[2] Even in the 1920s and 1930s, developer M. V. Hartranft and photographer-real estate salesman Harry Lamson would drive clients by the castle. The castle and walled gardens made extensive use of the "free building materials."[3] Dr. Smith's lavish gardens, which included banana trees, proved that Eden could be created in the barren, rocky soil of Tujunga.

Virginia Tenney Smith was born in Vermont on March 20, 1860. Her life prior to attending Boston University School of Medicine is unknown. In an age when few women would even dare to dream of becoming a doctor, Virginia Smith accomplished her career goal. In 1886, she entered Boston University as a junior in a three-year program.[4] By 1887, she was a third-year student in four-year program. After writing her thesis on diphtheria, she graduated from the university's School of Medicine on June 6, 1888. Her one-year residency was at a hospital in Arlington, a suburb of Boston, and from there she moved to Detroit, Michigan. In 1901, Dr. Smith was licensed to practice medicine in California. By 1904, she came to Los Angeles and in 1907 she received a degree from the College of Osteopathic Physicians and Surgeons there.[5] She left the area in 1912 for a two-year assignment in Brookline, Massachusetts. However, in 1915, she returned to California and opened a practice at 3441 South Flower Street in Los Angeles.[6]

In 1921, with the completion of her own sanitorium and hospital at the southwest corner of Michigan Avenue (Foothill Boulevard) and Hillhaven Avenue, she moved to Tujunga. While living in the Blarney Castle, Dr. Smith continued to practice medicine and operated at the hospitals in the Los Angeles area, including Pacifica Hospital. Often she would send her surgery patients to her sanitorium in Tujunga for recuperation.[7]

There are no known photographs of Dr. Smith from her days in Tujunga. Local resident Virginia Gaiger recalls she did not participate in club or group activities.[8] Some neighbors also recall that she drove a heavy sedan and that her ability to drive and maneuver the machine was a wonder to all who observed her.[9] Fate was not kind to Dr. Smith, though, and, after living in the Blarney Castle only two years, her brilliant career came to an abrupt and tragic end.

One morning, upon rising from bed, Dr. Smith suffered a massive cerebral hemorrhage. This would later be complicated by meningitis. "Dr. Smith was alone

Earliest known photograph of Dr. Smith's castle. It is a small-scale replica of Ireland's famous Blarney Castle. It was built of local stone and retains its original wrought iron window ornamentation.

at her home at El Centro [Valmont] and Monte Vista [Tujunga Canyon Boulevard] when the attack came, but from all evidence she rose from her bed, walked down the stairs and out the back door, knocking down articles on the way as she clutched blindly for support, and finally fell on the paved courtyard at the rear of her home. In falling she seemed to have struck her head on a stone, for when she was found, some time later by her neighbor, Mrs. Jessica Jonderton, she had a deep cut in her scalp and blood congealed in her hair and on the stone."[10]

Dr. Frances Hanken, a friend, removed her from the courtyard of the Blarney Castle and placed Dr. Smith in her own sanitorium. When Dr. Smith regained consciousness, she could not speak and was not expected to live. Other doctors, including a brain specialist, were called in to diagnose and treat Dr. Smith. They declared she had suffered a massive stroke and was not the victim of foul play as the neighbors suspected.

Within six months of her stroke, Dr. Smith had recovered her speech and was able to take limited car rides and visits from her friends. Within one year, her progress reports disappeared from the area's newspapers. In 1930 she sold the sanitorium to John Moren, who operated the hospital as a hotel until 1943. Thus was the dramatic end of Dr. Smith's brilliant medical career.

Many local residents would be surprised to learn that she lived another twenty-six years, the last seven of which were spent in Long Beach, California. On August 6, 1949, Dr. Virginia Smith passed away at her home at 360 West Ocean Boulevard.[11] Her ashes were placed beside the ashes of her companion, Kathryn E. Stone, in the Columbarium of Prayer at Forest Lawn Memorial Park in Glendale.[12] By an odd twist of fate, her "Blarney Castle" became far better known than any of her medical career contributions and accomplishments.

Notes

[1] Legend says Dr. Smith built the castle after viewing the Blarney Castle on a tour of Ireland. It was, in fact, built by a Los Angeles businessman and was two years old when Dr. Smith bought it. Author's interview with Tom Theobald, November 20, 2002.

[2] The castle was featured on Tujunga's Historic Home and Garden Tour in 1976 and 1993.

(*above*) The exotic garden on the paved patio to the rear of the castle, c. 1923. *Courtesy of the Los Angeles Public Library.*

(*right*) In back of the vine-covered castle was a walled garden with a long vista looking west over the lower levels of the valley. Note the wrought iron gate and ornamental window coverings, c. 1923.

[3] The actual stonemason who built the Blarney Castle remains a mystery. Stonemasons George Harris and James Livingston would claim it was their masonry creation.
[4] Boston University established the School of Medicine in 1873 by merging with the New England Female Medical College, which had been founded in 1848 as the first medical college for women in the world. (http://www.bumc.bu.edu/departments).
[5] Obituary, Dr. Virginia Smith, *Los Angeles Times*, August 7, 1949.
[6] Boston University School of Medicine Catalog, 1888–1924.
[7] "Mrs. Leo Smith Recovering from Major Operations," *The Record-Ledger*, June 21, 1923.
[8] Author's interview with Sunland resident, Virginia Gaiger, June 2001.
[9] Bicentennial Historic Tour Brochure, 1976. Bolton Hall Museum.
[10] "Apoplexy Strikes Dr. Virginia Smith—Well Known Physician Lies Unconscious with Little Hope of Recovery." *The Record-Ledger*, October 11, 1923.
[11] Certificate of Death, State of California. Certificate of Vital Record, County of Los Angeles. August 8, 1949.
[12] Forest Lawn Interment Index, Dr. Virginia T. Smith, MD DO, August 8, 1949.

FOUNDING SISTERS

Only known photograph of the interior of Dr. Smith's castle, c. 1923.
Courtesy of the Los Angeles Public Library.

By 1929, the vine-covered Blarney Castle was featured in newspapers and magazines as an example of the artistic stone creations in the area. *The Record-Ledger.*

By the 1940s the Castle had become famous and sported a wooden "Blarney Castle" sign over the front door, c. 1940s. *Courtesy of the Los Angeles Public Library.*

FOUNDING SISTERS

Pen and ink drawing of the Blarney Castle. Artist unknown, c. 1976.

In the early 1930s, a cement tower was added to the north side of the castle, c. 1992. *Courtesy of Author.*

388

> Under New Management   Phone Sunland 121
>
> ## *Tujunga Valley Sanitorium and Rest Home*
>
> MR. and MRS. HOMER SPARKS, Props.
>
> ALTITUDE 2000 FT.—LOTS OF SHADE—MOUNTAIN WATER—
> RATES REASONABLE
>
> 154 W. Michigan,   TUJUNGA, CALIF.

Dr. Smith's Tujunga Valley Sanitorium, located at 7254 Foothill Boulevard in Tujunga, c. 1920s

FOUNDING SISTERS

(*left*) In 1930, the Tujunga Valley Sanatorium and Hospital became the Tujunga Valley Hotel.

(*below*) The Tujunga Valley Hotel in 1940.
Both courtesy of Forrest Theriot.

Flora Peet White
1879–1960

Several visitors to Bolton Hall Museum have reported a sudden drop in the air temperature when they entered the rear of the building. Often, when photographs are taken inside the main hall of the museum, an unexplained white streak appears on the print.[1] From 1980 through 1992, Bolton Hall had live-in caretakers who reported seeing objects move of their own accord. Prior to the writing of this story, visitors to Bolton Hall were assured that no one had ever died in Bolton Hall and that there were no ghosts circulating from room to room in the historic museum.

On April 18, 1953, Flora White, her husband, Mark, and their niece, Anita Peet Geyer, were enjoying an evening of dancing at Bolton Hall. This was the social hour of the meeting of the United Spanish War Veterans and Auxiliary.[2] After having a dance with his niece, Mark went to the kitchen to get a drink of water. While there, he suffered a massive heart attack and died instantly before horrified friends and family.[3] On an evening filled with fun and laughter, Mark White became the only person of record to expire inside the Clubhouse.

Flora Adelaide Peet was born on February 21, 1879, to Frederick Peet of New York and Abigail Barker of Wisconsin. Flora and her brother were born in Manchester, Iowa.[4] The events of her childhood are not recorded or remembered. When Flora was in her early twenties, she married Mark White of Gerber, Iowa.

In May 1918, Mark and Flora moved to Los Angeles in response to Marshall Hartranft's extensive midwest advertising push for "The Little Lands."

> We settled at 232 Monte Vista Boulevard (now 10238 Tujunga Canyon Boulevard), with a million dollar view to the west. We built a two-room cabin and a mountain retreat until February of 1920, when we decided to build a home and live here. This was not easy for we had to bring a carpenter from town near our home on 69th Street (Los Angeles) and all building materials from Glendale or Los Angeles. There were no paved roads, even Foothill Boulevard was a dirt road and there were less than 300 homes between La Crescenta and San Fernando. During the first year, electricity was just coming in. Prior to this, it was the "pioneer and his lantern" who lighted the way to the Colonial Dances[5] or an occasional church social, both of which were held in "The Town Hall" erected when the Colony was founded in 1913.[6]

When they first arrived in Tujunga, both Mark and Flora were managers of the Bramble Funeral Home on Michigan Avenue (Foothill Boulevard). After two years of mortuary work, Mark left and became a supervisor with the Postal Service at the main arcade in Los Angeles. He retired in 1934. Flora became the owner of the funeral home after just two years and renamed the business White Funeral Parlor.

Along with being a full-time businesswoman, Flora became active in her new community's social and philanthropic clubs. In 1924, she was elected president of the Tujunga Women's Club and in 1936, became the chairwoman of the History and Landmark unit of the club. Her love of history and fascination with Cali-

Back row (*left to right*) Floyd Peet (brother), Floyd's wife, Mark White, Flora White.
Front row (*left to right*) Fred (father), Ralph (nephew), Anita (niece),
Abigail, c. 1900. *Courtesy of Anita Peet Geyer.*

fornia's early years prompted her to decorate her home for luncheons and dinner parties using an early California rancho theme. She assisted the Women's Club when they sponsored plays at Manzanita Park, showcasing the romantic life of the California missions. This hard working businesswoman became the first Worthy Matron of the Order of Eastern Star, Tujunga Chapter No. 445, in April 1925.[7]

Flora's family and friends often visited from Iowa, enjoying her warm hospitality. Her parents came to visit one winter and stayed for a year. While Flora tended to her frail father on Valentine's Day, 1933, he passed away of a heart attack. Her mother returned to Iowa to bury her husband there.[8]

"The Boys of '98 or the United Spanish American War, asked their wives to organize an auxiliary and again, I was honored when asked to head that organization."[9] By 1953, the organization included just thirty-two members, with Flora joining Hilda Livingston as one of the few surviving charter members.

Flora's niece, Anita Peet Geyer, remembers her as a highly intelligent, focused woman, who was very business-like in her manner. Anita came to California and opened Peet's Stationery Store in Montrose. After Anita's passing in November 1997, the towns of Montrose and La Crescenta were recipients of her bequests of over one million dollars.

In June 1960, Flora passed away quietly at her home, Whitehaven, after a long life dedicated to community service.[10] She and her husband, Mark, were devoted to Tujunga and were proud to be a part of its early growth.

(*above*) In 1920, Mark and Flora were managers of the Bramble Funeral Home, located at what is now 7257 Foothill Boulevard. The building was considered "a masterpiece of rustic charm."

(*right*) Mark White in his later years. *The Record-Ledger.*

Notes

[1] Several photographs, taken by the Author at monthly meetings of the Historical Society, contain a white cloud next to standing members.

[2] "Mark White Drops Dead of Heart Attack at Meeting," *The Record-Ledger* (April 13, 1953).

[3] Author's interview with Anita Peet Geyer at Peet's Stationery Store in Montrose. November 10, 1995.

[4] Record of Funeral. June 11, 1960. Bades Mortuary, Tujunga.

[5] The Colonial Dance Club held monthly dances at Bolton Hall, at which all participants were required to dress in costume and dance in the style of that era. Chancellor Livingston remembers that, at the time, all cars carried shovels in their trunks so as to be able to put out fires quickly. Once, while a colonial dance was going on, a large fire broke out. Everyone vacated the Clubhouse and the men fought the fire in knee britches and colonial costumes.

[6] "Beauty of Hills Was First Lure," *The Record-Ledger* (July 25, 1956).

[7] "Order of Eastern Star Chartered in 1925; White First Worthy Matron," *The Record-Ledger* (May 21, 1953).

[8] "Fred Ellsworth Peet Obituary," *The Record-Ledger* (February 16, 1933).

[9] "Stewart Heads Spanish War Veterans Auxiliary," *The Record-Ledger* (May 21, 1953).

[10] Record of Funeral, op. cit.

FOUNDING SISTERS

Tujunga Branch of

The Bramble Funeral Home

Reverent Christian Service

Local Managers—

Mr. and Mrs. Mark W. White
Monte Vista Boulevard
Just north of El Centro   Phone Sunland 12-J-1

Main Office and Chapel

1249 South Flower St.
Los Angeles

Fully Equipped For All Local Work

AMBULANCE SERVICE
PRIVATE CHAPEL

Tujunga Undertaking Co.

TELEPHONE SUNLAND 33 or 732

W. F. BROWN   MRS. MARK WHITE
Managers

(*clockwise from top*) 1922 Tujunga Telephone Directory advertisement for the Bramble Funeral Home.

In 1928, the funeral home was bought by Fred Bade and moved to Tujunga Canyon Boulevard, c. 1952. *Courtesy of Bades Mortuary.*

A *Record-Ledger* advertisement for Tujunga Undertaking Co., managed by Brown and White, c. 1926.

Flora White (*far left*) in a program "Belles of Early California," presented to the Tujunga Women's Club. This undated photograph is the only surviving one of the interior of the building that stood on Samoa Avenue. *The Record-Ledger* (May 15, 1952).

Alma at the age of 48 years, c. 1902.
Her youngest child was born when she was 46 years old.
Courtesy of Kendra Wieman Smith.

Alma Florence Wieman
1854–1939

Her college professors warned her that William Henry Wieman was "wild and erratic" and she should consider "a more stable suitor." The strong-willed and independent Alma chose William and embarked on a life of adventure and achievement.

Alma's mother, Jeannette Storms, married Nelson Wallace Morgan in 1852 in Chelsea, Michigan. Nelson was a wagon maker in Lima Center, Michigan. The Morgan family could trace their roots back to 1624, when Robert Morgan homesteaded 60 acres in the first settlement of Salem, Massachusetts.[1] After their first children, twins Alma and Albert, were born in 1854, the Morgans moved to Kansas. When the Civil War broke out, Nelson enlisted in the 1st Kansas Regiment and served with them throughout the war. Jeanette, having just had her third child, Minnie, moved back to her parents' home in Chelsea, Michigan. At the close of the war, their second son, Melvin, was born and the family returned to Kansas.[2]

Alma was fifteen years old when the family moved to Irving, Kansas. They drove across the plains in a covered wagon drawn by two yoke of oxen. Another family accompanied them, driving a horse-drawn covered wagon. The third accompanying family was that of a Methodist minister and they followed by train. The three families homesteaded 80 acres each in this unsettled portion of Kansas, four miles from Irving. In 1870, Jeanette's last child, Ralph, was born. Sadly, three years later, Minnie died at the age of twelve years.

Alma always longed to continue her schooling and attend college. It was a financial impossibility until Park College opened in Parksville, Missouri, and allowed their students to work their way through school. In 1875, Alma realized her dream and joined William, along with fifteen other students in the first class of Park College. Perhaps an early feminist, she noted in her diary that she resented the fact that women students had to do menial work—laundry with "sad irons," wash boilers, and scrub boards—while the men were able to earn their money by preaching in church pulpits. Alma knew she was equally qualified to preach.

It was at Park College where Alma fell in love with William "Willy" Henry Wieman. She kept his passionate letters to her until the day she died. For some unrecorded reason, William was asked to leave Park College. He transferred to Drury College in Springfield, Missouri. Alma graduated in 1879 in the Park institution's first graduating class. The following year, she was employed as the principal of the Irvine Public School and stayed one year. Alma then became a teacher at Park College.

On September 5, 1883, Alma married William, who had just finished his seminary courses and taken his first pastorate at Rich Hill, Missouri.[3] Henry, their first child was born there. The family then moved to Irving, Kansas, where Ernest and Stella were born. In 1888, the Wiemans moved to Corning, Kansas (sixty miles north of Topeka), where Reverend Wieman served as pastor of the Presbyterian Church for the next five years. He would be a minister on Sunday and a farmer

(*far left*) Alma Morgan Wieman. Undated photograph.

(*left*) William Henry Wieman. Undated photograph. *Both courtesy of Kendra Wieman Smith.*

all other days of the week. Little is recorded of Alma's stay in Corning but we can assume that with the addition of two children, Drury Park and Lois Hazel, Alma's days were full.

Two years before her family left Kansas, Alma's two younger brothers, Ralph and Wallace, and their wives, Ruth and Frances, had answered an ad in the newspaper for land near Delano in the San Joaquin Valley, California. William was once again getting restless and decided to move to California and join his brothers-in-law. In February 1892, William and Alma loaded themselves, their five children (ages infancy to eight years), William's father John Henry, household goods, and farm equipment in one-half of a freight car attached to a train headed on a 1,700-mile journey to California. On March 4, 1893, the crowded boxcar arrived in Delano. They were met by Wallace and Ralph Morgan with horses and wagons, then driven twenty miles in a rainstorm to Mira Monte. Within a few months, a temporary house was built for the Wiemans on Albert Morgan's homestead of open prairie, eight miles from Delano. Fortunately, William was an expert carpenter and stonemason and soon had a permanent home constructed near an artesian well. They planted wheat and William began preaching on a circuit of seventy miles by horseback.

> They had a vision of an agricultural utopian Christian community with 4 or 5 other families they settled in Mira Monte. The dream of a utopian community ended there when the artesian well first brought alkali to the surface and then went dry. The group of families stayed together for a move or two, with their shared communal ideal. One of their sojourns was in Bakersfield, in its wild boomtown days after oil was discovered. Wallace Morgan, her brother who later edited the *Record-Ledger* in Tujunga, started a paper there, campaigned to reform the political corruption, and brought into being a City Manager form of government.[4]

After the disaster of the alkali well, William and Alma took their family and headed to the High Sierras with a light wagonload of food and clothing. There they would have water. They built a lean-to under the pines and the family enjoyed fresh fish and game. William left the family often as he scouted for a location to build a new home. He found a piece of irrigated land, in outwash from the mountains, at Orosi (near Sequoia National Park) and built a home. They

Alma's birthplace, a farm near Chelsea, Michigan.
Home built by grandfather, Abram Storms in 1834. *Courtesy of Kendra Wieman Smith.*

The Wieman home, located at 7078 Valmont Street, was built in 1913.

farmed the land, producing almonds and fruit to be dried and shipped east. They also produced two more children, Elton and Donald. Along with farming, William had a circuit of four churches that he served: Orosi, Dinuba, Visalia, and Tracey. As there was no high school in Orosi, the children attended school in Dinuba. No higher education was available in the valley at that time. Two hundred miles away, in Eagle Rock, outside of Los Angeles, there was a Presbyterian college the children could attend without paying tuition. Six of the eight Wieman children would graduate from Occidental College in Eagle Rock.

In 1904, William and Alma once again moved to Bakersfield to be near Alma's brothers. After five years, they moved to the Highland Park area of Los Angeles, near Occidental College. Alma used her home as a boarding house, with her parents and father-in-law among the boarders.

In April 1913, the Wieman family bought property in Tujunga. The long-talked-of permanent home was soon to be a reality. The arduous task of rock removal was accomplished and a beautiful two-story home was completed by William and his sons.

Except in front of stores on the main street there were no sidewalks, and the small patch of lawn in front of the Wieman house was almost the only one in town. The house was a landmark because it was two stories high and, in addition to the lawn, there was a flower garden with roses, a flowering pomegranate, bird of paradise, and a form of jasmine. A deep basin was carved out of the hard, dry earth to hold water, and not even weeds grew between the plants. The Wiemans had thirteen varieties of grapes, and fig, apricot, plumcot, quince, and mulberry trees. Wisteria vines grew to entirely cover the verandas on each side of the house. Son Don built a small, ornamental waterfall at one end of a veranda. By Tujunga standards at the time, this was one of the grander properties, standing at the corner of Valmont and Pinewood streets.[5]

William and Alma became active and leading members of the new colony. The colonists, mostly middle-aged and elderly, were anxious for moral and spiritual leadership. William organized a Church Federation to which all Protestant organizations were invited. In 1920, using his expert masonry skills, William built a small stone chapel at 7156 Valmont Street, across from Bolton Hall. Wieman Chapel stands today as a testament to their faith and leadership.[6] Alma led Bible classes that to this day are known as "the Alma Wie-

Wieman Chapel, at 7156 Valmont Street, was the first Methodist Community Church.
In the early 1950s, the stone walls were plastered over.

man Bible class." William's Church later became the United Methodist Church. In 1928, a large two-story church was built next to their Chapel.

Having pioneered their entire life, William and Alma were well acquainted with the hardships and joys of being "the first." They counseled the new colonists on farming, tree cultivation, house building, and the skills necessary to make the dreams of a utopian community, under the blue skies of Tujunga, come true. The couple was an inspiration to the new comers who soon became disillusioned with the soil and the economy.

The Wieman household was always active. The oldest children were out of the house and graduated from college, but William's father lived in a small cottage to the rear of the main house and would live there until his death at age 101 years. Daughter Stella went off to serve as a Red Cross nurse, in France, during World War I.[7] Upon her return, she became the school nurse and a teacher at Pinewood Elementary School, located across the street from her parent's home. Never married, she lived at home and took care of her mother in her later years. Stella also brought foster children from the County to live in the Wieman house.[8] She loved cars and was one of the first women in Tujunga to own one. After the War, she homesteaded 160 acres in Phelan and alone built herself a two-room house. She delighted in driving her friends to her desert hide-away.

Alma's other daughter, Lois, spoke fluent Spanish and taught home economics in a high school near the Mexican border. When her oldest brother Harry's wife became terminally ill, Lois was recruited to raise his five children. After years of care giving, she moved back to Tujunga to care for her mother and two foster children, Bobby and Esther.

The 1920s were a time of mobility and change. A car that in 1914 cost a person twenty-four months of wages now cost a mere three months wages. The Model T Ford was stronger than a horse and much easier to maintain. America was on the move, with their love of the automobile escalating. Unfortunately, William's fate would be disastrously linked to a Model T Ford. On October 3, 1920,

> . . . that day your father and mother [William and Alma] came to call on us [the Wallace Morgans], bringing two of their grandchildren with them. Your father drove down in an old Model T Ford. I remember distinctly how he looked: He wore a little cap, set jauntily on his head, and his whole manner and appearance were more buoyant, happy and care-free than I ever had seen before. When he left us he drove to the house where Harry and Anna were living at the time, left the children, and he and your mother started west on El Centro Avenue (Valmont). The grade was steep, and in some way your father lost control of the car, it turned sharply to the right and overturned. The crash left your mother unconscious but not seriously injured. Your father suffered injuries to his head, and he never regained consciousness. Except, perhaps, for the few seconds when he may have struggled to regain control of the car, that day had been one of the happiest of your father's life.[9]

William died the following afternoon and the town deeply mourned the loss of one of their spiritual leaders. Alma suffered a broken collarbone, two broken ribs, and lost the hearing in one ear. She would have to walk with a cane, a crutch, or with the assistance of a grandchild for the remaining years of her life.

In 1927, Alma participated in a most interesting national eugenics study, conducted by the Carnegie Institute of Washington. As the debate raged on as to whether one's environment or one's genes were responsible for the character of a person, Alma wrote a lengthy study of the physical and emotional characteristics of the Storms, Morgan, and Wieman families.[10]

As granddaughter Kendra (Eleanor) Wieman Smith recalled of Alma,[11]

> She was always involved in community affairs, always steadily busy, although never hurried or the least bit upset. She

---

> I have never been able to find out precisely what feminism is: I only know that people call me a feminist whenever I express sentiments that differentiate me from a doormat.
> —Rebecca West, 1913

Alma and William Henry, with grandchild, Florence, c. 1914.
Courtesy of Kendra Wieman Smith.

and my aunt always had foster children living with them, usually teenage boys, and from my perspective now, I think her equanimity was probably remarkable. Her children all respected her enormously, perhaps revered her and somewhere my father published "an intellectual biography." In it he speaks of her readiness to listen to the thoughts about many things, often having to do with religion, when he was quite young. She would encourage his thinking, but did not seek to impose views on him.[12]

Alma's last few years were spent as an invalid, cared for in her own home by her daughters, Lois and Stella.[13] At the age of 84 years, this modern-day pilgrim passed away from heart disease at her home on February 1, 1939.

With descendents living throughout the United States and the world, Alma left a legacy of exceptional children versed in the fields of education, theology and architecture, all with creative minds. Alma's gifts to the community were bountiful. Her unique mind and her pioneering spirit made her well loved and highly respected. She brought a spiritual voice to a quiet land.

Notes

[1] "The Family of William Henry Wieman and Alma Morgan Wieman," compiled by Alma Morgan Wieman and Lois Wieman, 1934.

[2] "Family Stories," collected by Robert Wieman, 1954.

[3] Letter to Viola Carlson from Kendra (Eleanor) Wieman Smith (Berkeley, California, May 25, 1984).

[4] "Family Stories," op. cit.

[5] Ibid.

[6] "Church Began at Bolton Hall," *The Record-Ledger*, September 19, 1974.

[7] At the Armistice of November 1918, 25,000 American women had served in some capacity in Europe. They served as secretaries, telephone operators, doctors, nurses and ambulance drivers as well as in YWCA canteens.

[8] "Family Stories," loc. cit.

[9] Wallace Morgan, "A Last Chapter in the Life Story of William Henry Wieman," 1954.

[10] In 1896, Franz Boas, an anthropologist at Columbia University, was one of the founders of the eugenics movement. Eugenics asked the question of whether genes or environment influenced human characteristics. In 1937, he retired from public life. After World War II, there was a backlash against eugenics and Franz Boas reversed his position and stated the mind at birth was *tabula rasa*, a blank slate.

[11] Eleanor Wieman married the internationally noted authority on world religions, Huston Smith, author of *The Religions of Man*, *The World's Religions*, *Why Religion Matters*, and *The Wisdom of Faith*.

[12] Letter to Author from Kendra (Eleanor) Wieman Smith, April 14, 2001.

[13] In the late 1930s, Stella built her own home on 400 acres of timbered property on the Alsea River in Oregon. The Morgans, Wiemans and foster children would often vacation at her cabin. After World War II, the sisters Lois and Stella retired to the Willamette Lutheran Home in Oregon. Lois passed away at the age of 89 years. Stella passed away at the age of 91 years. Only their brother Wallace (Tubby) survived them. The story of the Wieman brothers is a book unto itself.

October 20, 1923, was an exciting day—the cornerstone of Tujunga Grammar School (now Pinewood Elementary) was laid at the corner of Valmont and Pinewood Avenue. At the far right is Professor White (holding hat), Stella Wieman (white dress), and sister Lois to her right. Faculty, parents and students were all in attendance, c. 1923.

Across the street from the Wieman's home was Pinewood Elementary School, with an auditorium that seated 1,000, c. 1924.

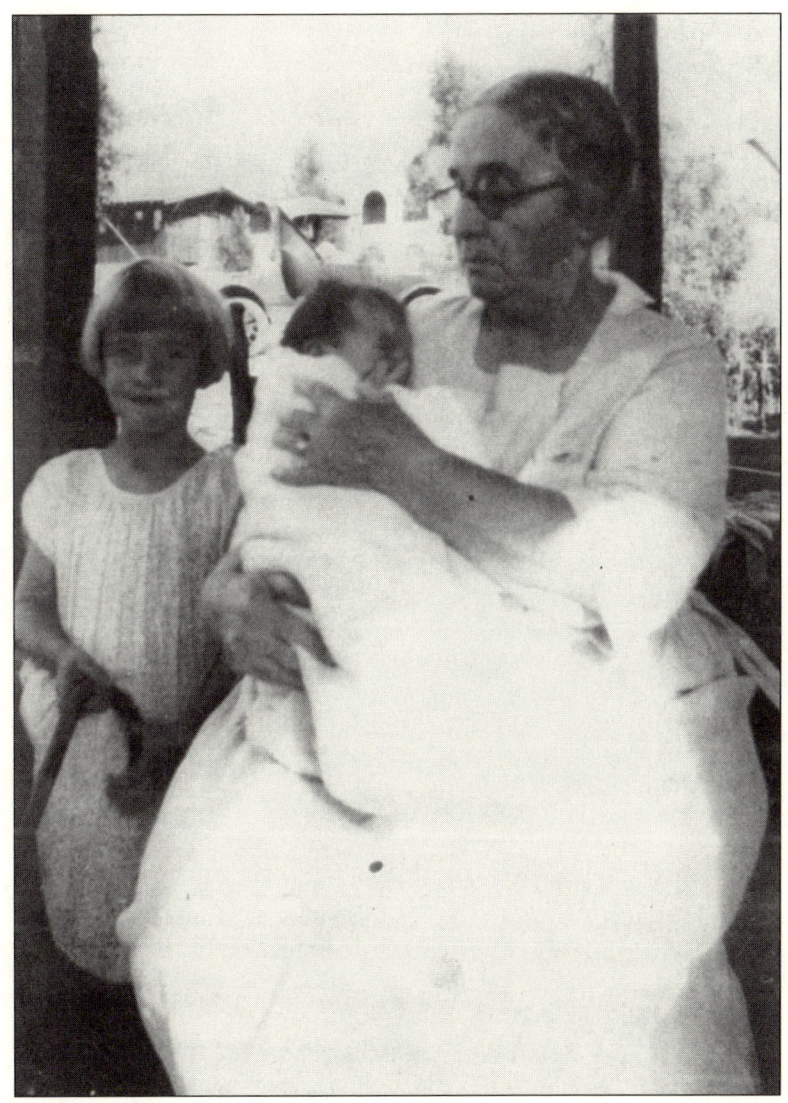

Alma with granddaughters Beverly (*left*) and Lois Franke.
She relished the role of grandmother. *Courtesy of Kendra Wieman Smith.*

Earliest known photograph of Jennie with husband James, c. 1890s.

Jennie Brocus Wornom
1851–1923

"It was about 1916 or 1917 that a small covered wagon drew up before our humble home at 6th and Soldam Avenue in Azusa. It showed signs of many a weary mile of travel behind it. The neighbor children, thinking the gypsies had come, ran and hid under their beds. But we were overjoyed with a visit from 'Parson' Wornom and his lady, 'Aunt' Jennie. They were indeed a treasure, well loved by so many and always spreading the 'Word' and giving a helping hand."[1] After coming to Monte Vista in 1903, the parson and his wife, Jennie, became the most beloved couple in the Monte Vista Valley.

Aside from being born in Franklin County, Pennsylvania, the details of Jennie's childhood are perhaps lost to time. We know that during the late 1890s she married James T. Wornom, who was sixteen years her senior. She had married into a family that could date their ancestry back to the 1700s in Kentucky. Jennie's new in-laws were the parents of fourteen children; James Thomas was their second child.[2] Born in Illinois, James entered into the Civil War in Company C of the 83rd Infantry on August 2, 1862. He left the service in Nashville, Tennessee, on June 26, 1865.[3] After Jennie's marriage to James, they traveled through Nebraska in their "house wagon" that was pulled by two horses. They made their way to the Northwest and spent the first years of their marriage there. James's father was a Methodist minister and the family was noted for their singing abilities. The petite Jennie joined her tall, raw-boned husband in song as they traveled the area in their horse-drawn wagon. As they "rode the circuit," spreading the Gospel, Jennie played a small, portable organ on the back of the wagon.

In 1893, the Wornoms came to California traveling in their "house wagon." They joined the many people who were eager to create the life they had envisioned. By 1903, when James and Jennie came to the Vale of Monte Vista, they pitched a tent under the shade of the mighty oaks in Sunland Park. Both were dedicated to serving the Lord and easing the burdens of their fellow men. Their first permanent Free Methodist Church was the small, abandoned Baptist Church located on the backside of Sunland Park. They conducted weekly services there, and when the soft-spoken Jennie entered from the back of the church, she was transformed, singing loudly and charismatically as she cast her eyes upward to the Lord. James would then enter and meet her at the alter, where they would embrace in a dramatic manner.[4] Jennie also taught the children's Bible class, and many remember her kindness and the occasional candy treats she would give them.

The childless couple became guardian of the valley's children and was always available to lend a hand to any family in need of help, be it physical or spiritual. Both Jennie and James were noted for their kind treatment and training of horses. The parson was said to have almost a mystical communion with horses. The wildest horse could be calmed under his guidance. Many a child was taught to ride and care for horses under his and

Jennie's tutelage. Their gentle touch and training methods brought them recognition as "horse whisperers." James also became known as a great horse trader. Sometimes the Wornoms rode their well-kept horses, but the animals are best remembered pulling the covered wagon the Wornoms used to travel California, spreading the Gospel at camp meetings and other Free Methodist churches.

In the early days of Monte Vista and Little Lands Colony, it was often very hot and there were few trees for shade. Many colonists, after a hard day of work, would spend the night on a cot outdoors. They remember hearing the clip-clop of horses' hooves and the raised voices of "Aunt" Jennie and Parson Wornom, making their way home, singing their favorite hymns: "We'll Never Say Good-Bye in Heaven," "Christ is Walking on the Waters," and their very favorite, "Lord I'm Coming Home—Never More to Roam."[5] The acoustics of the area magnified sounds so that a laugh or cough could be heard for miles. In the quiet of night, the singing of the coyotes and the evangelistic voices of the Wornoms filled the Valley.

It was 1913 when, after living in Sunland for ten years, the Wornoms moved to Hartranft's Little Lands Colony. In December 1921, the Wornoms built their own church, the Tujunga Union Gospel Mission, next to their home on North Sunset Avenue (Commerce) and Los Angeles Street (Apperson). Soon their chapel was filled to overflowing with local residents and visitors.[6]

For many years, Parson Wornom had begged his friend Marshall V. Hartranft to set aside land for his burial plot in the green Verdugo Hills he had grown to love. He told Marshall, "The Valley's setting up, Marsh. Nobody lives forever and some of us are getting along. I love these hills, Marsh, and I want to be buried in them." The busy developer had promised the Parson a hillside cemetery but had put the project on the back burner. On April 11, 1922, Marshall paid a visit to an ailing Parson, who whispered to his friend, "I'm almost ready for it, Marsh, have you got my cemetery yet?" When the Parson dozed off, M. V. Hartranft hurried back to his office and ordered his superintendent of construction to take all the men and mules and "throw" a road around the hill he had saved for his own home. The four-acre site, set aside for Hartranft's hillside mansion at the north end of Pinion Street, would be made ready for the parson's imminent death. The horse-trading parson would get his cemetery. The following day Marshall again went to his friend's home but it appeared to be too late. The Parson lay with his eyes closed and was breathing heavily. "Parson, it's Marsh," he implored. "Don't you know me?" There was no answer and with a heavy heart Hartranft turned toward the door. "Come back here," he heard a faint voice command. Startled, Hartranft stopped in his tracks. "You're conscious, Parson?" "I was playin' possum, how about that cemetery?" A relieved Hartranft assured Parson, "All ready for you." The parson sighed, "Thankie Marsh," and closed his eyes again. On April 19, 1922, the beloved Parson Wornom passed from this world.[7]

The passing of the parson from the green Verdugo Hills made the front page of the *Los Angeles Times*.[8] After three days of preparing a dirt road (Parson's Trail) to the top of Hartranft's hill, the town was ready to bury their beloved parson. Businesses and schools closed so all could attend his funeral. Hartranft kept his promise and provided a pageant of a funeral that would be remembered by all of the citizens. The parson's body was placed in his "house wagon" and driven by A. D. Kirchman up to the base of Parson's Trail. From there the neighbors bore his coffin on their shoulders up the steep trail to his final resting place, high on a hill above his adored valley. "A long procession followed, preceded by a squad of the American Legion, who fired a parting volley of gunfire high in the air."[9] Behind the casket, "The Parson's old horse walked with his bridle over his head. Slowly, sadly, the horse walked, his head almost to the ground. Behind him a forlorn group of sorrowing Colonists," and friends followed.[10]

Jennie, ill with breast cancer and broken-hearted, lived with Reverend Swaney and his family for the next year and a half. On October 25, 1923, just five days after her seventy-second birthday, Jennie Wornom joined her husband at their personal hilltop in the Hills of Peace Cemetery.[11] As her frail body was lowered into the grave, friend and neighbor John S. McGroarty spoke

(*above*) "Aunt" Jennie and Parson Wornom's Free Methodist Church in Sunland Park at Sherman Grove and Fenwick, c. 1913.

(*right*) The church, c. 1915.

FOUNDING SISTERS

Sunland and Tujunga's most beloved couple in their later years, c. 1914.

of "Aunt" Jennie and her strong Christian faith. He told of her great joy of attending cottage prayer meetings, winter revivals and summer camp meetings. She was a woman who wasn't afraid to show her faith. John envisioned the strong old parson of the Verdugo Hills sitting on his horse, erect in the saddle just as he used to sit when he road about the hills and valleys. Beside him was another horse, waiting with an empty saddle. "All the walls and ramparts of heaven were filled with shouting Christians. What a shouting of joy there was when the jasper gate swung open and the old Parson reached down and helped 'Aunt' Jennie up to the waiting saddle and they galloped away through the golden streets, across the ford to the river Jordan and into the green, green forest of heaven."[12]

A year later, George Harris (builder of Bolton Hall) would encircle the Wornom-Hatch "Pioneer Hill" with a wall of lava rock. Fortunately, the Wornoms and Hatches were protected from the ravishing floods that washed away the lower slope of the cemetery on February 9, 1978. Parson Wornom's niece drove from Arizona to check on her beloved aunt and uncle. In the summer of 2000, Boy Scouts and volunteers would build a stairway to "Pioneer Hill." The Wornoms remain on their knoll over looking the valley that they loved and traveled through in their horse drawn wagon so many years ago.

NOTES

[1] Letter to Donna Larson from Julia Granger Sharp (a Sunland resident in 1912), October 11, 1982.

[2] Letter to Viola Carlson from Aunt Jennie's niece, Flora Stevens, undated, McCook, Nebraska.

[3] Illinois State Archives. James T. Wornom Civil War Service Report (obtained by historian, Viola Carlson).

[4] Author's telephone interview with Viola Carlson. April 7, 1998.

[5] Viola L. Carlson, "Lord I'm Coming Home—Never More to Roam," Treatise (March 31, 1978).

[6] Don Ryan, "True Tales of Our City—Parson Wornom's Passing," The Foothill Leader (undated).

[7] California State Board of Health, Bureau of Vital Statistics, Certificate of Death. Dr. Virginia T. Smith of Tujunga, after nine days of care, certified he had died of chronic gastritis and septicemia.

[8] "Parson Laid to Rest in Hills—Loved Character Borne to Last Rest," Los Angeles Times (April 24, 1922).

[9] "Parson Laid to Rest in Hills," The Record-Ledger (April 20, 1922).

[10] Mabel Hatch, "The Old Parson and His Cemetery," The Green Verdugo Hills—A Chronicle of Sunland-Tujunga, Calif. And how it grew (Tujunga, California, 1952).

[11] California State Board of Health, Bureau of Vital Statistics. Certificate of Death, Dr. P. S. Traxler, Glendale.

[12] "Pioneers Go to Their Reward," The Record-Ledger (November 1, 1923).

JENNIE BROCUS WORNOM

Looking northeast on Apperson Street in Tujunga, "Aunt" Jennie and "The Parson of the Green Verdugo Hills." c. 1915.

Aunt Jennie and Parson Wornom are on horseback in front of the Tujunga Post Office, Gilbert's Gift Shop, and Dean's Pioneer Store. View southeast from the corner of Commerce and Valmont, c. 1915.

FOUNDING SISTERS

(*above*) The Wornoms covered wagon traveled to camp meetings and up and down the roads of southern California, c. 1919.

(*left*) American Legion members escort Parson Wornom to the base of the new Parson's Trail, c. 1922.

(*below*) Although many people had cars by 1922, it was fitting that Parson Wornom took his last journey to the newly built Verdugo Hills Cemetery in his covered wagon, pulled by his favorite horses, c. 1922.

412

(*right*) The Wornom's monument on "Pioneer Hill" in Verdugo Hills Cemetery.

(*below*) The Verdugo Hills Cemetery in 2002. Now maintained by The Friends of the Hills of Peace Cemetery Association. *Both courtesy of Author.*

Jean and Harry on the steps of their new home, c. 1910.

Jean Arnold Zachau

1885–1961

When the newly married Jean Zachau arrived to homestead her 73 acres on the northern rim of the Tujunga Valley, she brought with her a cow (given to her as a wedding gift), a two-horse wagon, and the determination to make a home for her new husband, Harry. While Jean and Harry were building their home, they lived in a wooden shack that was already on the land when they arrived. A plank on the rear of the shack had initials and the date 1902 carved into it.

Jean Arnold was born July 14, 1885, in Iola, Kansas.[1] Her father, a judge, moved his family of five children to Alhambra, California. While Jean was attending elementary school, she met her future husband in the fifth grade. Harry was born in Germany but had come to the United States when he was nine months old. His father was a doctor of podiatry. Harry and his three brothers and one sister moved to Alhambra, where his fate would be linked to the judge's daughter.

On Christmas Day 1909, Jean and Harry were married by her father in the Arnold home in Alhambra.[2] Harry worked for the railroad in Los Angeles, but he and Jean had a desire to leave the city life for the open spaces of the Tujunga Valley.

When the newlywed Zachaus arrived in Tujunga, it was wild country with heavy sage and greasewood plants covering the mountain slopes. Cougars, foxes, and coyotes roamed freely. There were no roads, just dirt trails wide enough for a wagon to get through. In the canyon behind their home, called Arroyo Hondo (deep canyon) and now officially named Zachau Canyon, Harry dug down to bedrock for water and laid pipe for an artesian well. The first water tank on the property consisted of four barrels placed high on a platform, reached by a wooden ladder. There wasn't any gas or electricity. Wood was used for cooking and heating and kerosene lamps used for lighting. Refrigeration of food was ingenious; they made use of a desert icebox. A wooden box was covered with burlap and a wooden frame, also covered with burlap, was built around the box. The burlap coverings were kept wet and then cooled by a breeze—no breeze, no refrigeration.[3] A mule train from Los Angeles brought groceries to either Roscoe (Sun Valley) or to Burbank.

After the backbreaking job of bringing water to the property and creating a road, Jean and Harry set about planting. They chose eucalyptus trees because of a scarcity of hard woods. They used "the oil from the leaves and bark to ward off colds, lumbago, pneumonia and mosquitoes. Later it was decided it was cheaper to get the oil from the drug store."[4] Their cow was traded for five pigs, which they attempted to raise along with turkeys, geese and chickens. They also had a vegetable garden.

> In order to make good on their homestead, the Zachaus had to have eight to ten acres under cultivation. They planted alfalfa for this requirement as well as for their livestock. The law allowing homesteaders to prove-up in three years instead of the previous five years, came along just in time for the Zachaus to prove-up in 1913 and have their papers signed by Woodrow Wilson, then President of the United States.[5]

415

This small frame building was standing on the property when Jean and Harry homesteaded 73 acres. (*left to right*) Bernard Zachau, Jean and Harry sit on steps. "1902" was carved on a plank at the rear of the house, c. 1910. *The Record-Ledger.*

In 1917, Harry and Jean moved to Arizona, where Harry worked in the smelter at a Douglas Airplane Plant during World War I. Their daughter, Jean, was born in Arizona in 1920. After her birth, the Zachaus returned to Tujunga and opened the Zachau Grocery Store on Michigan Avenue (Foothill Boulevard). The store was next to a barbershop run by Jim Greer and the Cozy Inn Restaurant, run by two sisters.[6]

In the winter of 1921, a snowstorm struck the entire Tujunga Valley. The vineyards and orchards were ruined. That didn't dampen the Zachaus' spirit. In the mid-1920s, their farm became famous for a salmon-pink gladiola named "Los Angeles." One year Harry paid $500 for a bushel of gladiolas bulbs; the next year the price plummeted to $5 a bushel! The fad of expensive garden flowers quickly passed.

Jean was happy in her role as homemaker and enjoyed canning vegetables and baking bread. Summer vacations were often spent visiting Jean's sister at her home on Balboa Island. Jean, a happy hearted woman, took great pleasure in outdoor entertaining at her farm. She also organized the wives of the Kiwanis members into the Sinawik Club. The ladies often met for luncheons and picnics in Sunland Park.

Jean Junior went to Palm Street Elementary School, which was a one-room schoolhouse on Mt. Gleason. She attended Pinewood Elementary School on Valmont for grades five through eight, and then graduated

416

Looking north on Hillrose Street towards the Zachau home.
Tujunga Canyon Boulevard in foreground, c. 1910. *The Record-Ledger.*

from San Fernando High School. After graduation, Jean Junior bought the Tujunga Rental Library and Gift Shop at 9917 Commerce Avenue (previously run by Frances Parcher). As a small child, Jean Junior had been a flower girl in Mrs. Carroll Parcher's wedding and had attended school with Marshall Hartranft's adopted children, Rosetta, Bud, and Dick. The Zachaus often enjoyed dining at the Hartranft's Lazy Lonesome Ranch.

Harry worked in real estate, and when Tujunga became an incorporated city in 1925, he served as commissioner of roads and commissioner of police and fire. That year, 1925, saw many changes in Jean's home and the town of Tujunga. Jean and Harry razed their first home and built their final residence on the same spot on Kyle Street, just off Tujunga Canyon Boulevard. They built the new house around the original fireplace and kept the original one-room shack as a workshop.[7]

Bolton Hall served as the City Hall of Tujunga for seven years. Harry recalled when Commerce Avenue was paved in 1926. The town had a big parade; everyone walked down the street carrying lanterns because there were no streetlights, and there was an all-day carnival with Ferris-wheels and merry-go-rounds. Tujunga had moved into the modern age and built their one and only float for the 1926 Rose Parade. Jean Junior was privileged to ride on the float. It was a banner year for this small city.

Get the Habit -- Trade at Zachau's

We are constantly adding to our extensive stock of merchandise, and you will find us well equipped to care for your wants.

We now have a supply of the FEDERAL FOOD PRODUCTS, the latest up-to-the-minute food creations; they're all going wild over it.

Comes in the form of COCOANUT CREME CUSTARD, CHOCOLATE DESSERT, KREAMLITE, CERRO BUTTER, LEMON PIE FILLING.

These are products for making instant pie fillings, puddings, cake fillings, the closest rival to apple butter, desserts and many other dainty dishes. Requires only a minute to make by adding water or milk, and saves the busy housewife many an anxious moment by always having on hand a tasty dessert that can be prepared in a moment's time. The price is 35c pe rcan, or three for $1.00, and you'll concede that it's the biggest value you ever got for your money.

H. W. ZACHAU

Highway, Tujunga   Phone 111-R

(*above*) H.W. Zachau General Merchandise store, facing State Highway (Michigan Avenue), now Foothill Boulevard, c. 1921.

(*opposite*) Both tourists and locals enjoyed the Pasadena Tournament of Roses, begun in 1890. Early floats were horse-drawn. On Colorado Blvd., the Tujunga float, designed by George Harris and covered in wild flowers from the Verdugos, took sixth place in the 1926 Tournament of Roses Parade. Jean Zachau, Jr., is seated on the float, far left. Note Vroman's Bookstore in background.

The twenties were an exciting time in Tujunga. Many civic organizations were formed and the popular Zachaus attended most of the social events. They often dined at John Steven McGroarty's home, Rancho Chupa Rosa. Harry shared John's view that Tujunga should not be annexed to the City of Los Angeles. Their battle was lost when Tujunga officially became a part of Los Angeles in 1932. Much Zachau land was lost due to high taxes and the city's claim for Zachau's spring water.[8] Because the Zachaus were against the annexation, Zachau Lane was changed to Las Lunitas Avenue. Harry became bitter and disillusioned. He once said, "My greatest mistake was that I didn't have a Ouiji board. I could have bought any land for $300.00 an acre and now, when cut into business lots, it sells for $9,000.00 an acre."[9] In 1936, Harry's father, Bernard, died and the Zachaus sold all but thirteen acres of their land. They kept their home and ten acres on the hill.

The forties were happier times for the family. Jean Junior married Tom Theobold in Yuma, Arizona, in 1941 and returned to Tujunga. They had two children and Tom would become the postmaster of Tujunga in 1959. He retained that position, with a break between 1961 and 1964, until 1968. Tom's mother, Jeanette, who passed away in 1960, had the distinction of obtaining the first building permit ever issued from the City of Tujunga on September 25, 1925.

In 1957, Harry passed away from pneumonia at the age of 73 years.[10] Jean passed away at her home of a heart attack in the summer of 1961.[11] She was the first woman homesteader of record in Tujunga, yet will always be remembered for her winning smile and friendliness.

Notes
[1] Record of Funeral. August 8, 1961. Bades Mortuary, Tujunga.
[2] Author's interview with Jean Zachau Theobold. October 2, 1996.
[3] "Harry Zachaus Moved Here in 1910 to Homestead 73 acres," *The Record-Ledger* (June 30, 1954).
[4] "Personality—Harry Zachau," *The Record-Ledger* (August, 1953).
[5] "Zachaus Lived in First Home Built in Tujunga," *The Record-Ledger* (May 21, 1953).
[6] "Fifteen Years Ago This Week," *The Record-Ledger* (December 10, 1953).
[7] "Harry Zachaus . . ." (June 30, 1954), op. cit.
[8] "Harry Zachaus . . ." (June 30, 1954), op. cit.
[9] Author's interview with Jean's son-in-law, Tom Theobold. February 11, 2001.
[10] Record of Funeral. November 29, 1957. Bades Mortuary, Tujunga.
[11] Record of Funeral, August 8, 1961, op. cit.

(*above*) Tujunga Fire chief Harry Rice holds the famous gladiolas at the Zachau farm, c. 1926. *The Record-Ledger.*

(*opposite, top*) In 1936, Jean and Harry's daughter bought The Tujunga Rental Library, located at 9917 Commerce Avenue. Frances Parcher had operated it, for the previous ten months. The two-year-old shop featured cards, gifts and a large stock of rental books. *The Record-Ledger* advertisement.

(*opposite, bottom*) Jean's son-in-law, Tom Theobold (center right) receiving the Presidential Proclamation declaring him Tujunga's official postmaster. He served from 1959 to 1961 and from 1964 to 1968. *The Record-Ledger* (1959).

FOUNDING SISTERS

(*above*) Jean and Harry at home in front of the original fireplace they built around in 1925, c. 1955.

(*below*) Jean's daughter, Jean, and her husband, Tom Theobald, at home on Zachau property—now Kyle Street, c. 1998. *Courtesy of Author.*

Appendixes

The Little Landers of Los Angeles

929 South Figueroa Street

Reply to
WM. E. SMYTHE

Los Angeles, California 1913.

LIST OF NAMES OF THE LITTLE LANDERS OF LOS ANGELES,

April 12, 1913,

AT THE LAYING OF THE CORNER STONE OF BOLTON HALL, LOS TERRENITOS.

Anson H. Burlingame	Mr. & Mrs. George Buck
Hattie "	Mr. & Mrs. Powell
Miss Mable Free	Two Children "
Miss Emma Craft	Mr. & Mrs. Fuller
Mr. & Mrs. Abbott Knight	Mrs. Culberson
Joseph Knight	Mrs. Morgan
Miss Annie L. Read	Mr. & Mrs. Wallace N. Morgan
Mrs. Mary G. Chase	Frances Morgan
Michael Jones	Mrs. Batie
Mrs. Cora Seavey	Mr. & Mrs. Slusher
Miss Sarah McMullen	Mr. & Mrs. Brundage
Solomon Trumpy	Mr. & Mrs. Philip Begue
Mrs. Bertha Williams	Five children "
John Stark	Mr. & Mrs. John W. Keeney
Mr. Zeigler	Mr. & Mrs. Charles Germain
Edward Thomas	Ralph German
Miss Mary Flickinger	John S. McGroarty
Mr. & Mrs. McWilliams	Edwin M. Spates, M.D.
Mr. & Mrs. Levi C. Doane	B.C. Sacksteder
Arthur H. Doane	J.S. "
Mrs. Caroline Brown	C.J. Sherer
Mrs. Fergerson	Louise Sherer
Mrs. Harrington	Richard "
Mr. & Mrs. Burns	Louise "
Mr. & Mrs. Proctor	Edward "
Mr. Lewis	Mr. & Mrs. Edward Forster
Mr. & Mrs. Fredrick Cowlirs	Mr. & Mrs. J.A. Ewing
Donald Cowlirs	Mr. & Mrs. Jack Cammer
Robert Cowlirs	Mr. & Mrs. J.P. McClement

FOUNDING SISTERS

Mr. & Mrs. Leo Lang
Margaret Lang
Geneva "
Charles Lang
Mr. & Mrs. J.C. Lang
Mr. & Mrs. Stokes
Floyd Stokes
Andry "
Mr. & Mrs. Puisinger
Baby "
Mrs. Hatty Hartranft
Marshal Hartranft Colby
Mr. & Mrs. W.G. Bellinger
Kenneth Bellinger
Mr. & Mrs. D. Dutton
Mr. & Mrs. M.E. Shorey
Prof. George M. Caldwell
Miss M.E. Caldwell
Johana Sommer
Mr. & Mrs. Henry Zachau
Mr. & Mrs. E.H. Johnson
Miss Rosetta "
" Gladys "
Miss Nina McMillen
Mr. & Mrs. A.D. Kirschman
H. Darwin "
Viola "
Wilma "
May "
Spencer "
Percy J. DeWello
Mr. & Mrs. T.W. Thomasson
Erick "
John M. Grosvenor
Harry "

Louise McClement
Flora M. Morgan
Bertha A. Baety
Bell "
Maude "
W.H. Delapp
Theresa Buford
W.F. Herington
Mr. & Mrs. M.V. Hartranft
Richard A. Hartranft
Mr. & Mrs. John MacVine
Mr. & Mrs. A.F. Wills
Mr. & Mrs. B. Schoneman
Elizabeth Voelker
Albert Wells
Fred Wells
Addison "
Herald Reed
Mr. & Mrs. J.F. Norman
R.B. Norman
C.A. Norman
L.G. Norman
Mr. & Mrs. W.R. Brewer
Mr. & Mrs. C.L. Lewis
" " J.J. "
J. Ellenburger
J. Ellenburger, Jr.
E. "
V. "

Appendix A: Population

Year	Los Angeles	California
1880	11,183	864,000
1890	50,395	1,213,398
1900	102,479	1,485,053
1910	310,198	2,377,549
1920	576,673	3,426,861*

Year	Tujunga
1913	300
1914	500
1915	625
1916	781
1917	976
1918	1,220
1919	1,525
1920	1,986
1921	2,482
1922	3,102
1923	3,877**

*Leonard and Dale Pitt, *Los Angeles A–Z, An Encyclopedia of the City and County*.
***The Record-Ledger of the Verdugo Hills*, February 1924.

Appendix B:
Sunland Rural Telephone Company

Year	No. of Telephones	No. of Emloyee
1908	22	1
1910	22	2
1913	26	2
1918	44	3
1923	165	6
1928	470	13
1933	504	12
1938	934	18
1943	1676	24
1948	4300	82
1953	6500	42

The Sunland Rural Telephone Company, located at the home of John Smart, one of the company's first stockholders. The house was near Oro Vista Boulevard and Fenwick Street in Sunland. By 1923 they had moved to an office on Apperson at Plainview, c. 1920.

> THE ANALYST OF CALIFORNIA is like a navigator who is trying to chart a course in a storm: the instruments will not work; the landmarks are lost; and the maps make little sense.
> —*Carey McWilliams*

Appendix C: Street Name Changes

When Tujunga became annexed to Los Angeles in 1932, the streets of the city were renamed.

1932 Name	Original Name	1932 Name	Original Name
Alene Drive	Ridge Lane	Helendale Avenue	Helena Street
Apperson Street	Los Angeles Street		Hart Avenue
	Hidden Oak Drive		Colby Avenue
Beckett	Mt. View Avenue	Hillhaven Avenue	Stephens Way
	Maiden Lane	Hillrose Street	Hill Street
	Citrus Avenue	Hirondelle Lane	Fisher Street
Betty Lou Lane	Kane Street		Golondrina Drive
Blanchard Canyon Road	Leona & Blanchard Canyon Road	Irma Avenue	Goleta Street
		Jardine Avenue	Harding Place
Breidt Street	Breidt Street	Las Lunitas	Zachau Lane
Cardamine Drive	Deneville Drive	Macrea Street	Sherwood Drive
Commerce Avenue	Sunset Boulevard	Marcus Avenue	Marshall Street
Day Street	Hillcrest Drive	McClemont Avenue	West View Avenue
Elmo Street	Woodruff Lane		McClemont Street
Fairgrove Avenue	Fairview Street	McGroarty Street & Place	Manzanita Drive
	Beulah Court	Memory Drive	Herbert Street
Fernglen Avenue	Griswold Street	Mountair Avenue	Cedar Street
Fitzroy Avenue	Fitzgerald Street	Mt. Gleason Avenue	Walnut Avenue
Foothill Boulevard	Michigan Avenue	Olcott Street	Olive Street
France Avenue	Frances Court	Owens Street	Halbert Street
Gish Avenue	Georgia Lane		Reed Avenue
Glory Avenue	Glorietta Avenue		Owens Avenue
	Farrel Street	Parsons Trail	Parsons Trail
Greeley Street	Greeley Street	Pinewood Avenue	Pine Street
Haines Canyon Avenue	Haines Canyon Road	Plainview Avenue	Palm Avenue
	Kings Highway	Provo Avenue	Proctor Road
Haywood Street	State Court	Quinton Lane	Queen Lane
	Haines Avenue	Redmont Avenue	Alden Drive

431

FOUNDING SISTERS

1932 Name	Original Name	1932 Name	Original Name
	Tujunga Avenue	Thousand Oaks Drive	Cutover Lane
Reid Street		Topley Lane	Orchard Way
St. Estaban Street	Los Robles Avenue		Orchard Drive
St. Estaban Way	Estaban Way	Tujunga Canyon Boulevard	Monte Vista Boulevard
	Estaban Road	Valmont Street	El Centro Street
Samoa Avenue	San Ysidro Road		Barclay Drive
Shady Grove Street	Marshall Court	Wentworth Street	North Street
Silverton Avenue	Belden Lane	Wilsey Avenue	Wilson Avenue
	Sycamore Avenue	Woodward Avenue	Third Street
Summitrose	Summit Avenue	Zitto Lane	Zitto Lane

Appendix D: Name Changes for the Sunland-Tujunga Area

Present Name	Old Name
Lake View Terrace	Tujunga Terrace
Shadow Hills	Hansen Heights
Sunland	Monte Vista
Sunland-Tujunga Area	Monte Vista Valley
	Vale of Monte Vista
Sun Valley	Roscoe
Tujunga	Rancho Tejunga
	Glorietta Heights
	La Ciudad de Los Terrenitos
	Little Lands Colony

> The past is never dead. It's not even past.
> —*William Faulkner*

Appendix E: Origins of the Little Landers

I. Foreign		
Austria	1	Marie Frish
Azore Islands	1	Anna Souto
England	1	Gertrude Maygrove
Finland	1	Hilda Livingston
Germany	1	Helena Fehlhaber
Romania	1	Anna Adam
Spain	1	Franciscoa Begue
II. California	2	Frances R. Morgan
		Frances M. Parcher
III. Other States		
Iowa	2	Mary Phillips, Flora White
Indiana	1	Zoe Gilbert
Kansas	2	Jean A. Zachau, Bertha Morgan
Maine	1	Myra Osgood
Massachusetts	3	Alice Carr Bolton, Marie Hansen, Alice Lamson
Michigan	7	Lillian Colby, Lydia May Dean, Mabel Hatch, Cora Belle Linaberry, Edna R. Buck, Nora H. Millspaugh, Alma Wieman
Missouri	1	Nana Mae Chapman
New York	4	Beth Pasko, Laura J. Bryson, Gladys Maygrove, Emma Mingay
North Carolina	1	Flora Morgan
Pennsylvania	7	Catherine Blake, Jennie Lichtenthaler, Ida McGroarty, Nannie Parcher, Helen Rutherford, Jenny Wornom, Anna Barclay Kirby
Vermont	1	Virginia Tenney Smith
Wyoming	1	Nellie Colby

Appendix F: And Their Name Lives On

Street Names in Parentheses Indicate Name Changed in 1932

Anna	Barclay (Kirby)	Barclay Drive (Valmont)—Sunland
Lillian & Nellie	Colby	Colby Street—Santa Monica
		Colby Canyon—San Gabriel Mountains
Rossi	Gish	Gish Avenue—Tujunga
Marie	Hansen	Hansen Heights—Shadow Hills
		Hansen Dam—Lake View Terrace
		Hansen Canyon—Angeles National Forest
		Marie Canyon—Angeles National Forest
Betty Lou	Hartranft	Betty Lou Lane—Tujunga
Rossetta	Hartranft	Rosetta Place—Sunland
Elizabeth	MacVine	McVine Street—Sunland
Ida	McGroarty	McGroarty Terrace—Tujunga
		McGroarty Street—San Gabriel
		Mt. McGroarty—Tujunga
		John S. McGroarty Auditorium—Verdugo Hills High School, Tujunga
Flora	Morgan	Flora Morgan Trail—Tujunga
Nannie	Parcher	Parcher Trail—Tujunga
Beth	Pasko	Pasko Lake (underground aquifer)—Sunland-Tujunga
		Pasko Park (base of San Ysidro cross)
Harriet	Smythe	Smythe Avenue—San Ysidro
		Smythe Elementary School—San Ysidro
Jennie	Wornum	Parson's Trail—Tujunga
		Wornum Avenue—Shadow Hills
Jean	Zachau	(Zachau Lane)—Las Lunitas—Tujunga
		Zachau Place—Tujunga

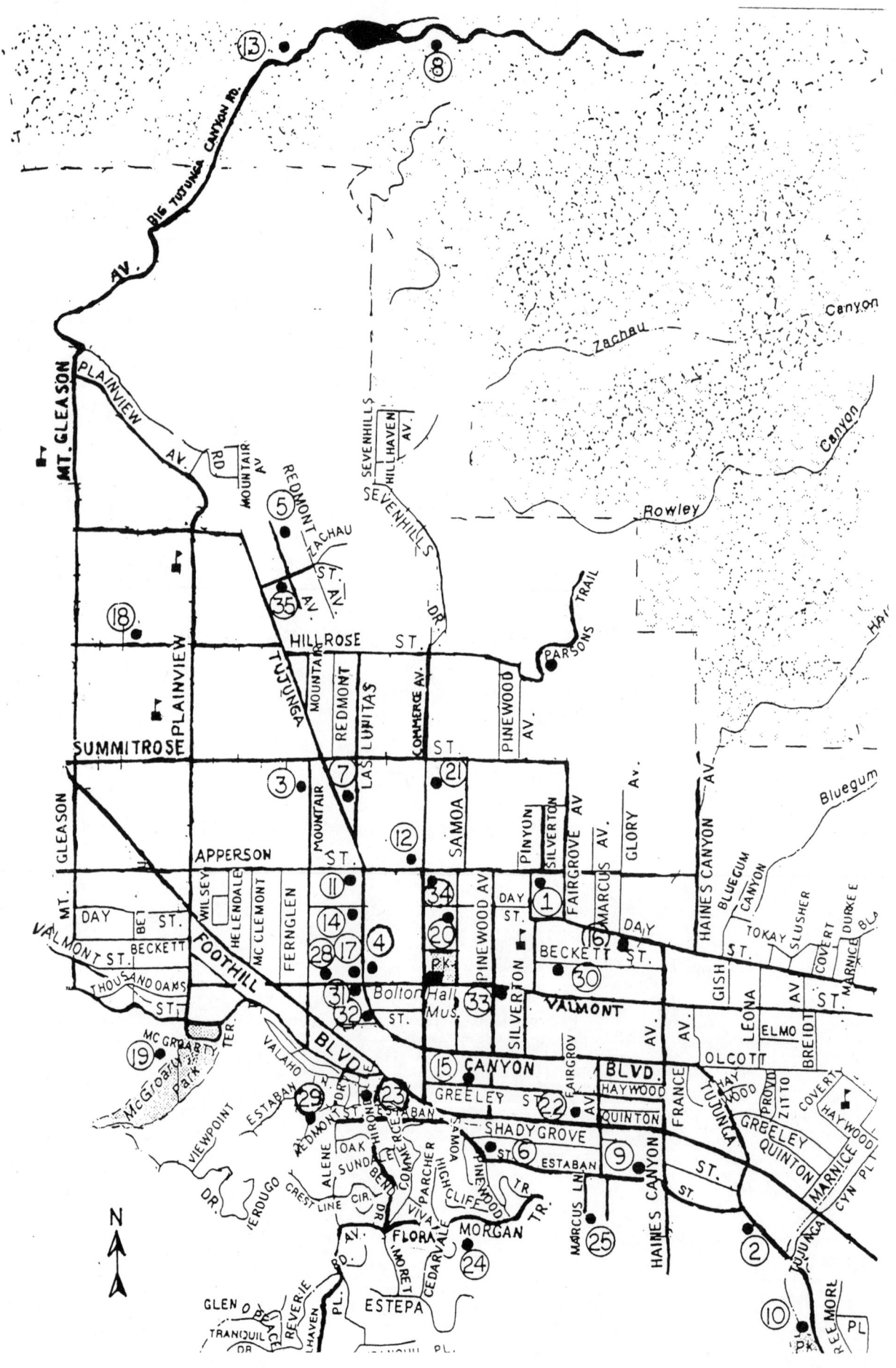

Appendix G:
The Tujunga Women's Heritage Trail

Homesites of the Early Women Pioneers

Site #	Name	Location
1	Anna Adam	Silverton
2	Franciscoa Begue	Tujunga Canyon Boulevard
3	Catherine Blake	Mountair
4	Alice Carr Bolton	Tujunga Canyon Boulevard
5	Laura Bryson	Mountair
6	Edna Buck	St. Estaban Street
7	Nana Chapman	Las Lunitas
8	Nellie & Lillian Colby	Big Tujunga Canyon (south side of road)
9	Lydia May Dean	St. Estaban Street
10	Helena Fehlhaber	Tujunga Canyon Boulevard
11	Marie Frish & Anna Souto	Tujunga Canyon Boulevard
12	Zoe Gilbert	Apperson Street
13	Marie Hansen (Hansen's Lodge) Bus.	Big Tujunga Canyon (north side of road)
14	Mabel Hatch	Tujunga Canyon Boulevard
15	Alice Lamson	Greeley Street
16	Jennie Lichtenthaler	Mt. View Avenue
17	Cora Belle Linaberry	Tujunga Canyon Boulevard
18	Hilda Livingston	Hillrose Avenue
19	Ida McGroarty	McGrourty Terrace
20	Gladys Maygrove	Samoa Avenue
21	Nora Millspaugh	Commerce Avenue
22	Emma Mingay	Foothill Boulevard (near Marcus)
23	Bertha & Flora Morgan	Hillhaven Avenue
24	Flora Morgan	Flora Morgan Trail
25	Frances R. Morgan & Frances Morgan Parcher	Marcus Lane
26	Myra Osgood	Tujunga Canyon Boulevard

FOUNDING SISTERS

Site #	Name	Location
27	Nannie Parcher	Marcus Lane
28	Beth Pasko	Valmont Street
29	Mary Phillips	Redmont at Valeho Lane
30	Helen Rutherford	Beckett Street
31	Dr. Virginia Smith	Tujunga Canyon Boulevard
32	Flora White	Tujunga Canyon Boulevard
33	Alma Wieman	Valmont Street
34	Jennie Wornam	Commerce Avenue
35	Jean Zachau	Kyle Street

Appendix H: Final Residence

ADAM, Anna	Grandview Memorial Park
	Glendale, California
BEGUE, Franciscoa	Calvery Cemetery
	Los Angeles, California
BLAKE, Catherine	San Bruno, California
BOLTON, Alice Carr	Grandview Memorial Park
	Glendale, California
BRYSON, Laura	Grandview Memorial Park
	Glendale, California
BUCK, Edna	Forest Lawn
	Glendale, California
CHAPMAN, Nana	Glenhaven Memorial Park
	Sylmar, California
COLBY, Lillian	Colby Ranch
COLBY, Nellie	San Gabriel Mountains, California
DEAN, Lydia May	Forest Lawn
	Glendale, California
FEHLHABER, Helena	Valhalla Memorial Park
	North Hollywood, California
FRISH, Marie	Glenhaven Memorial Park
SOUTO, Anna	Sylmar, California
GILBERT, Zoe	Kokomo, Indiana
HANSEN, Marie	Mojave, California
HATCH, Mabel	Verdugo Hills Cemetery
	Tujunga, California
JAMES, Anna	Forest Lawn
	Glendale, California
LAMSON. Alice	Forest Lawn Hollywood Hills
	Los Angeles, California
LICHTENTHALER, Jennie	Forest Lawn
	Glendale, California

FOUNDING SISTERS

LINABERRY, Corabelle	Grandview Memorial Park
	Glendale, California
LIVINGSTON, Hilda	Forest Lawn
	Glendale, California
MAYGROVE, Gladys	San Diego, California
MCGROARTY, Ida	Calvery Cemetery
	Los Angeles, California
MILLSPAUGH, Nora	Riverside Cemetery
	Three Rivers, Michigan
MINGAY, Emma	Grandview Memorial Park
	Glendale, California
MORGAN, Bertha	Ashland, Oregon
MORGAN, Flora	Inglewood Cemetery
	Los Angeles, California
MORGAN, Frances R.	Grandview Memorial Park
	Glendale, California
OSGOOD, Myra	Forest Lawn
	Glendale, California
PARCHER, Frances	Grandview Memorial Park
	Glendale, California
PARCHER, Nannie	Grandview Memorial Park
	Glendale, California
PASKO, Beth	Inglewood Cemetery
	Los Angeles, California
PHILLIPS, Mary	California
RUTHERFORD, Helen	Forest Lawn
	Glendale, California
SMITH, Virginia	Forest Lawn
	Glendale, California
WHITE, Flora	Grandview Memorial Park
	Glendale, California
WIEMAN, Alma	Forest Lawn
	Glendale, California
WORNUM, Jenny	Verdugo Hills Cemetery
	Tujunga, California
ZACHAU, Jean	Glenhaven Memorial Park
	Sylmar, California

Appendix I: Photo Gallery

~ Where They Worked ~

WOMEN IN THE URBAN ECONOMY:
UNITED STATES FEMALES WHO WERE EMPLOYED
Percentage of total population

1880	1890	1900	1910	1920
14.7	17.4	18.8	23.4	21.1

The United States census revealed that 8 million women were employed in 437 different job classifications.

Source: Jensen, Lothrop, *California Women: A History*, 77.

WOMEN IN SELECTED PROFESSIONAL OCCUPATIONS
Percentage of all workers

Occupation	1900	1910	1920	1930	1940	1950	1960
Lawyers		1	1.4	2.1	2.4	3.5	3.5
College presidents, professors		19.0	30.0	32.0	27.0	23.0	19.0
Clergy	4.4	1.0	2.6	4.3	2.2	8.5	5.8
Doctors		6.0	5.0	4.0	4.6	6.1	6.8
Engineers					0.3	1.2	0.8
Dentists		3.1	3.2	1.8	1.5	2.7	2.1
Biologists						27.0	28.0
Mathmeticians						38.0	26.4
Physicists						6.5	4.2
Librarians		79.0	88.0	91.0	89.0	89.0	85.0
Nurses	94.0	93.0	96.0	98.0	98.0	98.0	97.0
Social Workers		52.0	62.0	68.0	67.0	66.0	57.0

Source: Cynthia Fuchs Epstein, *Woman's Place: Options and Limits in Professional Careers* (1970; reprint ed., Berkeley, California: University of California Press, 1971), p. 7.

Adams Olive Cannery

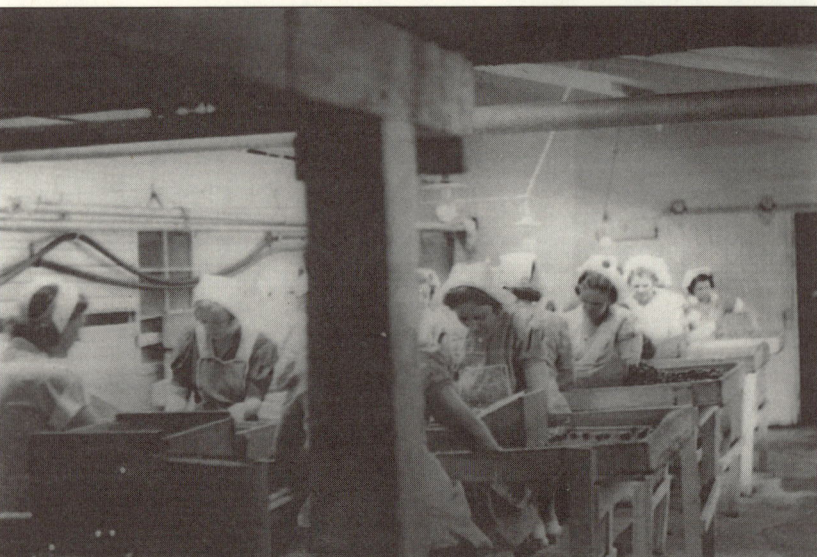

(*top, left*) This early 1920s photograph shows employees (primarily women) in front of the main building of the Adams Cannery.

(*above*) In this 1924 interior view of the Adams Olive Cannery, women sort olives that will grace the Thanksgiving dinner table of President Calvin Coolidge and other holiday dinner tables around the world. *Courtesy of Fred Adams.*

(*left*) The Adams Sunland Olive Cannery, located at Wentworth Avenue and Sherman Grove Avenue in Sunland, was the valley's largest employer until the late 1940s. Many a girl and woman worked either as summer help, full time, or during heavy canning seasons. The area ran out of olives in the early 1950s, and the Adams family moved the business to Strathmore, where they still produce Sunland Olives. *Photos courtesy of Fred Adams.*

APPENDIX I: A PHOTOGRAPHIC GALLERY

ANNIE M. KINDLER
Licepsed Real Estate Broker
300 E. Michigan Ave.   Tujunga
Phone Sunland 804

W. L. BOBO
Licensed Real Estate Broker

MARY Z. BOBO
Fire Insurance
Sunset and Highway

In The
TUJUNGA
VALLEY----

¶ 1 Lemon, 2 Navel and 2 Valencia Orange Trees On the Home Place To Supply the Tonic and Keep the System in Buoyancy and Pep.

Avocados, Grapes, Figs, Peaches, Garden Vegetables and Poultry Products to Furnish Stamina and Satisfy the Epicurean Taste.

Flowers and Roses Ever Blooming in the Door Yard for Beauty and Culture.

Rarefied Air and Abundant Sunshine for Unexcelled Body Building.

Moderate Altitude for Deep and Easy Respiration.

Gorgeous Mountain Scenery to Elevate and Inspire.

Within the Metropolitan Area and School District Of Los Angeles.

Water, Gas, Electricity; Local and Long-Distance Telephone Service.

Convenient, Up-To-Date, Business Establishments and Local Delivery.

Churches, Grammar Schools, Banks, Mail and Transportation Facilities.

Public Recreation Grounds; Outdoor Sports; Vigor for Young and Old.

An Exquisitely Tempered All-Year-Round Climate.

These are but a few of the many advantages enjoyed on a $500 homesite in the Tujunga Valley. Terms to suit.

Verdugo Hills Realty Co.
Corner Michigan and Walnut
TUJUNGA, CALIFORNIA

REAL ESTATE
Men and women enjoyed the profession of real estate sales equally.

(*right*) In this 1929 *Record-Ledger* real estate advertisement, the bounty of the harvest was apparent.

443

FOUNDING SISTERS

Genevieve Adams

Realtor

LEASES—RENTALS
LOANS - INSURANCE

165 W. Summit Avenue
TUJUNGA

Phone Sunland 1199

REAL ESTATE
(*left*) Annette Kellerman's real estate office in Rainbow Valley, near Wentworth Avenue and Foothill Boulevard, c. 1924. *Courtesy of Forrest Theriot.*

In this 1925 photograph of the members of the Tujunga Valley Realty Board, women are seen as an integral part of the realtors of the Valley. (*left to right*) Captain Robbins, Leo Lang, Bruce Anawalt, George Aiken, Mr. Goode, Mr. Kirschner, Major Pat Blake, Leo Smith, M.V. Hartranft, George Buck, unidentified woman, Bertha Morgan, Dr. Buck, Harry Zachau, Maggy Kautz, Mrs. Pratt, Genevieve Adams, an unidentified man and William Bobo. *The Record-Ledger.*

444

APPENDIX I: A PHOTOGRAPHIC GALLERY

Hollywood Comes to Sunland-Tujunga

(*above*) By 1918, the film companies had discovered the rustic and picturesque Big Tujunga Canyon, c. 1920s. *The Record-Ledger.*

(*right*) Sunland's Lancaster Lake and its rural scenery provided the background for many films. Local residents and their animals were often employed as "extras." Appearing on the silver screen was fun and profitable, c. 1926.

(*below*) In the 1920s and 1930s, Hollywood came to Sunland-Tujunga. Local women and children were employed as extras in the movies. Monte Vista Park and Big Tujunga Canyon were favorite spots for filming. This photograph is the movie set in Sunland Park for Mary Pickford's first talking movie, *Coquette.* Her efforts won her the Best Actress Oscar, c. 1929.

445

(*left*) A *Record-Ledger* advertisement for a trip to Santa Catalina Island, 26 miles off the Los Angeles coast, c. 1920.

(*above*) "They dared to show their ankles." Unidentified group of Tujunga ladies frolic in the surf.

～ Amusements ～
Catalina & the Beach

Tujunga ladies on a drive to the beach along Pacific Coast Highway, c. 1915.

APPENDIX I: A PHOTOGRAPHIC GALLERY

Mt. Lowe Railway

For 45 years, the trip to Mt. Lowe on the Incline Railway was a fun ride. Three hotels greeted guests at the top, c. 1915.

447

Tourists could choose to visit the ostrich farms in Los Angeles, Hollywood or Pasadena, c. 1915. *From Author's collection.*

Ostrich Farms

A visit to an ostrich or alligator farm was a "must see" for tourists in this southland advertisement from *The Early Sunset Magazine 1898–1928*. *Courtesy of Sunset Publishing Corporation.*

The Cawston Ostrich Farm and Feather Factory

One of the most interesting spots in Southern California

WE grow hundreds of ostriches just like this splendid bird, and tend them as carefully as the Middle West cattle grower looks after his prize-winning beeves. We are repaid for our trouble when we pluck the ostriches' magnificent plumage, full of life and lustre, which is developed in our factory on the farm into the finest ostrich feather goods the world produces.

We sell ostrich feather goods at producers' prices, all delivery charges prepaid. You save middlemen's profits and import duty. Satisfaction guaranteed or money refunded.

OUR NEW CATALOGUE

Free on request. An entertaining story of the farm with handsome halftones of farm scenes. Contains also illustrations and prices of Cawston Tips, Plumes, Boas, Stoles, Fans, Etc.

REPAIR DEPARTMENT

Do not destroy your old ostrich feather goods. Our Repair Department can restore their original beauty and usefulness at small cost. Send them to us.

P. O. Box 52,   South Pasadena, California

APPENDIX I: A PHOTOGRAPHIC GALLERY

Lady Liberty and Uncle Sam grace this float in the 1908 Fourth of July Parade.
The Monte Vista Hotel in Sunland is in the background. In a more innocent time, America's birthday was celebrated
with parades, races, ball games and fireworks. Sunland-Tujunga continues to have a parade down Foothill Boulevard each July 4th.

Parades

Looking west on Foothill Boulevard (Michigan) as Tujunga celebrates the end of World War I. *The Record-Ledger, c. 1918.*

449

FOUNDING SISTERS

Monte Vista Park

(*above*) The wedding of Jim and Alta Adams in Monte Vista Park in Sunland in 1902. Every resident of Sunland was at the affair.

(*opposite, top*) The stand in Monte Vista Park was used for Sunday concerts and plays. "Wan O'the Woods" play, c. 1915.

(*opposite, bottom*) In 1912, The Ladies Improvement League installed these cooking grills in Monte Vista Park, Sunland, c. 1917.

APPENDIX I: A PHOTOGRAPHIC GALLERY

Compliments of
RICE'S BUNGALOW CAFE
at the Big Oak Park
in Sunland

and

RICE'S BILLIARD PARLOR
425 S. Sunset Blvd.
In Tujunga

RICE'S
Bungalow Cafe and Grocery

Meals from 7 a. m. to 8 p. m.

Phone Sunland 623

Opposite Monte Vista Park
Sunland, Calif.

RICE'S CAFE
In the 1920s, Nancy and Harry Rice ran a popular cafe in Monte Vista Park.

APPENDIX I: A PHOTOGRAPHIC GALLERY

Twin Pines

(*above*) John Johnson's Monte Vista Inn, located at the corner of Fenwick Street and Sherman Grove Avenue in Sunland, became a popular dance pavilion (renamed Twin Pines in the early 1920s). The building was razed in 1964, c. 1921. *The Record-Ledger* (June 18, 1964).

(*below*) A close up view of the popular "Tin Lizzie." c. 1915. *Unknown source.*

DANCING
WEDNESDAY and SATURDAY
NIGHTS
TWIN PINES
SUNLAND
Best Music—Free Auto Parking—Lucky Spot Dances

453

Travel

(*above, left*) Unidentified photograph of local ladies visiting friends in Los Angeles on a "Tally Ho." c. 1903.

(*above*) An unidentified couple traveling the dirt road to Shadow Hills (Hansen Heights) in a 1913 Stevens Racing Car. Due to the rough roads, the cars frequently broke down or had flat tires. A trip to Los Angeles via automobile took over three hours on the route through Tujunga, Montrose, Glendale (Tropico) to San Fernando Road, c. 1913. *The Record-Ledger.*

(*left*) Foothill Boulevard entering the western edge of Tujunga, c. 1920.

(*below*) Dr. Spates' daughter, her husband and a friend, Elizabeth Clark (right) on a trip from Long Beach to Tujunga, c. 1915.

APPENDIX I: A PHOTOGRAPHIC GALLERY

Transportation

(*top*) The Sunland Stage made the trip from Sixth and Main Streets in Los Angeles to Tujunga and Sunland, c. 1915.

(*above*) The Jitney Bus ("Leaping Lena")—to La Crescenta to catch the Glendale Trolley. Percy Dewello, driver, c. 1916.

(*below*) Looking north on Brand Boulevard and Broadway at the Pacific Electric Station, c. 1916.

455

FOUNDING SISTERS

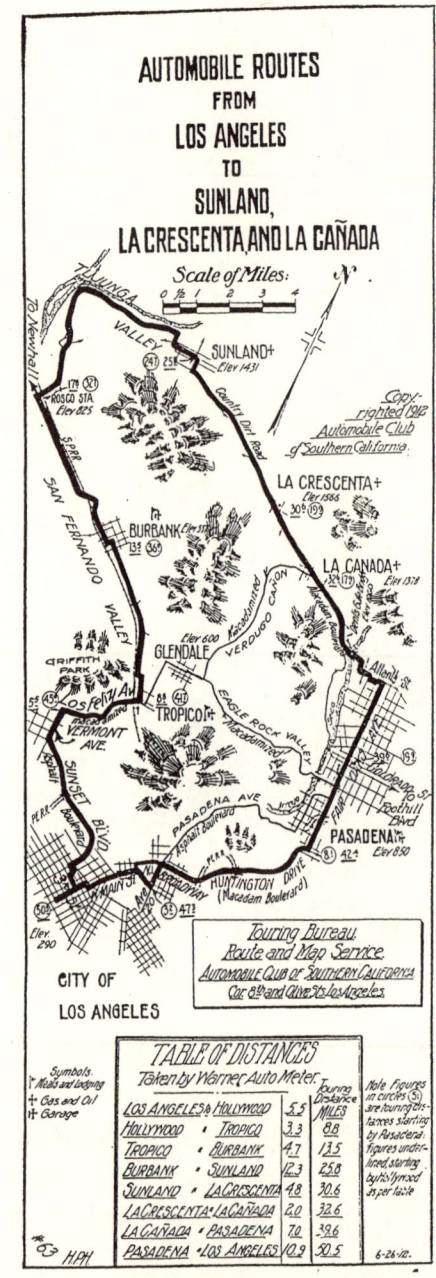

Transportation

(*clockwise from left*) Before 1916, the two entrances to Tujunga were on a dirt road. With the advent of the Automobile Club of Southern California, strip maps appeared in their monthly magazine, *Touring Topics*, and car trips became popular. Map dated 6-26-12. *Courtesy of Automobile Club of Southern California.*

The Glendale Depot where travelers caught the "jitney" to Tujunga from Glendale. The Tujunga taxi is parked alongside the depot, c. 1920.

The eastern entrance to Tujunga was through Montrose. Corner of Honolulu Avenue and Verdugo Road. "End of the line" for the Pacific Electric Car. Eventually the line extended westward to Pennsylvania Avenue in La Crescenta. The olive green car was nicknamed "Ding Dong Dinky" and its last run was December 30, 1930, c. 1919.

1922 advertisement in the *Record of Verdugo Hills*.

456

APPENDIX I: A PHOTOGRAPHIC GALLERY

Transportation

(*above*) The A.J. Richardson home at 7441 Valaho Drive, served as a bus barn for the first buses to travel from Tujunga to Glendale. It began operating in 1916. Mr. Richardson sold it to the Motor Transit Line and later the Pacific Electric Company bought and operated the system.

(*left*) March 13, 1924, advertisement for the Glendale and Montrose Railroad. *The Record-Ledger*.

(*below*) A.J. Richardson's impressive fleet of auto "stages" parked at the base of the Verdugo Mountains, c. 1920s.

457

FOUNDING SISTERS

Transportation

(*top*) In the 1920s and 1930s, the Richardson Transportation Co. provided auto stages to Sunland and Los Angeles. The Stage Office at the southeast corner of Foothill Boulevard and Commerce Avenue. *The Record-Ledger* (July 1, 1971).

(*left*) This 1923 advertisement encourages people to see the sights of southern California. *The Record-Ledger*.

APPENDIX I: A PHOTOGRAPHIC GALLERY

Unidentified woman next to a replica of the El Camino Real Bell, marking the route to the San Fernando Mission and the Buena Ventura Mission. The Automobile Club of Southern California promoted the restoration of the bells and markers along the King's Highway as early as 1905. By the 1920s, the motoring public could enjoy the restored historic route from San Diego to Paso Robles, c. 1928. *Courtesy of the Automobile Club of Southern California.*

FOUNDING SISTERS

```
COZY CUP INN
Garden of the Moon, Tujunga
In the Shade of the Oaks
Hours of Service
Lunch,         11:30 to 3:00 p. m.
Dinner:              5:30 to 7:30
Breakfast            6;30 to 9:30
```

Garden of the Moon

(*left*) The Garden of the Moon provided a family outdoor recreation center for dancing, food and "side shows" such as a gypsy fortuneteller and silhouette artist booths. In October, a yearly Moon Festival was held, c. 1925. *Courtesy of Catherine Blake.*

(*below*) A busy July 4th weekend at Garden of the Moon, c. 1924.

(*below*) Garden of the Moon was Valley playground at southwest corner of Commerce Avenue and Foothill Boulevard. Dancing, picnicking, and bootleg drinking were main attractions, c. 1925.

```
Garden of The Moon
Open Air
DANCING
Wednesday and Saturday Nights
Mr. and Mrs. W. A. Ross, Proprietors
8 to 12                          Good Music
```

```
GARDEN of the MOON SODA FOUNTAIN
      GEORGE M. BURGESS, Proprietor
      Home made ice cream, per qt. 50c
      Double decker cones, each,    5c
   ORDERS TAKEN FOR BULK ICE CREAM
```

460

APPENDIX I: A PHOTOGRAPHIC GALLERY

LANCASTER LAKE
Margaret and Edgar Lancaster take a boat ride on their lake,
situated at Sherman Grove and Hillrose Avenue in Sunland, c. 1926.

Lancaster Lake in Sunland was a popular spot for picnics and boating from 1925 to 1950, c. 1926.

461

FOUNDING SISTERS

JEWEL THEATRE
(Formerly Tujunga Valley Theater)

Opening Notice!

On July 8th at 8 p. m., the **JEWEL THEATRE** will be formally re-opened under new ownership and with a new policy.

A new $9000 **WURLITZER HOPE-JONES** Unified Organ will be installed and only the very best in pictures will be shown. We will have a

Gala Opening

Wednesday at 8 p. m. Continuous Show until 11:30

STRONGHEART
The Wonder Dog
IN

"White Fang"

Now playing its premier at the Criterian, Los Angeles

Also BABY PEGGY in "PEG OF THE MOUNTED,"
The International News and a Larry Semon Comedy

Going to the Movies

(*above*) The Jewel Theater had a short life. Built in 1925 and closed in 1930, it was torn down in 1931. Tujungans then had to drive ten miles to Glendale to see a movie. Homer Martin built his law office on the site in 1937.

(*left*) On October 9, 1924, the Tujunga Theater was locked up due to financial problems. By July of the following year, the theater reopened as the Jewel Theater. It remained so from 1925 through 1930.

(*opposite, bottom*) The Jewel Theater located on Sunset Boulevard (Commerce Avenue) between Michigan Avenue (Foothill Boulevard) and San Ysidro Street (Valmont). The café next to the theater was replaced with another real estate office, c. 1927.

APPENDIX I: A PHOTOGRAPHIC GALLERY

HIKERS ATTAIN SUMMIT OF MOUNT SISTER ELSIE

Starting almost at sunrise a party of young people hiked from the mouth of Haines canyon to the summit of Mount Sister Elsie last Sunday where they ate lunch and spent the afternoon in exploration of the mountain top.

The climb is a stiff one but the whole party felt that the glorious view of Southern California stretching out on all sides from the peak was more than worth the exertion.

Upon their return the young people enjoyed a delicious dinner served by Mrs. Wilmot Parcher.

Those included in the party were Mrs. Leverett Sacre, Miss Louise Sacre, Miss Edna Martin, and Miss Fan Greggory of Hollywood, and Miss Helen Franke, Miss Frances Morgan, Don Wieman and Carroll Parcher of Tujunga.

HIKING & CAMPING

(*above*) Elizabeth MacVine (*on white horse*) enjoys shooting a tin can in the air while on a camping trip to the Big Tujunga Canyon, c. 1910.

(*far left*) Article in *The Foothill Leader*, c. 1920s.

(*left*) This 1923 advertisement shows "what a civilized woman wears when she wants to get away from, it all. This blouse and knickers combo can be worn for hiking, camping and horseback riding. *The Record-Ledger.*

APPENDIX I: A PHOTOGRAPHIC GALLERY

> For I write not histories but lives: the showiest deeds do not always delineate virtue and vice, but often a trivial action, a quip or a prank will reveal more of character than the fiercest slaughters, or greatest parades, or sieges of cities.
> —*Plutarch*

CAMPING

(*left*) Motorists could escape to the desert, beach or mountains. Auto camps offered a place to set up a tent, buy provisions and enjoy the great outdoors. Advertisement for Summit Glen Auto Camp. *The Record-Ledger* (1925).

(*top*) In this 1910 photograph, Elizabeth MacVine strikes an "Annie Oakley" pose while on a camping trip with good friends, Alfred and Clara Blumfield, and children, Russ and Elizabeth, in Big Tujunga Canyon.

(*above*) Good friends the MacVines and Blumfields on a camping trip to the Big Tujunga Canyon. (*left to right*) Alfred Blumfield, Leonard MacVine, Elizabeth MacVine, George MacVine, and children, Russ and Elizabeth Blumfield. Note the jug to the right of the picnic table, c. 1910.

FOUNDING SISTERS

Big Tujunga Canyon

(*above*) Fording the Big Tujunga River en route to fun and adventure, c. 1920s.

(*left*) The newly completed bridge (more than 900 feet long and 22 feet above the stream bed) over the Big Tujunga River enabled motorists to travel to the San Fernando Valley throughout the year, c. 1922.

(*right*) Entrance to Big Tujunga Canyon. Photograph taken from Ardizzone Ranch. Note spelling of Tujunga Canyon, c. 1918.

(*below*) In 1929, the new high road was completed, thus avoiding the 23 crossings of the Big Tujunga River.

> I only went out for a walk and finally concluded to stay out till sundown, for going out, I found, was really going in.
> —*John Muir*

APPENDIX I: A PHOTOGRAPHIC GALLERY

Big Tujunga Canyon

(*top right*) Wildwood Lodge and Resort was a popular spot for picnics and dancing in the 1920s and 1930s. It became a favorite retreat during the Prohibition era. It was completely destroyed by the March 1938 flood. Once owned by the Justice family, the land was deeded to the United States Forest Service in 1973.

(*above*) A meadow of lupine flowers in Big Tujunga Canyon, c. 1930s.

> Civilization is a stream with banks. The stream is sometimes filled with blood from people killing, stealing, shouting and doing things historians usually record, while on the banks, unnoticed, people build homes, make love, raise children, sing songs, write poetry.
>
> The story of civilization is what happened on the banks. Historians are pessimists because they ignore the banks for the river. —*Will Durant*

467

APPENDIX I: A PHOTOGRAPHIC GALLERY

Big Tujunga Canyon

(*above*) Mrs. Carlson and daughters, Dorothy and Ruth (*left to right*), in the swimming hole on the Johnson family property in Big Tujunga Canyon.

(*opposite, top*) The swimming hole in Big Tujunga Canyon was a favorite spot. Edward Forster (*center*), Sylvester (*left*) and Mildred (*right*), c. 1915. *Courtesy of Jeraldine Saunders.*

(*opposite, bottomI*) Unidentified group enjoys fishing in the Big Tujunga Canyon, c. 1910.

FOUNDING SISTERS

~ Health Care ~

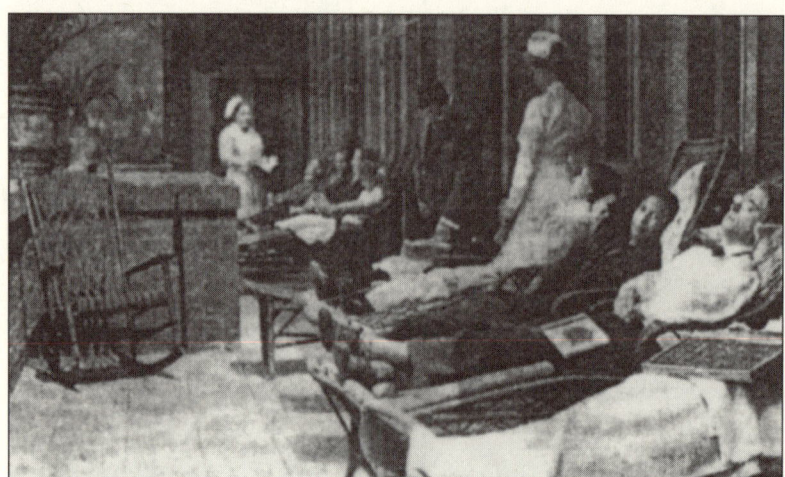

(*top*) In 1902, Barlow Sanitarium opened at Elysian Park in Los Angeles. It was for indigent patients suffering from tuberculosis and for the periodic smallpox epidemics. *Courtesy of Barlow Respiratory Hospital.*

(*above left*) Barlow patients receiving the "fresh air cure." Very few people were cured. Not until 1940 and the advent of antibiotics would a cure be found. *Courtesy of Barlow Respiratory Hospital.*

(*left*) A 1914 *Los Angeles Times* advertisement for Lydia E. Pinkham's (1819–1883) Vegetable Compound. Home remedies and a few over-the-counter preparations were all the Little Landers had in the way of health care.

470

APPENDIX I: A PHOTOGRAPHIC GALLERY

Hits Stone Wall To Avoid A Collision

DR. BAIN WRECKS OWN CAR BUT PREVENTS DAMAGE TO OTHER MACHINE

Dr. Leonard Bain of the Tujunga Emergency hospital is in bed with severe cuts and bruises on his chest and about his face and arms and his Buick touring car is badly wrecked as a consequence of a collision with a stone wall in front of Dr. Virginia Smith's residence at Monte Vista and El Centro streets last Sunday evening.

Dr. Bain was driving west on El Centro in answer to a professiooal call to Sunland when he saw another machine coming south on Monte Vista at a rapid pace. To avoid colliding with the other car the doctor deliberately swerved his machine to the left knowing that he was heading straight into a wreck against the stone wall. His purpose of preventing injury to the other machine and its occupants, however, was fully accomplished.

Dr. Naylor of Los Angeles, who happened to be at the Emergency hospital, dressed Dr. Bain's injuries.

(*far right*) Dr. Bain's car collides with Dr. Virginia Steven's wall and he goes to his own hospital. *The Record-Ledger* (1925).

(*below*) Tujunga Emergency Hospital. This stone building was located at the southeast corner of Apperson and Commerce. From the mid 1920s to the early 1970s it was the only hospital in Sunland-Tujunga.

CAMP CREEMORE
JANET KNIGHT
HOME FOR CONVALESCENTS
Conducted by Graduate Nurses

San Ysidro at Los Angeles
Sunland 1611   TUJUNGA

ROCK-DELL MOUNTAIN HOME
For Convalescents
NENA JOLIDON CROAKE
205 N. San Ysidro, Tujunga
Bet. Los Angeles and Summit Sts.
Phone Sunland 144

471

Mrs. M. C. Darwin
Graduate Nurse

Junction of West Michigan Avenue, Manzanita Drive and Hillhaven Road

We are Prepared to Care for

CONVALESCENTS, OBSTETRICAL CASES, NERVOUS CASES, MILD MENTAL CASES

Electronic Baths   Electronic Treatments

Each case under care of your own personal physician, or professional services furnished as desired

---

RANCHO HINATA BUNGALOWS

An institution for the care and successful treatment of asthma and serious nervous and chronic diseases.

Modern 3 room and bath, completely furnished separate bungalows to let. Bath, hot water heaters, electricity and phones if desired.

Pure and nutritious blood, being the basis of all health, success and happiness, Dr. Spates' treatment embodies the giving of osteopathic treatments, simple, vegetable medicines, a correct but not a starvation or faddish diet and considerable **common sense.**

Tenants may secure their nurses and have their physicians if they desire for every possible courtesy will be extended to all physicians.

For reservation of bungalows address

E. M. SPATES, M. D. D. O.
R. F. D. 11, Box 537; Phone Sunland 265, or
931 Black Bldg., L. A.; Phone 62786

OSTEOPATHIC PHYSICIAN
DR. LUCENA E. TURNER

Office, 150 Michigan Ave.   Office Phone
(Bide-a-Wee)   2044-J-4
Hours: 10-12 A. M., 2-5 P. M., and by Appointment
Women and Children   Acute and Chronic Diseases

(*above*) In 1929, Rancho Hiñata became The Palms Sanitarium, still run by Dr. Spates. *The Record-Ledger.*

Seperate Bungalows   Every Modern Convenience

Spacious Attractive Grounds

THE PALMS SANATORIUM

Corner Palm and Los Angeles, Tujunga. Phone Sunland 984

SPECIALIZING IN TREATMENT OF ASTHMA
All Cases Not Contagious Accepted

Los Angeles Office, 931 Black Bldg. Phone TUcker 2786

APPENDIX I: A PHOTOGRAPHIC GALLERY

(*top*) In the early 1930s, a portion of the Begue property became the Hotel Tujunga, a health resort located on St. Estaban Road.

(*middle*) In 1929, Rancho Hiñata became The Palms Sanitarium, still run by Dr. Spates. *The Record-Ledger.*

(*bottom*) After Dr. Spates built this wall of native stone, the State of California decided to widen Foothill Boulevard, thus putting his wall in the middle of the Boulevard.

473

FOUNDING SISTERS

HILLCREST SANITARIUM

3923 MARKRIDGE ROAD   **LA CRESCENTA**

TEL: FLORIDA 3-9963

The Hillcrest Sanitarium with its 15 buildings is situated in the foothills of the Sierra Madre Range at an elevation of 2300 feet in La Crescenta overlooking the valley of La Canada, Tujunga and Sunland.

The Sanitarium gives care and treatment to 156 geriatric patients

In 1927 the Sanitarium was designed, built and equipped for the treatment of tuberculosis and chest diseases. The United States Health Department reported this locality as the most equitable climate in the United States, being most beneficial for individuals afflicted with chest diseases.

Sufferers from asthma, hay fever, bronchitis and allied chest diseases frequently obtained complete relief after a short stay at the Sanitarium.

During the second World War the Sanitarium was operated by the Olive View Sanitarium and the County of Los Angeles operated it for specialized cases of tuberculosis.

In 1948 the Board of Directors of the Hillcrest Sanitarium abandoned the treatment of tuberculosis and dedicated it solely for the treatment of incompetent old age patients and patients with other minor nervous ailments.

Three new completely fireproof buildings are soon to be constructed to take care of the ever growing needs of the greater Los Angeles area, which will increase the capacity to 241 patients. Future plans also include the erection of a hospital within the beautiful landscaped gardens of the 40 acre tract belonging to the institution.

The Board of Directors consist of

    Dr. Chas. Coghlan, President

    Dr. M. Gecht, Vice President

    Mr. Roy Jellison, Vice President

    Mr. H. Lainck, Secretary-Treasurer

    Mrs. Jean Korton, Asst. Secretary

    Mr. E. Anderson, Director

    Mr. J. Rachal, Director

Their plans are to build this institution into a facility to care for all patients suffering from physical or nervous disorders.

Tujunga Rest Home
365 North Sunset Ave.
Sunland 563

Soma Mineral Baths

Given for Rheumatism, Neuritis, and all Diseases caused by Autointoxication.

ELECTRIC AND VIOLET RAY TREATMENTS GIVEN ALSO.

(*below*) The Hillcrest Sanitarium, located on Markridge Road between LaCrescenta and Tujunga. The high, dry air was beneficial to asthmatic and tubercular patients.

"There's A Wealth of Health in the Sunland-Tujnuga Valley"

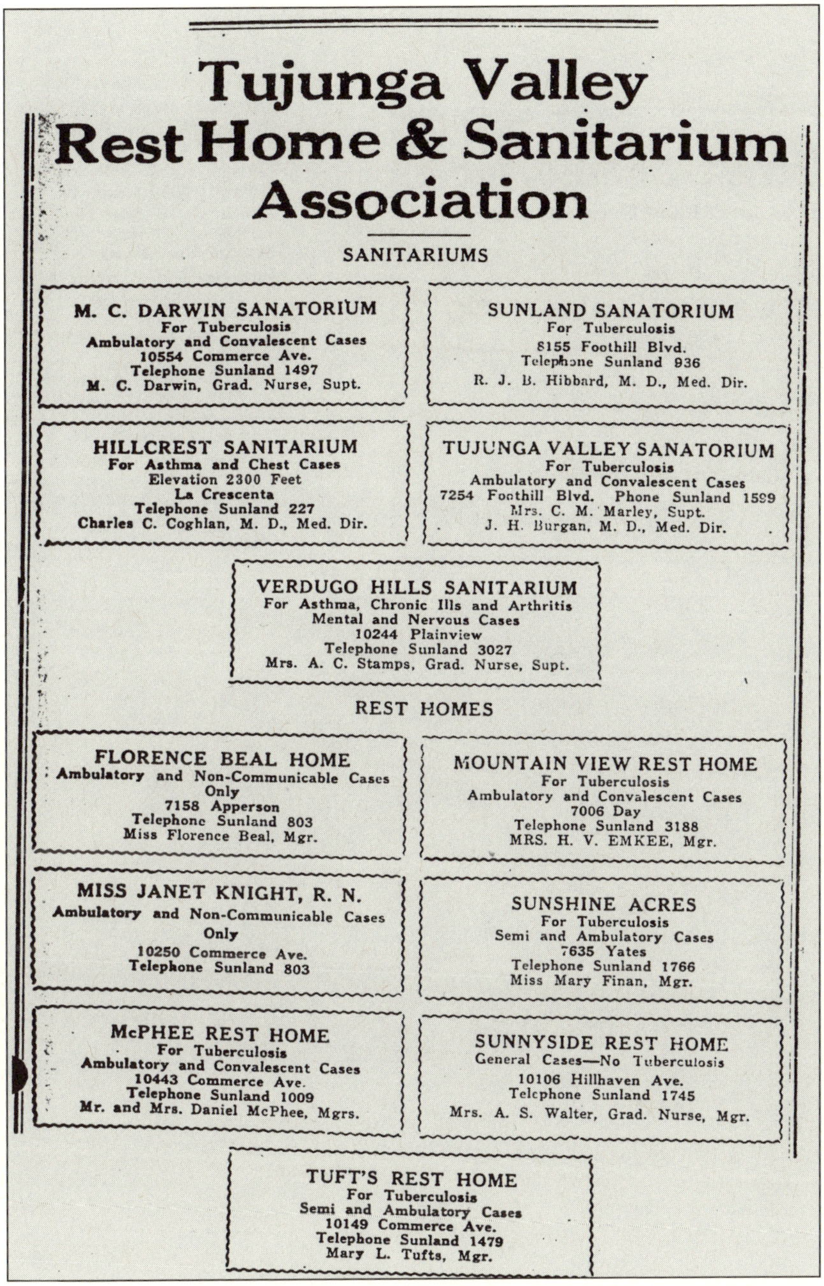

APPENDIX I: A PHOTOGRAPHIC GALLERY

Tujunga Valley Rest Home & Sanitarium Association

SANITARIUMS

M. C. DARWIN SANATORIUM
For Tuberculosis
Ambulatory and Convalescent Cases
10554 Commerce Ave.
Telephone Sunland 1497
M. C. Darwin, Grad. Nurse, Supt.

SUNLAND SANATORIUM
For Tuberculosis
8155 Foothill Blvd.
Telephone Sunland 936
R. J. B. Hibbard, M. D., Med. Dir.

HILLCREST SANITARIUM
For Asthma and Chest Cases
Elevation 2300 Feet
La Crescenta
Telephone Sunland 227
Charles C. Coghlan, M. D., Med. Dir.

TUJUNGA VALLEY SANATORIUM
For Tuberculosis
Ambulatory and Convalescent Cases
7254 Foothill Blvd. Phone Sunland 1599
Mrs. C. M. Marley, Supt.
J. H. Burgan, M. D., Med. Dir.

VERDUGO HILLS SANITARIUM
For Asthma, Chronic Ills and Arthritis
Mental and Nervous Cases
10244 Plainview
Telephone Sunland 3027
Mrs. A. C. Stamps, Grad. Nurse, Supt.

REST HOMES

FLORENCE BEAL HOME
Ambulatory and Non-Communicable Cases Only
7158 Apperson
Telephone Sunland 803
Miss Florence Beal, Mgr.

MOUNTAIN VIEW REST HOME
For Tuberculosis
Ambulatory and Convalescent Cases
7006 Day
Telephone Sunland 3188
MRS. H. V. EMKEE, Mgr.

MISS JANET KNIGHT, R. N.
Ambulatory and Non-Communicable Cases Only
10250 Commerce Ave.
Telephone Sunland 803

SUNSHINE ACRES
For Tuberculosis
Semi and Ambulatory Cases
7635 Yates
Telephone Sunland 1766
Miss Mary Finan, Mgr.

McPHEE REST HOME
For Tuberculosis
Ambulatory and Convalescent Cases
10443 Commerce Ave.
Telephone Sunland 1009
Mr. and Mrs. Daniel McPhee, Mgrs.

SUNNYSIDE REST HOME
General Cases—No Tuberculosis
10106 Hillhaven Ave.
Telephone Sunland 1745
Mrs. A. S. Walter, Grad. Nurse, Mgr.

TUFT'S REST HOME
For Tuberculosis
Semi and Ambulatory Cases
10149 Commerce Ave.
Telephone Sunland 1479
Mary L. Tufts, Mgr.

In 1934, the Tujunga Valley Sanatorium joined a host of sanitariums and rest homes in Tujunga. Tujunga Telephone Directory.

Hillcrest Sanatorium

Between LA CRESCENTA and TUJUNGA

For

TUBERCULOSIS and ASTHMATIC PATIENTS

HELIOTHERAPY---X-RAY

New, Modern Buildings

Fifty Rooms   Telephone Sunland 127

Sanitariums

Arcady Rest Home 10555 Hillhaven	1196
Beal Florence Home 7158 Apperson	803
Darwin M C Mrs 10554 Commerce	1497
Emkee Mountain View Rest Home 7006 Day	3188
Finan Mary E 7635 Yates	1766
Hillcrest Sanitarium La Crescenta	227
Knight Janet Rest Home 10250 Commerce	803
McPhee Rest Home 10443 Commerce	1009
Rockywold Rest Home 10243 Samoa	809
Sunland Sanatorium 8155 Foothill blvd	936
Sunnyside Rest Home 10106 Hillhaven	1745
Sunshine Acres Sanitarium 7635 Yates	1765
Tufts Mary L Tubercular Home 10149 Commerce	1479
Tujunga Valley Sanatorium 7254 Foothill blvd	1599
VERDUGO HILLS SANITARIUM 10244 Plainview	3027
Walter A S Mrs 10106 Hillhaven	1745

(*above*) "Mountains of Health" in Tujunga: road sign on the north side of Foothill Boulevard west of Lowell, removed in the early 1970s.

Tujunga Timeline

5 million years B.C.	Pleistocene Epoch; marine fossils deposited in Tujunga Valley.	1830	Population of Los Angeles is now 770 persons.
10,000 B.C.	Shoshonean Indians occupy the Los Angeles Basin.	1834	Secularization of missions; properties break up and are now managed by a civil administration.
435 A.D.	Tongva Indian village established at Orcas and Foothill in Lake View Terrace.	1840	Rancho Tujunga is granted to Lopez brothers.
1542	Juan R. Cabrillo expedition enters San Pedro Bay and claims for king of Spain.	1842	Francisco Lopez discovers gold under the "Oak of Golden Dreams" in Placerita Canyon, six years before John Marshall's discovery in Coloma, (northern) California.
1769	Gaspar de Portola and Father Juan Crespi expedition into San Fernando Valley.		
1769–1822	The Spanish Period; thirty ranchos granted.	1845	Lopez brothers traded Rancho Tujunga to San Fernando Mission Indian Miguel Trifuño; the battle of Cahuenga fought;
1771	Father Junipero Serra founds the San Gabriel Mission.		
1774	Juan Bautista de Anza first to make overland journey to California from Sonora.		Pío Pico becomes first governor of California.
		1848	John C. Fremont signs treaty between Americans and Californios; population of Los Angeles is now 1,300 persons.
1776	San Gabriel Mission moves to present location.		
1781	Governor Felipe de Neve and eleven families (forty-four men, women, and children) found Los Angeles (La Reiña de los Angeles).	1849	Gold discovered in northern California, beginning of the great gold rush; treaty between America and Mexico making California a U.S. territory is signed in Guadalupe, Hidalgo, Mexico.
1790	Population of Los Angeles is 139 persons.		
1797	San Fernando Mission founded by Father Fermin Lasuén.	1850	California admitted to the Union as 31st state; Los Angeles population is now 1,610 persons.
1812	Severe earthquake damages San Gabriel and San Fernando Missions.		
1822	Spanish rule of California gives way to Mexican government.	1851	United States Land Commission begins investigating ownership of

FOUNDING SISTERS

	Mexican land grants; most landowners lose property to creditors and to pay high legal fees.	1884–1886	100 towns are platted in Los Angeles County, of those, 62 disappeared.
1855	First official Los Angeles Schoolhouse built at 2nd and Spring Streets.	1885	Park Hotel established in Monte Vista (Sunland).
1857	Powerful earthquake near Fort Tejon, collapsing buildings from Los Angeles to Ventura.	1886	Elegant Monte Vista Hotel opens in Monte Vista (Sunland). United States president is Grover Cleveland.
1858	The Butterfield Overland Mail Company stage line links Los Angeles to eastern United States.	1886–1887	Railroad rate war; 120,000 people arrive in Los Angeles in one year.
1860	Los Angeles gets its first telegraph line; Abe Lincoln receives 356 votes to his opponent's 1,700 in Los Angeles for United States presidential election.	1887	Monte Vista Post Office established.
		1888	Glorietta Heights (Tujunga) platted by King, Dexter, and Gilbert.
		1889	United States president is Benjamin Harrison (1889–1893)
1861	Severe flooding in Southern California, many farms and cattle destroyed.	1890	Dr. Homer Hansen builds cabin in Big Tujunga Canyon; first Tournament of Roses parade held in Pasadena; Jane Addams and Ellen Starr start Hull House in Chicago; Settlement House Movement begins.
1862	Beginning of severe drought in Los Angeles area destroys the cattle industry.		
1863	Smallpox epidemic kills many on new Southland Indian Reservations.	1890–1920	The Progressive Era—social reform in work, politics, women's suffrage.
1865	The Civil War ends; Los Angeles now has 13,000 residents and is described as "filthy and lawless."	1891	Caroline Severance founds the Friday Morning Club as first women's club in Los Angeles; Jane Addams creates settlement house in Chicago.
1867	Pedro Ybarra files homestead claim in Big Tujunga Canyon.	1892	Alfred Adams, Sr., starts Adams Olive Cannery in Sunland; farmers and laborers form Populist Party.
1870	Ann Willden Johnson and husband Neils homestead 160 acres in Chatsworth; Emma Johnson (their eighth child) first white child born in San Fernando Valley.		
		1898	Spanish-American War.
		1900	Automobile Club of Southern California founded; population of Los Angeles is now 102,479 persons.
1876	San Fernando tunnel is completed; the Southern Pacific Railroad links San Francisco to Los Angeles; telephone is patented.	1900–1909	Immigrants arrive at Ellis Island in New York City at the rate of 100 people per hour.
1878	Clara Foltz is admitted as first woman lawyer to California Bar.	1901	Pacific Electric Railway (PE) incorporated; Angels Flight railroad in downtown Los Angeles begins. On September 6, while visiting the Pan-American Exposition in Buffalo, New York, President William McKinley assassinated by Detroit-born Leon Czolgosz, claimed to be seduced by anarchist Emma Goldman's oratorical powers.
1848	Married Women's Property Bill is introduced; first Women's Rights Convention is held.		
1882	American Red Cross is founded.		
1883	Page and Howes buy 2,200 acres of Rancho Tujunga.		
1884	Bertrand, Phillip and Franciscoa Begue buy property in Tujunga.		

478

TUJUNGA TIMELINE

1902	Vice President Theodore Roosevelt becomes president.
1903	Wright brothers achieve first powered plane flight at Kitty Hawk, North Carolina.
1904	St. Louis World's Fair; Abbot Kinney establishes the city of Venice, California, and builds elaborate canals.
1906	Earthquake and fire devastate San Francisco; Fehlhabers establish ranch on Tujunga Canyon Boulevard in Tujunga.
1907	Los Angeles voters approve a $23 million bond to build aqueduct from Owens Valley to Los Angeles; Marshall and Louise Hartranft arrive in Sunland and build Lazy Lonesome Ranch.
1907–1927	Peak period for the building of "California bungalows" in Tujunga and the Los Angeles area.
1908	The birth of the Sunland Rural Telephone Company.
1909	"In the Power of Sultan" considered the first motion picture made in Los Angeles, thriller filmed by Stella Adams and Hobart Bosworth at 8th Street and Olive Street in the yard of a Chinese laundry. United States president is Howard Taft (1909–1913).
1910	President Wilson signs proclamation establishing Mother's Day nationwide; women hold one-quarter of all jobs; progressive Republican Hiram Johnson becomes governor of California; first national air meet held at Dominguez Ranch; unionist bombs the Los Angeles Times building, 20 killed; Harry and Jean Zachau homestead 73 acres in Tujunga.
1911	Triangle Shirtwaist fire in New York; California women granted the right to vote.
1912	John Steven McGroarty's *Mission Play* opens in San Gabriel; the unsinkable R.M.S. *Titanic* sinks; Girl Scouts of America is founded; Caroline Severance first woman in California to register to vote. Harriet Quimby, first woman to fly the English Channel, buried at Valhalla Cemetery in North Hollywood, California.
1913	March—first six lots of Little Lands Colony sold (considered the anniversary of the Colony for many years). April—cornerstone at Bolton Hall laid as 209 people attend ceremony. August—Bolton Hall completed; a corner established as "Tujunga Library, the second library in San Fernando Valley." September—large forest fire above Tujunga. November—opening ceremony of Mulholland's Los Angeles Aqueduct; town of Montrose established. December—Sunland Library opens. 16th Amendment authorizes income tax. United States president is Woodrow Wilson (1913–1921).
1914	Panama Canal opens; World War I begins; Dean's Pioneer Store opens in Tujunga; Little Lands Colony Post Office opens; major flooding in Tujunga; Job Harriman establishes Llano del Rio Co-operative Colony, 45 miles from Los Angeles; Henry Ford starts first assembly line.
1915	Four hundred check dams completed in Haines Canyon; State takes over construction of Michigan Avenue (Foothill Boulevard); greater part of San Fernando Valley annexed to Los Angeles City; San Diego holds exposition; *Lusitania* torpedoed by Germans.
1915–1933	The Ridge Route through the Tehachapi Mountains is established.

479

1916	The colony's cooperative store closed; four inches of snow falls in the region in January; Cornelius Johnson kills last California grizzly bear in Big Tujunga Canyon; Margaret Sanger opens first birth control clinic in United States; Little Lands Colony becomes Tujunga.
1917	United States enters World War I; fifteen men from Tujunga go to war (all return safely); Adams Cannery in Sunland cans tomatoes and peaches for armed services; one of the coldest winters on record; Tujunga population is 1,000 people; Sunland population is 250 people.
1918	Pandemic influenza kills 500,000 Americans and 100 million worldwide; World War I ends; Hansen Heights annexed to Los Angeles; United States adopts Daylight Savings Time.
1919	President Woodrow Wilson suffers a massive stroke at White House. Wife Edith Galt Wilson and Dr. Grayson conspire to keep condition from world.
1919–1933	18th Amendment prohibits manufacture and sale of liquor.
1920	United States women win the right to vote; the *Record-Ledger* in Tujunga starts publication; population of southern California surpasses northern area of the state; population of Los Angeles is now 576,673 persons; radios arrive in America's homes.
1921	Garden of the Moon hosts the first Moon Festival; total rain for the season is 23.02 inches; bridges over Tujunga Wash constructed.
1922	First Easter sunrise service at Hollywood Bowl; six inches of rain falls in January; *The Verdugo Foothill Record Newspaper* combines with the *Crescenta Valley Ledger*; Bolton Hall sold to American Legion; outdoor dance pavilion, Twin Pines, opens in Sunland; Verdugo Hills Cemetery opens.
1923	Los Angeles Memorial Coliseum is completed; first Easter sunrise service under the Cross of San Ysidro in Tujunga; emergency hospital opens in Tujunga; Tujunga celebrates tenth anniversary; first city telephone directory of the Tujunga Valley published; Tujunga's funeral parlor opens; Jewel Theater on Commerce completed. United States President Harding dies in office.
1924	Tujunga Library moves to Valmont Street; 100-gallon still raided by Feds; population of Sunland is 1,500 people; Tujunga has 1,014 registered voters, Sunland has 491. Ex-President Wilson succumbs to illness. "The machinery is just worn out," he states before dying.
1925	Lancaster Lake in Sunland opens; Tujunga's float wins a prize in the Pasadena Rose Parade; zinnia is declared the official flower of Tujunga; Tujunga becomes a city of the sixth class on April 21; population of Los Angeles is 896,000 persons.
1926	Los Angeles Public Library opens downtown; rainfall in Tujunga is 27.37 inches; Monte Vista annexed to Los Angeles City and name changed to Sunland; Rose Parade broadcast over radio for first time; a jail is built at the rear of Bolton Hall; the area from Haines Canyon to Lowell Avenue was annexed to the City of Tujunga; the ornamental street lights on Commerce were installed; 425 tons of olives are packed by Adams Olive Cannery.
1932	Tujunga annexed to City of Los Angeles; population of Tujunga 4,500 persons.

In Gratitude

They say that there is a book inside every individual; so many people helped to coax this book out of the author that it must be many books. The late historian Viola Carlson urged me to pursue the idea of a history of the colorful lives of Tujunga's early women pioneers. Her guidance was vital in the early days of the "little project." Her premature death did not put an end to the encouragement I received from her.

I will always be indebted to the late Dr. Edwin Carpenter, who shared with me his photographs and extensive knowledge of the Verdugo Hills Cemetery. The late Dr. John Houk offered his vast experience of life on Tujunga Canyon Boulevard and his summers spent on the Fehlhaber Ranch. Our car trips together and photo-taking journeys will never be forgotten.

My sincere thanks go to Virginia Renner, Reader Services Librarian; Jennifer A. Watts, Curator of Photographs; and the knowledgeable staff at the Henry E. Huntington Library in San Marino, California; Dace Taube, Curator the Regional History Collection, Department of Special Collections, University of Southern California; and Mary W. Elings, Pictorial Archivist, The Bancroft Library, University of California, Berkeley. I am indebted to Morgan Yates for his assistance and guidance through the extensive map and photo collection of the Automobile Club of Southern California.

My deepest gratitude goes to Iberia Brogmus, Alline Merchant, and all the reference librarians at the Glendale Public Library; the staff at the Montrose Public Library; the Pasadena Public Library; the Riverside Municipal Library; Jeannine Pedersen; Catalina Island Museum Society, Inc.; the Seaver Center for Western History Research; the Natural History Museum; and Carolyn Cole, Photo Archivist at the Los Angeles Public Library. A special thank you goes to Diane Catlin of the Santa Fe Spring Public Library for providing information on the first Little Lands Colony and the Big Flood of 1916.

Some stories and photographs would have remained lost to time had not an individual gone the extra mile to locate the materials. Nick Lamerse of the *Oakland Tribune* spent months locating the photograph of Nan Chapman boarding her marriage plane. I remain indebted also to Cliff Johnson of the Angeles National Forest, Regional Collection in Arcadia, and Bill Dougherty and Lisa Gezelter of the National Archives and Records Administration—Pacific Southwest Region, for the maps and homestead information. Brian Kielbasa of Tempe, Arizona, brought the existence of the Tuna Detention Camp to my attention. He shared his extensive research on the plight of the 706 Polish refugees during World War II. They had made a brief stop in Tujunga en route to a new life in Mexico. I salute the man who understands marathon research.

On the local scene, a bouquet of thanks goes to the librarians and staff of the Sunland-Tujunga Public Library; Laurelle Geils, Director of the McGroarty Cultural Arts Center; and my friends and colleagues at Bolton Hall Museum in Tujunga who gave so generously of their time. Their professionalism will always be appreciated. Had it not been for the comprehensive assistance offered by Sue McCoy, Robert Burke, Juanita Fullford, and Louis Brousseau at Bade Mortuary in Tujunga, the project would have come to a grinding halt early on. Mark and Cindy McConnell and Kevin were most gracious, allowing me to step back in time when I visited Camp Colby, walked the grounds, and photographed the graves of Nellie and Lillian Colby.

A very special thank you goes to the one individual who answered more questions than should ever be allowed, the late Thomas Theobald (1916–2003), retired postmaster of Tujunga. Our car trips and telephone conversations made the entire book come alive. His incredible memory and propensity toward a little "inside gossip" always made for exciting research. Tom's knowledge of addresses and biographic sketches of individuals was inexhaustible. Tom's wife, Jean Zachau Theobald, was of great assistance identifying photograph contents and her keen memory of life in Tujunga in the 1920s and 1930s was invaluable.

Early Sunland resident Elizabeth Blumfield Schell shared her extensive knowledge of Sunland, the Big Tujunga Canyon, the Adams and Blumfield families, and "doodlebugs" right up to the time of publication. On-site information was obtained from La Cañada, Tujunga, and Sylmar rancher Fred Petrotta (1899–1994), whose family had land on Tujunga Canyon Boulevard across the street from the Fehlhaber and Begue's homes. Our six-hour road trip through La Cañada, Montrose, La Crescenta, Tujunga, Sylmar, and Lake View Terrace will never be forgotten. The memory of ninety-five-year-old Fred jumping out of the car in Little Tujunga Canyon to kill a rattlesnake will remain vivid. I don't believe I will ever meet a more colorful and delightful gentleman. He was a "Little Lander" in his heart all his days.

A specific expression of gratitude goes to historian and retired Verdugo Hills High School teacher Richard Thomas. He graciously provided information and the photograph of the House of Hoo-Hoo that was moved from the Panama Pacific International Exposition in San Francisco to Cupertino. His extensive knowledge of the exposition and the eventual Little Landers Clubhouse in Cupertino was a boon to the Little Landers story. Gail Hugger, Cupertino librarian, was most helpful in discovering the Monte Vista Newsletter of 1916.

Marcie Albright, Historian at the First Methodist Church in Tujunga and Pam Wollenciej, of Our Lady of Lourdes Catholic Church in Tujunga, provided church histories and members' stories.

The expertise of Julie Ward and Shirley at Sunland Print and Copy assured the quality of the photograph copies. Nick Bartrosouf at M and N Graphics in Sunland assisted in the clear reproduction of many batches of photographs.

Under the observant eye of Penni Bessenbacher, the manuscript was edited and prepared. Her enthusiasm for the "little project" never waned, and she kept me going through some difficult challenges.

Sunland artist Martine Prado provided the original maps of the Indian village locations, the design of the Tuna Detention Camp, and the homes of Tujunga's early women pioneers. We are indebted to him for a fine collection of original maps.

I am most grateful to my husband, Richard, who, for the last twelve years, endured a project that was always "almost complete." As the homemade dinners and clean house disappeared, he took over the jobs without complaint.

My greatest regret is that the people who most inspired me to write this book did not live to see its completion. Viola Carlson, Fred Petrotta, John Houk, and Tom Theobold remained my main cheering section after the death of my parents.

Most importantly, I would like to thank the relatives of the women pioneers, who so generously took the time to invite me into their homes to share their remembrances, photographs and genealogies. Their help and guidance assured that the voices of Tujunga's early pioneer women would not be lost. They made the journey a joy.

Selected Bibliography

I. Southern California

Baur, John. *The Health Seekers of Southern California*. San Marino: Huntington Library, 1959.

Bell, Horace. *Reminisces of a Ranger, or Early Times in Southern California 1881*. Los Angeles: Anderson, Ritchie & Simon, 1965.

Carpenter, Edwin H. *Early Cemeteries of the City of Los Angeles*. Los Angeles: Dawson's Book Shop, 1973.

Clealand, Robert Glass. *The Cattle on a Thousand Hills*. San Marino: Huntington Library, 1951.

Comer, Virginia L. *Los Angeles, a View from Crown Hill*. Los Angeles: Talbot Press, 1986.

Davis, Margaret Leslie. *Rivers in the Desert: William Mulholland and the Inventing of Los Angeles*. New York: HarperCollins, 1993.

Davis, Mike. *City of Quartz*. London: Verso Press, 1990.

Dumke, Glen S. *The Boom of the Eighties in Southern California*. San Marino: Huntington Library, 1991.

Engh, Michael E. *Frontier Faiths—Church, Temple and Synagogue in Los Angeles 1846–1888*. Albuquerque: University of New Mexico Press, 1992.

Fogelson, Robert M. *Fragmented Metropolis: Los Angeles, 1850–1930*. Cambridge: Harvard University Press, 1967.

McGroarty, John Steven. *California of the South: A History*. Chicago, Los Angeles: S.J. Clark, 1931.

McWilliams, Carey. *Southern California: An Island on the Land, 1946*. Santa Barbara: Peregrine Smith, 1973.

Nadeau, Remi. *City-Makers: The Story of Southern California's First Boom, 1868–1976*. Los Angeles: Trans-Anglo Books, 1965.

———. *The Water Seekers—Revised Edition*. Santa Barbara: Crest Publishers, 1997.

Newmark, Harris. *Sixty Years in Southern California, 1853–1913 . . . The Reminiscences of Harris Newmark*. Boston: Houghton Mifflin, 1916.

Nordhoff, Charles. *California: For Health, Pleasure, and Residence a Book for Travelers and Settlers*. New York: Harper & Brothers, Publishers, 1875.

O'Flaherty, Joseph. *An End and a Beginning: The South Coast and Los Angeles, 1850–1887*. New York: Exposition Press, 1972.

Pitt, Leonard, and Dale Pitt. *Los Angeles A to Z—An Encyclopedia to The City and County*. Berkeley: University of California Press, 1997.

Rasmussen, Cecilia. *LA Unconventional. The Men and Women Who did LA Their Way*. Los Angeles: Los Angeles Times Publishing, 1998.

Reisner, Marc. *A Dangerous Place—California's Unsettling Fate*. New York: Pantheon Books, 2003.

———. *Cadillac Desert—The American West and Its Disappearing Water*. New York: Viking Penguin, Inc., 1986.

Robinson, W. W. *Los Angeles*: Title Insurance and Trust, 1935.

Rolle, Andrew. *California, A History* (Revised and Expanded Fifth Edition). Wheeling, Illinois: Harlan Davidson, Inc., 1998.

Saunders, Charles Francis. *The Southern Sierras of California*. Boston: Houghton Mifflin Co., 1923.

Starr, Kevin. *Americans and the California Dream 1850–1915*. New York: Oxford University Press, 1973.

———. *Inventing the Dream—California Through the Progressive Era*. New York: Oxford University Press, 1985.

Sullivan, Noelle. *It Happened In Southern California*. Helena, Mont.: Falcon Publishing Co., Inc., 1996.

Thornton, Gerald F. *The Los Angeles Almanac 2001*. Montebello, Calif.: Given Place Publishing Co., 2001.

VanDyke, Theodore S. *Millionaires of a Day: An Inside History of the Great Southern Boom*. New York: Howard and Hulbert, 1890.

Woolsey, Ronald C. *Migrants West—Toward the Southern California Frontier*. Sebastopol, Calif.: Grizzly Bear Publishing Company, 1996.

Workman, Boyle. *The City That Grew, As Told to Caroline Walker, 1840–1936*. Los Angeles: Southland Publishing, 1935.

Wrobel, David M. *Promised Lands—Promotion, Memory, and the Creation of the American West*. Lawrence: University Press of Kansas, 2002.

II. Local History

Hatch, Mabel. *The Green Verdugo Hills—A Chronicle of Sunland-Tujunga and How It Grew*. Tujunga, Calif.: The Record-Ledger Press, 1952.

Jorgensen, Lawrence C. *The San Fernando Valley—Past and Present*. Los Angeles: Pacific Rim Research, 1982.

Leadabrand, Russ. *A Guidebook to the San Gabriel Mountains of California* (Revised Edition). Los Angeles: Ward Ritchie Press, 1970.

Lombard, Sarah R. *Rancho Tujunga—A History of Sunland/Tujunga, California*. Burbank: The Bridge Publishing, 1990.

Oberbeck, Grace J. *History of Crescenta—La Cañada Valleys—a story of beginnings put into writing*. Montrose, Calif.: The Ledger, 1938.

Pauley, Kenneth, ed. *Rancho Days in Southern California—an Anthology with New Perspectives*, "Rancho Tujunga, a Mexican Land Grant of 1840" by Viola Carlson, pp. 63–78. Studio City, Calif.: Westerners, Los Angeles Corral, 1997.

Pozzo, Mary Lou. *Hollywood Comes to Sunland-Tujunga 1920–1995*. Tujunga, Calif.: Bolton Hall Museum, 1995.

Robinson, John W. *The San Gabriels—The Mountain Country from Soledad Canyon to Lytle Creek*. Arcadia, Calif.: Big Santa Anita Historical Society, 1991.

Robinson, W.W. *The Story of the San Fernando Valley*. Los Angeles: Title Insurance and Trust Company, 1961.

III. The Utopian Experience

Anderson, Henry S. "The Little Landers' Land Colonies: A Unique Agricultural Experiment in California." *Agricultural History* 5, no. 4 (October 1931): 139–150.

Carey, John, ed. *The Faber Book of Utopias*. London: Faber and Faber Limited, 1999.

Chu, Henry. "Instead of Utopia, It Left a Lot of Lots to Be Desired." *Los Angeles Times* (January 8, 1996), pp. B1, B6.

Gilman, Charlotte Perkins. *Herland: A Lost Feminist Utopian Novel*. New York: Pantheon, 1915, Revised Edition, 1979.

Greenstein, Paul, Nigly Lennon, and Lionel Rolfe. *Bread and Hyacinths: The Rise and Fall of Utopian Los Angeles*. Los Angeles: California Classic Books, 1992.

Hall, Bolton. *A Little Land and a Living*. New York: The Arcadia Press, 1908.

———. *Life and Love and Peace*. New York: The Arcadia Press, 1908.

Hawthorne, Nathaniel. *The Blithedale Romance* (Revised Edition). New York: Norton Company, 1978.

Hine, Robert V., *California Utopian Colonies*. San Marino: Huntington Library, 1953.

Klimko, Frank. "Utopia in San Ysidro—Little Lands Colony, Born in 1909, Washed Away in 1916." *San Diego Union Tribune* (February 10, 1997), p. B1.

Lee, Lawrence B. "Little Landers Colony of San Ysidro." *Journal of San Diego History* 21 (1975), pp. 26–51.

Polton, Josiah. "Stories of the Little Landers." *Little Farms Magazine* 1 (October 1911): 6, 22.

Pourade, Richard F. *Gold In the Sun*, The History of San Diego Series, Vol. 5. San Diego: Union-Tribune Publishing Company, 1965.

Smythe, William E. *City Homes on Country Lanes*. New York: The MacMillan Co., 1921.

———. *The Conquest of Arid America* (Revised Edition). Seattle: University of Washington Press, 1969.

IV. Women's Studies

Armitage, Susan, and Elizabeth Jamison, eds. *The Women's West*. Norman: University of Oklahoma Press, 1987.

Beeton, Beverly. *Women Vote in the West: The Woman Suffrage Movement, 1869–1896*. New York: Garland Publishing, 1986.

Blair, Karen. *The Clubwoman as Feminist: True Womanhood Redefined, 1868–1914*. New York: Holmes and Meir, 1980.

Brown, Dee. *The Gentle Tamers: Women of the Old West*. Lincoln: University of Nebraska Press, 1958.

Butruille, Susan G. *Women's Voices from the Western Front*. Boise, Idaho: Tamarack Books Inc., 1995.

Bouvier, Virginia M. *Women and the Conquest of California 1542–1840*. Tucson: The University of Arizona Press, 2001.

Collins, Gail. *America's Women—400 Years of Dolls, Drudges, Helpmates and Heroines*. New York: William Morrow, 2003.

Cott, Nancy F., ed. *No Small Courage—a History of Women in the United States*. New York: Oxford University Press, 2000.

Dubois, Ellen, and Karen Kearns. *Votes for Women: A 75th Anniversary Album*. San Marino: Huntington Library, 1995.

Faber, Doris. *Petticoat Politics: How American Women Won the Right to Vote*. New York: Lathrop, Lee & Shepard Co., 1967.

Fischer, Christine. *Let Them Speak for Themselves: Women in the American West 1849–1900*. Hamden, Conn.: Shoe String Press, 1977.

Garbutt, Mary Alderman. *Victories of Four Decades, 1883–1924*. Los Angeles: Women's Christian Temperance Union of Southern California, 1924.

Holmes, Kenneth. *Covered Wagon Women: Diaries and Letters from the Western Trails, 1840–1890*. Glendale: Arthur H. Clark, 1988, vols. 1–8.

Hurtado, Albert L. *Intimate Frontiers: Sex, Gender and Culture in Old California*. Albuquerque: University of New Mexico Press, 1999.

Jensen, Joan M., and Gloria Ricci Lothrop. *California Women: A History*. San Francisco: Boyd and Fraser Publishing, 1987.

Levy, Jo Ann. *Unsettling the West—Elizabeth Farnham and Georgiana Bruce Kirby in Frontier California*. Berkeley: Hayday Books, 2004.

———. *They Saw the Elephant—Women in the California Gold Rush*. Norman: University of Oklahoma Press, 1992.

Lunardino, Christine. *What Every American Should Know About Women's History—200 Events That Shaped Our Destiny*. Hallbrook, Mass.: Bob Adams, Inc., 1994.

Luchetti, Cathy, and Carol Olwell. *Women of the West*. St. George, Utah: Antelope Island Press, 1982.

Lystra, Karen. *Searching the Heart—Women, Men, and Romantic Love in Nineteenth Century America*. New York: Oxford University Press, 1989.

Maggio, Rosalie. *The New Beacon Book of Quotations by Women*. Boston: Beacon Press, 1996.

SELECTED BIBLIOGRAPHY

Miedzian, Myriam. *Generations—A Century of Women Speak About Their Lives.* New York: Atlantic Monthly Press, 1997.

Moynihan, Ruth, and Susan Armitage. *So Much To Be Done—Women Settlers on the Mining and Ranching Frontier.* Lincoln: University of Nebraska Press, 1990.

Myers, Sandra L. *Westering Women and the Frontier Experience, 1800–1915.* Albuquerque: University of New Mexico Press, 1982.

Niederman, Sharon. *A Quilt of Words: Women's Diaries, Letters and Original Accounts of Life in the Southwest, 1860–1960.* Colorado: Johnson Books, 1988.

Nunis, Doyce, ed. *Women in the Life of Southern California—An Anthology.* Los Angeles: Historical Society of Southern California, 1966.

Rassmussen, Valija, and J. Diane Cirksena. *Women in the Progressive Period—Social Reconstruction II.* St. Paul, Minnesota: Upper Midwest Women's History Center, 1997.

Ross, Pat. *The Kinship of Women—A Celebration of Enduring Friendship.* Kansas City, Missouri: Andrews and McMiel, 1997.

Rothman, Sheila M. *Women's Proper Place.* New York: Basic Books, 1978.

Rowbotham, Sheila. *A Century of Women—the History of Women in Britain and the United States.* New York: Viking-Penguin, 1997.

Seagraves, Anne. *Daughters of the West.* Hayden, Idaho: Wesanne Publications, 1996.

———. *High-Spirited Women of the West.* Hayden, Idaho: Wesanne Publications, 1992.

Tinling, Marion. *With Women's Eyes—Visitors To The New World 1775–1918.* Norman: University of Oklahoma Press, 1993.

Trager, James. *A Women's Chronology—A Year-by-Year Record, from Prehistory to Present.* New York: Henry Holt and Company, 1994.

Turkington, Carol. *The Quotable Woman.* Philadelphia: Running Press Book Publishers, 1991.

Wertheimer, Barbara M. *We Were There: The Story of Working Women in America.* New York: Pantheon Books, 1977.

V. Native Americans

Forbes, Jack D. *Native Americans of California and Nevada.* Healdsburg, Calif.: Naturegraph Publishers, 1969.

Harrington, John Peabody. *California Indian Field Notes.* Los Angeles: University of California Los Angeles, Anthropology Department, 1966.

Heizer, Robert F. *The Indians of Los Angeles County: Hugo Reid's Letters of 1852.* Los Angeles: Southwest Museum, 1968.

Heizer, R. F., and M. A. Whipple, eds. *The California Indians: A Source Book.* Berkeley: University of California Press, 1971.

Hitt, Marlene. *Earliest Inhabitants of Rancho Tujunga.* Tujunga, Calif.: Marlene Hitt, 1997.

Johnson, Bernice Eastman. *California Gabrielino Indians.* Los Angeles: Southwest Museum, 1964.

Kroeber, A.L. *Handbook of the Indians of California* (Revised Edition). New York: Dover Publications, 1976.

Mathes, Valerie Sherer. *Helen Hunt Jackson and Her Indian Reform Legacy.* Norman: University of Oklahoma, 1997.

McCowley, William. *First Angelinos—Gabrielino Indians.* Novato, Calif.: Ballina Press, 1996.

Miller, Bruce. *The Gabrielinos.* Los Osos, Calif.: Sand River Press, 1991.

Walker, Edwin F. "The Dig at Big Tujunga Wash." Los Angeles: Southwest Museum, *The Master Key Magazine* 29, no. 6 (November 1945).

———. *Five Prehistoric Archeological Sites in Los Angeles County California.* Los Angeles: Southwest Museum, 1951.

VI. Ethnic Los Angeles

Acuna, Rodolfo. *Occupied America—A History of Chicanos,* 2nd Edition. New York: Harper and Row Publishing, 1982.

Allen, James P., and Eugene Turner. *The Ethnic Quilt: Population Diversity in Southern California.* Northridge, Calif.: The Center for Geographic Studies, 1997.

Armenian Assembly of America. *The Armenian Community of California: The First Hundred Years.* Los Angeles: Armenian Assembly Resource Center, 1982.

Balderrama, Francisco E., and Raymond Rodriguez. *Decade of Betrayal—Mexican Repatriation in the 1930s.* Albuquerque: University of New Mexico Press, 1995.

Bond, Max. *The Negro in Los Angeles.* San Francisco: R and E Research Associates, 1972.

Bunch, Lonnie. *Black Angelenos: The Afro-American in Los Angeles, 1850–1950.* Los Angeles: California Afro-American Museum Foundation, 1988.

Camarillo, Alberto. *Chicanos in a Changing Society: From Mexican Pueblos to American Barrios in Santa Barbara and Southern California, 1848–1930.* Cambridge: Howard University Press, 1979.

Chinn, Thomas W., H. Mark Lai, and Phillip P. Choy. *A History of the Chinese in California.* San Francisco: Chinese Historical Society of America, 1969.

Condit, Ira M. *The Chinaman as We See Him and Fifty Years of Work for Him.* Chicago: Fleming H. Revell, 1900.

Daniels, Roger. *The Politics of Prejudice: The Anti-Japanese Movement in California and the Struggle for Japanese Exclusion.* Berkeley: University of California Press, 1962.

———. *Coming to America—A History of Immigration and Ethnicity in American Life.* New York: Harpers Perennial, 2nd Edition, 1990.

DeGraf, Lawrence B. "Race, Sex and Regions: Black Women in the American West, 1850–1920." *Pacific Historical Review* (May 1980).

DeGraf, Lawrence B., Kevin Mulroy, and Quintard, Taylor, eds. *Seeking El Dorado—African-Americans in California.* Los Angeles: Autry Museum of Western Heritage, 2001.

DelCastillo, Richard G. *The Los Angeles Barrio, 1850 1890: A Social History.* Berkeley: University of California Press, 1979.

Deverell, William. *Whitewashed Adobe—The Rise of los Angeles and the Remaking of its Mexican Past.* Berkeley: University of California Press, 2004.

Flamming, Douglas. "African-Americans and the Politics of Race in Progressive-Era Los Angeles," *California Progressivism Revisited.* Berkeley: University of California Press, 1994.

Hayden, Delores. "Biddy Mason's Los Angeles." *California History* (Fall 1989): 86–99.

Hosokawa, Bill. *Nisei: The Quiet Americans.* New York: William Morrow and Company, Inc., 1969.

Ichioka, Yuji. *The Issei: The World of the First Generation Japanese Immigrants, 1885–1924.* New York: Free Press, 1988.

Kashima, Tetsuden. *Judgment Without Trial: Japanese American Imprisonment During World War II.* Seattle: University of Washington Press, 2003.

Katz, William L. *Black Women of the Old West.* New York: Atheneum Publishers, 1995.

Keneally, Thomas. *The Great Shame—and the Triumph of the Irish in the English-Speaking World.* New York: Anchor Books—Random House, Inc., 1998.

Lawson, Inada. *Only What We Carry—The Japanese American Internment Experience.* San Francisco: California Historical Society of America, 2000.

Lockyear, William R. "The Celestials and the Angels: A Study of the Anti-Chinese Movement in Los Angeles to 1882." *Historical Society of Southern California Quarterly* 42 (September 1960): 245.

Lothrop, Gloria Ricci. *Los Angeles Profiles—A Tribute to the Ethnic Diversity of Los Angeles.* Los Angeles: The Historical Society of Southern California, 1994.

Lothrop, Gloria R., and Chi Siamo. *The Italians of Los Angeles.* Pasadena: Tabula Rasa Press, 1981.

Monroy, Douglas. *Rebirth—Mexican Los Angeles From the Great Migration to the Great Depression.* Berkeley: University of California Press, 1999.

Pearlstone, Zena. *Ethnic—L.A.* Beverly Hills, Calif.: Hillcrest Press, 1990.

Pitt, Leonard. *The Decline of the Californios: A Social History of the Spanish-Speaking Californians, 1846–1890* (Revised Edition). Berkeley: University of California Press, 1998.

Rios-Bustamonte, Antonio. *An Illustrated History of Mexican Los Angeles, 1781–1985.* Los Angeles: Chicano Studies Research Center University of California, 1986.

Sandberg, Neil C. *Jewish Life in Los Angeles: A Window to Tomorrow.* Lanham, Maryland: University Press of America, 1986.

Sandmeyer, Elmer C. *The Anti-Chinese Movement in California.* Urbana, Illinois: University of Illinois, 1973.

See, Lisa. *On Gold Mountain—The One-Hundred-Year Odyssey of My Chinese-American Family.* New York: First Vintage Books, 1995.

Vorspan, Max, and Lloyd P. Gartner. *History of the Jews in Los Angeles.* San Marino: Huntington Library, 1970.

Waldinger, Roger, and Mehdi Bozormehr, eds. *Ethnic Los Angeles.* New York: Russell Sage Foundation, 1996.

Yoo, David K. *Growing Up Nisei: Race, Generation and Culture Among Japanese Americans of California, 1924–1949.* Urbana: University of Illinois Press, 2000.

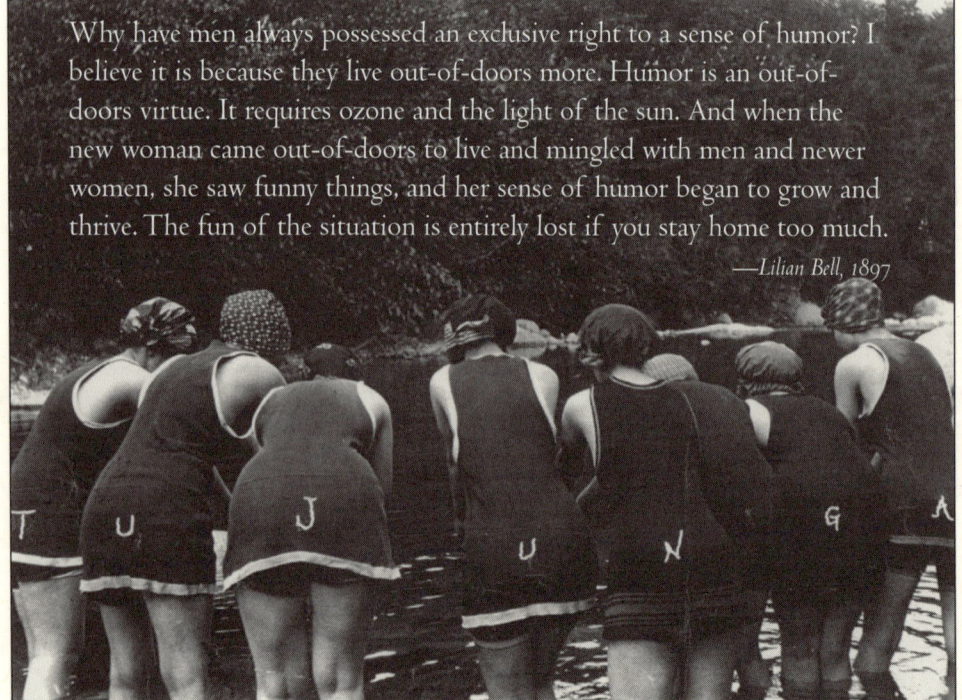

A group of Tujunga ladies frolic in the Big Tujunga Canyon, c. 1920s.

Index

Abe, Mabel, 139, 140. *See also* Tsumori, Mabel; Tuna Canyon Detention Center
Acton, Calif., 198
Adam, Anna, 144–146
Adam, George, 144–146
Adams, Elmer, 319
Adams Olive Cannery, 114, 442
African Americans: Jim Crow laws, 132; Little Landers Colony restrictions, 133. *See also* Ku Klux Klan
Aiken, Dorothy, 55, 444
A.J. Richardson Motor Transit, 457
Al Reeds Sandwich Shop, 24, 25
Alexander, David W., 38
Alien Land Laws. *See* Japanese, Alien Land Laws
Alligator Farms, 44
Alvarado, Juan B., 38
American Legion Post #250, Bolton Hall purchase of, 22; turkey shoot, 151; Legion Hall, 351; Wornum funeral, 408, 412
American Water Company, 357, 358. *See also* Haines Canyon Water Co.; Osgood, Myra
Anaheim, 377, 379
Ardizone family, 114, 286
Argay, Joe, 201–203, 205
Arroyo Seco, 198, 247
Arthritis, 145, 365
Auto Camping, 465

Ashby, Fredrick, 173–178, 323
Asthma, 107, 110n. 6–9, 261, 295, 296, 319, 320, 338, 360, 361, 472, 474–476. *See also* Sunair Home
Australia, 111, 112, 117n. 1, 3
Automobile Club of Southern California, 32, 456, 459

"Back to soil" movement, 61
Bades Mortuary, 9, 394, 482. *See also* White, Flora
Bailey, Gilbert, 210
Bakersfield, 347, 348, 400
Balloon (gas), 198–201. *See also* Colby, Lillian; Colby, Nellie
Bancroft, Hubert Howe, 95, 129
Barclay, Anna (Kirby), 33, 45, 53
Barclay, Frank, 32, 45. *See also* Monte Vista Hotel
Barclay, LuLu, 319
Barlow Sanitorium, 107, 470. *See also* Tuberculosis
Baum, Frank L., 59
Begue, Franciscoa, 148–153, 286, 319
Begue, Philip, 113, 114, 153, 286, 319, 357
Begue's Barbeque, 156, 157
Bell, Horace, 94, 103n. 5
Bella Union Hotel, 39
Bellamy, Edward, 61
Bellamy, Francis, 60
Benton, Arthur B., 241n. 8
Big Tujunga Canyon, 197–199,

243–247; water rights in, 68–69; Fern Caves, 123; road to, 466; fishing at, 468, 469
Birds Acres, 263, 265, 280. *See also* Hatch, Mabel; Linaberry, Cora Belle
Blake, Catherine, 162–168, 170
Blake, Ida May, 164, 168
Blake, Pat, 162–164, 167–169, 444
Blanchard Canyon, 68, 149, 357
Blarney Castle, 382, 384–388. *See also* Virginia Smith
Bloomfield, Ed, 53
Blue Gum Canyon, 68, 69
Blumfield, Clara and Alfred, 465, 482. *See also* Schell, Elizabeth (Blumfield)
Boas, Franz, 44, 401, 402n. 10
Bobcats, 319
Boesen, Victor, 107, 110n. 6
Bolton, Alice Carr, 172, 173–177
Bolton Hall (building), as clubhouse, 19, 101; bell of, 22–23, 124, 125n. 6; horse trough of, 22; laying cornerstone of, 70, 209, 263, 425–426; health services at, 110n. 7; City Hall, 339; ghosts of, 391; Dedication Ball of, 188–189, 286
"Bonnie Brae," 288–290. *See also* Livingston, Hilda; Livingston, James
Boston University School of Medicine, 383, 385n. 4–6. *See also* Smith, Dr. Virginia

487

Boulevard Christian Church, 288. *See also* Livingston, James
Bramble Funeral Home, 391, 393, 394
Brunke, Ray, 271–272, 275
Bryarly, Mary, 38
Bryarly, Wake, 38
Bryson, Carl, 179, 180n. 4, 181–182
Bryson, Laura, 179, 180, 183. *See also* Rosie the Riveter
Buck, Arthur, 186n. 2
Buck, Edna Belle, 185–189
Buck, George, 185–189, 190, 191, 444
Buck, Leslie, 190, 327
Burbank, 333, 334, 415
Bureau of Indian Affairs, 303. *See also* McGroarty, John S.
Burnam, Daniel H., 59

Cabrillo, Juan, 127
Cabrini, Mother, 55
California, island of, 126; name origin, 127; seal of, 130
California for Health, Pleasure and Residence, 40. *See also* Nordhoff, Charles
California Forestry Board, 63, 121
California Fruit Growers Exchange, 54. *See also* Sunkist
California Home Extension Association, 52. *See also* Hartranft, Marshall V.
Californios, 31, 32
Camp Colby, 482
Camp Creemore, 16–17, 471
Cañedo, Rafaela, 38
Cape Horn, 148, 150
Carlson, Mel, 33
Carlson, Viola, 31, 33, 54, 56, 293, 306n. 9, 410n. 2, 4, 481
Carney, Doc., 211, 321
Carr, Harry, 44
Carry Act (1894), 62. *See also* Irrigation
Castle Hi–Yan–Ka, 371–374. *See also* Phillips, Mary
Catalina Island. *See* Santa Catalina Island
Cattle on a Thousand Hills. *See* Cleland, Robert Glass

Ceferatt, Gilbert, 140
Celis, Don Eulogio de, 130
Cereus, Night Blooming, 229
Chapman, Nan Mae, 192–194, 481
Check Dams, 112
Chilao Flats, 129, 151. *See also* San Gabriel Mountains
Chinese, census of, 127; Massacre (Los Angeles, 1871), 128; occupations, 128; laundry (Tujunga), 134
Church Federation, 400. *See also* Rev. William Wieman, United Methodist Church
City Home and Country Lanes, 73. *See also* William E. Smythe
Civil Conservation Corps (CCC): La Tuna Canyon, 138, 139; Big Tujunga Canyon, 249–250; Haines Canyon, 344
Civil War, 40, 66, 333
Clark, Tom, 202
Cleland, Robert Glass, 32, 56, 117n. 2
Cobery, Art, 345
Colby, Delos, 197, 199, 200
Colby, Lillian, 196, 197, 201–202, 206. *See also* Balloon (gas)
Colby, Nellie, 196, 200, 201
Coldwater Canyon, 197. *See also* Colby, Delos
College of Osteopathic Physicians and Surgeons (Los Angeles), 383. *See also* Virginia Smith
Colonel Harper's Middle Ranch, 33, 55
Colonial Dance Club, 393
Colorado River, 111
Conquest of Arid America, 63. *See also* William E. Smythe
Coronet Magazine, 107. *See also* Victor Boesen
Corrigan, Cora, 56, 57, 181
"coughing pilgrims," 40
Cox, John, 39
Coyotes, 111, 286, 319, 408
Crescenta Valley Ledger of Montrose (1922), 35
Crescenta Valley Mining Company, 149
Crescenta Valley Historical Society, 345

Cross of San Ysidro, 240, 241, 301. *See also* Gilbert, Zoe
Cupertino Colony. *See* Little Landers Colony—Cupertino

Daly, Marcus, 296, 306n. 6. *See also* McGroarty, John S.
Dark Canyon, 247
Davidson, Arnold, 367
Darrow, Clarence, 59, 247
DaSilva, Ida May (Blake), 164, 170
De La Ossa, Rita, 38
DeMille, Cecil B., 33, 56n. 15
Dean, Charles, 213
Dean, Darius, 208
Dean, Lydia May, 209–214, 320–321, 348
Debs, Eugene V., 60, 90n. 2
Desert Ice Box, 415. *See also* Zachau, Jean
"Ding Dong Dinky" car, 456. *See also* Pacific Electric Interurban Railway
Disney, Walt, 59, 60, 334
Dominguez, Juan Jose, 31. *See also* Rancho San Pedro
Drought of 1887, 61
Drought of 1890, 61
Dundee (ghost towns), 43

E. Campus Vitus, 37
Eagle Rock, 34, 111, 440. *See also* Wieman, Alma
Earthquake faults, 123
Earthquakes, Fort Tejon (1857), 123; Santa Barbara (1925), 123–124; Long Beach (1933), 124
Easter Sunrise Service, 240, 241
Eastern Star (Chapter 445), 145, 338, 392, 293
Eby, Mr., 191
El Camino Real bell, 38, 459
El Cajon, 66
El Centro, 288
El Descanso Ranch, 149, 151, 152. *See also* Begue, Franciscoa
Elfin Woods, 351. *See also* Morgan, Wallace
Ellenberg, Elsie, 3, 129–130

INDEX

Ellenberg, Frances, 3, 129–130
Elysian Park (Los Angeles), 470
Encino (Village of), 93, 103n. 1
"Escrow Indians." See Real Estate
Eucalyptus trees, 112, 117n. 1, 3, 4, 118, 282
Eugenics, 44, 401, 402n. 10. See also Wieman, Alma
Exposition Park (Los Angeles), 9, 145

Fages, Pedro, 31
Falvey, Father, 216, 305, 315
Fehlhaber, Helena, 215–220, 226, 286
Fehlhaber, Herman, 113, 218, 221, 222, 226, 286
Fehlhaber–Houk Park, 218, 219n. 14, 230, 231
Feliz, Martin, 33, 95
Fern Caves, 123, 244, 251. See also Big Tujunga Canyon; Hansen, Marie
Fern, Maidenhair. See Fern Caves
Fernandeño, 92–103, 128–131
Fire Station, 342
Fisher, Gotlieb, 124, 288
Fitzgerald Ranch (Seven Hills), 116, 286, 290, 292
Flint, Sen. Frank P., 247, 297
Flood of 1914 (Tujunga), 124. See also Dean, Lydia M.
Flood of 1916 (San Ysidro), 71–73. See also Hatfield, Charles
Flood of 1934 (New Year's Eve), 217, 219n. 11, 250, 339, 340, 341, 345
Flood of 1938 (March), 218, 250, 253, 255
Flora Morgan Trail, 338, 436, 437
Flu epidemic of 1918 (Spanish), 86, 480
Forster Brothers (Ed, Jake, Joseph), 286, 302
Free, Mabel, 213, 214
Free Methodist Church (Sunland), 409. See also Wornum, Parson James; Wornum, Jennie
Frish, Marie, 232–236

Gabriclinos. See Native Americans, Tongva Indians
Garden of Eden, 111
Garden of the Moon, 323, 460

"Gente de Razon," 31, 51n. 4
German–American Bund, 136
Geyer, Anita Peet, 391–392, 393n. 3. See also White, Flora
Ghosts. See Mark White
Ghost Towns (Dundee, Joyful, Ivanhoe, Lordsburg, Ramona, Raymond), 43
Gilbert, Zoe, 105, 237, 242, 323. See also Cross of San Ysidro
"Gilded Age," 60
Gilmour, Florence, 124
Gish, Rossi, 175
Glassell, Andrew, 31, 39
Glendale, 209, 333, 352, 360, 363, 391
Glendale High School, 286, 351
Glendale–Montrose Railway, 14–15, 52, 457
Glendale Sanatorium, 352
Glendale Suburban Electric System. See Glendale–Montrose Railway
Glenwood Mission Inn, 297, 298
Glorietta Heights (Tujunga), 54, 80, 286
Glorietta School, 153, 340
Goats, 86, 380; San Ysidro, 71; kids, 177; Nubian, 213. See also Kraft, Emma
Gold, 36–37
Goldman, Emma, 66, 68n. 28, 91
Gompers, Samuel, 60
Grapes (Tokay, Black Prince, Malaga, Zinfindel, Cornishon), 150, 215, 216, 228
Grant, Ulysses S., 70
Greeley, Horace: Greeley Street, 90n. 11–12, 173; Temperance Colony (Co.), 61
Greenfield, Grace, 319, 326. See also Maygrove, Galdys
Green Verdugo Hill, a Chronicle of Sunland–Tujunga, 261. See also Hatch, Mabel; Morgan, Wallace

Haines Canyon, 68–69, 102, 148–149, 211, 286, 357
Haines Canyon Water Company, 124, 357–358
Hall, Bolton (author), 58, 60–61, 90n. 8, 173

Hansen Dam, 250, 256, 257
Hansen Heights (Shadow Hills), 248
Hansen, Homer, 243–253
Hansen, Marie 243–259
Hansen marriage, 243, 251
Hansen Ranch Lodge, 248–249, 252, 467
"Happy Books," 295, 306n. 3. See also McGroarty, Ida
Harriman, Job, 54, 66, 68, 297
Harris, George W., 24, 59, 75–76, 90, 91n. 42, 385n. 3, 410
"handkerchief farming," 75
Hartley, Pearl Parker (Hayward), 86, 91n. 42
Hartranft, Hetty, 56n. 38
Hartranft, Marshall V., 52, 54, 63, 69, 70, 75–76, 191. See also Lazy Lonesome Ranch, Western Empire Home Extension Plan
Harvest Home Festival, 114
Hatch, Henry, 261–265, 267
Hatch, Hiram, 191, 265, 267
Hatch, Mabel, 103n. 17, 105, 113, 120, 260–267, 410n. 10
Hatfield, Charles M., 70, 71–73, 91n. 35–37
Hathaway Home for Children, 56n. 15. See also Paradise Ranch
Hayrides, 319
Hayes, John R., 68. See also Progressive Movement
Hayward Heath Colony, 70, 84–86, 91n. 31, 40–42
Health–climate, 107–109
Hellman Bank (Los Angeles), 323
Hillcrest Sanitarium, 474–476
Hills of Peace Cemetery. See Harris, George; Hatch, Mabel; Verdugo Hills Cemetery; Wornum, Pastor James; Wornum, Jennis
Hiking, 205, 464
Hindenborg Park, 136
Hines, Robert V., 90, 91n. 50. See also Utopianism
History of San Diego, 65, 91n. 23. See also Smythe, William E.
Holiday Lake, 258. See also Hansen Dam

489

Homesites (women's), 436, 437–438
Hoof and Mouth Disease, 107
Hoover, Leon, 31, 38
Hoover, Vincent, 38
"Hope of the Little Lands" Tablet, 82, 90
Horse Thief Trail, 149–150, 216, 219
Horses (trough), 22
Hotel Tujunga, 158–159, 473. *See also* Begue, Franciscoa
Houk, John, 216, 219, 230, 231, 481
Houk, Martha, 275
Hoyt, Silas, 124, 246
Hughes, Barbara, 184
Hughes, Harry, 184

"immigrant trains," 41
Indians (East), 132
Industrial Revolution, 60
Industrial Workers of the World, 65, 68–69, 90*n*. 2, 91*n*. 27. *See also* Wobblies (San Diego)
Irrigation: William E. Smythe, 61–72; Carey Act (1894), 62; National Irrigation Congress, 62; Newlands Reclamation, 62; Conquest of Arid America, 63; San Ysidro, 66
Ivanhoe. *See* Ghost Towns

James, George Wharton, 129
Japanese, Agriculture, 132; Alien Land Laws, 132, 135*n*. 28; *Ozawa v. United States*, 132; Internment Camps, 133, 139; Discrimination, 137; Tuna Canyon Detention Camp, 138, 139
Jewel Theater, 462. *See also* Tujunga Valley Theater
Jim Crow Laws. *See* African Americans, Jim Crow laws
Jitney Bus (Leaping Lena), 455–456
Johnson, John, 453
Johnson, Marjorie, 266*n*. 8, 281*n*. 2
Johnson, Mary Ann, 69. *See also* Big Tujunga Canyon, water rights in
Johnson, Hiram, 65, 66
Jump, Anna, 48, 56*n*. 35
Jump, Sid, 48, 56*n*. 35. *See also* Park Hotel

"Just California" (poem), 299. *See also* McGroarty, John S.
Joyful, 43. *See also* Ghost Towns

Karvis, Jackie, 42
Kirby, Anna (Barclay), 31, 33, 52, 54
Kiwanis, 101, 241, 416. *See also* Smith, "Singing Jimmie"; Gilbert, Zoe
Klondike (Alaska), 198
Kraft, Emma, 213, 214. *See also* Goats, Nubian
Ku Klux Klan, 133–134, 135*n*. 31, 136. *See also* Little Lands Colony—Tujunga (Los Terrenitos)

La Bow, Marie, 24, 25
La Crescenta, 218–219, 234, 289, 319, 339, 345, 391, 392
La Tuna Canyon, 138, 139
Ladies Improvement League, 450, 451
Lakeview Terrace, 248. *See also* Hansen, Homer; Tejunga Terrace
Lamson, Alice, 26, 268–275, 280
Lamson, Harry, 269–275
Lancaster Lake (Sunland), 445, 461
Lancaster, Paul, 319
"Landing of Pilgrims," 238. *See also* Zoe Gilbert
Lang, Leo, 191, 286, 444
Lazy Lonesome Ranch, 112, 186, 238, 285, 301, 417
Le Mesnager Winery, 114
Lemons (seedless), 377, 380. *See also* Rutherford, Helen; Sunkist
Lewis, J. S., 90, 238
Lichtenthaler, Jennie, 276, 277–279, 377–379
Linaberry, Cora Belle, 265, 280–283. *See also* Birds Acres
Lincoln, Abraham, 211, 367, 377
Little, Roger, 33
Little Landers Colony—Cupertino, 86, 88, 89, 90
Little Landers Colony—Hayward, 70, 84–86
Little Landers Colony—San Ysidro, 65–67, 70–75
Little Landers Colony—Standish, 63, 64

Little Landers Colony—Tujunga (Los Terrenitos), 17–20, 22, 81, 91*n*. 51, 99, 174, 361, 434, 435, 437, 439–440
Little Landers Magazine, 66, 69
Little Landers Movement, 61
Little Tujunga Canyon, 33
Livingston, Chancellor, 265, 285, 290, 293
Livingston, James, 284–290
Livingston, Hilda, 284–294, 392
Llano del Rio, 54, 66, 68, 297
Lombard, Sarah, 9, 259, 373. *See also* Rancho Tujunga
Longfellow, Henry, 269
López Adobe, 33, 55–57. *See also* Carlson, Viola; Watt, Ethel Duquette
López, Catalina, 37–38
López, Claudio, 34
López, Francisco, 30, 34–35
López, Geronimo, 37
López, Maria L. Cota, 34
López, Pedro, 34–35, 38
López Station, 34, 37
Los Angeles Aqueduct, 16–17
Los Angeles Chamber of Commerce, 43, 52, 61, 79
Los Angeles County, official seal of, 130
Los Angeles River, 123
Los Angeles Times Newspaper: bombing of, 65–66, 68; open shop fight, 65, 68. *See also* Carr, Harry; Otis, Harrison Grey
Los Angeles water, 16–17, 111, 123
Los Pobladores, 37
Los Terrenitos Colony. *See* Little Landers Colony—Tujunga (Los Terrenitos)
Lordsburg. *See* Ghost Towns
Lothrop, Gloria Ricci, 56*n*. 23
Lukens, Mt., 150, 253*n*. 10
Lummis, Charles, 32, 111, 129. *See also* Out West Magazine

Maclay, Edward, 130
MacVine, Elizabeth, 31, 53, 55–56, 464, 465
MacVine, John, 56

INDEX

"Manifest Destiny," 43, 61
Manzanita Park. *See* McGroarty Park
Martin, Homer, 264, 277, 462
Mauk, Earl, 48
Maygrove, Constance (Bing), 316, 318, 320, 322, 323, 327
Maygrove, Dorothy, 51, 265, 316–317, 320, 322, 326
Maygrove, Gertrude, 265, 316, 321, 322. *See also* Monte Vista Band
Maygrove, Gladys, 51, 56n. 36, 265, 316, 318, 320–322, 324, 326–327. *See also* Monte Vista Band
Maygrove, R. Walter, 265, 316–317, 323. *See also* Monte Vista Band; Porter's Catalina Island Marine Band
McGroarty, Ida, 125, 171, 294–315. *See also* Rancho Chupa Rosa
McGroarty, John S., 32, 129, 191, 295, 303–304, 359
McGroarty Cultural Arts Center, 481
McGroarty Park, 307
McHale, Margaret, 305, 306n. 5
McWilliams, Carey, 69, 91n. 29, 430
Mellus, Francis, 38
Mexican–American War, 36
Mexican Revolution, 65–66
Miller, Frank, 297. *See also* Glenwood Mission Inn
Millionaires Club of Happiness and Contentment, 191, 286, 362
Millspaugh, Nora, 114, 328, 331, 328–331
Mingay, Emma, 333
Mingay, Henry, 332–335
Mining: Placerita Canyon, 35; Klondike (Alaska), 198; copper, 296
Mission Play, 32, 44, 298, 299, 300, 303. *See also* McGroarty, John S.
Mission Playhouse, 44, 298, 300, 302, 304–305
Mission San Gabriel, 34
Model A Ford, 372
Model T Ford, inside front cover, 265, 319–320, 401, 453
Montalvo, Garcia de, 127
Monte Vista. *See* Little Landers Colony—Cupertino
Monte Vista Band, 286, 325. *See also* Maygrove, Gertrude; Maygrove, Gladys; Maygrove, R. Walter
Monte Vista Hotel, 32, 46, 49–50, 56n. 29, 77. *See also* Frank Barclay
Monte Vista Inn, 453
Monte Vista Park (Sunland), 52, 445, 450–452
Montrose, 344, 392
Morgan, Bertha, 336–342, 444
Morgan, Flora, 9, 336–338
Morgan, Frances M., 347, 350, 352, 354–355, 360, 417, 464
Morgan, Frances R., 346–352, 355, 398
Morgan, Wallace, 175, 191, 261, 267, 306,n. 17, 347, 352, 355, 362, 398, 401
Mormon Colony (San Bernardino), 54
Motor Transit Stage, 458. *See also* Richardson, A. J.
Moulton, Mrs., 202, 203. *See also* Colby, Lillian
Mount Gleason Sanitarium, 289
Mount Lowe, 447
"Mountains of Health" sign, 476
Movie Industry, 52, 445
Mueller, Captain, 198, 200. *See also* Colby, Delos; Colby, Lillian; Colby, Nellie
Muir, John, 111, 466
Mulholland, William, 111
Muuhonga Village, 94, 96

National Panic of 1873, 40, 61
Native Americans, 93–98, 103, 129–130, 132–133
Newlands Reclamation Act (1902), 62
New Plymouth Colony (Idaho), 62, 91n. 17–19
New Year's Eve Flood (1934), 217
Nieto, Manuel, 31
Nixon, Richard M., 352
Noonan, May, 24, 25
Nordhoff, Charles, 40, 56n. 22

Oak Glen Ranch. *See* Morgan, Flora
Oak Grove, 216. *See also* Fehlhaber, Helena
Oak of Golden Dream, 36–37. *See also* Placerita Canyon
Occidental College (Eagle Rock), 111, 400. *See also* Wieman, Alma
Oil, 52, 277
Old Heritage Wine. *See* Le Mesnager Winery
Old Times Week, 145, 146, 289
Olive Cannery, 114, 442
Olmstead, Frederick L., 59
Olvera, Augustin, 38
"Open Shop," 68
Opid's Camp, 202. *See also* Colby, Lillian
Oranges, 43, 45
Osgood, Myra, 280–283, 356–357
Ostrich Farms (Cawston's), 306, 441, 448
Otis, Harrison Grey, 52, 297, 305, 408
Our Lady of Lourdes Church, 163, 166, 171, 305, 312–314
Out West Magazine, 32, 63, 111, 129

Pacific Electric Interurban Railway, 39, 44, 285, 377, 455, 456
Palm Street Elementary, 416
Palms Sanitorium, 472–473. *See also* Spates, Dr. Edwin
Panama Canal, 180–181n. 4. *See also* Bryson, Carl
Panama Exhibition (San Diego), 66, 320
Parades (Fourth of July), 449
Paradise Ranch, 33, 56n. 15
Parcher, Carroll, 360, 362, 417, 464
Parcher, Frances (Morgan), 347, 348, 360
Parcher, Nannie, 359, 464
Parcher, Wilmont, 359, 360, 361, 362
Park Hotel, 45, 48, 51, 56n. 35. *See also* Barclay, Anna; Jump, Sid; Willis, Ben
Parker, Harold, 200, 203. *See also* Colby, Delos; Colby, Lillian; Colby Nellie
Pasco Park, 241, 367
Pasko, Beth, 365–369
Pasko, Edgar, 365–366, 367n. 4
Patton, George S., Sr., 297
Payne, Theodore, 113
Perner Family (Sunland), 131

Petrotta Family, 113, 319, 482
Phelan, Calif., 401. *See also* Wieman, Stella
Phillips, Mary, 370–375
Phillips, Ray, 371–375
Photography, 269. *See also* Brunke, Ray; Lamson, Harry
Pico, Governor Pío, 32
Pinewood Elementary School, 372, 401, 403, 404, 416
Placerita Canyon, 35–37
Plainview Elementary School, 416
Pledge of Allegiance to Flag, 60
Poet Laureate (California), 305–306
Pomroy, Francis Muir, 305, 306n. 25
Pluviculture, 71, 73. *See also* Hatfield, Charles
Pneumonic Plague, 109
Population (Statistics), 427
Porter, G. K., 130
Porter's Catalina Island Marine Band, 317. *See also* Maygrove, Walter
Postcards, 54
Post Office, 19, 174–176, 177n. 7, 178, 193, 195, 419
Potpourri Jar Gift Shop, 366, 368
Poultry, 114. *See also* Frish, Marie; Rutherford, Helen; Souto, Anna
Powell, John Wesley, 62, 91n. 16
Prado, Martine, 94, 139, 436, 482
Preemption Act of 1841, 56
Progressive Era (1900–1926), 60, 213
Progressive Movement, 68
Prohibition, 215
Pueblo of Los Angeles, 34, 36, 38, 41

Rabbit Gulch, 319. *See also* Maygrove, Gladys
Record–Ledger Newspaper (1922), 317, 349, 350, 351, 359
Record of the Verdugo Hills (1920)
Rainfall (statistics), 122
Rainmaking. *See* Pluviculture
Ramona Pageant, 32, 306n. 11
Rancho Chupa Rosa, 191, 301–302, 306n. 20, 308–310, 311, 419. *See also* McGroarty, Ida
Rancho Hiñata, 472, 473. *See also* Spates, Dr. Edwin
Rancho de Cahuenga, 38
Rancho La Cañada, 32, 38
Rancho Los Alamitos, 32
Rancho Los Nietos, 31
Rancho Providencia, 38
Rancho San Francisco Xavier, 35
Rancho San Pedro, 31
Rancho San Rafael, 31
Rancho Temescal, 37
Rancho Tujunga, 31, 38, 39, 40, 41, 96
Real estate, 42–43, 443–445
Real Estate Covenant, 132
Red Cross, 362–363
Reynolds, Jerry, 35, 36, 56n. 17
Rice, Harry, 420
Rice's Bungalow Café, 452
Richardson, A. J., 457, 458
Roca, Rogério, 130
Roscoe "flag stop," 14, 415
Rose Parade (1922/1926), 350, 417–419
Rosie the Riveter, 180, 184. *See also* Bryson, Laura
Rostand, Herb, 170
Rowley, Dorothy, 47, 56n. 32–33, 327
Rowley, Quinton, 47
Rowley, Robert, 47, 56n. 30, 124, 125n. 5, 131
Rowley, Virginia, 47, 286
Runnymede Colony, 88
Rutherford, Helen, 376–381
Rutherford, Robert Owen, 377–381

St. Luke's of the Mountains Church, 341
San Andreas Fault, 123
San Fernando Fruit Growers Association, 380. *See also* Rutherford, Helen
San Fernando Mission, 96, 130
San Fernando Valley, 34, 42, 55, 98, 127, 383
San Fernando Valley High School, 417
San Fernando Valley Historical Society, 38
San Gabriel Mountains. *See* Camp Colby
San Joaquin Valley, 297, 347, 398
San Ysidro Colony: creation of, 63; bad publicity of, 68, 69; produce of, 70
San Ysidro (St. Isador), patron saint, 55, 56n. 40, 241, 301
Sanger, Phil, 380. *See also* Goats, San Ysidro
Santa Catalina Island, 317–318, 446, 481
Santa Clarita Valley, 35
Santa Fe Railroad, 41, 127
Saunders, Jeraldine, 164
Sawtelle Veteran's Hospital, 334
Serra, Fr. Junípero, 303
Seven Hills (Tujunga), 286
Shadow Hills, 54, 248, 454. *See also* Hansen Heights
Sharp, Julia Granger, 101, 410n. 1
Sherman, Moses, 31
Sierra Madre Fault, 123
Sims, Earl (stage), 238, 286
Sinawick Club, 241, 416. *See also* Kiwanis
Sister Elsie, 149, 158
Sister Elsie's Peak, 160, 238, 249, 253, 339, 464
Smallpox Epidemic: in Los Angeles, 32, 111; worldwide, 149
Smith, Houston, 355, 402n. 11
Smith, "Singing Jimmie," 100, 101, 103n. 20
Smith, Leo, 444
Smith, Dr. Virginia, 382–389
Smothers, Howard, 290
Smythe, Harriet, 65, 66, 73, 91n. 39
Smythe, Margaret, 65, 71, 72, 73
Smythe, William E., 61–75
Socialism, 66, 297. *See also* Job Harriman
Soule, John, 90n. 12. *See also* Greeley, Horace
Southern Pacific Railroad, 13, 14, 40, 127
Southwest Museum, 97
Souto, Anna, 232–236
Spanish–American War, 201, 391, 392

INDEX

Spanish Period (1784–1822), 31
Spahr, Carl, 152
Spates, Dr. Edwin, 105, 110n. 5, 319, 454. *See also* Rancho Hiñata, The Sanitorium
Standish Colony, 63, 90n. 20–22. *See also* Little Lands Colonies—Standish
State Federation of Women's Clubs, 213
Strawberry Peak, 197, 205. *See also* Colby, Delos
Street Names, 431–432
Stone Masons. *See* Forster Brothers (Ed, Jake, Joseph); Harris, George; Livingston, James
Stuart, Roberta, 57
Sunair Home for Asthmatic Children, 110n. 8
Sunkist, 54, 380
Sunland Rural Telephone Company, 429

Tally-Ho, 243, 454
Temple Workman Bank (Los Angeles), 40
Tennis Courts, 49, 329
Tent Living, 24–25, 191, 270, 286
Terry, Nella, 104
Theobald, Jean (Zachau), 416–417, 419, 422, 482
Theobald, Tom, 90, 281n. 4, 342, 384, 419, 420, 421, 482
Theriot, Alice, 377, 378
Theriot, Forrest, 214, 339, 373–375, 376–381
Thoreau, Henry David, 60
Thorsen, Mrs. Knute, 378, 379, 381
Tia Juana, 64, 69
Tin Lizzies, 265, 453
Tonello, Fr. Joseph, 163, 166, 241
Tongva Indians, 92–104
Tortoises, 370, 372, 378. *See also* Phillips, Mary; Rutherford, Helen
Touring Topics (journal), 101
Tourist Train, 285
Townsend Plan, 303, 306n. 23. *See also* McGroarty, John S.
Treaty of Guadalupe Hidalgo (1848), 32

Trifuño, Miguel, 31, 38
Tsumori, Mabel, 139, 140. *See also* Tuna Canyon Detention Center
Tuberculosis, 107, 193, 277, 377
Tujunga Board of Trade, 362
Tujunga Canyon Dam, 249, 254
Tujunga Emergency Hospital, 471
Tujunga Grammar School, 401, 403, 404. *See also* Pinewood Elementary School; Wieman, Stella
Tujunga Hotel, 159. *See also* Begue
Tujunga Public Library, 364
Tujunga Rental Library, 417, 420, 421
Tujunga Song, 239. *See also* Gilbert, Zoe
Tujunga Terrace, 247. *See also* Hansen, Homer; Lakeview Terrace
Tujunga Timeline, 477–480
Tujunga Undertaking Company. *See* White, Flora
Tujunga United Methodist Church, 400
Tujunga Valley Hotel, 390. *See also* Smith, Dr. Virginia
Tujunga Valley Realty Board, 242, 444
Tujunga Valley Sanitorium, 389
Tujunga Valley Theater, 462, 463
Tujunga Village, 38, 96
Tujunga Wash, 156
Tujunga Water & Power Company, 247, 249
Tujunga Women's Club, 113, 211, 212, 336, 395
Tuna Canyon Detention Center, 138, 139, 481
Turner, Fredrick J., 59, 90n. 1
Twain, Mark, 60
Twin Pines, 453

Union Gospel Mission (Tujunga). *See* Wornum, Pastor James; Wornum, Jennie
United Methodist Church. *See* Wieman
United States Land Commission, 32
University of California Los Angeles, 341

Utopian Colonies, 54, 60, 61, 63–65, 90n. 6
Utopianism, 60, 61, 90n. 7, 91n. 29, 91n. 50, 398

Vale of Monte Vista, 105, 175, 433
Vallejo, General M.G., 129
Vasquez Canyon Trail, 247
Vaughan, Slim, 234
Verdugo Hills Cemetery, 265, 266, 267, 408, 410n. 8–12, 412, 413. *See also* Hatch, Mabel; Wornum
Verdugo Hills Golf Course, 139. *See also* Tuna Canyon Detention Center
Verdugo Hills Hebrew Center, 233, 234n. 4
Verdugo Hills High School, 140, 213, 218
Verdugo Hills Transportation Company, 456
Verdugo, Jose Maria, 31, 38
Verdugo Wash, 217
Veterans of Foreign Wars, 265
Villa, Poncho, 68
Vinol Tonic, 114
Volsted Act of 1920, 114
Vroman's Book Store, 419

Ward Walling Store, 321
Watt, Ethel Duquette, 31, 33, 56, 57
Weeks, Charles, 88
Weeks, Moses L., 42
Western Empire Home Extension Plan, 66, 69
Western Empire Magazine, 105, 110n. 1
Western Empire Suburban Farms Association, 69, 286
Whelan, John, 112, 117
White, Flora, 391–395
White Funeral Home, 391
White, Mark, 391–393
Wickiup Creek (Big Tujunga Canyon), 197. *See also* Colby, Delos
Wicks, Moses, 31, 40, 42
Wieman, Alma, 348, 396–402, 405
Wieman, Eleanor (Kendra), 355, 401, 402n. 3, 402n. 11–12

493

Wieman, Lois, 398, 401, 402n. 13
Wieman, Stella, 249, 397, 401, 402n. 13, 403
Wieman, Rev. William Henry, 51, 397, 398, 399, 402
Wildwood Lodge, 467
Willis, Ben, 51. *See also* Park Hotel
Wilson, Woodrow, 415
Wobblies (San Diego), 65
Women's Christian Temperance Union (W.C.T.U.), 114, 119n. 10, 330. *See also* Millspaugh, Nora
Women's Work, 441. *See also* Adams

Olive Cannery, Movie Industry, real estate, work statistics
Wollard, Jack, 266n. 1
Woodruff, Ensign & Mary, 119, 319
Woods, Julia Smythe, 74, 90n. 9
Work statistics, women, 441
World War I, 114, 163, 202, 213, 224, 239, 269, 271, 286, 288, 290, 291, 362, 401, 402, 449
World War II, 184, 323, 372, 481
World's Fair (Chicago), 59
Wornum, Parson James, 261, 40, 408–409, 411–412, 413
Wornum, Jennie, 407–410, 411

Writer's Rendezvous, 367. *See also* Beth Pasko

Yang-na Village, 96
Ybarra Ranch, 247
Yucca Plant, 113, 120, 121

Zachau Canyon, 415
Zachau, Harry, 286, 414–419, 444
Zachau, Jean (Sr.), 286, 414–419, 422
Zalvidea, José, 96
Zinnia, 117, 119
Zitto, Victor, John, 113, 286
Zulu Cars, 41

Founding Sisters:
Life Stories of Tujunga's Early Women Pioneers, 1886–1926
by Mary Lou Pozzo
has been produced in an edition of 1,500 copies.

The typeface used is Centaur.
Design by Ariane C. Smith under the direction of Robert A. Clark.
Printing by Thomson-Shore, Inc., of Dexter, Michigan.

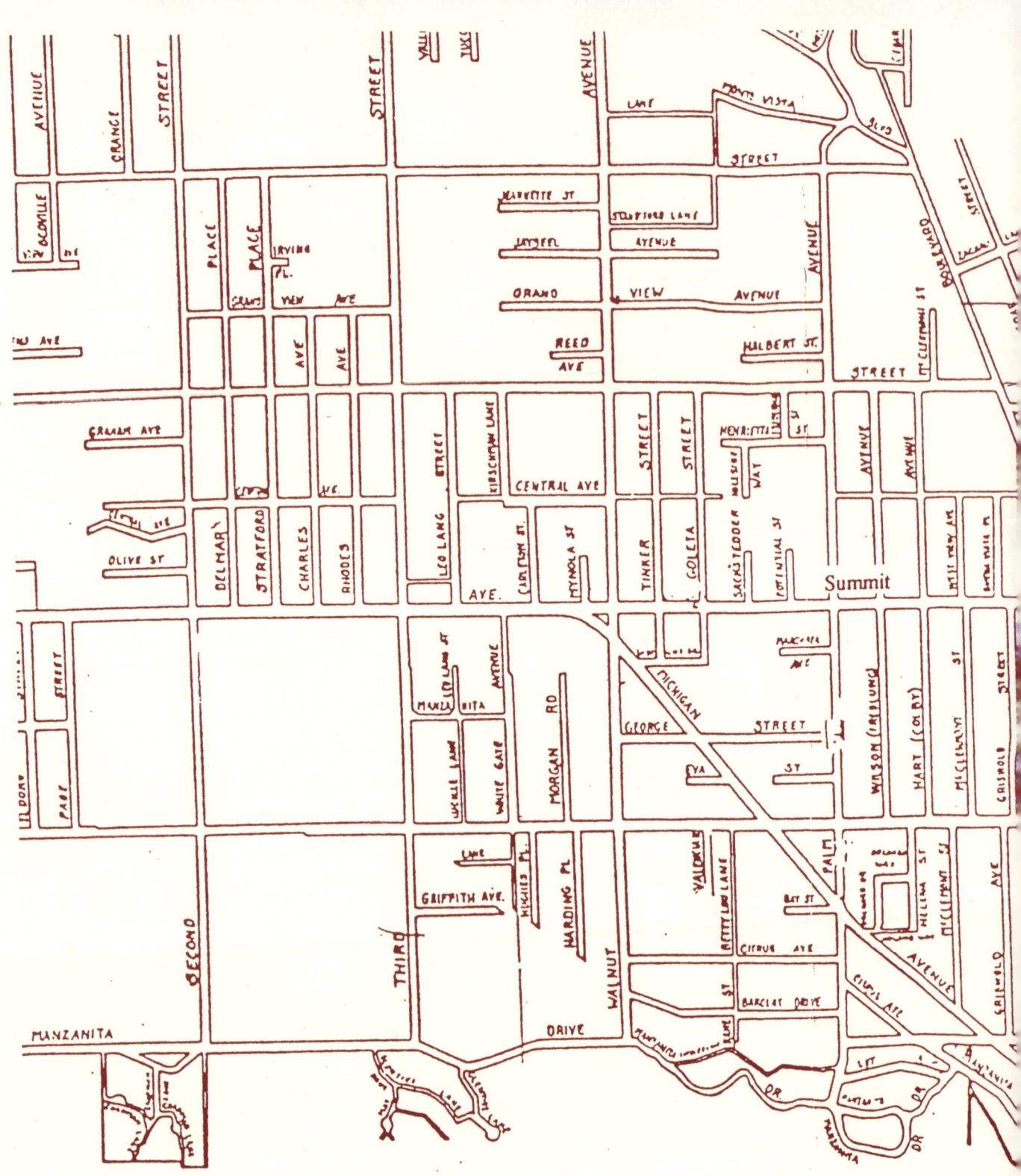

— MAP OF —
— TUJUNGA-VALLEY — CITY OF TUJUNGA —
AND
— BY NEWTON L. ELWELL 1925 —